New perspectives on the Shakespearean world

This book is published as part of the joint publishing agreement established in 1977 between the Fondation de la Maison des Sciences de l'Homme and the Press Syndicate of the University of Cambridge. Titles published under this arrangement may appear in any European language or, in the case of volumes of collected essays, in several languages.

New books will appear either as individual titles or in one of the series which the Maison des Sciences de l'Homme and the Cambridge University Press have jointly agreed to publish. All books published jointly by the Maison des Sciences de l'Homme and the Cambridge University Press will be distributed by the Press throughout the world.

Cet ouvrage est publié dans le cadre de l'accord de co-édition passé en 1977 entre la Fondation de la Maison des Sciences de l'Homme et le Press Syndicate de l'Université de Cambridge. Toutes les langues européennes sont admises pour les titres couverts par cet accord, et les ouvrages collectifs peuvent paraître en plusieurs langues.

Les ouvrages paraissent soit isolément, soit dans l'une des séries que la Maison des Sciences de l'Homme et Cambridge University Press ont convenu de publier ensemble. La distribution dans le monde entier des titres ainsi publiés conjointement par les deux établissements est assurée par Cambridge University Press.

New perspectives on the Shakespearean world

RICHARD MARIENSTRAS

Translated by

JANET LLOYD

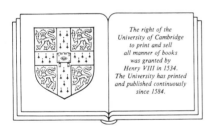

The right of the
University of Cambridge
to print and sell
all manner of books
was granted by
Henry VIII in 1534.
The University has printed
and published continuously
since 1584.

CAMBRIDGE UNIVERSITY PRESS

Cambridge
London   New York   New Rochelle   Melbourne   Sydney

EDITIONS DE LA MAISON DES SCIENCES
DE L'HOMME

Paris

Published by the Press Syndicate of the University of Cambridge
The Pitt Building, Trumpington Street, Cambridge CB2 1RP
32 East 57th Street, New York, NY 10022, USA
10 Stamford Road, Oakleigh, Melbourne 3166, Australia
and Editions de la Maison des Sciences de l'Homme
54 Boulevard Raspail, 75270 Paris Cedex 06

Originally published in French as *Le Proche et Le Lointain*
by Les Editions de Minuit 1981
and © 1981 by Les Editions de Minuit
First published in English by Editions de la Maison des Sciences de
l'Homme and Cambridge University Press 1985 as *New perspectives on the
Shakespearean world*
English Translation © Maison des Sciences de l'Homme and Cambridge
University Press 1985

Printed in Great Britain at the University Press, Cambridge

Library of Congress catalogue card number: 85–5759

British Library cataloguing in publication data

Marienstras, Richard
New perspectives on the Shakespearean world.
1. English literature – Early modern, 1500–1700
– History and criticism
I. Title II. Le proche et le lointain. *English*
820.9′003   PR421

ISBN 0 521 25265 2
ISBN 2 7351 0101 0 (France only)

WD

Contents

Contents

Acknowledgements

I should like first to express my gratitude to the late and deeply lamented Professors Michel Poirier and T. J. B. Spencer. From Michel Poirier, my research supervisor, I received much valuable advice and encouragement to pursue my Elizabethan studies. T. J. B. Spencer was always ready to enter into discussion whenever I met him.

Jean Jacquot, with whom I was privileged to work and to teach for many years, allowed me to profit from his incomparable experience in research work and showed me quite exceptional warmth, sympathy and generosity. His recent death was a profound bereavement to all his friends and disciples.

Many friends have, on many occasions, helped me with their views: Maurice Charney, William R. Elton, Eric Hobsbawm, Léon Poliakov, Pierre Vidal-Naquet, Ian Willison, Abraham Semsz and many others.

I owe much to the members of the 'groupe de recherches théâtrales et musicologiques' of the C.N.R.S. (Centre National de la Recherche Scientifique), my colleagues at the Charles-V Institut anglais, the members of the study group on the history of racism; also to a number of students at the Charles-V Institut and to many students at the écoles normales supérieures.

My wife has read and reread the chapters of this book with great patience. Robert Ellrodt is largely responsible for the final form of the book and without Jérôme Lindon, its French publisher, it would have been both longer and less readable.

Georges Groussier was so kind as to check the entire text in detail, correcting many errors and suggesting many improvements.

I am extremely grateful to the English translator of this book, Janet Lloyd, whose patient and precise labour made this edition possible.

Nothing could have been achieved without the help of the Bibliothèque Nationale, the British Library, the Library of Congress and the Folger Shakespeare Library.

All through the production phase of the English version I have worked closely with Linda Randall, a most dedicated subeditor of the C.U.P., who saved me from many lapses, errors and inconsistencies. Without the benefit of her expertise this book would be much more imperfect than it is.

viii

Introduction

This study is devoted to certain aspects of Elizabethan ideology and to the way these are used in Shakespeare and a number of other dramatic works of the period. The following themes are considered: the forest and hunting; the relations between the king, the kingdom, his subjects and foreigners; sacrifice and bloodshed. The poacher, the foreigner, the sacrificial victim and the outlaw are all beings 'set apart' compared with beings who are 'near' and whose 'nearness' is defined by custom, laws and allegiance to the sovereign. The forest is a royal domain legally and geographically set apart, since it is not controlled by the common law of the realm. The king, master over his forests, is 'set apart' from his subjects by reason of his status, which is at once natural and supernatural, and also by reason of the wild nature which he alone takes on and perpetuates, whilst the other inhabitants of the kingdom must be preserved from wildness by the exercise of will and right reason. The sacrificial victims are excluded beings – deviants, foreigners, figures who are harmful to the city, or purely innocent, the targets of unnatural forces.

Hunting reflects the complex relations between culture and wildness. The hunter possesses a technique which he uses against the animal; but man's ferocity may reverse the original relationship and switch the wildness to his side. Furthermore, ever since ancient times, hunting has been a metaphor for the pursuit of fugitives, for the pursuit of love and of the absolute.

A number of simple oppositions may be used here, the pertinence of which has been shown by Claude Lévi-Strauss and Mary Douglas:[1] the opposition between nature and culture, between the near and the far, between the continuous series and the unique event or one that disrupts the series, between sacrifice and the sacrilegious, the pure and the impure, nurture and poison. They appear at both narrative and semantic levels; they help to clarify family relationships, differences or conflicts between social and ethnic groups, as well as conflicts within the self.

In order to avoid the difficulty presented by the fact that 'the work studied and the analyst's thought reflect each other', to use Claude Lévi-Strauss'

1

expression, and so that we may be able to distinguish 'what is simply received from the one and what the other puts in',[2] controls quite independent from the conscious elaborations of the analyst have been used: essentially, information derived from history, from accounts of voyages, from theological works and, also, from legal documents, the importance of which is often underestimated in connection with literary analysis.

The aim of this book is not, however, to discover structures that can be formalised in a fashion similar to those that anthropologists construct on the basis of myths or rules of kinship. There are three reasons for this.

First, if a myth is 'structured rigorously at every level',[3] like a crystal, a literary work, for its part, appears rather as 'a geological formation extending over dozens of kilometres . . . , and we cannot exclude the possibility that certain literary productions may be just as subject to contingencies, to the interplay of probabilities as, for example, a heap of stones or a landfall'.[4]

The second reason has to do with the way that works in the Elizabethan period were composed. Making constant use of allegory, homology, equivocation and being, furthermore, subject to censorship, they could often make themselves understood in a covert fashion only by means of metaphors and allusions. One of the tasks of the student is to formulate hypotheses, however conjectural, as to the meaning or multiple meanings that they suggest. This is why, unlike literary works which are longer lasting, works of criticism are destined to lose their relevance with time, constantly giving way before new interpretations.

The third reason has to do with the very purpose of literary criticism. This is not only to contribute to the advancement of some hypothetical science of literature but also to establish a number of connections between the work and the period in which the critic is living; he must restore intelligibility to those aspects of the work which are increasingly losing it and make it possible for the reader's sensibilities and emotions once again to be stirred by it. This means that he cannot be satisfied solely with methods that are or claim to be objective. He has a duty to move and touch the heart so that when the reader turns from the work of criticism to the work of art itself he, like readers in the past, may in his turn be convinced and carried away by it. These tasks may be contradictory but their conflictual union perhaps provides a better definition of literary criticism than some method rigorously established and too systematically applied – or surreptitiously flouted.

This study has drawn upon a large body of discourse and opinions borrowed from the critical tradition, the human sciences and writers of the Renaissance as well as modern authors. The links between them are, it must be confessed, arbitrary ones to the extent that they stem from one man's choice and experience of life. The works of the past make demands upon not only our knowledge of the texts but also what we, personally, have made of ourselves in the world. Our commitments and our passions, our honesty and our deceptions are at the same time paths that lead us to the literary works and obstacles that deny us access to them. For each of us the paths and the obstacles are different and that is why, though we may read the same work or look at the same painting, we never see the same things.

Furthermore, I would establish a clear-cut difference between a work of art (be it written, pictorial or musical, etc.) and criticism. First, because commentaries neither extend nor provide a sequel to the artistic form of the works, their contributions are purely discursive. Secondly, because while a confrontation with time must take place in all narratives, that confrontation is central to the creative work but not to the work of criticism. Organising time in a story or tale and describing how time is organised or affects the story are two totally different procedures.

Literary criticism does no more than devise devious paths of access to literature. These paths are necessary, however, if we wish to remain aware of the differences which divide the present from the past. And our awareness of the diversity of works, men and cultures depends upon our ability to sense that the past, although ours, is also a stranger to us.

To be sure, one might, in the name of the universality of human nature, blur both the particular historical features of the work and also the fact that we ourselves belong to a particular time, place, society and group. But it is quite possible, on the contrary, to exalt those very facts and emphasise the extent to which the work is rooted in its own time and to which the commentator belongs to his, in such a way that the commentator, in an effort of sympathy, eventually gets through to the work despite having earlier distanced himself from it – insofar, at least, as he was capable of doing so.

The duel between art and nature is one of the main themes of Shakespeare's sonnets.[5] It is of major importance in *King Lear*.[6] Frank Kermode has shown the part it plays in *The Tempest*.[7] The argument between Polixenes and Perdita in *The Winter's Tale* (IV, iv) is famous. The contrast between the two terms is used by Shakespeare to illustrate the creative activity of man in general – whether, wisely, he imitates the natural order or, foolishly, departs from it – and to indicate the respective roles of education and innate talents or, to put it another way, custom on the one hand and natural law on the other. 'Nature' and 'custom',[8] 'art and nature' and 'nurture and nature', 'title' and 'parts',[9] 'blood' and 'virtue'[10] are just a few of the terms used to express this opposition. But these antitheses are not made as obvious as contrasts between clearly defined primary colours. Hiram Haydn, simplifying, notes four different concepts of nature in the Renaissance.[11] One of the dominant ideas was that of divine reason: as applied to man, this supposed that free-will established a balance between the elements and the humours. And the king, dominating the social edifice as the head dominates the body, was seen as the agent who regulated public imbalances. He was the 'fountain of justice', and his magical powers[12] were the visible sign of his function as social healer.[13] He was not simply the 'artisan' of health, the 'ape of nature',[14] he used the means of a unique and privileged art to which he was the heir in accordance with rules both natural and supernatural.

The king was believed to be endowed with a double nature, both secular and priestly, and also with a double body – one physical, the other immaterial, the latter being immortal and mystically linked to the body politic.[15] But there were also both civilised and wild sides to the king. The sovereignty that he exercised over wild spaces and civilised ones alike, the allegiance that both subjects and outlaws owed him were justified first and foremost by the prerogative that gave him the power to condemn and to absolve both that which was within and that which was outside the jurisdiction of common law – the power to declare war and, having done so, act where the force of law 'hath a cessation', to use Francis Bacon's words. But sovereignty and allegiance were also justified by a mythical idea that relates to the origin of his power. It is an idea that James I in 'The Trew Law of Free Monarchies' (1598) expressed as follows: 'When the Bastard of Normandie came into England and made himself king, was it not by force and with a mighty army?'[16] So the exclamation that Christopher Marlowe puts into the mouth of his Machiavelli is altogether in tune with the ideas of the time:[17]

> Many will talke of Title to a Crowne.
> What right had *Caesar* to the Empire?
> Might first made kings, and Lawes were then most sure
> When, like the *Dracos*, they were writ in blood.[18]
>
> (*The Jew of Malta*, 18–21)

The advice that Machiavelli gave his Prince was well and truly applied:

Now, there are two ways of resolving conflicts: violence and the law; the latter is the proper method of men, the former for beasts. But since the law is often inadequate for the purpose, it becomes necessary to have recourse to violence. A ruler must nicely judge the proportion of man to beast required. The writers of antiquity illustrated this by an allegory when they recorded that Achilles and many other Grecian princes were sent to Chiron, the Centaur, for their education. The appointment of a tutor who was half man and half beast clearly implies that a ruler needs some of the attributes of both to survive. Since then, a prudent ruler must from time to time know how to handle his affairs in a bestial way, the beasts he should take as models are the fox and the lion, because the lion's strength alone will avail him little against gins, nor the wiles of the fox against the ferocity of wolves.[19]

According to the 'Elizabethan world picture', the legitimate king was above all a civilising hero.[20] But a king who founds his right upon conquest is related to the wild beast: blood is the cement that holds his laws together.

To be sure, this view of a king both wild and civilising, representing at the same time nature and culture, the supernatural and wildness, was at odds with plenty of other ideas at the beginning of the seventeenth century, in particular with those of Sir Edward Coke for whom the common law of the realm dated from time immemorial and could not therefore have originated in violence.[21] The great Jacobean jurist nevertheless did not deny that, although 'the common law hath admeasured the king's prerogative',[22] the royal prerogative constituted an essential privilege of the Crown, the origins of which were lost in the mists of time. John Manwood, more absolutist than Coke, to some extent overlooked these limits when he declared that the Sovereign could still, at the end of the sixteenth century, create a forest at will on the land of any of his subjects. His *Treatise and Discourse of the Lawes of the Forest* stresses the wild character of the monarch. He presents us with a hunter-king, the master of the wooded spaces where the beasts of the forest, in the security that he procures them, wait to be hunted by him and put to death, that is to say sacrificed, according to his pleasure. The ritual of the killing of the stag is homologous to sacrifice which, according to René Girard,[23] itself is a mimetic action in which social violence, in a symbolised recollection of its original founding and unleashing, can be manifested without danger to the body politic.

Sacrifice was a theme on which the Elizabethans were well-informed. Polemics relating to the Transubstantiation, descriptions of biblical sacrifices prefiguring the Crucifixion and travellers' tales about pagan sacrifices all abounded and were relevant to the questions that beset protestants on the subject of their own relations with the sacred.

They did feel the need to make a distinction between the episodic nature of sacrifice and the serial nature of social violence. Yet in the protestant view, blood sacrifice was a manifestation of barbarity at the very heart of civilisation.

In Shakespeare, social violence mechanically pursues its devastating course: a first murder (or offence) is followed by a second murder to avenge the first, and then a third to avenge the second. It is an ever-expanding spiral: in the history plays, it originally concerns only the nobility but it soon envelops the whole people, as divided in its loyalties as in its family relationships, up until the moment when the accumulated evil is invested particularly and specifically in a criminal scapegoat, a Richard III or a Macbeth, whose killing and dismemberment marks the beginning of a new era.

Four of the present studies are on the subject of sacrifice. *Titus Andronicus* presents the sacrifice of an enemy of Rome which is the origin of a subsequent chain of atrocious acts of vengeance. In *Julius Caesar*, Brutus presents the assassination of Caesar by the conspirators as a sacrifice. This unique immolation is supposed to restore to Rome its original virtues and make it possible for all Romans to participate in political society. But this view of a sacrifice is immediately challenged: Antony and the Roman *plebs* interpret it as a sacrilege, a 'butchery', and civil war flares up again. In

Macbeth, the sacred is discovered through sacrilege. The murder of the legitimate king polarises in Macbeth's person all the evil diffused throughout the kingdom, for the tyrant attracts to himself the resentment and hatred of all. Macbeth thereupon becomes the carrier of defilement, conscious of the evil he commits; and he also becomes the one whose expulsion from the realm of nature liberates the whole land. The deaths of two kings, Duncan and Macbeth, constitute the axis of the tragedy whose evolution passes from a sacrilege to an expiatory sacrifice. Finally, in *'Tis Pity She's a Whore* by John Ford, Giovanni celebrates a kind of private sacrifice when he presents the bleeding heart of his sister Annabella at the banquet of the notables. Here again, the sacred can be perceived in the horror of sacrilege whose very excess touches upon the absolute.[24]

Thus wildness can erupt at the very heart of the civilised. Neither the valiant Macbeth nor the virtuous Brutus nor the peerless Coriolanus nor the noble Othello can completely dominate the wilder side of their nature. It is not surprising then that Henry V and Prospero must resort to cunning and violence to save from chaos a society or individuals who would otherwise be torn apart by the struggle for power. At a time when newly discovered lands were providing a far distant setting for the wild nature which used to be found in the forests, Shakespeare situated it within the bounds of civilised, indeed of everyday, life.

This second opposition, between the near and the far, makes it possible to establish relationships between themes which look, at first sight, widely disparate: geographical localities, temporal sequences, ages widely distant one from another, kinship relations. Titus Andronicus, who offers Saturninus and Tamora a cannibal meal, turns out to be more wild in his vengeance than the Goths in theirs. The 'civilisation' of Rome is under less threat from an invasion than from an ill-chosen monarch's marriage to a foreign woman. Othello is unable to resist the solicitations of Iago but the real evil lies at the heart of the city, not in the heart of the Moor of Venice. Caliban, the offspring of a witch and an incubus, acts in conformity with his ineducable nature. But what of Sebastian and Antonio, ready to kill for power, who are the degenerate product of civilisation? In every case, the near is more dangerous than the far. Internal corruption, as in *Hamlet* or *Timon of Athens*, can only be checked by violence. Alternatively, as in *Coriolanus*, violence shatters the fabric of the social body and reveals itself at the heart of what had been considered as the highest virtue.

But this opposition between the near and the far also makes other analyses possible. Thus incest, which is a union between beings who are too close, can be considered as a symmetrically inverted homologue of the murder of one human being by another close to it. After Duncan's murder (*Macbeth*, II, iii, 138–9), Donalbain speaks to Malcolm of 'the near in blood / The nearer bloody'. In *The Life and Death of Jack Straw* (1594) civil war is explicitly compared to incest:

> What meanes these wretched miscreants,
> To make a spoile of their owne country men:
> . . . to trouble England thus
> Well may I tearme it insest to the Land. (II, 603–4, 607–8)[25]

In *Hamlet*, Claudius' first speech provides a striking example of a manipulation of the theme of the near and the far, in terms of the family, rhetoric and time:

> Though yet of Hamlet our dear brother's death
> The memory be green, and that it us befitted
> To bear our hearts in grief, and our whole kingdom
> To be contracted in one brow of woe,
> Yet so far hath discretion fought with nature,
> That we with wisest sorrow think on him
> Together with remembrance of ourselves:
> Therefore our sometime sister, now our queen,
> Th' imperial jointress to this warlike state,
> Have we as 'twere with a defeated joy,
> With an auspicious, and a dropping eye,
> With mirth in funeral, and with dirge in marriage,
> In equal scale weighing delight and dole,
> Taken to wife. (*Hamlet*, I, ii, 1–14)[26]

Claudius is justifying himself for having flouted custom and nature and brought the time of the nuptials too close to that of the funeral rites. This proximity in time is the result of a conflict between reason and nature, wisdom and grief, a conflict which has made it oddly possible to combine the thoughts owed to the deceased with interest in one's own advancement. It is an association which prefigures another, one so scandalous indeed that, in announcing it, the two terms involved are carefully distanced from one another; the subject and the object are set far apart: 'our sometime sister' (line 8) 'have we' (line 10) 'taken to wife' (line 14). The incestuous relationship is interrupted by an interminable parenthesis in which a series of oxymorons denote contradictory and unnatural feelings or situations: 'defeated joy, an auspicious and dropping eye, mirth in funeral, dirge in marriage, in equal scale weighing delight and dole'. The subversion or rottenness of the kingdom of Denmark is thus signified by a series of associations which upset the temporal, family and social distances imposed by nature and custom and which are the consequence of one man's murder by a next of kin. The subversion is accompanied by a disregard for the rules of proper timing: Horatio, who has returned to Denmark for the funeral rites of the old king, is astonished that Gertrude's marriage should have followed so hard upon their heels:

> Thrift, thrift, Horatio! The funeral baked meats
> Did coldly furnish forth the marriage tables. (I, ii, 180–1)

As Richard Hooker wrote:

'There is', saith Solomon, 'a time for all things, a time to laugh and a time to mourn.' That duties belonging unto marriage and offices appertaining to penance are things unsuitable and unfit to be matched together, the Prophets and Apostles themselves do witness. Upon which ground as we may right well think it marvellous absurd to see in a church a wedding on the day of a public fast, so likewise in the selfsame consideration, our predecessors thought it not amiss to take away the common liberty of marriages during the time which was appointed for preparation unto and for exercise of general humiliation by fasting and praying, weeping for sins.[27]

Time is in the hands of superior powers. The way in which it is divided up and exerts pressure upon the destiny of men should be accepted by men. In order to win the hand of the daughter of the king of Antioch, Pericles must, on pain of death, solve the riddle that masks the incestuous relationship between the daughter and the father. Pericles indicates that he has solved the mystery; he is then obliged to flee to save his life.[28] Once he has discovered the unnatural union of two closely related beings, he is doomed to a long period of wandering in distant lands. Many adventures separate him from his wife and daughter with whom he is only reunited right at the end of this strange romance: the hero, now grown old, is saved because he does not question the gods.

In *'Tis Pity She's a Whore*, the unnatural association between brother and sister is a homologous and inverted expression of the feud which exists between human beings in a city perverted by egoism and injustice. A society in which so many evils are rife has lost all sense of the proper distances which each social creature must respect to ensure its safeguard. No one any longer knows his place so everyone acts in accordance with his overriding passion, his own self-interest or a debased concept of honour.

These strange or unnatural associations and these painful, scandalous or salutary separations are provided with a suitable framework by the theme of the voyage. To go far away from what is close or draw near to what is distant is to reverse man's customary relation to his social and natural environment. In *Othello* and *The Tempest* Shakespeare developed the theme of this paradoxical and dangerous relationship in mutually complementary and opposite ways.

In *Othello* he presents a protagonist whose origins, appearance and valour all make him foreign to the city, but who is needed by the city to defend it against the Turkish threat. But Othello carries off Desdemona and marries her. An organic relationship is added to the relationship set up by service and the city cannot tolerate it. Mary Douglas writes: 'A double moral standard is often applied to sexual offences. In a patrilineal system of descent, wives are the door of entry to the group. In this they hold a place analogous to that of sisters in the Hindoo caste. Through the adultery of a wife impure blood is introduced to the lineage.'[29] 'Impure blood' threatens to defile Venice: the blood of a foreigner, a barbarian, a Moor.

The Calvin affair has a particular significance with regard to the status of foreigners. Elizabethan society was inegalitarian and stratified by strongly marked differences between the various classes and ranks. But it was also capable of conceiving of absolute standards of otherness. Our reporter on the affair, Sir Edward Coke, proposed a classification for the various categories of foreigners: friendly foreigners, temporary enemies, enemies in possession of safe-conducts and perpetual enemies. The first three categories imply differences only of degree, the last a difference of nature. The perpetual enemies were Jews, Turks, heretics and pagans. They belonged not to the natural order but alongside the devil himself.

While most 'perpetual enemies' lived far away, beyond the seas, in fabled or only recently discovered lands, some were enemies from within, traitors, like Iago. The man convicted of treason was declared unworthy to live and the king could refuse him the remarkable boon of simply being beheaded or hanged. The killing of a traitor was a ritual that excluded him not just from society but from the very order of nature. His dismembered limbs were returned to the elements. This is how, in 1606, Sir Edward Coke, in his capacity as attorney general, described the fate awaiting the conspirators of the Gunpowder plot:

For first after a traitor hath had his just trial and is convicted and attainted, he shall have his judgement to be drawn to the place of execution from his prison as being not worthy any more to tread upon the face of the earth whereof he was made: also for that he hath been retrograde to nature, therefore is he drawn backward at a horse-tail. And whereas God hath made the head of man the highest and most supreme part, as being his chief grace and ornament, . . . he must be drawn with his head declining downward, and lying so near the ground as may be, being thought unfit to take benefit of the common air. For which cause also he shall be strangled, being hanged up by the neck between heaven and earth, as deemed unworthy of both, or either; as likewise, that the eyes of men may behold, and their hearts contemn him. Then is he to be cut down alive, and to have his privy parts cut off and burnt before his face as being unworthily begotten, and unfit to leave any generation after him. His bowels and inlay'd parts taken out and burnt, who inwardly had conceived and harboured in his heart such horrible treason. After, to have his head cut off, which had imagined the mischief. And lastly his body to be quartered, and the quarters set up in some high and eminent place, to the view and detestation of men and to become the prey for the fowls of the air.[30]

Othello was written before the Calvin trial and has no relation with this constitutional affair. But the legal case[31] and the dramatic work both appear in a society with its own particular views of inclusion and exclusion: Othello, who is treated socially as a hateful foreigner as soon as he marries Desdemona, ends up by behaving as the unnatural being he has been told he is: the role that Iago makes him play is that of the 'perpetual enemy'.

The concept of the 'perpetual enemy' stands in opposition to the whole scale of gradations that range from 'temporary enemy' to the subject invested with all the liberties granted to those who bear allegiance to the king. In his 'An Advertisement Touching An Holy War', Francis Bacon has one of his protagonists declare that there are some nations (for example those which practise human sacrifice) which are 'outlawed and proscribed by the law of nature and nations, or by the immediate commandment of God'. Sir Edward Coke's 'perpetual enemies' would certainly appear to fall within this category. To take action against them, 'there needs no intimation or denunciation of war . . . , all these formalities the law of nature supplies'.[32]

One of Shakespeare's last plays takes place on an almost deserted island where Caliban, who believed himself king of it, is displaced by Prospero, the banished duke of Milan. The 'good' savage proves ineducable and attempts to ravish Miranda. The tempest called up by Prospero wrecks on the island a selection of figures from Neapolitan and Milanese society who plan to set up their own government there at the price of murder and the burning of books. The parallel between the wildness of the civilised and the wildness of Caliban is followed through right up to the point at which Prospero, with the disguised violence of his magic, imposes his law upon them all. Near or far, power must in the end be exercised, for the nature of man is depraved. But these men, who deserve forgiveness despite their depravity, or perhaps because of it, themselves determine the very nature of power: one must use it without weakness, act by force and cunning, be both beast and man so that men may remain human.[33] However, such a concept, altogether in conformity with authentic Machiavellianism, is not admissible within the Elizabethan or even the Jacobean context; but it can still be suggested – with whatever reticence, horror, disgust or resignation is felt necessary.

The difficulty of exercising authority during a period of social, political and ideological mutation is a question that constantly preoccupies Shakespeare. The fact is that authority must be both lawful and legitimate and since the usurpation of Bolingbroke this double condition has no longer ever seemed to be fully satisfied.[34] Henceforth, as Harry Levin puts it, 'the dilemma of authority . . . is to prevent ideal communities from ever coming into existence, or to prevent existing communities from ever becoming ideal'.[35]

1. The forest, the wild and the sacred: a study of *A Treatise and Discourse of the Lawes of the Forest* by John Manwood

1. Mucedorus: the wild man in the forest

In a comedy published in 1598, Mucedorus, prince of Valencia, disguises himself as a shepherd the better to woo Princess Amadine of Aragon, famed for her beauty. In the first act Amadine is walking in a forest in Aragon in the company of Segasto, whom her father wishes her to marry. A bear appears and chases them. The unworthy suitor takes to cowardly flight. Mucedorus, sword in hand though in his shepherd's disguise, emerges from the wings with the severed head of the bear[1] which he offers as a token of homage to Amadine. With gratitude and relief she accepts this gift. It comes in useful again in the second act to prove the valour and innocence of the shepherd-prince when he is unjustly accused of murder by the dastardly Segasto.

In the third act Segasto manages to get Mucedorus exiled. Amadine determines to follow the man who has won her heart. They arrange to meet under the beech tree close to which the bear was killed, near a well. Amadine is the first to arrive. But the man she meets is not Mucedorus but Bremo. Bremo is a wild man, a man of the woods, a resurgence of the medieval *homo sylvestris*.[2] He has already introduced himself to the audience, in a monologue:[3]

> Who knowes not Bremoes strength,
> Who like a king commandes within these woods?
> The beare, the boare, dares not abide my sight,
> But hastes away to save themselves by flight:
> The christall waters in the bubbling brookes,
> When I come by, doth swiftly slide away,
> And claps themselves in closets under bankes,
> Afraide to looke bold *Bremo* in the face:
> The aged oakes at Bremoes breath doe bowe,
> And all things els are still at my command.   (III, iii, 6–15)

11

Salem Academy and College
Gramley Library
Winston-Salem, N.C. 27108

What favour shewes this sturdie sticke to those,
That heere within these woods are combatantes with me?
Why, death, and nothing else but present death.   (II, iii, 21–3)

Bremo is nature's master. He holds sway over wild beasts, his strength is prodigious; with a puff of breath he can make oak trees bend. His only weapon is his cudgel. And he is a cannibal. Upon seizing Amadine, he immediately exclaims:

A hapie prey! Now, *Bremo*, feede on flesh.
Dainties, *Bremo*, dainties, thy hungry panch to fill!
Now glut thy greedie guts with luke warme blood!
Come, fight with me, I long to see thee dead.   (III, iii, 16–19)

Amadine, naturally enough, refuses to fight and Bremo wants to devour her. But in conformity with the accepted idea that baser creatures are sensitive to beauty,[4] he realises that 'some newe-come spirit, abiding in [his] breast, sayth "spare her, Bremo, spare her, do not kill" '. And he goes on to say:

I think her beawtie hath bewitcht my force
Or else with in me altered natures course.   (III, iii, 52–3)

He forces Amadine to follow him to share his forest kingdom. At this point Mucedorus, who is being pursued by Segasto, is obliged to change his disguise: he now adopts that of a hermit, a man who lives in 'some lone abode within these woods'. He equips himself with a pilgrim's walking staff and decides to remain close to the well so that he can drink to the health of the lost Amadine in its waters. In this forest retreat he meets Mouse, a country bumpkin – a comic character involved in the sub-plot; Mouse declares that the best place to be is not a forest but a kitchen when it's a matter of eating, and a buttery when it's a matter of drinking. He promises the hermit that, if he will come and visit him, he will give him 'a piece of beef and brewis knockle deepe in fat' (IV, ii, 79).

As if to underline the oppositions between their different cuisines and modes of life, in the following scene Bremo plies his suit with Amadine. He promises to crown her with ivy, to feed her on quails and partridges, blackbirds, larks, thrushes and nightingales (not specifying whether the meat will be raw or cooked), on goat's milk, fresh spring water and 'all the dainties that the woodes afforde'.[5] He undertakes to strew the paths of the forest where she walks with flowers and to teach her to 'chase the hart', 'kill the deer' and 'rouse the roe'.

Mucedorus arrives upon the scene. In his hermit's disguise he is unarmed and unable to put up a fight. Of course Bremo wants to kill him but relents before Amadine's pleas. Mucedorus becomes the monster's servant: an inversion of the situation of Prospero and Caliban. Mucedorus tries in vain to convert the man of the woods, to civilise him: like Caliban, Bremo proves ineducable, culture has no hold over his nature, he remains 'a blodie butcher'.[6] Mucedorus flatters Bremo and the man of the woods teaches the hermit how to use his cudgel. Needless to say, Mucedorus makes the most of these lessons: he hits Bremo on the head and kills him. He then abandons his second disguise and reveals himself to Amadine as the shepherd. Without knowing he is really a king's son, Amadine's choice falls upon him rather than Segasto. And this brings the comedy to an end.

We may distinguish a series of very simple, obvious oppositions: Bremo's cudgel is opposed to the sword of the shepherd-prince and also to the walking staff of the hermit-prince. The 'wild' cuisine of Bremo – in which the 'raw' and the 'moving' predominate – is different from the boiled foodstuffs Mouse suggests to Mucedorus and also from the hermit's diet. The running water drunk by Bremo is opposed to the still water (from the well) of the hermit and also to the – fermented – beer of Mouse. The wild man can learn nothing from the civilised man but the latter can learn from the savage.

Moreover, Mucedorus passes through a series of trials and apprenticeships: his victories are evidence of a nature in which cunning, force, asceticism and chivalry are united. In every episode his civilised nature triumphs and is confirmed. In conformity with the contemporary manuals of behaviour, Mucedorus combines the virtues of the active life with those of contemplation. He is both knight and hermit, at the same time courtier, man of the people and man of the woods. His disguises identify him with a pastoral nature that is reassuring and temperate, and also with a higher nature, as is indicated by his transformation into a hermit. His civilised nature is opposed to that of Segasto which is deceitful, and also to the wildness of Bremo, in three ways: his is (1) a better nature, (2) a civilised nature acquired and controlled and (3) a nobility both inherited and merited.

Bremo, for his part, is the incarnation of pure wildness, the wildness that was believed to have existed before laws were imposed upon the world. That is Mucedorus' theme when he attempts to persuade Bremo to renounce his ways:

> In time of yore, when men like brutish beasts
> Did lead their lives in loathsom celles and woodes
> And wholy gave themselves to witlesse will,
> A rude unruly rout, then man to man
> Became a present praie, then might prevailed,
> The weakest went to walles:
> Right was unknowen, for wrong was all in all.
> As men thus lived in this great outrage,
> Behould one *Orpheus* came, as poets tell,
> And them from rudenes unto reason brought,
> Who led by reason soone forsooke the woods.
> Insteade of caves they built them castles strong;
> Citties and townes were founded by them then:
> Glad were they, they found such ease,

And in the end they grew to perfect amitie;
Waying their former wickednesse,
They tearmd the time wherein they lived then
A golden age, a goodly golden age.
Now, Bremo, for so I heare thee called,
If men who lived tofore as thou dost now,
Wilie in wood, addicted all to spoile,
Returned were by worthy *Orpheus'* meanes,
Let me like *Orpheus* cause thee to returne
From murder, bloudshed and like crueltie.   (IV, iii, 72–95)

The reference to Orpheus – no doubt derived from Horace's *Ars poetica* – makes Mucedorus a civilising hero: unable to deflect Bremo from his wildness, as Orpheus would, he kills him with his own weapons: in other words, he assumes Bremo's wildness in order to make it rebound against the wild man. It is both paradoxical yet hardly surprising that the role of the temporary wild man should be taken by a hermit: this figure, at the upper pole, fills an analogous role to that of the wild man, at the lower. The same point is amusingly made in Boccaccio[7] where Brother Albert, having enjoyed the favours of Lisette in his disguise as the angel Gabriel, is obliged to assume the appearance of a man of the woods before eventually being thrown into prison: a moralistic inversion of the positive role usually attributed to the hermit or 'man of god'.[8]

A number of themes described by Pierre Vidal-Naquet and Jacques Le Goff[9] in their analysis of *Yvain ou le Chevalier au Lion* can be detected here, in a somewhat degraded form. The giant cowherd whom Yvain meets in the course of his quest is 'an authentic wild man', master of the forest, who, assuming an ambiguous role, guides the knight along the path of discovery despite the fact that he is ugly and resembles a Moor.[10] In contrast to his role, Bremo represents a dangerous, even fatal, wildness. His own role is symbolic rather than mythical, for in *Mucedorus* the oppositions are conscious and ideological, whereas they hardly ever are in *Yvain*. The civilised state which is opposed to the wildness of Bremo is diversified and carefully arranged into a hierarchical order: nobles have different natures and merits from common men and Mouse, the bumpkin, who is situated at a low level in the civilised world (he turned tail when confronted with the bear and does not understand the solitary asceticism of the hermit) is nevertheless superior to Bremo.

For the opposition between the wild man and others is an absolute one. It manifests itself in 'present time' (Mucedorus and Bremo come face to face), but Bremo's wildness is an 'anachronism' (see lines 90–5), a vestige of the past, of the time when men were moved by their instincts alone. The play in which he appears is a romance and the tendency of this literary genre is towards a resolution in which all the characters eventually discover themselves to be in a world now reconciled. But Bremo is killed. Like the bear, he is irretrievable. He has proved himself incapable of adapting to progress.

In *Mucedorus*, the framework for the wild life is the forest. Ever since the Middle Ages the forest had been the natural setting for chivalric or initiatory adventures, the place *par excellence* opposed to the civilised, to reason and to humanity and which at the same time, by virtue of the trials to which it subjects those who venture into it, makes it possible to rediscover, in a regenerated and superior form, that from which it has set them apart.[11] Can we take it that it had the same role in England at the end of the sixteenth century? This seems doubtful even though in some cases it still provided a refuge for outlaws and masterless men.[12] In Shakespeare, despite the role played by the forest in *Titus Andronicus*, the important initiatory space is located within man himself (*Hamlet*) or else it is abstract, topographically ill-defined even if outside the city (*King Lear*, *Timon of Athens*, *Coriolanus*). The woods in which the Greek lovers of *A Midsummer's Night's Dream* get lost, or the Forest of Arden, are only metaphorical places of wildness: what is discovered there is a kind of amorous licence, an 'animality' which is a property of civilised man and a constant part of his nature. As for the outlaws in *Two Gentlemen of Verona*, *As You Like It* or *Cymbeline*, they do not find it easy to make their pastoral disguises pass unnoticed. These woods are rather places for individual discoveries, romantic refuges from the corruption of the Court or the force of the mighty. In other words, the tradition of the forest as a refuge is maintained. In contrast, the 'wild' forest, as presented with its inhabitants in Spenser's *Faerie Queene*, in particular in the episodes of Amoret (IV, vii, 5ff) and of Serena (VI, ciii, 35 and ff),[13] really hardly exists in Shakespeare, who reverses the role that the forest played in earlier fictions: for the civilised, it provides a welcoming refuge and the life that we see unfolding there briefly is that of the 'civilised wildness' of the Court or the town. The only wild man or savage ('salvage . . . slave') in Shakespeare is Caliban, and he lives not in a forest but on a faraway island. As L. Carrive has noted[14] 'wild or hostile nature is not a subject for poetic inspiration' at the beginning of the seventeenth century.

So it is quite legitimate to investigate how the forest was considered towards the end of Elizabeth's reign. For *Mucedorus* was one of the most popular plays of the period. Between 1598 and 1668, it was reprinted sixteen or seventeen times and there is evidence to show that it enjoyed considerable success;[15] it was even performed outside London after the theatres were closed in 1642. So the concept of the wild man in his forest was flourishing in the popular imagination even if the literary treatment of such themes marked them with a certain unreality. So what was the position of the forest itself, what was its status, whom did it shelter and, above all, what was its symbolic role?

2. The forest in retreat

First it should be remembered that the wooded areas, clearly more extensive than today, were receding as they began to be intensively exploited to answer the needs of naval construction and furniture-making and also for the iron, glass and dyeing industries. A number of forests, in particular the Forest of Dean and those of Sussex and the Western Midlands, were particularly affected. The Elizabethans were well aware of the fact: they complained about it in official correspondence, declaring that they respected the forest even while exploiting its wood.[16] On the subject of the damage suffered by the Forest of Arden, Drayton writes:

> For when the world found out the fitness of my soil,
> The gripple wretch began immediately to spoil
> My tall and goodly woods and did my grounds enclose:
> By which in little time my bounds I came to lose.[17]

In his *Description of England*, William Harrison, for his part, said:

We have in these daies diverse forrests in England and Wales, of which some belong to the king and some to his subjects . . . [he cites twenty-five of these] and which although they are far greater in circuit than manie parkes and warrens, yet are they in this our time lesse devourers of the people than these latter, sith beside much tillage, many townes are found in each of them, whereas in parks and warrens we have nothing else than either the keepers and warreners lodge, or at least the manor place of the chief lord and owner of the soile.[18]

Once the forest became threatened rather than threatening, once it 'lost its bounds' and tracts of it were cleared, a change in its symbolic role was inevitable. Even in the Middle Ages, men were aware of that, as is shown by the Norman poet Wace who, in his *Roman de Rou*, notes that forest clearance has brought about the disappearance of fairies, deer and other marvels that used to be there:

> Là alai jo merveilles querre
> [I went there to seek for marvels]
> Fol m'en revinc, fol y alai,
> Fol y alai, fol m'en revinc
> Folie quis, pour fol me tinc.
> [What I sought was mad and I realise I was mad].[19]

Human penetration was similarly diminishing or eliminating the physical place for wildness. And yet the need for such a place, in the imagination, was a pressing one. We can see that from John Manwood's legal treatise first published in 1592 and whose title, in the 1598 edition, reads as follows: *A Treatise and Discourse of the Lawes of the Forrest: Wherein is declared not onely those Lawes, as they are now in force, but also the originall and beginning of Forrestes; And what a Forest is in his owne proper nature, and wherein the same doth differ from a Chase, a Park or a Warren . . . Also a Treatise of the Purallee, declaring what Purallee is, how the same first began, what a Purallee man may do, how he may hunt and use his owne Purallee, how far he may pursue and follow after his chase, together with the lymits and boundes, as well of the Forrest, as the Puralley.*[20]

It is rather a daunting book of over 500 pages but, as Manwood himself writes, it was to prove useful given that 'the greatest part of them [the forests] are spoiled and decayed: and also that verie little, or nothing, as yet is extant concerning the Laws of the Forest'.[21] It is a significant confession. The task is not so much one of description as one of promotion and restoration. It is a matter of appealing to the past, to tradition, to the formidable body of forest laws (as distinct from the common law) to restore to the royal forest in material fact the role that Manwood believes it should by rights play on a symbolic and a political level. For Manwood, like Drayton, is indignant that the bounds of the forest are no longer recognised, that the 'pourallees' around the forest are growing larger and that not only the inhabitants of these 'pourallees' but even 'strangers' from London go hunting in the very heart of the forest and, 'even when those wild beasts [are] unseasonable', carry off the remains of the animals they have killed (pp. 378–9).

This view of poaching, like that of the dwindling forest areas, is confirmed by other sources of evidence.[22] Poaching, which had been in the past and was to be a century later[23] so severely repressed, was at this period common practice. It went on day and night, by means of nets, traps or an assortment of weapons. This was because, in the first place, there was no other way to obtain game; game which, as William Harrison puts it, was 'neither bought nor sold, as in other countries, but mainteined onelie for the pleasure of the owner and his friends'.[24] Secondly, because the nobles were careful to fence off their parks and warrens, extending the area that they covered to the detriment of crop-growing – which aroused the indignation of Harrison who declared that the proliferation of animals was depopulating the realm. And thirdly, because the royal forests about which Manwood is so concerned were so badly guarded and had manifestly lost both their wild and their sacred character.

Harrison and Manwood each have different preoccupations. The one deplores the extension of feudal parks and warrens to the detriment of crops (for these areas were not necessarily wooded); the other denounces the 'abuses and daily outrages' to which the royal forest and the beasts that dwell within it were subjected. We can detect a measure of ecological consciousness here, for Manwood was not without practical experience in respect of the forest. But the fact is that his treatise is a kind of legal-cum-ideological poem, putting forward a particular vision and theory where forestry law and the forest were concerned.

John Manwood was a jurist attached to Lincoln's Inn. But he was also game-keeper of Waltham Forest and judge for the New Forest (Hampshire).

He owned land in Essex, land which had previously been part of the priory of Blackmore (in the parish of Bromfield), dissolved under Henry VIII. He is eloquent in praise of the functions and dignity of the judge of the forest. Shortly before his death in 1610, he wrote a brief 'Project for improving the Land Revenue of the Crown by inclosing Wasts'[25] and submitted it to Sir Julius Caesar, the chancellor of the exchequer. He belonged to the new class that swelled the ranks of the landowners following the dissolution of the monasteries and, as we shall see, he shared the most absolutist tendencies of the Elizabethan world view.

His work is well known to jurists and historians. At the beginning of this century it was the object of a critical study by Turner, who examined medieval laws of the forest in the Introduction to his *Select Pleas of the Forest*.[26] It was used by Charles Petit-Dutaillis in his long historical study 'La Forêt et le droit de chasse en Angleterre au Moyen Age',[27] by William Holdsworth in his great history of English law,[28] by a number of historians and by authors of regional studies on the English forests. However, none of these works consider the symbolic content of the treatise or even its political aspects, which Edward Coke did not fail to note. This chapter will be concerned with these last two points. It will also include some remarks on the animals for which the forest provided a refuge.

3. Legal space, real space

What, according to Manwood, is a forest? He defines it in terms more complex than those noted by Petit-Dutaillis at the beginning of his study, which we quote below:

A Forest doth chiefly consist of these four things, that is to say, of vert, venison, particular laws and priviledges, and of certain meet officers appointed for that purpose, to the end that the same may the better be preserved and kept for a place of recreation and pastime meet for the royal dignity of a Prince.

Manwood follows up that definition with this:

A Forest is a certain Territory of wooddy grounds and fruitful pastures, priviledged for wild beasts and fowls of Forest, Chase and Warren, to rest and abide in, in the safe protection of the King, for his princely delight and pleasure, which Territory of ground, so priviledged, is meered and bounded with unremovable markes, meers and boundaries, either known by matter of record, or else by prescription: And also replenished with wild beasts of Venerie or Chase, and with great coverts of Vert, for the succour of the said wild beasts, to have their abode in: For the preservation and continuance of which said place, together with the Vert and Venison, there are certain particular Lawe [*sic*], Priviledges and Officers, belonging to the same, meet for that purpose, that are onely proper unto a Forest, and not to any other place. (I, 1, pp. 40–1)

Manwood then provides a commentary to his definition which shows that in his eyes all these elements are interdependent, on the legal level as well as in reality. Privileged 'fruitful pastures' are necessary as without them the beasts would run away and be killed by hunters, and this would mean 'the utter destruction of the forest' (I, 3, p. 42). The privileged conditions that the animals enjoy make the difference between a forest and a simple wood where the animals would not 'have a firm peace' (p. 43). Furthermore, this area is bounded by 'unremovable markes' which are: (1) sometimes vertical, such as hills or churches; (2) sometimes at ground level, such as rivers or roads; (3) sometimes boundary zones or limits separating the forest from some landmark which represents its boundary but which, although all boundary markers are a part of the royal domain, might alarm the animals; a house or a windmill are *ad terrorem ferarum Domini Regis*, 'a terror or a fear unto the wild beasts of the forest', not a place of safety or refuge for them. The king has no interest in them; it is therefore necessary to interpose a suitable distance ('a meer of the forest') to ensure the peace of the animals (I, 3, p. 47). It is also important to restock the forest with 'wild beasts of Venerie or Chase' (I, 3, p. 49) as, without animals, it would be no more than a wooded piece of land ('A . . . territory of wooddy grounds') (I, 3, p. 50). Conversely, without the forest, it would be impossible for the animals to live in peace: so neither the 'coverts of vert' nor the springs which make it possible for the vegetation to grow should be destroyed.

During the Middle Ages the purpose of the barons' conflicts with the king was to restrict the royal privileges, considered exorbitant. Then, it was necessary to protect men against the royal forest. Here, the position is reversed: it is necessary to protect the forest against men so that it can, in the first place, perpetuate itself and, secondly, continue to provide a shelter for animals. If a windmill strikes fear into the king's beasts, a distance or protective frontier must be interposed between those animals and the threat that the buildings of men impose upon them.

However, 'markes, meers and boundaries' would never be enough to establish a sufficient distance between what is forest and what is not. At the end of his treatise Manwood reminds the reader what a pourallee (or purlieu) is: a territory adjoining the forest and indicated by recognised and declared markers. From a historical point of view, these were forest zones that had been disafforested – that is to say that between the beginning of the thirteenth and that of the fourteenth centuries they lost their status as forest-land. Having gone into the history of the matter, Manwood nevertheless shows that the purlieu was an area which allowed certain privileges to those who owned that land or were tenants there: on their own land they could cut the wood and hunt. However, for everybody else the purlieu remained a part of the forest. So, if a wild animal reached a purlieu, it belonged to the king except if hunted and killed by the landlord of the terrain in which the kill took place. And Manwood spells out the rules of hunting which are extremely restrictive for the inhabitant of the purlieu: he cannot hunt at night or on a Sunday or during a month when the deer 'are great with fawn' (XX, p. 377) (a fence-month), or for more than three days a week, or with any persons other than his own servants, or during a period less than forty days after the end of the royal hunt (which causes the animals to take refuge in the purlieu) or during a period of less than forty days before such a hunt begins (so as not to put them on their mettle). And whenever he can go hunting, he must always start the hunt in the purlieu, not bar the path of the beast to the forest in such a way as to prevent it from finding refuge there, and not follow his hounds into the forest unless they have already seized the beast before it crosses the boundary and it has dragged them beyond it (XX, 9, pp. 376–7).

There are thus two intermediary zones between the forest and the outside world: the purlieu and its own boundaries which, in the case of, for example, a river or a road, are already a part of the forest and therefore a 'sanctuary' for the animals.

4. Sanctuary and wildness

'Sanctuary' is the term that Manwood himself uses. He points out that the words *silva* and *saltus* (wood) are often translated as 'forest'. But it does not necessarily follow that just any wood is a forest. It is only a forest if the king has granted it the privilege of sheltering fallow deer and other wild animals against all attack, 'for them to rest in firm peace'. 'And such a wood so priviledged is called by Budaeus in his second booke *De Philologia, Silva sacrosancta*, a priviledged wood for wild beasts to be safe in. And in another place, he calleth a Forest *saltus sacrosanctus*' (II, 4, p. 68).

In chapter XVIII, devoted to hawking in the forest, Manwood again says: 'The Forest . . . is . . . a Sanctuary and Priviledged place for the peace and safety of all manner of wild fowls . . . ' (p. 275).

The term 'sanctuary' is normally used to refer to the right of asylum. The expression 'privileged place' is used to denote the places where the right of asylum can be exercised: churches, essentially, and a few sanctuaries.[29] This right had been recognised in England ever since the Saxons' conversion to Christianity: a person accused of a crime (with the exception of treason and sacrilege) could, having taken refuge in a sanctuary, make his confession, adjure the realm and leave England for a foreign country without further harassment.[30] The right was limited by Henry VIII but was not abolished until 1623, by James I.[31]

The jurist Manwood is obviously referring to this right of asylum when he uses terms such as 'Sanctuarie' and 'Priviledged place'. The forest thus takes on the character of a sacred place: the animal becomes untouchable, as it were removed from the jurisdiction of the common law, like a man who has taken refuge in a sanctuary. There are striking similarities between the topography of the forest and that of the setting for a pastoral. Walter R. Davis describes the latter as follows:

The pattern formed by the subdivisions of this setting [of the Renaissance pastoral romances] may be graphically if roughly imagined as a center with two concentric circles surrounding it, implying a kind of purification of life proceeding inward: from the gross and turbulently naturalistic outer circle, to the refined pastoral inner circle, and then to the pure center of the world. The center is always supernatural, usually either a shrine like the Cave of the Nymphs or the dwelling of a magician. It may be the actual dwelling place of the God.[32]

The severity of the punishments inflicted before the promulgation of the Forest Charter[33] (enucleation, castration . . .) to repress offences against venison or against the 'vert' is a clear enough indication that such infractions of the law were considered as sacrilegious acts. Words evoking the withdrawn, mysterious and sacred character of places of refuge for animals make their appearance very early on in English juridical literature. Speaking of offences against the 'vert', that is to say infractions committed, so to speak, against the person of the forest, Manwood declares that the 'vert' must be preserved as it is what makes the forest beautiful: one must respect it *propter decorem*, 'for the comlinesse and beauty of the same in a forest'. Moreover, if a forest loses its 'vert' it ceases to be a forest, for it soon loses its animals: to destroy the 'vert' is to destroy the venison. 'The wild beasts of the forest have their secret counsel houses in the greatest thick woods, where they do most chiefly delight to take their rest or, as Budé puts it, *in silvis impeditissimis sunt conciliabula ferarum, ubi gaudent requiescere ferae*' (VI, i, p. 119).

Now, as early as the twelfth century, in the *Dialogus de Scaccario* (Dialogue of the Exchequer), Richard Fitz Nigel was of the opinion that whatever is done according to the laws of the forest is not just in an absolute sense, only just according to the laws of the forest, for the latter do not stem from the common law of the realm. He nevertheless wrote: *in forestis etiam penetralia Regum sunt, et eorum maximae deliciae*.[34] The *penetralia* are the sanctuaries, the mysteries, the places that are most withdrawn. Manwood speaks of the animals in the forest as Fitz Nigel spoke of the king, withdrawing into the most impenetrable (*impeditissimus*) coverts to find sacred refreshment. The analogy between animal and king is detectable in Manwood's text. The king's relationship to wild animals is a natural one, stemming from the fact that he is subordinate to none, except God. There is a famous sentence in Bracton where the great medieval jurist establishes that the king is subject to God and the laws or, as he puts it, 'The King is under the law.'[35] Manwood alters its meaning slightly to put the stress on king's absolute preeminence in the realm:

The king or Soveraign Governor of a Realm, is the most excellent and worthiest part or member of the body of the Commonweale next unto God: as Bracton saith, *Ipse autem Rex non debet esse sub homine, sed sub Deo et Lege, quia lex facit Regem*. The King ought not to be under man, but under God and the Law, because the law doth make him a King. (II, 2, p. 54)

Through his diligence, pains and care, the king ensures peace and security for all. Thanks to his efforts and watchfulness, the realm can experience pleasure and joy. That is why:

the Law do attribute unto him all honour, dignity, prerogative, and pre-eminence: which prerogative doth not only extend to his own person, but also to all other his possessions, goods, and chattels beside: And therefore in respect of his continual care and labor, for the preservation of the whole Realm, being the residue of the body, the Laws doe allow unto the King, amongst many other priviledges, this pre-rogative, to have his places of recreation and pastime, wheresoever he will appoint: for, it is at the liberty and pleasure of the king, to reserve the wild beasts and the game to himself for his onely delight and pleasure, in such priviledged places where he will have a firm peace appointed for them. (II, 1, p. 55)

The political nature of Manwood's argument is apparent in this passage: not even John Cowell, in his *Interpreter* (burnt by the common hangman in 1610 on account of a number of absolutist remarks),[36] includes within the royal prerogative the king's right to plant forests wherever he pleases. But Manwood develops a logical justification: just as the law authorises the king to enter the property of any of his subjects if mines of gold or silver are discovered there, similarly it also authorises him 'to make a Forest even at his will and pleasure' (p. 55). Quite apart from the fact that gold and silver are things so excellent that the law attributes them 'to the most excellent person [in the realm] which is the King' (p. 56), these are also things that belong to nobody;[37] they are therefore wild, just as game is. So the king can dispose of them as he will:

And although men may kill such wild beasts in their wildnesse, when they are found wandring, being out of any Forest, Park, Chase, or Warren: Yet no man hath any property in them, untill they have killed them; for during the time of their wildnesse, they are *Nullius in rebus* and they then must needs be said to be *in manu domini regis*, in the King's possession: And then the King may priviledge them in any place where hee will appoint, to prohibit any man to kill or destroy them. (II, 1, p. 57)

To justify this special relationship between the king and wild animals, Manwood goes back to the period prior to the reign of Edgar (959–75) when inhabitants would destroy the woods around the places where they lived so as not to be attacked by wild beasts. These then took refuge further off in the huge wooded tracts of land: 'so that I do gather . . . that the first beginning of forest in England was *propter defectum inhabitantis populi*, for want of people to inhabit those vacant places wherein wilde beasts were' (II, 2, p. 63).

Commenting on this passage, one might say that only the king had authority over wild places which were situated 'outside' the law, far from all property and tenure. Charles Petit-Dutaillis notes that *Foresta* comes from *foris* and means: 'terrain located outside, forbidden to domestic animals, subjected to special conditions by royal proclamation'.[38] But he also remarks that the 'Forest' – a hunting area reserved for the king – probably did not antedate the Conquest. Manwood's historical considerations are, in effect, ideological. In his eyes, the king's relationship to wild animals, as to wild places, is founded upon natural law: it presents analogies with the allegiance that links subjects to their king,[39] which is said to have existed before the establishment of positive laws. Since he is a 'corporation sole',[40] that is to say a person both individual and collective, historical and trans-historical, who forms a diachronic collectivity together with his predecessors, the king derives his prerogative (and his relationship to the realm, the territory, the wild spaces and the cultivated or urbanised areas) from his very status, which is founded upon natural law. In other words, the king and his prerogative have both immemorial and presently existing roots. Manwood cites Fitz Nigel once more to establish this point more firmly, justifying royal 'refreshment' (hunting and retreat to the forest) by his need to escape from the Court, the place for things civilised and for agitation, in order to rediscover the breath of natural freedom:

For Kings and Princes do resort to the forest for their pleasure of hunting, having for that time laid aside all cares, to the end that they might there be refreshed with some quiet, being wearied with the continual business of the Court, they might (as it were) breath a while for the refreshing of their free liberty. And thereupon it cometh to pass that such offenders in Forests, for their offences are subject unto the only Judgement and determination of the King. (XXIV, 1, p. 487)

If the forest is the place of sacred 'refreshment' for the king, hunting is *par excellence* his recreative, punitive and civilising activity. The king is mediator between the civilised and the wild because he participates in both: 'We read in the 16. of Jeremy, where the Prophet threatneth the wicked, that God will send hunters to hunt them from the hills, and the mountains, and from the caves, wherein they were' (IV, 7, p. 107). And Manwood specifies: 'The Prophet useth this metaphor of a *Hunter*, because that a Hunter doth so greedily pursue after the wild beasts, that by the pursuing of them he doth make them yield themselves unto him from their wildness, to become even obedient unto him' (XVIII, 10, p. 299).

It should be noted that this function of the king as a civilising hero can only be understood in relation to his authority over the wild spaces, spaces where he is master, owner and also dependent (since it is indispensable for him to make these periodic returns to 'natural liberty'). It is, admittedly, only his civilising function that is picked out as a theme: it represents the visible, illuminated face of the hunter-king. But a shadowy face is also discernible: while he is hunting, he, like a hound, 'greedily' pursues his prey to overcome – or kill – it. There is wildness too, then, in his nature. It is a feature that appears in the definition that Gervase Markham gives of hunting:

a curious search or conquest of one Beast over another, pursued by a naturall instinct of enmity, and accomplished by the diversities and distinction of smells onely, wherein *Nature*, equally dividing her cunning, giveth both to the offender, and offended, strange knowledge both of offence and safety. In this recreation is to be seene the wonderfull power of God in his creatures, and how far rage and policie can prevaile against innocency & wisedome.[41]

Furthermore, the king's authority over wild spaces and animals is not unconnected with certain constitutional theories relating to the power of the king over conquered lands and kingdoms. In 1581 the House of Commons had Arthur Hall imprisoned for denying that the Commons went back to time 'immemorial'. If they did not they must have been created by some authority other than themselves as was claimed by the Reverend Dr Blackwood in his *Apologia pro Regibus* (1581) where he maintained that after the Conquest the power of William the Conqueror over possessions and men was absolute: those Anglo-Saxons who had retained their property held it only at his pleasure. And Blackwood went on to compare the situation of the Anglo-Saxons to that of the Indians after the Spanish conquest.[42]

Before his accession to the throne of England, James I himself declared in his 'Trew Law of Free Monarchies' (1598) that the kingdom of Scotland had been conquered and founded by Fergus before any parliament existed: 'And so it follows, of necessity, that the kings were the authors and makers of the laws and not the laws of the kings'.[43] James I went on to say that this statement was equally valid for England:

When the Bastard of Normandie came into England and made himself king, was it not by force and with a mighty army? Where he gave the Law and tooke none, changed the Lawes, invested the order of government, set down the strangers his followers in many of the old possessours roomes, . . and their old [Norman] lawes which to this day they are ruled by are written in his language and not in theirs; and yet his successors have with great happiness enjoyed the Crowne to this day; whereof the like was also done by all them that conquested them before.[44]

Francis Bacon, for his part, wrote in 1596 (although he changed his mind later on) that the ancient laws of England had been established by the Conqueror who 'got by right of conquest all the land of the realm into his own hands' and redistributed it as he wished.[45]

It is easy to see the relation that exists between war, conquest, hunting, the right of possession and, one might add, absolutism. The quarry that the king pursues so 'greedily', to use G. Markham's expression, might be game in the forest near at hand, distant man or some far-off land, or subjects unfortunate enough to incur his displeasure and who are inadequately protected by the law.

J. W. Allen has some ironical comments to make upon James I's argument: Was Fergus king even before he 'conquered' Scotland? For what reason did his men recognise the whole conquered land to be *his* property? Did the invaders bring with them no sort of law? And then, if Fergus was an absolute monarch before he left Ireland, the origin and nature of his monarchy was wholly independent of his conquest of Scotland. So the argument has no historical basis: it is simply a way for James I to proclaim that the king has sovereign and absolute power not only over the country but also over all its inhabitants. He will certainly not deprive them of their lives unless there exists a law that authorises him to do so, but that law will be one that either he himself or one of his predecessors has promulgated and he subjects himself to it – thus showing restraint and mercy – simply because it is his good pleasure to do so.[46]

Here we touch upon a controversial constitutional problem.[47] Whatever the practical politics of James I – and of Elizabeth before him – theories relating to absolute monarchy and to limited monarchy co-existed under the reign of the Tudors and Stuarts.[48] When he claimed that the king had a right to plant forests as he pleased, John Manwood was inclining towards the side of the absolutists. He implies that right depends upon force, and law upon conquest: in short, that the civilising function of the monarch only begins to be exercised after he has manifested his 'wildness' in order to master whatever is wild. Just as victorious war defines the relationship of a people to an enemy which is inferior to it – either because it is less civilised or more savage, or because its civilised nature had degenerated – similarly hunting defines man's relationship with wild nature. 'The hunter is first the predatory animal such as the lion or the eagle, second the cunning animal such as the snake or the wolf . . . and, third, he who possesses a skill, which is precisely what neither the lion nor the wolf do possess.'[49]

5. The protection of the forest

The forest is not only a wooded territory protected by confines, frontiers and purlieus, that is to say by physically perceptible spaces. Its legal status, that is, the immaterial protection it enjoys, is outside the common law of the realm. The space in which this was deployed was thus 'set apart' materially, legally and symbolically.

Manwood takes delight in describing the laws that protect the forest and the various individuals and legal rulings that should ideally stand guard over it, identifying and punishing all offences committed against it. The hierarchy of judges and forest authorities, whose almost total disappearance over the years Manwood deplores, was as follows: the territory of the kingdom was divided into two sectors, the one to the north of the Trent, the other to the south, each being entrusted to a forest judge. The forest 'wardens' – also known as 'stewards' or 'bailiffs' – each looked after one particular forest or group of forests.[50] Foresters were game-keepers as were 'foresters in fee', either in the service of the king or employed as subordinates by the wardens. The 'woodwards' (private foresters) looked after woods held by private individuals within the confines of the royal forest. The 'vert' and venison in these holdings had to be preserved for the king's hunt. 'Regarders' were sworn-in knights, chosen for the most part by the sheriffs: entrusted with a temporary mission of enquiry, they inspected or 'regarded' the forest every three years. 'Verderers' were knights or important tenants with possessions in the forest 'chosen by the Kings writ' (four for each forest, usually) and sworn to bring offenders before the forest court sessions and attend sessions of forestry justice.

The hierarchy as a whole was responsible for the surveillance of the forest, the collection of taxes and the administration of forestry justice. Manwood also describes the courts: among others, the court of attachment which was supposed to meet every forty days in each forest (every forty-two days according to Turner[51]) and judge minor offences, and the court of 'justices in eyre' which had in former times held session every three years but which in Manwood's time no longer sat – a fact that he deplores as without these journeying judges the entire system of forestry justice was paralysed or unbalanced.

All this personnel was responsible for administration, surveillance and repression in the forests. The royal desire to preserve this domain of prerogative had given rise to a considerable body of jurisprudence over the centuries, with the result that offences are described in astonishing detail. The 'vert' was divided into three sectors: the 'over vert' (upper wood), the 'nether vert' (the underbrush) and the 'special vert' (the wild berries upon which the deer fed). Destruction of such bushes carried heavy penalties. In point of fact, everything was 'special vert' in a royal forest – although that was not the case where enclaved woods and land within the forest were concerned. Then, of course, there were hunting offences, prohibitions against the possession of hounds the pads of whose front paws were not cut, and of nets and shares. Finally 'pourpresture' (encroachment upon the forest either by building or enclosure) was forbidden, as was 'waste' – that is to say the cutting of wood and in particular the clearing of land and the uprooting of trees for the purposes of cultivation. 'Vert' and venison were thus protected on every side: higher up, lower down and also on the forest edges. During the Elizabethan period offences were only punished by fines or, in default, by a year's prison sentence. But the memory of the old punitive measures lingered on. The forest remained 'outside', a concrete sign of what is 'faraway' and forbidden. The conservation and permanence of that sign was therefore of great political and symbolic importance.

6. The beast and the outlaw

In this connection, Manwood recalls two legal practices which confirm the sacred character of the forest and its special physical and legal nature. First, it is most important, he says, that the limits of the forest should be known to everybody. For if a man comes to be accused of killing a beast of the forest, the spot where the beast was killed is crucial: 'If that it were killed out of the Forest . . . [it must be] no offence to the Forest Laws' (VII, 2, p. 129).

Similarly, if a forester sees a man in the forest 'and after hue and cry made to him, to stand unto the peace, will not yield himself, but doe flie or resist' (VII, 2, p. 130), then if the forester kills the interloper within the limits of the forest he will not be accused of murder. For 'the killing of such an offendor within the limits of the forest, or without, maketh it felony, or no felony' (VII, 2, p. 130). Inside the forest the recalcitrant trespasser places himself in the position of a wild animal hunted by the king: his killing is legitimate. The expression used is 'after hue and cry made to him', for which Littré provides the gloss that he would be pursued to the sound of the horn and with loud cries, as in a hunt for a wild beast. Edward Coke confirms that 'the offence must be committed within the Forest' if appeal is to be made to these *verba dolentis*.[52] The expression goes back to a very ancient practice when pursuing criminals. The call to pursuit could be raised by private individuals, constables or officers of the peace. The officer of the peace would then be acting as though he held a mandate from a magistrate: in other words, he acted in the name of the king. Those who joined him had the right to apprehend the pursued man – who might, however, later be recognised to be innocent. If he took refuge in a house they could force the door if refused entry. A man thus found himself in a wild space where the common law of the realm did not apply, he became an outlaw, a hunter turned quarry, a man 'with the head of a wolf', according to Bracton's definition referred to by Cowell,[53] who has forfeited the benefit of the protection of the king and the law. All inhabitants in the country were obliged to lend assistance to the officer of the peace in his pursuit; if they did not do so they were collectively fined by the local court.[54] With this whole pack of men on his heels, the delinquent was 'turned into a wild thing' within the entire territory of the forest so that, as Manwood puts it, 'from Town to Town, Village to Village and place to place, within the limits and bounds of the Forest' (p. 313), the poacher would be relentlessly pursued.

The pursued man could find a temporary refuge only outside the forest: there, once again protected by the common law of the realm, he could only be arrested with a warrant. However – and this is a clause of capital importance – just as, when hounds held the quarry and were dragged along by it, they could be followed by the inhabitant of the purlieu into the forest itself in order to make the kill, similarly, if the forester did not lose sight of the trespasser, he could continue to follow him and apprehend him outside the forest.

These two symmetrical and inverted pursuits make it possible to say that 'wild places' were not simply a matter of a topographical location but resulted from a complex configuration: (1) a spatial relationship, (2) a relationship to the law, (3) a relationship to wildness and to the sacred, (4) a relationship between two agents directly opposite in character or situation, now as of hunter and quarry, now as of pack of hounds and quarry, now as of owner and owned beast – but an opposition which might also disappear when the scene of the pursuit changed. The opposition is neatly underlined by Manwood when he specifies that in cases of infraction against the laws of the forest there can be no distinction between principal agent and accomplices: where a number of persons have taken part all equally are considered to be principal agents of the transgression: 'None are accessaries in the trespasses of the Forest, but all are principals' (XIX, 5, p. 312).

7. The beasts of the forest

Many distinctions, however, exist within the forest. In the commentary that Manwood provides, along with his definition of the forest, he notes that the forest is not a privileged place for all kinds of animals indiscriminately, only for those which belong to 'the forest', 'the chase' or 'the warren'.

The difference between these three concepts – challenged by Petit-Dutaillis – is stressed most strongly by Manwood. It stems from the fact that a forest 'doth differ from a Chase [or a Warren], that is to say in particular Laws, in particular Officers [and particular animals], in certain Courts, that are incident unto a Forest' (p. 52), and he goes on to say:

> As a Forest in his own proper nature is the most highest franchise of noble, and princely pleasure, that can be incident unto the Crown and Royal dignity of a Prince, so the next in degree unto it is the liberty of a franke Chase. A Chase in one degree is the self same thing that a Park is, and there is no diversity between them, save only that a Park is inclosed, and a Chase is always open and not inclosed, and therefore the next in degree unto a frank Chase is a Park. The last and next in degree unto a Park is the liberty and franchise of a free Warren. (I, 5, pp. 52–3)

From a historical point of view these distinctions are easily explained: there were feudal chases and warrens which were inferior in dignity to the royal forest.[55] What is important here is that Manwood, faithful to his hierarchical vision of Elizabethan society, sets up a graded scale similar to that for living creatures. Furthermore, adopting the widely held view that what is superior contains and includes what is inferior, he specifies that a forest is at one and the same time a forest, a chase and a warren, or rather that 'because a Forest in dignity is both highest and the greatest franchise, being also a general and compound word, the same doth comprehend in it, a Chase, a Park, and a free Warren' (I, 5, p. 53). So killing a beast of the warren in the forest is an offence punishable according to the laws of the forest.

Finally, he classifies the beasts of the forest into three categories:

Beasts of the Forest	Beasts of the Chase	Beasts of the Warren
The hart	The buck	The hare
The hind	The doe	The coney
The hare	The fox	The pheasant
The boar	The martyn	The partridge
The wolf	The roe	

(IV, 1, 2, 3, pp. 91–6)

This classification has been challenged by Turner.[56] He claims that the law did not distinguish between the male and female of the red deer on the one hand and those of the fallow deer on the other. He maintains that if the words 'beasts of the forest' have any legal meaning they must refer to all those animals that were covered by the special laws of the forest and that the laws relating to red deer were the same as those relating to fallow deer: the two species should be placed in the same category. He notes that in the thirteenth century the roebuck was still one of the beasts of the forest but that it was excluded during the reign of Edward III and classified instead as a beast of the warren because it put other members of the deer family to flight. Furthermore, Turner says, the hare should not appear among the beasts of the warren as, except on rare occasions, it was not protected by the laws of the forest. Finally, Turner thinks it absurd to include the wolf in this category: far from being protected, it was considered a harmful beast that should be exterminated. He thus maintains that there were only four 'beasts of the forest': red deer, fallow deer, roebuck and boar and – in certain exceptional circumstances – the hare.

Turner's classification is strictly legal. Manwood's is traditional, legal and symbolic. It would appear to be based upon (1) Elizabethan legal memories,[57] (2) the classifications of William Harrison, Guillaume Budé, and a number of treatises on hunting[58] and (3) on a number of explicit symbolical and cynegetical considerations designed in advance to refute objections of the kind that Turner makes.

Manwood notes that the distinction between the red hart and hind on the one hand and the fallow buck and doe on the other can be justified by reference to the Psalms[59] and the kinds of terrain that these creatures prefer as their haunts – for the red deer the depths of the forest, for the fallow deer 'the fields, the hills and the mountains' (IV, 1, p. 97). The former are 'beasts of the woods', the latter 'beasts of the fields'. As for the wolf and the fox, Manwood admits that Canute's *Forest Constitutions* (actually an apochryphal work)[60] excluded them from the classification as they are harmful to men and are predators: nevertheless, he says, in the old days game-keepers included the wolf among the beasts of the forest and the fox among those of the chase 'for the Estimation that Kings and Princes have had of them, and for the noble pastime in the hunting and chasing of them' (IV, 1, p. 93).

Thus, the king's 'pleasure' is an essential element in Manwood's classification, as is the animal's aptitude to be hunted and to provide choice game. Biblical references are used to support his argument and to provide supplementary justifications for the hunt; every day Solomon treated himself to the meat of both red and fallow deer for his royal meal; Esau became Isaac's favourite son because he was a 'cunning' hunter (Genesis 15); God sends hunters in pursuit of the wicked (Jeremiah 16). 'Hunting in Forests, Chases, and such like priviledged places of pleasure, is only for Kings, Princes, and great worthy personnages, and not for mean men of mean calling or condition' (IV, 7, p. 107).

As Turner points out, Manwood's classification is not really legal; but it is traditional. J. Charles Cox has shown that it may have originated from some verses that appear in the preface of two treatises on hunting transcribed around 1440,[61] in which the animals are classified according to the ways in which they are tracked down and rousted out and according to whether they were hunted in the woods or in the open country. To Manwood's mind, the forest and hunting are linked in the same way as are the forest and prerogative. The wild, the sacred, the right of protection and of hunting (that is to say, ritual killing), the legal space and the territorial space together form an articulated whole for which the king is at once guarantor, beneficiary and emblem. The contiguity of the wild and the sacred is clearly indicated by the double role assigned to the forest: a place of sacred refreshment and refuge for the king and for beasts; a place of return to the wild when the hunt takes place, when only the king is empowered to kill or have the animal killed. By extension, this possibility of suffering death also applies to such of the king's subjects as have contravened the laws of the forest by usurping his prerogative.[62] For this concept of royalty both wild and sacred to be altogether meaningful, it was essential that it should not be territorially circumscribed, which is why Manwood maintains that, once the wolves were exterminated, all wild animals belonged to the king, wherever they might be, and that the king had the right to create new forests throughout the length and breadth of the realm, at his pleasure, even though the last attempt to do so, under Henry VIII, had been a failure.[63] Manwood's work is a deliberate if precarious reaffirmation of a symbolic system in the process of collapsing. The forest is used to confirm the supra-natural dimension of royalty while at the same time royalty provides confirmation that the forest has a similar dimension and nature.

8. The sacrifice of the red stag and the retreat of the wild

Manwood does not stop at dividing the beasts of the forest into separate categories. He lists the correct terms to designate the animals at their different ages (IV, 5); he gives the specific dates when the beast is 'in season', that is to say when it may be hunted; he enumerates the specific terms used to describe the various groups of animals and the verbs used in respect of the various species to indicate that they are rousted or flushed out. In short, within his juridical work he includes a little treatise on hunting.

He is particularly interested in the red stag which he places in a category of its own. He gives the names by which the animal is known at each year of its existence.[64] Thus, when it is five years old it is a 'stag'; when it is six, it is a 'hart'.[65] But it is never called a stag if the king or queen are hunting it: in that case it is always a 'hart'. Manwood notes that Canute's ancient Forest Charter described the 'hart' as a royal wild beast: *fera regalia*, otherwise known as a 'hart royal'. He goes on to tell us that if a beast hunted by the king escapes from the forest, the king can make a proclamation in the villages of the vicinity to the effect that nobody should harm it and that specially designated forest guards should return it to the forest. In such cases, the beast is called a 'hart royal proclaimed'. Manwood cites the case of a man who, under Henry VII, was accused of killing a 'hart proclaimed'; but, he adds, the accusation was dismissed as it proved impossible to establish exactly where the proclamation had been made (IV, 5, p. 100).

Within the confines of the forest no one could hunt the stag coursed by the king or kill it, except the king himself and his hunters. Outside the forest it became untouchable as if, once marked out for sacrifice, the beast became a part of the monarch's belongings, even outside the sanctuary that the forest represented for it.

Finally, Manwood lists the seasons for all the beasts of the forest.

Beast	Beginning of season	End of season
Red deer (stag)	24 June (Saint John)	14 September (Holy Cross)
Red deer (hind)	14 September (Holy Cross)	2 February (Candlemas)
Fallow deer (buck)	24 June (Saint John)	14 September (Holy Cross)
Fallow deer (doe)	14 September (Holy Cross)	2 February (Candlemas)
Roebuck (male)	Easter	29 September (Michaelmas)

Roebuck (female)	29 September (Michaelmas)	2 February (Candlemas)
Hare	29 September (Michaelmas)	24 June (Saint John)
Boar	Christmas	2 February (Candlemas)
Wolf	Nativity	25 March (Annunciation)
Fox	Nativity	25 March (Annunciation)

Actually, these dates vary slightly from one source to another. The hunting season for the three predatory or dangerous beasts, the boar, the fox and the wolf, began on Christmas Day and ended at Candlemas in the case of the boar, soon after the beginning of spring for the wolf and the fox. The hunting of roebuck began on Easter day, the hare could be hunted for three-quarters of the year, from Michaelmas to Saint John's day. The hunting of the red and fallow does began when the stag hunting was over. The red stag could only be hunted between Saint John's day and 14 September, the day of the Holy Cross.

The most obvious opposition is that which exists between stag hunting and the hunting of the predatory animals. The boar, theoretically hunted between Christmas and Candlemas, is the winter beast which dies when Carnival time begins. The symbolism of the boar is extremely complex.[66] The other two predatory beasts are hunted until springtime.

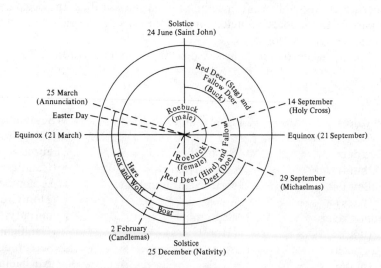

The hunting seasons, according to Manwood

The stag season begins at the summer solstice and ends shortly before the autumn equinox. Midsummer day follows the period when witches and evil spirits are at large. The coming of the stag thus corresponds with the departure of the evil spirits. The hunting of the stag comes to an end at the moment of the Exaltation of the Holy Cross when, according to the *Golden Legend*,[67] death becomes everlasting life and the Cross and the Blood of Christ perform miracles. Both dates speak for themselves.[68]

The ritual nature of stag hunting is evident from the way in which its trail is discovered and the ways it is chased and set at bay. But it is the way that it is cut up that is most revealing in this respect. In his treatise on hunting, George Turbervile describes the French and the English ways of cutting up a hart.

In the French manner, when a hart is killed the hunters sound their horns, the hounds are allowed to bite at the beast and are then put on the leash. The chief huntsman takes his knife and cuts off the front hoof of the hart which he presents to the king or chief personage present or to some lady whom he desires to honour. Green branches are cut and spread on the ground, the hart is placed on its back with its legs in the air. First its testicles or 'doucets' are cut off and hung from a forked stick already prepared for them. Then it is skinned. An incision is made from throat to abdomen, then various careful slits and the hide is removed. Once the hart has been skinned – except for the head – the huntsman asks for a bottle of wine and takes a draught, otherwise the venison would rot. The prince, who has been presented with a brazier, and a sauce made with wine and spices, has the pieces already cut roasted. They are eaten in such a fashion that princes may be 'rejoicing and recreating their noble mindes with rehersall which hound hunted best and which huntsman hunted moste like a woodman: calling theyr best favoured hounds and huntsmen before them and rewarding them'.[69] Then the huntsman again takes up his knife and cuts up the hart; he spreads the hide on the green foliage strewed on the ground and cuts off other choice morsels, one being the tongue which is offered to the king. Various morsels are then distributed to the hunters. Some, such as the heart, are given to the hounds, which are also rewarded in other ways, in particular with bread, cheese and milk mixed with the blood of the hart. It is clear that in the cutting up of the hart two kinds of gift may be distinguished: the honourable gifts, for the king and the hunters, and the rest – the pieces flung to the hounds.

In England, it is the prince or queen or chief personage in the hunt who first, having dismounted, touches the dead hart with a knife presented by the chief huntsman, to see how thick and good the flesh of the hart is. Then the head is cut off, this task generally falling to the chief personage in the hunt. Sometimes the head is cut off attached to the entire neck, to reward the hounds. The delicate morsels, such as the 'doucets', are also presented to the prince, but on a handkerchief. If the cutting of the shoulder is clumsy the chief huntsman is judged to be 'no handsome woodman'. There is an engraving in Turbervile's treatise showing a huntsman or nobleman offering Queen Elizabeth a knife for her to 'try' the flesh of the killed beast.

In reality, though, that was not always the way things happened. The hunt could turn into a veritable slaughter of game. At Cowdrey, in Sussex, with Lord Montecute in 1591, the queen was present at the pursuit and dismemberment by greyhounds of sixteen fallow buck: 'sixteen bucks, all having fayre law [that is to say a start of roughly twenty metres], pulled downe with greyhounds in a laud or law'.[70] On another occasion,

> Her Highness took horse and rode into the park, at eight o'clock in the morning, where was a delicate bowre prepared, under the which were her highness musicians placed; and a cross-bow, by a nymph, with a sweet song, was delivered into a hands, to shoot at the deere: about some thirty in number were put into a paddock, of which number she killed three or four, and the Countess of Kildare one.[71]

The habit of killing game without danger of failure, purely for the pleasure of killing, was fairly general. In a poem entitled 'Squyr of lowe degre', the king of Hungary promises his daughter that, if she comes hunting, the game, trapped in a net, will be easy to slaughter:

> Ye shall be set at such a tryst
> That hert and hynde shall come to your fist.[72]

As can be seen, the sacrificial ritual of the hunt may still be respected in the forests; but in the parks (and in the forests too when nets were used) the hunt was more of a slaughter – a butchery as Antony says in *Julius Caesar*. And it should be remembered at this point that the forest was also a park and a warren, as has been seen above.

So it would appear somewhat doubtful whether the forest described by Manwood – a forest subject to such careful verbal regulations yet in reality so little guarded and so often violated by intruders – was really still a shelter for 'the wild'. Despite the success of *Mucedorus*, contemporaries seem to have been aware of the situation, for they had invented or brought back into use an intermediate category where animals were concerned, in-between the domesticated and the wild.

In his *Description of England*, William Harrison, complaining of the proliferation of enclosed parks where fallow deer destined for the hunt are raised, writes:

> It is doubted of manie whether our bucke or doe are to be reckoned in wild or tame beasts or not. Plinie deemeth them to be wild. Martial is also of the same opinion, where he saith, '*Imbellas damae quid nisi praeda sumus*' [Inoffensive fallow deer, but for the fact that we are prey]. And so in time past the like controversie was about bees, which the lawyers call '*feras*' . . . But Plinie attempting to decide the quarell calleth them '*Medias inter feras et placidas aves*' [Bees in between the wild and and the peaceful].[73]

This legal allusion has a bearing upon a subject much discussed at this period: to whom did wild beasts, found objects, wrecks, etc., belong? Manwood is quite categorical: just as the king can enter the lands of his subjects when gold or silver mines are found there and can thereupon dig there at his good pleasure, so can he, according to law, create forests at his good pleasure so that beasts may rest there in firm peace (II, 1). This means that the king can at any moment decide that the beasts on such or such land belong to him. The point of declaring an animal to be wild was to prevent it, wherever it might be, from being the property of anyone but the king. That is what Manwood declared in Chapter II and he repeats it in Chapter XIV, 1 (p. 216): 'The king, by his Prerogative Royal, may afforest the demesne woods and lands, pastures and waste soyl of every man within this Realm, wheresoever he will'.

But Sir Edward Coke, the intransigent defender of the common law of the realm during the Jacobean period, held a different view. With impressive firmness he maintains, in the fourth part of his *Institutes of the Laws of England*, that since the time of Henry II the king has had no right to establish forests on the domain of his subjects. For, he says,

the common law hath so admeasured the king's prerogatives that they should not take away nor prejudice the inheritance of any. But we agree that all the lands of the subject are originally derived from the Crown. And therefore when the ancient kings had the most part in their own hands or at least great Desarts, waste and woody grounds for want of habitation, they might make what Forests it pleased them therein, which may be a reason and cause of a lawfull beginning, and therefore a Forest may be by prescription good in law over other men's grounds.[74]

In short, to discover or rediscover the wild forest, the forest that the king can create at his pleasure, one must go back to the origins, to the real or fictional constitution of property in the kingdom. The forest and the royal prerogative are now circumscribed and limited by the rights of other men, by their lands and by the laws: in other words, by the most important forms of civility.

Manwood, although with different intentions, puts forward a similar historical account: he refers to a period – an imaginary one – when all beasts *ferae naturae* ' . . . were the Kings only, in whose ground or land soever they were in any place, in the Realme' (II, 2, p. 64); and it was only later on that they ceased to belong to the king unless they were within his domain or his forest. According to Manwood, however, they could always become his property again, since the king had the right to establish forests at his good pleasure.

This problem of the ownership of wild beasts and treasures that belonged to nobody, which Hugo Grotius was soon to tackle in his great work,[75] is evidence of the fact that, in the royal forest, the sacred is associated with the wild, the more clearly so given that the common law of the realm, bourgeois civilisation and cultivated nature were progressively pressing closer upon them, and gradually making them both disappear wherever the dominion of the law, of civility and of culture was becoming more absolute. R. H. Tawney has written that in the sixteenth and seventeenth centuries we can detect a tragic (or perhaps pathetic, if not 'hysterical', according to Christopher Morris) attempt to reaffirm a system that was fast disappearing.[76]

The common ground reserved for wildness was shifting not only in reality but also in literature. Shakespeare's exiles or 'brigands' (*The Two Gentlemen of Verona, As You Like It, Cymbeline*) are to be found in wild places that pastoral conventions and the author's irony make unreal. The fact is that now the place for the wild is situated beyond the seas or, in a domestic English context, in madness, in individual transgressions, popular revolts or collective disorders. It is no accident if *King Lear* is sometimes called an inverted pastoral. The time when the action is supposed to be taking place, a past and almost mythical period, makes it possible to restore to nature some of its wild and inhuman characteristics. But what is important above all is that the space in which this wildness is unleashed is outside the city; it is an imaginary space where natural and civilised laws are suspended, transgressed or set aside. The wild becomes internal; its place is at the heart of men who live at the heart of civility.

9. Conclusion

The interest of Manwood's work lies in the fact that it tackles both legal and factual matters. For Manwood the forest is both a natural space and a legal concept. Thus, he teaches us to become aware of the tangled web which all reality presents: we cannot entirely separate facts from human constructions or reality from what is imagined or symbolised. He also helps us to understand that ideology is not a construction which can be detached from the facts or reality that it interprets. Its elements of truth and untruth, and all the parts of it that constitute a vision of the world without which nothing would be discernible or significant, are all inextricably intertwined.

The work is made up of a compilation of legal judgements, edicts and precedents that can be read as a historical presentation of the laws relating to the forest and the constitutional and political problems raised by the existence of the forest ever since its real or imaginary origins. But Manwood reorganises this material from a perspective that is peculiar to his own period and his own options. Some of the latter are conscious and betray political aims or ecological interests, but others are unconscious: thus, the relation between the pursuit of the outlaw and that of the beast hunted in the purlieu only emerges under analysis, as does the homology between the geographical situation of the various spaces of the forest and those described in pastoral. And other correspondences too might be cited. For example, at Beverley, Durham, Ripon and elsewhere, those who violated the privileges of a sanctuary were liable to sanctions, the severity of which increased in proportion to the proximity to the centre of the place where the violation took place. J. Charles Cox notes that at St-John-de-Beverley, the area of refuge extended over a radius of one and a half miles around the church. This was divided into six zones: while an infraction committed in the outermost zone was punishable by a fine, nothing, in the old days, could atone for an offence committed within the sixth and innermost zone, where the altar was located – nothing, short of the life of the sacrilegious individual.[77]

Thus, if the structural relations between hunting, pursuit, wildness, sacrilege and the sacred that Manwood describes are relevant to the forest and its inhabitants, they are also pertinent to other places[78] and creatures.

APPENDIX I
The 'seasons' for the animals

The dates that determine the beginnings and the ends of the 'seasons' for the various animals are to a large extent arbitrary and from one source to another there are considerable variations. Here is a table showing these variations.

Animal	Source	Beginning of season	End of season
Stag	Twici Manwood	24 June (Saint John)	14 September (Holy Cross)
	Edward of Norwich	8 July	Not specified
		3 May (Holy Cross) (France)	14 September (Holy Cross) France)
Hind	Twici Manwood	14 September (Holy Cross)	2 February (Candlemas)
	Sources other than Twici and Manwood	14 September (Holy Cross)	6 January (Epiphany)
Buck	Manwood	24 June (Saint John)	14 September (Holy Cross)
	Dryden (*see* Twici)	8 July	Not specified
Doe	All sources	14 September (Holy Cross)	2 February (Candlemas)

Roebuck	All sources	Easter	29 September (Michaelmas)
Roebuck (female)	All sources	29 September (Michaelmas)	2 February (Candlemas)
Hare	Berners Manwood	29 September (Michaelmas)	24 June (Saint John)
	Dryden (*see* Twici)	29 September (Michaelmas)	2 February (Candlemas)
	Edward of Norwich	In all seasons	
	Ferrières	March and April (Hunting with hounds)	
		May and June (Trapping)	
	Fouilloux	Mid-September–Mid-May (France, sixteenth century)	
	Edward of Norwich	Mid-September–Mid-May (England, sixteenth century)	
Boar	Manwood Twici	Christmas	2 February (Candlemas)
	Ferrières	29 September (Michaelmas)	11 November (Saint Martin)
	Bormann	14 September (Holy Cross)	11 November (Saint Martin)
	Berners	Nativity	Purification of the Virgin Mary
Wolf	Manwood Berners	Nativity	25 March (Annunciation)
Fox	Manwood	Nativity	25 March (Annunciation)
	Twety	8 September (Nativity of the Virgin Mary)	25 March (Annunciation)
	Berners	Nativity	25 March (Annunciation)
	Wardrobe Accounts of Edward I	1 September	19 November

Source: Edward of Norwich, Second Duke of York, *The Master of Game* (trans. of the treatise by Gaston de Foix (alias Gaston Phoebus), eds. William A. and Florence Baillic-Grohman, London, 1904, pp. 188–9. With this edited text, the publishers also produced a superb study on hunting.

Reference list of hunting books cited in the table (in chronological order)

Wardrobe Accounts of Edward I: *Liber quotididnus Contrarotulatoris Garderobae. 28 Edward I, A.D. 1299–1300*, Society of Antiquaries of London, London, 1787, p. 308.

Twici (or Twiti), Guillaume, *Le Art de Vénerie* (first half of fourteenth century), published as *The Art of Hunting, by William Twici, Huntsman to King Edward the Second.* (*MSS. Phillipps, No. 8336.*) [*now in British Library, Add. MS 46919*] *With Preface, Translations, Notes, and Illustration*, by H. Dryden, Daventry, 1863.

Ferrières, Henri de, *Les Livres du roy Modus et de la royne Ratio* (*c.* 1354–76), vol. 1: *Le Livre des deduis du roy Modus*; vol. 2: *Le Songe de pestilence*, ed. G. Tilander, Société des Anciens Textes Français, 2 vols., Paris, 1932.

Twety, Guillaume and Gyfford (or Giffard), John, *Le Venery de Twety* (an early fifteenth-century version of the *Vénerie*, in the Cottonian MS, Vespasian B. XII, fols. 5–9, at the British Library), eds. Thomas Wright and J. O. Halliwell, in *Reliquiae Antiquae*, 2 vols., William Pickering, London, 1841–3, vol. 1, pp. 149–54.

Edward of Norwich, Second Duke of York, *The Master of Game* (*c.* 1420), trans. of the *Livre de Chasse* by Gaston de Foix (alias Gaston Phoebus), eds. William A. and Florence Baillie-Grohman, London, 1904.

Bernert, Dame Juliana (see Julians Barnes), *The Boke of Saint Albans* (containing several treatises) (printed at St Albans in 1486), facsimile edn with introd. by William Blades, London, 1881.

Fouilloux, Jacques du, *La Vénerie* (1561), ed. Gunnar Tilander, *Cynegetica*, 16, E. G. Johanssons, Karlshamn, 1967.

Manwood, John, *A Treatise and Discourse of the Lawes of the Forest*, 4th edn enlarged by W. Nelson, London, 1717.

Bormann, Ernst, *Die Jagt in den altfranzösischen Artus- und Abenteuer-Romanen*, N. G. Elwert, Marburg, 1887.

Recent editions of Twici and Berners are as follows:

La Vénerie de Twiti (French and English versions), ed. Gunnar Tilander, *Cynegetica*, 2, Almqvist and Wiksells, Uppsala, 1956.

Boke of Huntyng (by Juliana Berners, or Julians Barnes), ed. Gunnar Tilander, *Cynegetica*, 11, E. G. Johanssons, Karlshamn, 1964.

2. The forest, hunting and sacrifice in *Titus Andronicus*

Shakespeare's interest in the themes of hunting, the forest and sacrifice – or the sacrificial act insofar as it can be represented or evoked on stage – can be clearly seen in *Titus Andronicus*.[1]

While Saturninus and Bassianus are engaged in a struggle for power, Titus makes his triumphal entry into Rome. He has conquered the Goths and brings back prisoners with him: Tamora, queen of the Goths, her three sons Alarbus, Chiron and Demetrius, and Aaron the Moor. Alongside four living sons, he also brings back the bodies of his own twenty-one sons who have been killed. To appease their shades, Lucius asks that a Goth be sacrificed before the bier of his brothers and Titus grants his request:

> *Lucius*: Give us the proudest prisoner of the Goths,
> That we may hew his limbs, and on a pile
> *Ad manes fratrum* sacrifice his flesh
> Before this earthy prison of their bones,
> That so the shadows be not unappeas'd,
> Nor we disturb'd with prodigies on earth.
> *Titus*: I give him you, the noblest that survives,
> The eldest son of this distressed queen. (I, i, 96–103)

This sacrifice corresponds to what Shakespeare and his audience considered to be Roman custom.[2] Its purpose was to spare the living the anger of the dead and prevent the occurrence of disastrous prodigies.

Tamora begs that her eldest son be spared:

> Stay, Roman brethren! Gracious conqueror,
> Victorious Titus, rue the tears I shed,
> A mother's tears in passion for her son:
> And if thy sons were ever dear to thee,
> O, think my son to be as dear to me.
> Sufficeth not that we are brought to Rome,
> To beautify thy triumphs, and return
> Captive to thee and to thy Roman yoke;
> But must my sons be slaughtered in the streets

> For valiant doings in their country's cause?
> O, if to fight for king and commonweal
> Were piety in thine, it is in these.
> Andronicus, stain not thy tomb with blood:
> Wilt thou draw near the nature of the gods?
> Draw near them then in being merciful;
> Sweet mercy is nobility's true badge:
> Thrice-noble Titus, spare my first-born son.   (I, i, 104–20)

First Tamora refers to the similarity of the feelings that a father and a mother should feel for their respective children. To this argument, which appeals to the humanity common to both conqueror and conquered, she then adds another: patriotism should be respected even in an enemy. She adjures Titus not to defile this tomb with blood: pity, not intransigence or harshness, is a virtue worthy of the gods and it is also a sign of true nobility.

A few comments are necessary at this point. Although the Elizabethan public may have believed that the souls of the dead sometimes returned to harass the living,[3] it could hardly have believed that a human sacrifice had ever really been necessary to appease the anger of the dead. In the words of Philip Brockbank: 'Resistance to the ancient cult of sacrifice is an important and necessary strain in both humanist and Christian tradition'.[4] On the other hand, revenge, which is a disguised form of sacrifice and which obliges the avenger to 'take the law into his own hands' even though he has no legal (or possibly even moral) right to set himself up as an agent of justice, did sometimes take place in real life and was often acted out with great success in the theatre.[5]

Tamora's arguments – humanitarian, patriotic and with their appeal to the virtues of nobility – were familiar and probably convincing to the Elizabethan public. In contrast, Titus' reply:

> Patient yourself, madam, and pardon me.
> These are their brethren whom your Goths beheld
> Alive and dead, and for their brethren slain
> Religiously they ask a sacrifice:
> To this your son is mark'd, and die he must,
> T'appease their groaning shadows that are gone.   (I, i, 121–6)

must have seemed specious in the eyes of Christians. 'Religiously they ask a sacrifice': that calls to mind Lopez de Gomara's remark that the Indians 'were growne even to the highest hill of crueltie under the colour of devout and religious persons'.[6] Tamora's exclamation: 'O, cruel, irreligious piety!' may well have been in tune with the feelings of some of the public even if that public could understand that the sacrificial act simply masked a desire for vengeance. Lucius' two rejoinders must have confirmed those feelings:

> Away with him, and make a fire straight,
> And with our swords, upon a pile of wood,
> Let's hew his limbs till they be clean consum'd.   (I, i, 127–9)

> See, lord and father, how we have perform'd
> Our Roman rites: Alarbus' limbs are lopp'd,
> And entrails feed the sacrificing fire,
> Whose smoke like incense doth perfume the sky.   (I, i, 142–5)

In *The Discoverie of Witchcraft* (1584), Reginald Scot speaks of the 'barbarous impiety' of the Indians who 'sacrifice such of their enemies as they have taken in warre'.[7] In *Titus Andronicus*, the emphasis placed on dismemberment, on entrails burning on the sacrificial fire and perfuming the heavens like incense, must have been shocking to a public which disapproved of the cruelty of pagan customs and whose own religious ceremonies, moreover, had been made more sober after the Reformation. Furthermore, the barbarity of Rome is compared in the play by Chiron to that of the Scythians, and Demetrius assimilates Titus to the tyrant of Thrace, promising his mother that the day will come when vengeance will be possible.

This human sacrifice takes place at the moment when the power in Rome is in dispute; it may be seen as Titus' first mistake. The second is his refusal to assume the power that is offered to him and his decision to get his supporters to vote for Saturninus. The third is to take Saturninus' side when the latter seeks to marry Lavinia, already promised to Bassianus, and to kill his son Mutius because he revolts at this breaking of an earlier promise. All the horrors that are then perpetrated in the play have these events as their origin: the dismemberment of Alarbus is followed by the severing of the hands and tongue of Lavinia, the hand of Titus and the heads of Quintus, Martius and finally also of Demetrius and Chiron. Despite the often precious language and verbal flourishes which have surprised or shocked so many commentators,[8] it was hardly possible to take a detached attitude before the horror of this series of mutilations, the climax of which is the cannibal meal that Titus offers Tamora. 'To chop, to lop, to hew, to cut' – the words recur so often, accompanied by images or visible 'tableaux' produced on the stage, that the text propped up by these visible signifiers which have a greater force and longer lasting impact than the words themselves, acquires an almost realistic violence.

Although the human sacrifice does not occur on stage it is clearly introduced into the play to produce a shock effect. The fact that an act of 'religious barbarity' takes place in a city regarded in the sixteenth century as the very symbol of civilisation suggests that Shakespeare was already adopting a Christian point of view to judge and describe events happening before the advent of Christianity. But were such horrors really only conceivable in a pre-Christian civilisation? In *Henry VI*, Part III, the great families of England contending for power perpetrate similar cruelties. Thus, when Queen Margaret, Clifford and Northumberland have taken the duke of York prisoner (I, iv), the queen orders that he be stood on a molehill, he who

> . . . raught at mountains with outstretched arms,
> Yet parted but the shadow with his hand.[9]

Then she insults him at length, mocking his sons, particularly the youngest one, Edmund, duke of Rutland, assassinated though still a child. The queen hands York a handkerchief soaked in Rutland's blood, for him to wipe away his tears. And so that the analogy with the crucifixion should not pass unnoticed, after the handkerchief, which recalls the sponge proffered to Christ, a crown (or a garland) made of paper is offered to York:

> York cannot speak unless he wear a crown.
> A crown for York! and, lords, bow low to him:
> Hold you his hands whilst I do set it on.   (I, iv, 93–5)

The queen stays the hand of Clifford – who is for striking York down immediately – so as to prolong his torments. Thereupon York laments the death of Rutland so poignantly that Northumberland can barely 'contain his tears'. Then York compares his enemies to cannibals:

> That face of his the hungry cannibals
> Would not have touch'd, would not have stain'd with blood;
> But you are more inhuman, more inexorable,
> O, ten times more than tigers of Hyrcania.   (I, iv, 152–5)

Revolting as the attitude of the queen and Clifford is, it is nevertheless in conformity with the inexorable fatality that rules the actions of avengers. In a similar fashion, in *Titus Andronicus*, sacrifice, which is in conformity with the customs of the city, is an expression of family piety. However, as Alan Sommers points out, that piety is an 'insufficient virtue' for it is devoid of pity;[10] Shakespeare himself, in making Northumberland react with such emotion, clearly makes the point that vengeance should have its limits.

Having shown himself pitiless with regard to Tamora and blind where Saturninus is concerned, Titus later finds himself at the mercy of the woman whose pleas he so implacably rejected. Political authority in Rome falls into the hands of his enemies. There then ensues a reign of injustice, that is to say chaos. Altogether in conformity with habitual cycles of revenge, a chain of reprisals and counter reprisals is set in motion. But the acts of revenge which punctuate the play should not be considered simply as criminal for here the atrocities also have a mediating value, similar to that of sacrifice, and when the cycle is completed it restores order to Rome 'through the sacrificial tragedy and the death-ritual of the feast'.[11]

The action now moves from Rome to the forest. At the end of the first act Titus invited Saturninus to hunt the panther and the stag with him (I, i, 494). But Titus, who sees himself as the hunter, is soon to become the hunted beast. The monologue delivered by Aaron, who remains on stage alone after the first act, represents the pivot of the action. Servility is no longer appropriate since now Titus holds his imperial mistress captive (II, i. 13). The plan of revenge now put forward is not simply to strike the Andronicus family, as Tamora had suggested to Saturninus. It is to drag the whole of Rome down into chaos and also to strike at Saturninus. Aaron thus declares himself as the perfect villain: he has also the negative and satanic characteristics of the conventional Moor, together with his guilty lust: he plans to have his pleasure with this queen,

> This goddess, this Semiramis, this nymph,
> This siren that will charm Rome's Saturnine,
> And see his shipwrack and his commonweal's.   (II, i, 22–4)

But personal – and, in Aaron's case, gratuitous – revenge comes first. He suggests to Chiron and Demetrius that they violate Lavinia. The parallel between the woman-hunt and the doe-hunt is thus established. And furthermore Aaron defines the forest as a place predestined by nature to the release of savagery:

> My lords, a solemn hunting is in hand;
> There will the lovely Roman ladies troop:
> The forest walks are wide and spacious,
> And many unfrequented plots there are
> Fitted by kind for rape and villainy:
> Single you thither then this dainty doe,
> And strike her home by force, if not by words:
> This way, or not at all, stand you in hope.   (II, i, 112–19)

What is being prepared will be 'a solemn hunting', a ceremony[12] but an atrocious one, 'a triumph of the forces of evil', to use Antonin Artaud's phrase,[13] a kind of spiritual plague: 'the troubled humours of the plague-ridden [are], as it were, the solid and material side to a disorder which, on other levels, is equivalent to all the conflicts, struggles, cataclysms and disasters that events bring us'.[14]

'The dainty doe' says Aaron. And Demetrius repeats it, when Titus invites him to the hunt:

> Chiron, we hunt not, we, with horse nor hound,
> But hope to pluck a dainty doe to ground.   (II, ii, 25–6)

The adjective is the same, 'dainty', a word used to describe an object of choice, something to eat, to hunt, to possess, to violate, to enjoy.[15]

Tamora, in her turn, enters the forest, there to meet Aaron. This natural setting in which she desires to sport with her lover is agreeable and pleasing, with birds singing in every bush and a breeze making the green leaves quiver (II, iii, 12–15). But that is a subjective view. Aaron tells Tamora that his thoughts are not of love: revenge is in his heart, death in his hand. Perfect villain that he is, he has thought it all out: the rape, the murder and the false accusations. The two lovers are surprised by Bassianus and Lavinia. Lavinia accuses Tamora of changing Saturninus into a stag and prays to Jupiter for the hounds to spare him! Chiron and Demetrius arrive upon the scene. Tamora, like an outraged Diana, urges her sons on to vengeance, that is to say to rape and murder. The forest reveals its evil power. It is a place where the violence of the instincts can be unleashed without restraint. Bassianus is assassinated by Demetrius and Chiron. And under the very eyes of Tamora, and with her approval, the two sons drag Lavinia off to rape her (offstage). To prevent her revealing the identity of her aggressors, they cut off her hands and remove her tongue. In an extra piece of plotting Aaron has buried some gold in the forest as a lure and thereby makes the blame for the assassination fall upon Martius and Quintus (two of Titus' sons).

The forest in which this hunt of the human doe takes place and where a man is thus killed like a beast symbolises an instinctual, evil and fatal force. Aaron is under the sign of Saturn, like Saturninus. Tamora is compared to Diana surprised by voyeurs, and the myth of Acteon to which she refers is transposed literally by Shakespeare, who has the doe violated and Bassianus killed by those dogs, Chiron and Demetrius. Aaron himself plays the role of an evil hunter, forcing Quintus and Martius into a trap, making them fall into the pit in which the body of Bassianus has been placed. Shakespeare makes considerable use of Ovidian themes: not just the story of Acteon, but that of Philomel too.

As mentioned above, some critics consider that the violence is somewhat distanced by the preciosity of the language. But that is to underestimate the theatrical force of the murders committed before the very eyes of the spectators, and above all the impact of the scenes of mutilation. Lavinia appears, her mouth bloodied and her hands severed. When Aaron suggests to Titus that he could save the heads of his sons by cutting off his hand, Titus agrees and mutilates himself right there before the audience. And it is before the spectators too that the heads of his sons together with his own severed hand are presented to him. The culmination of all these horrors is when Titus cuts the throats of Tamora's two sons, while Lavinia catches their blood in a basin. The cannibal feast is then prepared by Titus, dressed as a cook. The bones, ground to 'dust', are mixed with the blood to make a paste in which the heads of Chiron and Demetrius are cooked. They are then offered as a meal to Saturninus and Tamora, and Titus is careful to note that it is a meal 'whereof their mother daintily hath fed' (V, iii, 61). Titus is jubilant: the mother has eaten 'the flesh that she herself hath bred'. Tamora is then stabbed to death by Titus who has earlier also killed his own daughter to spare her living with the memory of the defilement she suffered.

Titus and Saturninus die, in their turn. When the cycle of family and personal violence comes to an end, so do the chaos and injustice that have ruled in Rome. Thanks to an army of Gauls which, for reasons that are none too

clear, has agreed to march on Rome under the command of the last of Titus'
sons, the city is restored to order and civil conviviality.

> *Marcus*: You sad-fac'd men, people and sons of Rome,
> By uproars sever'd, as a flight of fowl
> Scatter'd by winds and high tempestuous gusts,
> O, let me teach you how to knit again
> This scattered corn into one mutual sheaf,
> Those broken limbs again into one body;
> Lest Rome herself be bane unto herself . . .   (V, iii, 67–73)

Aaron and Tamora are punished as befits their crimes; Aaron is buried
alive and Tamora denied burial and thrown to the beasts and birds of prey,
for 'her life was beast-like and devoid of pity' (V, iii, 198).

The connections and comparisons in the narrative are most interesting in
this early work. The play begins at the moment when two rivals are contending for power and Titus returns in triumph to Rome. The opposition
between the two candidates is also an opposition between two types of
government: the one, Saturninus', is evil for it contains all the seeds of
tyranny; the other, through Bassianus, represents the Roman empire as
seen by medieval tradition, with an addition of republican ideals.[16] Shakespeare is at pains to show us the complex origins of the disorders that ensue.
A sacrifice, in conformity with the traditions of family and city, but pitiless
nonetheless; an ill-omened choice which places Titus at the mercy of the
barbarism that he has just vanquished outside Rome but traces of which still
exist in the heart of the city itself. Although the major opposition between
the first and second acts is between the civilised and the wild – between the
city and the forest – one can also discern the minor theme that wildness is not
absent from the customs of Rome while nature is not invariably a sombre
and doom-laden scene. The fact is that Tamora finds civilised arguments to
plead for the life of her son whose sacrifice Titus orders. And even Aaron is
concerned about what will happen to the child Tamora has conceived by him
and that he takes care of after leaving Rome.

In the forest, the hunt unfolds back to front in the manner made famous
by the myth of Acteon. The mutilations and dismemberments take place
both in the wild forest and in the now-barbarous city. The cannibal meal is
as it were an emblem of the events of the play as a whole: it is a hideous perversion of all relationships of proximity and it is, in effect, just such relationships of proximity and conviviality, so necessary to civilised life, that are
transformed, frustrated and undermined every time some bloody event
takes place on the stage. The close connection between – or succession of –
social disorder, sacrifice, hunting, defloration, madness, mutilation, murder
and cannibalism is thus not simply a chain of events representing a con-
cession to a public thirst for sensationalism; it is a series with a significance

of its own: *Titus Andronicus* can be seen as a structured repertory of the themes that Shakespeare was to exploit with greater maturity and depth in his later works.

3. Some reflections on sacrifice

1. Elizabethan attitudes to sacrifice

The meaning, function and forms of sacrifice hold a special place in the preoccupations of the Elizabethan consciousness. This is chiefly because this was a Christian civilisation where the crucifixion was the event around which all liturgy was organised: the sacrifice of Christ is constantly recalled in homilies, theological texts, iconographical representations and architecture.

The Reformation renewed the meaningfulness of the eucharistic ritual. How should the mass be celebrated? How should communion be administered? How should the presence of Christ in the bread and wine be understood? Luther and Calvin in effect deny that there is any sacrificial aspect to the mass, or at least the idea of any propitiatory sacrifice. They demand that communion be delivered in both kinds. There were countless arguments about what really happens when one eats and drinks in the course of the communion. Calvin rejects Zwingli's view which is that, in communion, the believer is commemorating the sacrifice of the Cross in a purely symbolic and spiritual fashion. He also rejects the catholic theory of transubstantiation according to which the substance of the bread and wine is annihilated to give place to the real presence of the body and blood of Christ. Instead, he envisages a presence that is both spiritual and real: the faith of the communicant transforms the bread and wine into a true spiritual offering. The stress is laid upon faith, there is no direct or material relationship between the body and blood of Christ on the one hand and the bread and wine on the other.

Following the Forty-two articles of 1553, the confession of faith promulgated by Henry VIII and abolished by Mary Tudor, the Thirty-nine articles, adopted in 1563 and ratified in 1571 by Elizabeth, constitute the doctrinal charter of the Church of England. Papist errors and a part of catholic teaching are repudiated. The Scriptures become the only authority in matters of faith. Only two sacraments are recognised: baptism and communion. Compulsory celibacy for priests is abolished. Services must be held in English. The twenty-eighth article specifically states that transubstantiation 'is repugnant to the plain words of Scripture, overthroweth the Nature of a Sacrament and hath given Occasion to many Superstitions. The Body of Christ is given, taken and eaten in the Supper only after an heavenly or spiritual Manner. And the Mean whereby the Body of Christ is received and eaten in the Supper is Faith.'[1]

The promulgation of the Forty-two articles followed by that of the Thirty-nine had given rise to many theological polemics in which catholics and protestants argued their various positions. The question of transubstantiation occupies a place of primary importance in these and gives rise to many disagreements over sacrifice. In the polemic involving John Jewel, the bishop of Salisbury, and Thomas Harding, who had abandoned protestantism and taken refuge in Louvain, Harding maintains that Christ was offered to his father in three ways: figuratively; in reality, with the shedding of blood; and sacramentally or mystically. He adds that all the sacrifices of the Old Testament in their various ways prefigured this particular sacrifice. He goes on to observe that Christ was truly offered up on the Cross; and that sacramentally or mysteriously Christ is offered up to his father in the Church's sacrifice, in the form of bread and wine, truly and in all reality: his very body and blood are really present.[2]

Bishop Jewel replies that at the time of the laws of Moses, the priests and Levites were offering up to God oxen, calves, rams and goats; with the blood they sprinkled the book, the instruments of priesthood, the whole tabernacle and all those present; as Saint Paul says, in the ceremonies relating to those laws, 'without shedding of blood is no remission of sin' (Heb. ix) (p. 719). In a similar fashion, Jewel goes on to say, the pagans used to kill their beasts and offer them up to their idols – sometimes as many as a hundredfold in a single day. Sometimes they went further and used human blood in their sacrifices. Erechtheus of Athens and Marius of Rome killed and offered up their own daughters in honour of Pallas. In the honour of Saturn, the nobles of Carthage killed and offered up in a single sacrifice seventy of their own male children. 'In respect of these gross and fleshly and bloody sacrifices, our Christian sacrifices in the gospel, because they are more spiritual and proceed wholly from the heart, are called unbloody.'[3]

The protestant bishop opposes the 'blood' sacrifices of the pagans, Jews and catholics to the non-blood sacrifices of the protestants and emphasises that once Christ had been sacrificed on the Cross no other blood sacrifice was ever again necessary. This idea is constantly repeated. Thus, Bishop Hooper writes:

I believe that Jesus Christ by the sacrifice of his body, which he offered upon the tree of the Cross, hath defaced and destroyed sin, death and the devil, with all his kingdom; and hath wholly performed the work of our salvation, and hath abolished and made an end of all other sacrifices; so that from thenceforth there is none other propitiatory sacrifice either for the living or the dead, to be looked for or sought for, than the same: for by this one only oblation hath he consecrated for ever all those that are sanctified.[4]

Long explanations on the first sacrifices are also to be found in Henry Bullinger's *Decades*. In 1586, in the province of Canterbury, Archbishop Whitgift ordered that every minister of religion in charge of a parish who did not hold the qualification of Master of Arts, Bachelor of Law or a licence to preach publicly,

shall before the second day of February next provide a Bible, and Bullinger's *Decade* in Latin or English, and a paper booke, and shall every day read over one chapter of the Holy Scriptures, and note the principal contentes thereof briefly in his paper booke, and shall every weeke read over one Sermon in the said *Decades* [fifty in all], and note likewise the chief matters therein contained in the said paper.[5]

The sixth sermon of the third *Decade* is entirely devoted to 'the sacraments of the Jews' and 'their sundry sorts of sacrifices'. Bullinger points out that Cain, Abel, Noah, Shem, Abraham and Isaac all offered up sacrifices. He notes that the pagan sacrifices of the Gentiles resembled those of the Jews: it is therefore conceivable that the 'great patriarchs' of the Gentiles may each have taught their respective nations how to make sacrifices, in accordance with the lesson they themselves had received from their own ancestors Shem, Ham, Japhet or Noah. The various sacrifices shared a number of common features: they could only be made in one particular spot and had to be inspired by a pure faith; the animal had to be burned by a sacred flame, not by a fire lit in a profane manner; wild or impure beasts were not to be used, etc. Bullinger then gives a detailed description of the holocaust, in which the offered beast had its throat cut by the priest, its blood collected to be sprinkled around the altar, its hide removed (this was the portion of the animal reserved for the priests), and then all the rest was burned. He goes on to mention the oblation (an offering of food and drink) and expiatory sacrifices, etc.

His method of exposition, which is traditional, puts one in mind of what Erich Auerbach calls the 'figural' interpretation of the Old Testament, which consists in interpreting events as 'figures' or pre-figurations of the episodes described in the New Testament.[6] For instance, Bullinger devotes much space to the sacrifice of the scapegoat, which took place for the feast of atonement, on the tenth day of the seventh month of every year; its purpose was to wipe away, or cleanse, the collective sins of the entire people. He is not concerned to give a detailed description of the way in which this sacrifice was made as a full account of that appears in Leviticus; but he is anxious to interpret its meaning and mystery:

In that most pleasant glass was figured the whole passion, and effect of the passion, of Jesus Christ, our Lord and Saviour; which by that sacrifice was every year laid before the eyes and renewed to the minds of all the faithful church of God. For this manner of representing our redemption and salvation did please God, by sacraments, rather than by pictures, colours or by stage-plays . . . [7]

On that day the high priest officiated alone, with the aid of no more than two assistants, one to take the scapegoat away, the other to carry far away from the crowd the young ox and the second ram that were to be sacrificed. In Leviticus (xvi.17), there is an injunction stipulating that the high priest should be alone in the sanctuary to carry out the sacrifice. Bullinger interprets this as follows: 'For no man must be joined to Christ in finishing the work of our salvation and redemption. For he alone is the Saviour; . . . he alone was crucified for us. The patriarchs, prophets, apostles, martyrs and all other creatures are utterly excluded from having any thanks for our redemption and salvation.'[8]

Bullinger continues his description with a series of comparisons between the actions of Aaron and those of Christ. He notes that Aaron, having killed a bullock for himself and his family, drew lots before the entrance to the tabernacle, to decide which of the two rams should be sacrificed and which 'sent away as the scape-goat' into the desert:

The two goats do signify Christ our Lord, very God and very man, in two natures unseparated. He is slain, and dieth in his humanity; but is not slain nor dieth in his divinity. Yet he, being one and the same Christ, unseparated, is the Saviour of the world and doth work the redemption of us mortal men. So in the two goats was a mystery hidden. And for because, as Solomon saith, the lots are guided by the Lord's will, it was not without the especial will of the Father that the Son was sacrificed, and killed on the cross.[9]

Bullinger then compares the blood of the bullock and the ram that are slaughtered to the Blood of Christ: just as the high priest 'went within the veil' and seven times sprinkled the seat of mercy, so Christ entered not the tabernacle but heaven, and with his own blood obtained remission for our sins. When the high priest had placed the remaining blood on the golden altar surrounded by fumes of incense (for, says Bullinger, our redemption calls for both innocent blood and fervent prayer – as 'by the great quantity of smoke was noted the great efficacy of earnest prayer'), he emerged from the sanctum and gave the second ram to the man responsible for it, for him to lead it away into the desert. But first he placed his two hands upon the ram and on its head confessed the sins of the people, while the people themselves did likewise, repeating the confession phrase by phrase. Then, once all the sins had been laid on the head of the ram, it was sent off to carry away the sins of the whole people into the desert.

This was certainly the ceremony from which the Gentiles derived their ways of purging or disculpating the people. In Greek the process is known as *catermata*, in Latin as *piamina*:

For their manner was, in extreme perils, that one should give himself for all the rest, whom they took, and did either kill and burn upon the altar, or cast into the water; praying therewithal, that all their evil luck might go with him, and that the gods being pacified with the death of him might again be favourable to all the rest. But the wretches erred as far as heaven is wide: for Christ the Son of God was made sin for us, that is, he was made a sacrifice for sin, yea, he became a curse for us, that we by him might receive a blessing.[10]

And Bullinger adds that, if the scapegoat carried the sins away into the desert, this was not in order to make the sins disappear but so that they should no longer be laid at the door of the people: 'Sin is imputed to all them that are without the church, in the desolate wilderness. The convenient man, that should carry away the scapegoat, can be none other than Christ himself . . . And by dying he carried away conveniently the scapegoat, I mean the sin of all the world.'[11]

Bullinger concludes by insisting, as do most protestant preachers, upon the unique, definitive and sufficient nature of the sacrifice of Jesus.

The interest of Bullinger's text lies not only in the comparison he makes between the sacrifice of the scapegoat and that of Jesus on the Cross: it will have been noticed in passing that he interprets the sacrifices of the Gentiles, that is to say the pagans, as an imitation of the sacrifices practised by the Jews; also that he is familiar with the customs of the Greeks and Romans. Given that Bullinger's *Decades* were one of the texts that were recommended reading for the instruction of the Anglican clergy, we may take it that the Elizabethans were far from uninformed on these matters. Lastly, we must note how strongly he stresses the paradoxical nature of the sacrificial victim: the victim is made sin, is made a sacrifice for sin, then becomes a curse for humanity so that, by him, humanity may receive a blessing.

Jewel and Bullinger were not the only churchmen or preachers to pronounce on sacrifice. Similar reflections are to be found in John Hooper, Hugh Latimer, Matthew Parker, William Perkins and others. One interesting example is the sermon preached in 1585 by Edwin Sandys, archbishop of York and primate of England.[12] He covers the familiar and well-trodden ground of rebellion against princes, reprehensible because it is an insult to God who has chosen them to govern. This theme is illustrated by a number of biblical examples: Jeroboam, who plotted against Solomon and revolted against Rehoboam. And, of course, Absalom and Achitophel; the point being that it is generally people of standing who stir up rebellion.[13] The humble are pushed on by the great, for if they revolted on their own they would seldom succeed.

Sandys insists that treason can never be pardoned because:

It is the nature of the wicked, the longer they continue in sin, the less to be weary of it . . . there is no end of their malice . . . The obdurate heart of Pharaoh will never be mollified. Tigers will not be tamed: it is almost impossible that one, which hath drunk of the cup of that harlot, should retain in his heart any drop of loyal blood.[14]

Those who think to rise up against God and their prince must repent:

So long as ye continue in the hardness of your hearts, though you offer him all the beasts upon a thousand hills, it is all in vain. Repent and 'offer up the sacrifices of righteousness' [Lev. iv] . . . The rebel Absolon offered sacrifice in Hebron; but in vain because his heart was full of treason. Antichrist reneweth his oblations every day; but to what purpose, so long as he mindeth murder, stirreth rebellion . . . [15]

Sandys then explains what a sacrifice is and who are the priests who can offer it: 'Sacrificing is a voluntary action, whereby we worship God, offering him somewhat in token that we acknowledge him to be the Lord, and ourselves his servants.'[16]

There can be no sacrifice without a priest. Sandys notes that the Scriptures define three kinds of priesthood: the priesthood of the Levites, Aaron for example; royal priesthood 'figured in Melchisedeck and verified in Christ';[17] and a spiritual priesthood as found generally among all Christians: they must sacrifice to the Lord with their goods (make charitable gifts); with their bodies (which must resist sin); and with their souls (by having contrite hearts disposed to prayer and praise).

The close association of the themes of treason and sacrifice is remarkable: the traitor may make sacrifices but he will do so in vain, for his intentions belie his actions. Besides, the true traitor is 'irretrievable': treachery is an essential part of him just as wildness is essential to the tiger. Some of Shakespeare's villains are altogether in line with this definition: Richard III, Iago, Edmund; Brutus, on the other hand, is not. He can be compared to a priest whose task is dictated him by the (real or illusory) demands of the city.

Alongside these sermons and homilies, there are constant allusions to the sacrifice of Christ in the literary works of the period as in its dramatic tradition. The culminating point of the great medieval cycles is the Passion. The theme of 'Christ who died for our sins' also appears in Morality plays and in many Elizabethan dramas. *Dr Faustus* is a striking example.

But the Elizabethans had other sources of information on the practice of sacrifice. First, the Roman historians who, as we learn from T. J.-B. Spencer, were much admired. And Plutarch, of course; but also the rare works on Rome produced by English writers: the *Chronicle of all the Noble Emperors of the Romaines* (1571) by Richard Reynoldes; and *An Historical Collection of the Continual Factions, Tumults, and Massacres of the Romans . . .* (1601) by William Fulbecke.[18]

A proof of the interest evinced in sacrifices is the considerable space occupied by a description of them in the *Romanae Historiae Anthologia . . .* (1614) by Thomas Godwyn, a work written in English and reprinted twenty-three times between 1614 and 1696. It is divided into four books and the second is entirely devoted to Roman religion. Furthermore, one long chapter (I, 2, chapter 19) is entitled 'De veterum sacrifiis et ritu sacrificandi'. There is also a chapter on the *Lupercalia* (II, 2, 1) and another on the *Saturnalia*, etc.

Finally, travellers' tales provided another source of information. Although human sacrifice and cannibalism would be seen unfavourably, the fact that they were described contributed towards spreading the conviction that sacrificial acts were often practised throughout the world. Thus, allusions to cannibals are frequent in the collection of voyages by Richard Hakluyt.[19] But the existence of cannibalism, also attested – of course – by Montaigne's *Essays*, was already being criticised with horror and was illustrated by an engraving in the *Cosmographia* by Sebastian Muenster (1554).[20]

The English had also read the second part of the *Historia General de las Indias* (1552) by Lopez de Gomara, translated by Thomas Nicholas and published in London under the title *The Conquest of the West India* in 1578 and 1596.[21] This dealt with Mexican Indians, and cannibalism and sacrifice are there described in terms that must have made the reader shudder. Here are a few extracts:

The Divell did many times talke with the Priestes and with other rulers and particular persons, but not with all sorts of men. And unto him whome the Divel had appeared, was offered and presented great gifts. The wicked spirit appeared unto them in a thousand shapes, and fashions, and finally hee was conversant and familiar among them verie often . . . And because he commaunded them, they sacrificed such an infinite number of creatures.

So this ignoraunt people giving credite to the condemned spirite, were growne even to the highest hill of crueltie, under the colour of devout and religious persons.

The chiefest feast in the yere, when most men are sacrificed and eaten, is at the ende of everye fifti two yeares . . . The last day of the first moneth is called Tlacaxipeualiztli, on the whiche day were slaine a hundred slaves, which were taken in the warres, and after the sacrifice, their flesh was eaten in this order. All the Citizens, gathered themselves together in the high Temple, and then the Ministers or Priestes came and used certaine ceremonies, the which being ended, they tooke those which were to be sacrificed, by one and one, and laid them uppon their backes uppon a large stone, and then, the same being on live, they opened him in the breast, with a knife made of flinte stone, and tooke out his heart, which they threw immediately at the foote of the Aultar, as an offering, and anointed with the fresh bloud, the face of the God Vitzilopuchtli, or any other Idoll. This done, they pluckt off the skinnes of a certaine number of them, the which skinnes so many auncient persons put incontinent uppon their naked bodies, all freshe and bloudy . . . After the sacrifice ended, the owner of the slaves did carry their bodies home to their houses, to make of their flesh a solemn feaste to all their friendes, leaving their heades and hartes to the Priests.[22]

The English paid particular attention to works of this kind given that they were living at a time when their own navigators were in competition with the Spaniards. One of the most common themes in English travel literature at this time is that English colonisation will be less harsh and more humane for the natives than Spanish, because it will be protestant. But even protestant-ism would not allow that pagan sacrifices might be found acceptable.

Robert Burton can be read as an amplified echo to the vast number of works that he examined. He is much preoccupied with pagan customs, and the outraged indignation that he evinces while recording Spanish accounts of sacrifice illustrates the point we are making well enough:

It is wonderful to tell how the devil deludes them, how he terrifies them, how they offer men, and women, sacrifices unto him, an hundred at once, as they did infants in Crete to Saturn of old, the finest children, like Agamemnon's Iphigenia, etc. At Mexico, when the Spaniards first overcame them, they daily sacrificed *viva hominum corda e viventium corporibus extracta*, the hearts of men yet living, 20,000 in a year . . . to their idols made of flour, and men's blood, and every year six thousand infants of both sexes.[23]

It might be interesting to speculate on how the Elizabethan public reacted to accounts of representations of pagan sacrifices. There were at least two attitudes possible. First, a Christian might take the view that any super-stitious practice, all blood sacrifice, must be purely and simply condemned, either with horror or with pity.[24] Views as broad-minded as those of Montaigne, who considered that eating dead men was less odious than torturing the living, were not common. However, as R. M. Frye indicates, another attitude was equally possible: 'that characters whom Shakespeare has carefully shown to be pre-Christian are in fact to be interpreted as such',[25] that is to say, with the necessary perspective and comprehension. Frye's remarks seem both solid and sensible. On Lear's words to Cordelia, after the defeat of his army:

> Upon such sacrifices, my Cordelia,
> The gods themselves throw incense.[26]   (V, iii, 20–1)

Frye reminds us that, according to Calvin, pagans commonly believed that God only takes pleasure in sacrifices if they are offered with sincere inten-tions. Calvin similarly made the point that men ignorant of Christianity nevertheless sometimes believed in a God who ruled in heaven and who administered justice in the most unexpected way.[27] He also believed that the doorway of prayer was open to all mortals, even to unbelievers. Frye gives a few more examples taken either from Calvin or from Hooker and then adds that Shakespeare 'respects his pagan characters enough to give their paganism its due. That we should do so too seems advisable from the stand-point alike of historical theology and of literary criticism.'[28] Shakespeare was probably able to exploit 'a kind of tension between the Christian attitude of his public and dramatic expression, for the purpose of heightening interest in the development of a sympathetic stage character' within the framework of a pre-Christian world.[29] W. R. Elton, for his part, shows that the Renaissance was capable of judging pagan beliefs in four different ways:[30] (1) the *prisca theologia* was the view and behaviour of pagans who, by reason of their virtues, lived in a purity that prefigured Christianity: that view made quasi-Christians of them – Elton gives Cordelia as an example; (2) the aetheist or sceptical view, that is to say one to be condemned – that of Edmund in *King Lear*, for instance, or of Cicero in *Julius Caesar*; (3) the superstitious view, as embodied in Julius Caesar – Elton himself gives the example of Gloucester in *King Lear*; (4) a view that does not correspond to any of the above but results from man's reactions to events provoked either by a hidden providence or by chance or contingency – King Lear for instance, or Cleopatra

But the most radical view seems to be that of Reginald Scot in *The Discoverie of Witchcraft* (1584); his horror of sacrifices seems equalled only by his horror of catholics. In book XI of his work, he begins by denouncing the practice of augury on the part of the Hebrews and the Romans; he approves of Marcus Varro for considering extremely unclean gods who conceal their secrets in the intestines and guts of animals. He inveighs against the 666 sorts of sacrifices practised by the Egyptians and at the same time mocks at the Romans who 'had almost as manie' and at the Greeks as well as the Persians and Medes who followed them closely in such practices. He remarks that 'the *Indies* and other nations have at this instant their sacrifices full of varietie, and more full of barbarous impietie. For in sundrie places, these offer sacrifices to the divell, hoping thereby to moove him to lenitie: yea, these commonlie sacrifice such of their enimies, as they have taken in warre' (XI, i). He informs us that the Jews used a 'diabolical sacrifice, never taught them by *Moses*': they offered their children to Moloch, forcing their sons and daughters to run through fire (XI, ii).

The next chapter is entitled: 'The Cannibals crueltie, of popish sacrifices exceeding in tyrannie the Iewes or Gentiles'. In a marginal note Reginald Scot writes 'Against the papists abhominable and blasphemous sacrifice of the masse.' Here is the text:

The incivilitie and cruell sacrifices of popish preests do yet exceed both the Jew and the Gentile: for these take upon them to sacrifice Christ himselfe. And to make their tyrannie the more apparant, they are not contented to have killed him once, but dailie and hourelie torment him with new deaths; yea they are not ashamed to sweare, that with their carnall hands they teare his humane substance, breaking it into small gobbets; and with their external teeth chew his flesh and bones, contrarie to divine or humane nature; and contrarie to the prophesie, which saith: 'There shall not a bone of him be broken' (Psalms, 34, 20). Finallie, in the end of their sacrifice (as they say) they eate him up rawe and swallow him into their guts everie member and parcell of him: and last of all, that they conveie him unto the place where they bestowe the residue of all that which they have devoured that daie. And this same barbarous impietie exceedeth the crueltie of all others: for all the Gentiles consumed their sacrifices with fier, which they thought to be holie.

In the chapters that follow, Reginald Scot speaks of pagan superstitions concerning fire (XI, iv); he devotes two chapters to Roman sacrifices, the practice of augury and the most propitious moments for announcing auguries. And finally, the better to denounce the fraudulence of prophecy as practised in the ancient world, he observes that those who professed the art of prophecy never stooped so low as to make pronouncements for the poor or lower classes, declaring that only the great were worthy of their attentions.[31]

One final attitude may have been that described by J. L. Simmons.[32] It is a complicated, erudite version of the condemnation of paganism and hence of sacrifice. It can be traced to Saint Augustine and involves a description and assessment of the pagan world in the light of Christian historiography. In the Roman plays, above all in *Coriolanus*, the effect of such a description is that 'the ironies and perversities of the play serve to expose Rome's ultimate tragic plight'.[33] Simmons cites North's dedicatory epistle to Queen Elizabeth: 'If they have done this for heathen kings, what should we doe for Christian princes? If they have done this for glorie, what should we doe for religion? If they have done this without hope of heaven, what should we doe that looke for immortalitie?'[34] and then goes on to note that Shakespeare represents Rome as

a pagan world in which the characters must perforce operate with no reference beyond the Earthly City . . . All attempts to rise above the restrictions of man and his imperfect society are tragically affected by the absence of revelation and the real hope of glory. Implying this historical distinction, Shakespeare views his Roman world with the cosmic irony of what that world could not know.[35]

But is this not to attribute to Shakespeare the attitude of a Christian apologist to the point of rather forgetting the dramatic author who used Rome to reflect the later Renaissance breakdown of a belief in providence and 'the real hope of glory' that England was then living through?[36]

2. Sacrifice in *Julius Caesar*

Gathered in Brutus' house, the conspirators are about to finalise the details of their undertaking. Right from the start, Brutus seeks to dissuade them from swearing an oath to accomplish what they have resolved:

> No, not an oath. If not the face of men,
> The sufferance of our souls, the time's abuse –
> If these be motives weak, break off betimes,
> And every man hence to his idle bed.
> So let high-sighted tyranny range on,
> Till each man drop by lottery. But if these,
> As I am sure they do, bear fire enough
> To kindle cowards and to steel with valour

> The melting spirits of women, then, countrymen,
> What need we any spur but our own cause
> To prick us to redress? What other bond
> Than secret Romans, that have spoke the word,
> And will not palter? And what other oath
> Than honesty to honesty engag'd,
> That this shall be, or we will fall for it?
> Swear priests and cowards, and men cautelous,
> Old feeble carrions, and such suffering souls
> That welcome wrongs; unto bad causes swear
> Such creatures as men doubt; but do not stain
> The even virtue of our enterprise,
> Nor th' insuppressive mettle of our spirits,
> To think that or our cause or our performance
> Did need an oath . . . [37]
>
> (II, i, 114–46)

The point is that an oath would represent a commitment which would only bind the conspirators to one another, at the same time separating them from Rome and the very impulse that is urging them to action.[38] Now, for Brutus, the real commitment is the one that already binds them to Rome – to the Rome of the old virtues and liberties for which Brutus is, in the eyes of all, the spokesman and the incarnation. Because his cause is the cause of Rome, because he desires to act in the name of Rome as a whole against a tyranny which purports to be Rome but which is in reality a travesty of the city that will lay men open to death 'by lottery', Brutus wants only the cause itself to spur the conspirators on to restore a situation in which, as a result of Caesar's death, each man can once again find his proper place in the commonwealth. This is the point that Brutus is making in the Forum when Antony enters carrying Caesar's body: 'Here comes his body, mourned by Mark Antony, who, though he had no hand in his death, shall receive the benefit of his dying, a place in the commonwealth, as which of you shall not?' (III, ii, 42–5).

Such, in part, are Brutus' sentiments. But Shakespeare gives us to understand that this is not the whole story. The true Rome in whose name Brutus claims to be acting is a dream of the past projected into the future. At the present juncture, the Romans are not united. They stand neither wholly with Caesar nor wholly against him. In this respect, Brutus' opposition to the suggestion that Cicero be informed of the plot (II, i, 150–3) is significant, as is also the *placit* that Artemidorus seeks in vain to get Caesar to read (II, iii) in which all the conspirators are denounced. It is also significant that, at the very moment when Lucius comes to announce that Cassius, accompanied by men with covered faces, is asking to see him, Brutus himself is deploring in advance both the action to be committed and the clandestine precautions necessary for it:

> They are the faction. O conspiracy,
> Sham'st thou to show thy dangerous brow by night,

When evils are most free? O, then by day
Where wilt thou find a cavern dark enough
To mask thy monstrous visage? Seek none, conspiracy;
Hide it in smiles and affability:
For if thou path, thy native semblance on,
Not Erebus itself were dim enough
To hide thee from prevention. (II, i, 77–85)

The reason why the plot has to be clandestine is not simply that, to the minds of the Elizabethans, it is, as any conspiracy, essentially demoniacal; it is also because, within the fictional framework of the tragedy, the political opposition can no longer express itself openly: 'Marullus and Flavius, for pulling scarfs off Caesar's images, are put to silence' (I, ii, 282–3). In circumstances such as these, Rome is no longer Rome.

Beyond the immediate goal the conspirators have set themselves (some of them with misgivings),[39] namely the elimination of Caesar, the ultimate objective of the conspiracy is, for Brutus, the restoration of a community within which the old virtues and liberties will prevail and divisions be eradicated.[40] What was necessary was to restore health to the body politic and that could only be done at the cost of a painful operation, an exchange in which a man's life would be forfeit but the health of Rome restored. The task to be accomplished is defined as follows by Brutus and Caius Ligarius:

> *Caius*: What's to do?
> *Brutus*: A piece of work that will make sick men whole.
> *Caius*: But are not some whole that we must make sick?
> *Brutus*: That must we also. (II, i, 326–9)

When Brutus claims to be acting in the name of Rome this is more an expression of his desire than of reality: for only the future can tell if, depending on whether Rome supports or condemns the action in the offing, the conspirators will have acted in the name of the entire city or of only a faction of it. The political conditions are such that it is not possible to be sure whether he is or is not spokesman for the city; all he can do is blindly assume the role of spokesman, act without knowing, as if he already was what he can only become once the deed has been accomplished. In setting up the action in this fashion, Shakespeare takes us into the heart of the darkness and ambiguity inherent in any political action. And, given that the frame of reference for the play is not solely political, another reading is possible too, justified by the religious metaphors used by Brutus to describe the act that he is contemplating and subsequently accomplishes, an action that he has to view as a sacrifice.

This aspect of the work is superimposed upon others which might be said to complement it: thus, the assassination of Caesar by Brutus and Cassius and the hostility between them and Antony could, we should remember, be seen as a demonstration of a situation familiar enough to psychoanalysts: the three men can be considered as the sons of Julius Caesar, or as rival brothers. There is no reason why an interpretation of the sacrificial nature of the murder need be incompatible with one which sees Caesar both as a father-figure and as an autocrat justifying his own role and functions and the order that he imposes by means of drawing analogies with the order of the universe itself: that is what he is saying in the speech that he makes just before his assassination:

> But I am constant as the northern star,
> Of whose true-fix'd and resting quality
> There is no fellow in the firmament.
> The skies are painted with unnumber'd sparks,
> They all are fire, and every one doth shine;
> But there's but one in all doth hold his place.
> So in the world: 'tis furnish'd well with men,
> And men are flesh and blood, and apprehensive;
> Yet in the number I do know but one
> That unassailable holds on his rank,
> Unshak'd of motion . . .   (III, i, 60–70)

This political murder, sacrifice, the falling of a star, is presented for a moment as an attempt to replace an inhuman cosmic order with an order of a different kind, ruled by the will of men and a social ethic founded wholly upon contract.[41] The second half of the play shows that such an order appeared conceivable yet unattainable to Shakespeare: Rome refuses to accept the proposed contract, the new order envisaged is immediately challenged, Antony's speech in the Forum wins the day for the idea that the suppression of Caesar was neither a sacrifice nor a solemn act of rupture with the past, but a murder, a sacrilegious episode which must in its turn be expiated, which calls for bloody retribution. For Brutus, in contrast, Caesar's murder has to be an absolute beginning and an absolute end: that is why he rejects the advice of Cassius, who wants to do away with Antony at the same time as Caesar:

> *Cassius*: . . . I think it is not meet,
> Mark Antony, so well belov'd of Caesar,
> Should outlive Caesar: we shall find of him
> A shrewd contriver; and you know, his means,
> If he improve them, may well stretch so far
> As to annoy us all; which to prevent,
> Let Antony and Caesar fall together.
> *Brutus*: Our course will seem too bloody, Caius Cassius,
> To cut the head off and then hack the limbs,
> Like wrath in death and envy afterwards;
> For Antony is but a limb of Caesar.   (II, i, 155–65)

In a tirade that seems at first sight enigmatic, Brutus stresses the sacrificial nature of the proposed deed. He foresees a favourable reaction from the *plebs* provided Caesar alone dies and, without mandate, he assumes the role of sacrificer, asserting that it will eventually fall to him by universal consent. That particular aspect of any political action, namely that it can only prove its own soundness once it has been accomplished, although it is necessary to justify it in advance in order to accomplish it, is also present in his mind, overlaying his concept of the unique, timely and, as it were, definitive nature of the sacrificial act which marks an absolute end in the sense that no retribution is called for but which also marks an absolute beginning in a purified universe, a new departure. Some critics, Brents Stirling for one,[42] have imagined that Brutus is merely attempting to confer a kind of spurious dignity upon the assassination by raising it to the level of ritual and ceremony, but that is to reduce the sacrificial act to nothing more than a political or psychological expedient and to neglect its undeniable significance and its importance in the thematic construction of the play.

What *is* sacrifice? According to Claude Lévi-Strauss,[43] it is an act which establishes a renewed relationship between two separated orders, the sacred and the profane for instance. The relationship between the sacred and the profane, having been temporarily interrupted, is reestablished by rendering the victim sacred. The destruction of the victim, by again breaking the relationship, creating an irreversible fact, brings about, as it were, an empty space between the two orders; the superior order is then expected to fill the gap thus created by bestowing mercy or beneficence. In short, sacrifice is one particular form of exchange through which the beneficent hand of the almighty may be forced.

Sacrifice may also be expiatory or it may constitute a rite of communion. In the expiatory sacrifice, a human object is offered up to the sacred in order to win its indulgence or appease its wrath. In the rite of communion, a sacred object is shared out so that the sharers may penetrate its virtues and by so doing reinforce the cohesion or harmony of the inferior or profane partner in this communion.

The sacrifice presented in *Julius Caesar* incorporates all these aspects. First, with the choice of an elect and exemplary victim who, by virtue of his functions, is part human and part divine. When Brutus meets the conspirators, he says:

> Let's be sacrificers, but not butchers, Caius.
> We all stand up against the spirit of Caesar,
> And in the spirit of men there is no blood.
> O, that we then could come by Caesar's spirit,
> And not dismember Caesar! But, alas,
> Caesar must bleed for it. And, gentle friends,
> Let's kill him boldly, but not wrathfully;
> Let's carve him as a dish fit for the gods,
> Not hew him as a carcass fit for hounds.
> And let our hearts, as subtle masters do,

Stir up their servants to an act of rage,
And after seem to chide 'em. This shall make
Our purpose necessary, and not envious;
Which so appearing to the common eyes,
We shall be call'd purgers, not murderers.   (II, i, 166–80)

Not only does this speech define the act to be accomplished and how it is to be done; also, through the act itself, it defines the nature of the victim: Caesar must not be massacred as if by butchers and that is because Caesar is worthy to be offered up as a sacrifice. Correlatively, meanwhile, if accomplished as Brutus desires it to be, the act will establish Caesar as what he already is. One could here recall to mind the 'Thou marshall'st me the way that I was going' (II, i, 42) that Macbeth addresses to the imaginary dagger that leads him on or that he follows towards Duncan's room: actions are created by the human will but at the same time they are dictated or suggested to it. And their meanings either entirely or partially escape the agent that executes them.

So the victim of the sacrifice is to be unique; the action will be unrepeatable, a part of no series. Brutus is keenly aware of its expiatory nature as he exclaims: 'alas, / Caesar must bleed for it' (II, i, 171). He is conscious that he is killing an exceptional being and one that he loves. After the murder, he justifies himself as follows to Antony:

Our hearts you see not; they are pitiful;
And pity to the general wrong of Rome –
As fire drives out fire, so pity, pity –
Hath done this deed on Caesar . . .   (III, i, 169–72)

Only be patient till we have appeas'd
The multitude, beside themselves with fear,
And then we will deliver you the cause
Why I, that did love Caesar when I struck him,
Have thus proceeded.   (III, i, 179–83)

It is an expiatory act, then, agonising to perform, a costly gift to effect a renewal of things – for the sake of Rome: 'If there be any in this assembly, any dear friend of Caesar's, to him I say that Brutus' love to Caesar was no less than his. If then that friend demand why Brutus rose against Caesar, this is my answer: Not that I loved Caesar less, but that I loved Rome more' (III, ii, 18–23). Such are his words to the *plebs* of Rome to whom, later, he also declares: 'I slew my best lover for the good of Rome' (III, ii, 46). Later still, in acts IV and V, particularly during his quarrel with Cassius, he refers to the cruelty of the agreed sacrifice.

The third aspect of the sacrifice is the order to the conspirators, whom Brutus at this point addresses as 'Romans', to bathe their hands in Caesar's blood (an episode that is not to be found in the sources for the play). This action is the rite of communion:[44]

> . . . Stoop, Romans, stoop,
> And let us bathe our hands in Caesar's blood
> Up to the elbows, and besmear our swords:
> Then walk we forth, even to the market place,
> And, waving our red weapons o'er our heads,
> Let's all cry 'Peace, freedom and liberty!'   (III, i, 105–10)

All these aspects of the sacrifice are essential for a full understanding of it, given that Brutus' project is both a moral and a political one, and its moral aspect is permeated by religious overtones. Of all the conspirators, Brutus is the only one for whom morality is an absolute criterion[45] and who yearns for a city that is not governed only by force, passion and self-interest. In this respect, he stands in contrast to Antony who uses moral and religious considerations abundantly in his speech to the *plebs*, but does so to serve his political purpose. He also stands in contrast to Cassius who is a slave to his own feelings, resentment and appetites.

Brutus seeks to reestablish a social order in which history will unfold in accordance with the common and disciplined will of men united in their respect for recognised values. The success of his project depends upon the consent of Rome. A political project cannot succeed if it lacks the support of the city. And, similarly, a sacrifice cannot be considered to be such unless it is seen as such by the entire community. Only a general consensus can suspend the rule of secular laws and decide to transgress them in favour of sacred law – or law established in the general interest. Brutus presupposes that the consensus exists but his interpretation is proved false by Antony. The end of act II and the famous Forum scene in effect constitute what might be described as a dispute over interpretation on a sacred as well as a human level. Nothing could have better conveyed the equivocal status of the sacred at the end of the sixteenth century than the device of making the *plebs*, presented as the fickle and changeable mob, act as arbiter in this dispute. And, to add to this equivocation, Brutus' antagonist, though acting as a lawful or self-appointed avenger, will reap political profit from the disorder that he himself has helped to create.

After the assassination, Antony pretends to rally to the conspirators. But already, in his speech, in the way that he referred to the spilling of Caesar's precious blood, he has indicated that his interpretation of the assassination will not be the same as theirs. As G. Wilson Knight has remarked: 'In the spirit of men there is no blood' (II, i, 168), 'but in the blood of men there is spirit: hence the power of Caesar's blood throughout the play.'[46] The conspirators wanted to appropriate that power through their rite of communion following the sacrifice. But Antony changes the blood which they used to anoint themselves into a mark of sacrilege. Brents Stirling has indicated the various stages in this process of inversion[47] although it is not so much a matter of a 'counter-ritual', as he calls it, rather a tapping of what Wilson

Knight calls 'the strength' of Caesar's blood.[48] Faced with the conspirators, Antony already betrays the fact that the bloodshed with which their hands are stained has deprived him of his reasons for living, since their murderous daggers are 'made rich / With the most noble blood of all this world' (III, i, 155–6):

> Now, whilst your purpled hands do reek and smoke,
> Fulfil your pleasure. Live a thousand years,
> I shall not find myself so apt to die;
> No place will please me so, no mean of death,
> As here by Caesar, and by you cut off,
> The choice and master spirits of this age.   (III, i, 158–63)

As Stirling remarks, Antony makes a point of shaking each and every conspirator by the hand in such a way as to shake the solidarity that has united them in the sacrifice, picking out each of the men who have killed, individually:[49]

> I doubt not of your wisdom.
> Let each man render me his bloody hand.
> First, Marcus Brutus, will I shake with you;
> Next, Caius Cassius, do I take your hand;
> Now, Decius Brutus, yours; now yours, Mecellus;
> Yours, Cinna; and my valiant Casca, yours;
> Though last, not least in love, yours, good Trebonius.
> Gentlemen all – alas, what shall I say?   (III, i, 183–90)

Antony's irony is already detectable but it is in his next speech that the equivocation becomes glaring:

> That I did love thee, Caesar, O, 'tis true!
> If then thy spirit look upon us now,
> Shall it not grieve thee dearer than thy death,
> To see thy Antony making his peace,
> Shaking the bloody fingers of thy foes,
> Most noble, in the presence of thy corse?
> Had I as many eyes as thou hast wounds,
> Weeping as fast as they stream forth thy blood,
> It would become me better than to close
> In terms of friendship with thine enemies.
> Pardon me, Julius! Here wast thou bay'd, brave hart;
> Here didst thou fall; and here thy hunters stand,
> Sign'd in thy spoil, and crimson'd in thy lethe.
> O world, thou wast the forest to this hart;
> And this indeed, O world, the heart of thee.
> How like a deer, strucken by many princes,
> Dost thou here lie!   (III, i, 194–210)

The inversion is not as clear-cut as Stirling suggests; for the hunting and killing of the stag were heavily ritualistic operations: some morsels of the stag's flesh were delicately cut up as dishes fit for the gods; others were flung to the dogs. And only the king, or those he authorised to do so, could hunt in the forest. The hunter-king in pursuit of the hart was performing a ritual action. The poacher was usurping the royal prerogative.[50] Casca is not slow to seize upon the ambiguity of the description purveyed by Antony. He asks him if, despite his grief, for which nobody reproaches him, he counts himself as a friend of the conspirators: 'Will you be prick'd in number of our friends?' (III, i, 216) and Antony replies, slipping in yet another ironic phrase which covertly gives the lie to his declaration of friendship:

> *Antony*: Therefore I took your hands, but was indeed
> Sway'd from the point by looking down on Caesar.
> Friends am I with you all, and love you all,
> Upon this hope, that you shall give me reasons
> Why, and wherein, Caesar was dangerous.
> *Brutus*: Or else were this a savage spectacle.   (III, i, 218–23)

So there will have to be a confrontation. And, being without allies, Antony suggests that it be made before the people, with Caesar's body in full view of all (III, i, 228). As soon as he is alone, he produces the other interpretation to Caesar's murder: it was not a sacrifice at all, but an odious sacrilege, a sacrilege that cries out for divine vengeance:

> Woe to the hand that shed this costly blood!
> Over thy wounds now do I prophesy
> (Which like dumb mouths do ope their ruby lips,
> To beg the voice and utterance of my tongue),
> A curse shall light upon the limbs of men;
> Domestic fury and fierce civil strife
> Shall cumber all the parts of Italy;
> Blood and destruction shall be so in use,
> And dreadful object so familiar,
> That mothers shall but smile when they behold
> Their infants quartered with the hands of war,
> And pity chok'd with custom of fell deeds;
> And Caesar's spirit, ranging for revenge,
> With Ate by his side come hot from hell,
> Shall in these confines, with a monarch's voice,
> Cry havoc and let slip the dogs of war,
> That this foul deed shall smell above the earth
> With carrion men, groaning for burial.   (III, i, 258–75)

As Maurice Charney notes,[51] Antony's view is similar to that of the bishop of Carlisle in *Richard II* (IV, i, 136–49). But there is one difference: Antony determines to be the active agent of chaos. He, in his turn, with no mandate other than the one he finds spelled out in Caesar's wounds, for which he claims to speak, assumes the mission of finding human agents to serve his apocalyptic vision – in other words, to translate it into political terms.

Each in turn, before the people, Brutus and Antony present their own particular versions of the events. Each is partial, incomplete, and so dishonest. While Brutus may justifiably swear before the *plebs* to the purity of his own intentions, he cannot speak for the other conspirators whose motives we know to be personal, and so illegitimate. Only Brutus had the concern of the community at heart. And although Antony sets himself up as the avenger and apologist for Caesar, he twists the facts – for example his description of the crowning of Caesar is slanted to show that Caesar was not ambitious – and thereby unleashes a chaos the outcome of which he cannot foresee:

> Now let it work. Mischief, thou art afoot,
> Take thou what course thou wilt!   (III, ii, 262–3)

It is an apocalyptic moment when the words used seem to have run riot and no longer relate to the true facts: the poet Cinna is assassinated by the people just because his name is Cinna. Just as Brutus' intentions are betrayed and his actions deformed before our very eyes by the interpretation that is put upon them, so chaos deprives words of their meaning and living creatures of their essence. Each and every one has played, is playing or will play a double game. Once historical forces have determined that the act committed by Brutus was a sacrilege, the apocalypse, the agents of which they become the moment they give its meaning to Caesar's murder, is inevitably unleashed.

This mechanism is, as it were, inherent in Antony's demagogic rhetoric: (1) the conspirators have shed the 'costly' blood of Caesar; (2) that blood will be 'costly' to them.[52] Antony twists the sense that Brutus gave to Caesar's blood: no, Caesar was not ambitious, he was loyal to his friends, he paid the ransom of the captives he brought to Rome into the public treasury, three times he refused the crown, during the festival of Lupercalia. Antony prepares to read out Caesar's will – then thinks better of it, for if he did, 'the commons'

> . . . would go and kiss dead Caesar's wounds,
> And dip their napkins in his sacred blood,
> Yea, beg a hair of him for memory.   (III, ii, 134–6)

That blood has 'become that of a martyr or a saint'.[53] The speech evokes a cult of relics which, in protestant England, was a sign of superstition or demagogy. And to rouse the mob even more, Antony displays Caesar's cloak and describes each rent in it before at last revealing the martyr's corpse:

> Look, in this place ran Cassius' dagger through:
> See what a rent the envious Casca made:
> Through this the well-beloved Brutus stabb'd;
> And as he pluck'd his cursed steel away,

> Mark how the blood of Caesar follow'd it,
> As rushing out of doors, to be resolv'd
> If Brutus so unkindly knock'd or no;
> For Brutus, as you know, was Caesar's angel.
> Judge, O you gods, how dearly Caesar lov'd him.
> This was the most unkindest cut of all;
> For when the noble Caesar saw him stab,
> Ingratitude, more strong than traitors' arms,
> Quite vanquish'd him: then burst his mighty heart;
> And in his mantle muffling up his face,
> Even at the base of Pompey's statue
> (Which all the while ran blood) great Caesar fell.
> O, what a fall was there, my countrymen!
> Then I, and you, and all of us fell down,
> Whilst bloody treason flourish'd over us.
> O, now you weep, and I perceive you feel
> The dint of pity. These are gracious drops.
> Kind souls, what weep you when you but behold
> Our Caesar's vesture wounded? Look you here!
> Here is himself, marr'd, as you see, with traitors.   (III, ii, 176–200)

The sacrificers were no more than butchers. If Pompey's statue is bleeding, it is not because Caesar, at the beginning of the play, entered Rome 'in triumph over Pompey's blood' (I, i, 51) – the corpse or effigy of the victim bleeds anew in the presence of its assassin – but through a miraculous sympathy with the displayed corpse. And every wound suffered by Caesar will, through Antony's voice, call Rome to revolt and 'precipitate the total destruction of Brutus' republican ideal':[54]

> I tell you that which you yourselves do know,
> Show you sweet Caesar's wounds, poor poor dumb mouths,
> And bid them speak for me. But were I Brutus,
> And Brutus Antony, there were an Antony
> Would ruffle up your spirits, and put a tongue
> In every wound of Caesar that should move
> The stones of Rome to rise and mutiny.   (III, ii, 226–32)

These men have ceased to be men having a place in the commonwealth. Having invited the mob to pillage, Caesar's avenger will soon get ready to seize power for his own ends. Remember that, in answer to Cassius' question: 'Will you be prick'd in number of our friends?' (III, i, 216), Antony later responds: 'These many then shall die; their names are prick'd' (IV, i, 1). And he turns certain clauses of Caesar's will to his own profit. The final inversion of meaning occurs shortly before the battle of Philippi, when Antony insults the conspirators:

> Villains! you did not so when your vile daggers
> Hack'd one another in the sides of Caesar:
> You show'd your teeth like apes, and fawn'd like hounds,
> And bow'd like bondmen, kissing Caesar's feet;

> Whilst damned Casca, like a cur, behind
> Struck Caesar on the neck.   (V, i, 39–44)

Once again, as Stirling points out,[55] the dish destined for the gods becomes the carcass torn to pieces by the dogs. Antony, who in the past has spoken of a deadly hunt in pursuit of Caesar, now lists the beasts who were hunting him down: apes, hounds and curs . . . The hunted beast, like a mystical hart whose blood has miraculous properties, thus preserves its status of a victim of a quite uncommon kind.

Caesar's assassination has repercussions right up to the end of the play when Brutus and Cassius are brought to the pass of turning their swords against themselves in an evocation of the action they have accomplished – the action that their defeat now labels sacrilege in their own eyes and which consequently calls for retribution in which they must be both agents and victims.

> . . . Caesar, thou art reveng'd,
> Even with the sword that kill'd thee.   (V, iii, 45–6)

says Cassius as he dies. And Brutus, before the corpse of his friend, exclaims:

> O Julius Caesar, thou art mighty yet!
> Thy spirit walks abroad, and turns our swords
> In our own proper entrails.   (V, iii, 94–6)

Yet, as he dies, he says:

> . . . Caesar, now be still;
> I kill'd not thee with half so good a will.   (V, v, 50–1)

This brings us to a consideration of the equivocal status here ascribed to the sacred because of its close association with the political.

As early as the very first scene, which Brents Stirling sees as no more than an example of religiosity prefiguring the subsequent ritualistic or pseudo-ritualistic actions, the theme is already clearly stated. A crowd of artisans is preparing to celebrate the triumph of Caesar who has just defeated the sons of Pompey, as the feast of the Lupercalia is about to take place. The two tribunes, Flavius and Marullus, protest with indignation: they belong to Pompey's party and recall how the crowd earlier acclaimed Pompey just as it now prepares to fête Caesar, the general of the civil war. They ask the crowd to disperse, to repent, for this mark of disloyalty cannot fail to call down upon it the wrath of the gods who will plague the city. It would not be seemly to make this a festival day or to strew flowers before the steps of Caesar who comes in triumph, besmirched with the blood of Pompey. The crowd disperses in silence. It recognises its fault, Flavius declares, and he asks Marullus to strip the decorated statues of Caesar of their ornaments:

Marullus: May we do so?
You know it is the feast of Lupercal.
Flavius: It is no matter; let no images
Be hung with Caesar's trophies. I'll about
And drive away the vulgar from the streets;
So do you too, where you perceive them thick.
These growing feathers pluck'd from Caesar's wing
Will make him fly an ordinary pitch,
Who else would soar above the view of men
And keep us all in servile fearfulness.   (I, i, 66–75)

Notice Marullus' significant hesitation. Is it right to touch the statues and divest them of their ornaments now, at the time of the sacred festival of the Lupercalia? It doesn't matter, says Flavius, Caesar's sprouting plumage must be removed. Respect for what is sacred should not cause one to forgo political action. But we can sense that some transgression *is* involved, for the statues are decorated not only to celebrate Caesar's triumph but also for the religious festival. To act as Flavius suggests, against Caesar and in conformity with the loyalty due to Pompey, is to act sacrilegiously and betray the customs of Rome. It is here that the paradox and central theme of the play appears: to be faithful to one code of conduct – civic virtue – it is necessary to betray another – respect for religious customs. Brutus faces the same case of conscience: in order not to betray the Rome of the ancient virtues, he will betray and assassinate Caesar. But his action must be seen within the special context of the city, where it is impossible to separate politics from religion, where political assassination must naturally be either a sacrifice or a sacrilege.

As for the enigmatic nature of the supernatural manifestations in the play, two examples will suffice. Casca describes the storm that has descended upon Rome: it is as if the world 'too saucy with the gods, incenses them to send destruction'. He goes on to describe a number of extraordinary or fantastic events: the common slave who, raising his left hand, saw it burst into flame like twenty torches, yet was not burned; the lion seen in front of the Capitol; men in flames seen in the streets; a bird of night that appeared in the Forum in broad daylight. Casca is met by detached scepticism on Cicero's part; but when he later meets Cassius, the latter compares these terrifying apparitions with the monstrous character that the city has taken on under Caesar's government:[56]

Cassius: Now could I, Casca, name to thee a man
Most like this dreadful night,
That thunders, lightens, opens graves, and roars
As doth the lion in the Capitol;
A man no mightier than thyself, or me,
In personal action, yet prodigious grown,
And fearful, as these strange eruptions are.
Casca: 'Tis Caesar that you mean, is it not, Cassius?   (I, iii, 72–9)

The audience certainly expects these marvels to be premonitory. But another possibility is that they took place because of some extraordinary event which preceded them. The storm is no doubt a sign of the anger of the gods. But who can say whether that anger is manifested because of the civil war from which Caesar has emerged victorious, or because of the conspiracy being prepared against him?

A similar ambiguity hangs over Calphurnia's prophetic dream. Caesar has heard her cry out in her sleep: 'Help ho! They murder Caesar!' (II, ii, 3). Caesar tells Decius that Calphurnia has just dreamed that his statue, like a fountain with a hundred mouths, was spurting blood in which many Romans were dabbling their hands (II, ii, 76–9). She begs him not to go to the Capitol. But Decius reassures Caesar:

> This dream is all amiss interpreted;
> It was a vision fair and fortunate:
> Your statue spouting blood in many pipes,
> In which so many smiling Romans bath'd,
> Signifies that from you great Rome shall suck
> Reviving blood, and that great men shall press
> For tinctures, stains, relics and cognizance.   (II, ii, 83–9)

The audience knows that the assassination must take place but it is hard to determine whether it will be an act of retribution occasioned by the civil war against Pompey or an action of which the gods, with all these premonitory omens, are seeking to give warning. The very multiplicity of the signs (the soothsayer's warning, Artemidorus' *placit*) suggests rather that the gods are closing the ears of the man they desire to destroy. That the supernatural exists is not brought into question, only the ability of men to enter into relation with the sacred, which is presented to all and sundry in the form of enigmatic happenings.

This particular quality of the play may – as J. L. Simmons[57] suggests – stem from the fact that the action takes place in a Rome distanced by Shakespeare's Christian consciousness. The author is presenting characters whose lives only make sense within the framework of the city here on earth. If Brutus had assassinated Caesar within a Christian system of reference, he would have been a damned soul, not a tragic hero. His suicide is justifiable for, if he knows himself, he must recognise the real reason for his failure: his resemblance to Caesar.[58] It is a resemblance that many commentators have noticed, suggesting that Brutus is a 'spiritual dictator'.[59]

That interpretation is only partially convincing. It raises the problem of the relationship that one senses between the world of the play and a number of political and spiritual problems peculiar to the Elizabethan period. For England at that time was certainly a part of a Europe being pulled in two different directions between, on the one hand, the necessary actions and laws of the government of the city and, on the other, the Christian imperatives that relate to the government of souls.[60] It was an instance of the classic conflict between universal and providential history and history subject to contingency, to purely political or social necessity. It was a conflict between Machiavellian *virtù* and the virtue of a Christian prince, between a capacity to act in the light of one's knowledge of the nature of men and the world and – at times – the need to act in the light of the knowledge of oneself. In *Hamlet* and *King Lear*, Shakespeare was soon to show that, when it comes to action, it is not necessarily an advantage to know oneself and that just or morally acceptable action is rarely crowned with success.

That is why, even if Shakespeare manages to present, within a Roman context, characters who behave with credibility – that is to say, as pagans – he nevertheless at the same time uses this context and these characters to pose political problems that it would have been difficult to formulate if his subject had been English history. By taking a detour by way of Roman history, he makes it possible to escape from a situation in which the king rules by divine right and political problems must always be posed in Christian terms.

R. M. Frye points out that it is not necessary to integrate the characters from Shakespeare's Roman plays into a view where they can be seen from the Christian angle. The Elizabethans were not unaware that the enlightenment of moral law was not necessarily absent in pre-Christian days.[61] If, as J. L. Simmons suggests,[62] Brutus' fault stems from an aspiration to pass beyond or to ignore the reality of human imperfections or a desire to live in a world in which evil is without power, then his fault must have been shared by all those who, at the end of the sixteenth century, hoped to live under the rule of the ideal prince – that is to say a Christian prince – or those who dreamed of a new Jerusalem. However, as in *Julius Caesar*, these dreams and desires could not but be frustrated by reality.

This is why it seems correct to assume that through Brutus' failure Shakespeare is trying to express both the distant nature of the sacred and at the same time its still decisive role in the lives of men at the end of the sixteenth century. The sacrifice of Caesar becomes an execrable murder in the eyes of the *plebs* whereas – given that Brutus' interpretation of the deed was at first accepted – it might have become an act of justice and a rite of communion. It is Antony's demagogy that brings about the reversal in the *plebs*. And the deaths of Brutus and Cassius become a posthumous vengeance for Caesar only because they are defeated politically.

Thus, Shakespeare demonstrates the ineluctable warping that moral and religious intentions suffer as soon as they enter into the course of history: in this play, in which it for a moment plays the part of arbiter, the *plebs* is an image of what even the most noble desires and the most assured of political policies must come to terms with. But, given that the action, even if it failed, was at least attempted, Shakespeare is also indicating all the legitimate aspirations, exemplary virtues and inevitable bad faith that such an action is bound to presuppose. It is within the terms of this tension that the tragedy unfolds and is accomplished.

It situates the individual in a world where everything is variable, simultaneously constituting and destroying him. He is no longer a being who must choose between actions he knows in advance to be either good or bad, nor one who makes a choice in a world that his decision will in no way modify (and by 'world' we must understand both the material world and the world of moral values). He no longer acts like the character of a morality play. He no longer can perfectly well take action or achieve his own salvation through self-knowledge, for his salvation does not depend solely upon the power he exercises over himself; it also depends upon his power over other things and over the world. In circumstances such as these, after the moment of choice the decisions made may be both good and at the same time bad: only later will their particular virtues and vices be revealed.

The sacrificial aspect of Caesar's murder – and also its duplication in the suicides of Brutus and Cassius, which are presented as expiatory sacrifices – makes it possible to exonerate the heroes for whatever wrongs they may have committed: their faults were inevitable, for in this universe man's behaviour is inevitably bound to be faulty. Thus, the individual taking action or struggling in this world is described as a being whose exemplary quality stems from his ability to follow through his choices to the end and live out his passion absolutely. Neither lucidity nor blindness are fully relevant:[63] for the knowledge of oneself is linked with knowledge of other men and the world – and neither man nor the world can divest themselves of what within them is unfathomable.

4. Macbeth or the tyrant sacrificed

1. General considerations

L. C. Knights has described *Macbeth* as 'a statement of evil' in which the three principal themes, intimately connected in the work, are unnatural disorder (as opposed to the natural order), the reversal of values and deceitful appearances. Writing in 1933, he was reacting, with his emphasis upon the poetic, thematic and dramatic coherence of the play, against commentators of the A. C. Bradley school,[1] who judged characters according to their psychological depth. This made it difficult for them to integrate into their analyses of the play characters and scenes whose main function is to provide a contrast to the depiction of the personal, social and cosmic disorders unleashed by Macbeth and Lady Macbeth under the patronage of the witches: characters such as Duncan, Malcolm and Macduff or scenes such as the last in act IV, in which Malcolm and Macduff define the individual, moral and political norms that should govern the behaviour of an acceptable sovereign.

The fact is that these three themes emerge distinctly from the poetic and also the dramatic fabric of the tragedy. As formulated by L. C. Knights, however, what they are governed by is an antithetical logic – the logical law of the excluded middle. In L. C. Knights' terms, there is an implicit opposition between 'unnatural disorder' and 'the order of nature', between 'the reversal of values' and a situation in which these values would stand in contrast to each other in their normal antithetical fashion, between 'deceitful appearance' and something that might be called 'candid appearance'.[2] He thus favours such interpretations as give a strongly polarised slant to the problems in the play; but this theoretical formulation, in its turn, renders certain aspects of the work obscure.

In the very first scene three witches, or rather three 'weird sisters', introduce the theme of a confusion – rather than a reversal – of values: 'Fair is foul, and foul is fair', announcing that they will wait for Macbeth 'when the battle's lost and won'. Macbeth, acting as noble, valiant, almost super-human warrior, 'Bellona's bridegroom', has crushed Macdonwald's rebellion and defeated the Norwegian troops and the traitor Cawdor. He meets the witches and is told that he will take the title of the conquered traitor and also become king. This suggestion gives rise to a vision of possibilities which has already found realisation by the end of act II. Spurred on by Lady Macbeth to a course of action that he had already imagined, he assassinates the king, who is his guest and who had showered him with favours, and becomes in his turn king of Scotland. Duncan's two sons have fled. Imagined possibilities have become reality, but only in appearance. Macbeth has seized power; he has made himself master of crown, kingdom and history, but not an assured master. 'To be thus is nothing, but to be safely thus' (III, i, 47).[3] Macbeth has killed his guest, broken the link that bound him to his lord, killed his benefactor – subverting relationships which, within the system of the play, are natural relationships, as organic as those between the earth and growing plants. Macbeth uses familiar, almost domestic, terms to express the exclusion which from now on must be his lot. As he passes the door of the room in which Donalbain and another noble-man are resting, he hears the one exclaim 'God bless us' and the other reply 'Amen'. But for Macbeth it is now impossible to say 'Amen'.

'Consider it not so deeply', Lady Macbeth tells him, locating the region of his being in which the crime has rebounded to strike her husband.

> Methought, I heard a voice cry, 'Sleep no more!
> Macbeth does murther Sleep', – the innocent Sleep;
> Sleep, that knits up the ravell'd sleave of care,
> The death of each day's life, sore labour's bath,
> Balm of hurt minds, great Nature's second course,
> Chief nourisher in life's feast;   (II, ii, 34–9

The rhythm of life is changed, the rhythm that used to be punctuated by sleep, so salutary for existence, sleep which allows the body and soul to be born anew after the death of each day and man to participate in the banquet of life – that banquet in which Macbeth will never again be able to take part: henceforth, acting always in isolation, he is excluded from the social communion of the meal just as he is from the spiritual communion that makes it possible to say 'Amen'.[4]

Macbeth has subverted the relationship in which individual and social order can be expressed as a living and homological dependence of the cosmic order. And all in vain, since the violence that he used can impose no order upon his own nature or the trouble that he feels at the spectacle of the general disorder. Macbeth has seized material power and obtained the name of king:

> Upon my head they plac'd a fruitless crown,
> And put a barren sceptre in my gripe   (III, i, 60–1)

But he does not possess real power or that mystical authority which, within the symbolic system of the play, under the name and attributes of sovereignty, is able at every level to maintain the cohesion of the universal organism and the human microcosm. To use Wycliffe's terms, he has the *potestas* but not the *dominium*.[5]

This second theme is expressed in the work in a number of ways: first, through the chain of murders to which Macbeth is brought in pursuit of his declared end of reigning 'safely' and which, each time, produces the opposite effect: just as the two sons of King Duncan managed to flee, Banquo's son, Fleance, escapes the assassins hired by Macbeth to kill him at the same time as his father:

> *Murderer*: Most royal Sir . . . Fleance is scap'd.
> *Macbeth*: Then comes my fit again: I had else been perfect;
> Whole as the marble, founded as the rock,
> As broad and general as the casing air:
> But now, I am cabin'd, cribb'd, confin'd, bound in
> To saucy doubts and fears.   (III, iv, 19–24)

Fleance's escape is thus a dramatic means used to signify the serial nature of the violence employed within the general framework of crime. Given that Fleance has no further dramatic role to play in the remainder of the drama, the sole purpose of this episode is to show that violence cannot be an agent of order since any murder is inevitably just one of a series and can never give whoever orders it the certainty that he has, at last, accomplished his final transgression.

Following a further consultation with the witches, who make a number of equivocal prophecies – both true and false – the assassination of Lady Macduff and her children marks the beginning of a new phase. This killing is a gratuitous action impossible to justify on any rational grounds – in contrast to the previous one where it was a question of destroying a possible rival together with his rival offspring – but there is a link between it and at least two other aspects of the work. On the one hand it continues the series, and is in that respect profoundly logical; on the other, it marks a change in Macbeth's behaviour – the interval between his conceiving of the action and its realisation being shortened in the extreme:

> . . . From this moment,
> The very firstlings of my heart shall be
> The firstlings of my hand.   (IV, i, 146–8)

Hitherto divided within himself, Macbeth now achieves a kind of unity by accepting the role of murderous tyrant that Ross indirectly describes for Lady Macbeth:

> But cruel are the times, when we are traitors,
> And do not know ourselves; when we hold rumour

From what we fear, yet know not what we fear,
But float upon a wild and violent sea
Each way, and move . . . [6]   (IV, ii, 18–22)

Unable to make his power real, Macbeth plunges into a world where he has to multiply the bloody signs of his omnipotence: it is as if he is killing beings beyond his reach, beings that are no longer anything but signs for him. His solitude, underlined by the deception he practises even toward Lady Macbeth as soon as he has killed Banquo, and the fact that his only confidants, to whom furthermore he lies, are now assassins, marks the onset of his fundamental alienation now that he is separated both from the community of men and from that other equivocal community of the powers of evil whose listener he is, without being their ally. His separation from Lady Macbeth is final after the sleepwalking scene. Lady Macbeth's nerve has cracked; all she can do is relive now the murderous scenes of the past in her imagination whilst Macbeth, who has also lost all relationship with natural time, is cut off from both the past and the future – the future which for him can henceforth be nothing other than a constantly recreated present.

Seyton: The queen, my lord, is dead.
Macbeth: She should have died hereafter:[7]
There would have been a time for such a word. –
To-morrow, and to-morrow, and to-morrow,
Creeps in this petty pace from day to day,
To the last syllable of recorded time;[8]
And all our yesterdays have lighted fools
The way to dusty death. Out, out, brief candle!
Life's but a walking shadow; a poor player,
That struts and frets his hour upon the stage,
And then is heard no more: it is a tale
Told by an idiot, full of sound and fury,
Signifying nothing.   (V, v, 16–28)

The forest of Birnam is already marching on the castle of Dunsinane where Macbeth awaits the enemy: the witches' seemingly impossible prediction is coming true. Nature is mounting its assault on the place where the unnatural tyrant, who has forgotten what fear and natural feelings are, awaits. Like a sacrificed bear at bay before the dogs (V, vii, 1–2) Macbeth, unlike Brutus and Antony, will not commit suicide: the judgement of men, of posterity is of little concern to him.

Why should I play the Roman fool, and die
On mine own sword? whiles I see lives, the gashes
Do better upon them.   (V, viii, 1–3)

The mechanism of murder functions to the last. Macbeth has become a machine for destroying lives simply because they are lives: 'whiles I see lives . . . '; to kill for the sake of killing has become his nature. This aspect of mechanical inevitability is expressed the more forcibly in that Macbeth's desire has been to interrupt it; he has all along dreamed of a murder that would be the last; and that dream not only conveys the relation between him and the world of 'natural' values but also, in implicit contrast, indicates that Macbeth performs actions that are beyond his control. Jan Kott sensed the imperious logic of the chain:

> There is only one theme in *Macbeth*, a monotheme. That theme is murder. The story is reduced to its simplest form, to a simple image, a single division of roles: between those who kill and those who are killed. Ambition, here, is intention to murder, planning to murder. Fear is the memory of murders accomplished and horror at the necessity for yet another crime. The great murder, the real murder, the murder that starts the story, is the assassination of the king. Well, after that, killing is inevitable.[9]

The point is perhaps made too strongly but the logic is clear. Wilbur Sanders describes a similar logic when he writes that, in Scotland, nature is 'barbarically resistant to humanisation'.[10] There is a 'continuity' there between consciousness and climate; integrity is subject to 'powerfully distorting pressures'.[11] Macbeth's peculiarity is that he 'has to' kill Duncan because he is both 'child and savage',[12] incapable of sharing what he knows about himself yet with a 'terrible hunger' to impart that knowledge. Half spurning the action that he longs to commit before the murders of Duncan and Banquo, rushing into action with the murder of Lady Macbeth, he is reticent once again at the moment of his last fight with Macduff:

> Of all men else I have avoided thee:
> But get thee back, my soul is too much charg'd
> With blood of thine already.   (V, viii, 4–6)

This time Macbeth has to fight an enemy not of his own choosing and this constraint to which he is subjected stamps his forced action with an accompanying feeling of nausea. But it is not just that he feels sickened. What Shakespeare has done is paint 'the portrait of a maturity which has learned to live with the consequences of actions catastrophic and destructive in the extreme',[13] and Sanders points out that this daunting maturity is of more interest than the moral collapse of a man crumbling beneath the weight of guilt – which is the view too often taken by commentators. For nowhere else does Shakespeare present such a portrait.

Order, then, is finally restored with this killing in which the blood shed can at last be washed away by blood – the essential characteristic of a sacrifice – whereas the blood shed by Macbeth he could not wash away either by water or by blood[14] – the essential characteristic of sacrilege.

The return to order is also a return to reality, the restoration of normal, fruitful time, a new beginning for things and for growth. It is also an end to fear: the fear Macbeth felt both before and following Duncan's murder; fear of the night, of witchcraft, of nightmare, of the wolf:

> . . . Now o'er the one half-world
> Nature seems dead, and wicked dreams abuse
> The curtain'd sleep: Witchcraft celebrates
> Pale Hecate's off'rings; and Wither'd murther,
> Alarum'd by his sentinel, the wolf,
> Whose howl's his watch, thus with his stealthy pace,
> With Tarquin's ravishing strides, towards his design
> Moves like a ghost.   (II, i, 49–56)

Fear of blood, of the knock on the door, fear of the nearest of kin ('the near in blood / the nearer bloody'), of apparitions, of the dark, of baleful miracles (II, iv), fear of distant enemies, of anxiety, of 'scorpions [that fill] the mind' (III, ii, 36), fear such that one would destroy the whole world in order to suppress it:

> But let the frame of things disjoint, both the worlds suffer,
> Ere we will eat our meal in fear, and sleep
> In the affliction of these terrible dreams,
> That shake us nightly.   (III, ii, 16–19)

And, finally, fear of Banquo's ghost, in a pivotal scene after which there has to be killing without discrimination, fear transmitted to the entire kingdom up until the moment when Macbeth has become so sated that nothing any longer moves him:

> I have almost forgot the taste of fears.
> The time has been, my senses would have cool'd
> To hear a night-shriek; and my fell of hair
> Would at a dismal treatise rouse, and stir
> As life were in't. I have supp'd full with horrors:
> Direness, familiar to my slaughterous thoughts,
> Cannot once start me.   (V, v, 9–15)

Fear which, after he has experienced every shade of medieval and renaissance terror,[15] makes it possible for him to confront the last fight of all, and death.

The social and natural norms implicitly defined throughout the play are reestablished with the impending coronation of Malcolm, who creates a new rank of nobility, that of the earls, and whose thanes become 'the first that ever Scotland / In such an honour nam'd'. It is the beginning of a new world. In accordance with the witches' enigmatic pronouncement at the beginning of the play, Macbeth tried to have evil pass for good but now all the evil, concentrated in his own person, has at one stroke been suppressed.

The end of the play appears to confirm the interpretation of those who detect a moral and metaphysical antithesis at work in it. However, the antithetical terms are confused as often as they are opposed; the overall judgement passed on Macbeth should not be confused with the judgement passed upon him by his antagonists; the evil itself is a stage that has to be passed through before the good can be restored; and finally, the relationships between the various episodes are not simply logical but homological as well; the positive characters are secretly compared to the negative as are the most transparent situations to the most equivocal.

First, we should remember that the witches' declaration with which the play opens, 'Fair is foul, and foul is fair', is a proposition of which the multiple meanings are such that to interpret it simply as proclaiming a reversal of values is altogether inadequate. The indeterminate present tense employed makes it impossible to tell whether, in speaking thus, the witches are describing a general and permanent state of the world, the present state of the world, a state of the world that is imminent, or a wish for the future. But at all events, one can see that, in the play, this state of confused values exists already even before the decision to kill Duncan. Right from the very first scenes, the state of the world *is* a state of confusion in which thanes are deceivers ('No more that Thane of Cawdor shall deceive / Our bosom interest': I, ii, 65), and blood nobly shed or shed in a just cause is compared to the blood that was shed at Golgotha. Furthermore, things do not proceed in the direction of an ever-increasing confusion but on the contrary towards a separation, an increasingly clear-cut differentiation between good and evil and order and disorder, values which, in the last act, turn into political forces. So what Macbeth does is not pervert an initially pure situation but rather, by becoming the agent of all the evil and disorder at large in Scotland, make it possible for it to be crystallised and purged in his own person. Even as Macbeth sets himself up as tyrant, he is also setting himself up as the expiatory victim of the society he is crushing. The necessity that his destiny reveals is much more profound, more archetypal than the dictates of ambition, the thirst for power, the logic of murder and the prospect of damnation: it is the tragic necessity to assume upon himself, and himself alone, the murderous processes that dictate the course of history – the principal one being murder; it is the necessity to be invested with a role that could be described as the polarising of chaos.

What is it that makes it possible for Macbeth, despite all his crimes, nevertheless to mobilise our sympathy? What is it that makes him an exemplary individual and allows us to identify with him right to the last? A number of answers have been provided to this question. R. B. Heilman[16] basically takes into account the various ways the character has been presented, and underlines – among other things – that Duncan's murder is not shown on stage but conveyed to the audience through Macbeth's remorse (which stands in contrast to the pitiless attitude of Lady Macbeth); that the crimes that he commits and from which he distances himself show that he is not a naturally evil being; that each step that he takes further into cruelty is accompanied by signs of disorientation which arouse in the spectator a growing sympathy and understanding; that this character expresses himself in language the poetry of which is deeply moving; but that, in the end:

the reader ends his life with and in Macbeth in a way that demands too little of him. He experiences forlornness and desolation and even a kind of substitute triumph – anything but the soul's reckoning which is a severer trial than the world's judgement. He is not initiated into a true spaciousness of character but follows, in Macbeth, the movement of what I have called a contracting personality. This is not the best that tragedy can offer.[17]

This article implies a concept of tragedy which may seem too exclusively psychological and moral. The absence of any repentance or of that expansion of the soul which, according to Heilman, is prompted by an examination of conscience, in no way diminishes the stature and power of the character. Perhaps Shakespeare is saying something else: by emphasising the necessary and fatal nature of the actions described has he not made it possible for the spectator, through the destiny of a criminal and sacrificed individual – a sacrificial victim – to be relieved of the burden of historical violence in which he is an accomplice, in which he in some obscure way plays a part but which he cannot accept as an ineluctable element in his existence?[18] By making such a detailed study of fear, did he not make it possible for fear to be purged?

2. The role of the witches

Reading a play one cannot help wondering, 'How should this role be played?' It is a question that, here, is raised by the witches – not because a modern public would not believe in them: Orson Welles managed to make them astonishingly real; rather because questions are posed by their form, their functions and their nature. And modern criticism, which sees them as old women, witches, *parcae*, sybills or, as Holinshed put it: 'the goddesses of destinie, or else some nymphs or fieries, indued with knowledge of prophesie by their necromanticall science',[19] does not help to provide an answer: for these harmful creatures make true pronouncements, truly know the future and lead Macbeth to behave in such a way that the excesses to which they goad him on provoke in the spectator a revulsion which also turns against them.[20] Their relation to the verbal and thematic fabric of the play and the sequence of the action is much closer than, for instance, that of the Porter of Hell Gate, or the old man in act II, or the two doctors who appear at the end of the play, one to attend Macbeth, the other at Malcolm's side. But their place in the logic of the action and their influence upon the main protagonist are far from clear.

The principal difficulty seems to arise because one feels that their relationship with the protagonist should fit into some kind of sequential, rhetorical or psychological logic; that it should be an influence comparable, for example, to the influence Lady Macbeth exerts upon him. In default of any relationship of that kind, a number of divergent interpretations have been put forward. A. C. Bradley,[21] followed by others, maintains that they should be seen simply as old crones – so they leave the protagonist 'entirely free'. For E. M. W. Tillyard,[22] an all-powerful providence is at work in the play, against which Macbeth struggles in vain, just as he struggles in vain against disorder (which would appear to imply that Macbeth is not a free agent). For W. C. Curry,[23] the witches may not be able positively to determine men's thoughts, but they can incite them to this thought or that. This view is in conformity with the idea people had at the time, of Satan's influence over men. Wilbur Sanders[24] points out that the question 'what is it that impels a man to act?' seldom finds an unequivocal answer.

But the problem should not, in fact, be posed in those terms. When the witches first meet Macbeth, they greet him as follows:

> *1 Witch*: All hail, Macbeth! hail to thee, Thane of Glamis!
> *2 Witch*: All hail, Macbeth! hail to thee, Thane of Cawdor!
> *3 Witch*: All hail, Macbeth! that shalt be King hereafter!　　(I, iii, 48–50)

To Banquo, they predict:

> *1 Witch*: Lesser than Macbeth, and greater.
> *2 Witch*: Not so happy, yet much happier!
> *3 Witch*: Thou shall get kings, though thou be none:
> So all hail, Macbeth and Banquo!　　(I, iii, 65–8)

It is not long before the idea of murder enters Macbeth's head; it betrays itself through his distress and a gesture that prompts Banquo to say:

> Good Sir, why do you start, and seem to fear
> Things that do sound so fair?　　(I, iii, 51–2)

and later on in the form of a possibility envisaged in the course of a monologue:

> My thought, whose murther yet is but fantastical,
> Shakes so my single state of man,
> That function is smother'd in surmise
> And nothing is, but what is not.　　(I, iii, 139–42)

It is an idea that comes to him again in another monologue (I, iv) and in a letter to Lady Macbeth (I, v). It is subsequently pondered and argued out more fully (I, vii) and rejected (I, vii, 31). It is Lady Macbeth who finally persuades Macbeth (I, vii) and who, at the end of act I, devises the plan for the murder, when she looks forward to what will have to be done in order to kill Duncan. In this speech, she uses techniques of persuasion (I, viii, 35–73) which are in keeping with the Elizabethan norms of credibility. The feeling that Macbeth has been influenced by the witches assails the spectator some time between scene iii and scene vii. But because it is only after Lady Macbeth's speech that Macbeth appears convinced, only then that the relationship between cause and effect, speech and conviction, is clearly established, the spectator may arrive at the conclusion that it is a human rather than a supernatural agent that spurs Macbeth on to action.

The relationship between the witches' prediction and Macbeth's declared thoughts is, to use Roland Barthes' term,[25] one of 'consecution' rather than consequence. The illusion that the spectator may have been under between scene iii and scene vii is one that both Lady Macbeth's speech and the presence of the witches help to create. As Barthes points out: 'In that case the story would be a systematic application of the logical error expressed in scholastic philosophy as *post hoc, ergo propter hoc*, which could well be the motto of destiny, for which the story is simply providing a language.'[26]

Actually, the impression of causality created in scene vii is no less misleading than that created in scene iii. It is quite possible to imagine Macbeth reacting with a refusal when presented with those very same arguments without our sense of verisimilitude being in the slightest strained. In either case the relationship is truly one of 'consecution' – although in the second case the means of persuasion seem more normal, more credible, more in line with our cultural expectations, and so more logical.

It does not seem very likely that Shakespeare can have been unaware of the difference between the means used in the two cases: in other plays he makes use of similar discrepancies to create similar effects, with the purpose of creating an illusion of free determination, even while placing the agents of the action in a situation of constraint. Here, the presence of the witches partly exonerates Macbeth to the extent that the real evil appears to be located outside him – just as the mere presence of Iago partly exonerates Othello in the eyes of the spectators. That presence allows Shakespeare to show how evil can be incorporated in a human and historical agent. The illusion of free determination is an artistic device to make it possible to overcome the divide separating a conceptual opposition from a chain in which events succeed one another inevitably, constituting a series. It is always Macbeth who acts – freely – but at the same time it is always the witches who are acting through him. Sometimes Shakespeare uses intermediaries posted at intervals throughout the play: thus, before Macbeth is convinced, Lady Macbeth goes altogether over to the side of the witches (I, v, 38–54). Sometimes he provides motivation for Macbeth's decisions in the information he has received from the witches: the reason that Macbeth decides to assassinate Banquo is, apparently, that he fears lest his son, Fleance, should succeed him. In the second interview, the warning, 'Beware Macduff', might have provided the motivation for his expressed desire to do away with Macduff, but his decision to assassinate all the members of his house stems neither from the logic of the action nor from outside persuasion.

Then one could appeal to the logic of murder. With J. I. M. Stewart, one could say that for Macbeth the abyss of evil is so deep that all he can do is throw himself into it: for it 'truly is crime, not the crown, that is irresistible to him'.[27] The fact is that the play secretly provides another law, which Macbeth obeys: the relations between the various episodes are not simply logical but analogical too. Thus, in the account that the first witch gives her companions in act I, scene iii, she relates how a sailor's wife who had some chestnuts in her lap refused to give her any although she herself was eating them, and even bade the witch be gone. The witch tells her companions that she will change herself into a rat without a tail, summon up unfavourable winds and make the sailor live an accursed life, depriving him of sleep and making him waste away.

This somewhat enigmatic story clearly serves to indicate the malevolent and harmful character of the witches: because she has been denied something to which she had no right, the witch is going to punish a third person by supernatural means. But that explanation is a superficial one. For this story must be compared to another. In act III, scene iv, after the apparition of Banquo's ghost and the disorderly departure of his guests, Macbeth realises that, although invited, Macduff did not come to the banquet. When he learns that he has taken refuge in England (IV, i), so escaping death, the tyrant has his wife and children killed.

The first story can be summarised as follows: the one who refuses (to offer) a gift of food is punished through her husband who is far away from her. The second: the one who refuses (to accept) a gift of food is punished through his wife who is far away from him. In both cases what is refused is part of an exchange. In the first case, the agent of the undeserved punishment is a bearded woman ('You should be women, / And yet your beards forbid me to interpret / That you are so'!: I, iii, 45–7). In the second the agent is one who believes the witches have made him sterile ('Upon my head they plac'd a fruitless crown, / And put a barren sceptre in my gripe': III, i, 60–1). Compared with Lady Macbeth, Macbeth is 'feminised', the reverse of the witches with their beards.

The homological relationship between the two stories confirms that it is not only through the action that Shakespeare establishes a connection between the witches and Macbeth. If it is true that Macbeth assumes the entire burden of evil indicated in the play, and that his death is an expiatory rite, it is not surprising that his actions conform to the schema provided by the witches. Modes of behaviour that are in conformity with the norms of good or of order and those that are in conformity with the norms of chaos are thus compared at a number of levels of discourse. Just as Macbeth is an inversion of Edward the Confessor, the miracle-working king who could act as a healer, when Macbeth vainly seeks aid from his doctor, his behaviour sets up in the memory of the spectator a confused echo of the behaviour of the first witch. At the beginning of the seventeenth century a character from tragedy could no longer be a supernatural being or an incarnation of the devil if he was to carry conviction. Whatever demoniacal elements were revealed in the course of history in the natural order and in daily existence had to be circumscribed, exorcised and expelled in their human manifestations. In our discussion of the sacrifice in *Julius Caesar* we referred to the special status of the sacred at the end of the sixteenth century: it is to that same status that we must appeal to explain the relationship established between the essence of evil and its manifestation through a dignified and serious dramatic action.

Let us examine the formal and poetic means Shakespeare uses to create and sustain the illusion of the deviant nature of the witches. In act III, scene iv, after the apparition of Banquo's ghost, Macbeth's guests disperse. Macbeth has been unable to eat or to drink from the cup that he lifted; he has repeated that he is so far advanced on the path of bloodshed that there can be no going back and that he has decided to seek out the witches once more. In act III, scene v, Hecate meets them. This scene is usually taken to be an interpolation. In act III, scene vi, Lennox is talking with another lord: we learn that the subjects of Macbeth are ready to revolt and that a coalition is being formed against him in England. In act IV, scene i, the witches are boiling up a cauldron into which they toss all kinds of ingredients. G. Wilson Knight has shown that this 'witches' meal' is an inversion of the banquet that never took place. Although Macbeth may be invited to this second banquet, in the end he will be excluded from it: the witches exist on an equivocal, metaphorical, ontological level at which human agents cannot participate directly.

Before Macbeth's entrance, the witches are chanting a song:

1 Witch: Thrice the brinded cat bath mew'd.
2 Witch: Thrice, and once the hedge-pig whin'd.
3 Witch: Harpier cries:– 'Tis time, 'tis time.
1 Witch: Round about the cauldron go;
In the poison'd entrails throw. –
Toad, that under cold stone
Days and nights has thirty-one
Swelter'd venom, sleeping got,
Boil thou first i' th' charmed pot.
All: Double, double toil and trouble:
Fire, burn; and cauldron, bubble.
2 Witch: Fillet of a fenny snake,
In the cauldron boil and bake;
Eye of newt, and toe of frog,
Wool of bat, and tongue of dog,
Adder's fork, and blind-worm's sting,
Lizard's leg, and howlet's wing,
For a charm of powerful trouble,
Like a hell-broth boil and bubble.
All: Double, double toil and trouble:
Fire, burn; and cauldron, bubble.
3 Witch: Scale of dragon, tooth of wolf;

Witches' mummy; maw, and gulf,
Of the ravin'd salt-sea shark;
Root of hemlock, digg'd i' th'dark;
Liver of blaspheming Jew;
Gall of goat, and slips of yew,
Sliver'd in the moon's eclipse;
Nose of Turk and Tartar's lips;
Finger of birth-strangled babe,
Ditch-deliver'd by a drab,
Make the gruel thick and slab:
Add thereto a tiger's chaudron
For th'ingredience of our cauldron.
All: Double, double toil and trouble:
Fire, burn; and cauldron, bubble.
2 Witch: Cool it with a baboon's blood:
Then the charm is firm and good.   (IV, i, 1–38)

These thirty-eight lines are divided up as follows: three introductory lines
(one for each witch), non-rhyming; a strophe of six lines (couplet rhymes),
and a refrain of two lines; a strophe of eight lines, and a refrain; a strophe of
thirteen lines, and a refrain; a concluding couplet.

With two exceptions, all the words are monosyllables or disyllables. The
lines are trochaic tetrametres, not iambic pentametres as in the bulk of the
play. They are rhymed. The strophes are irregular, although the refrain provides a recurrent theme. The fashion in which they grow progressively
longer is clearly designed to create a spell-binding atmosphere. The poem –
not counting the purely grammatically functional words – contains about
one hundred and forty words, sixty-three of which appear nowhere else in
the play.

The various ingredients that the witches toss into the cauldron themselves
have evil connotations. But every reference points back to a unique signified
meaning; in every case we are offered one part torn from a whole, itself a
deviant one.

The opposition between the natural and the unnatural whole – a combination of monstrous elements each of which is a part torn from a natural
organism – is a clear enough indication of what the witches are about: they
are out to recreate a whole, following a recipe and laws that are theirs alone
– instead of integrating themselves with the organism that the cosmos represents, and ascertaining , through this very integration, that it remains what
it is or what it should be. Macbeth's attempt to found the order of the realm
upon his own personal will, having himself decapitated the socio-natural
organism by eliminating its sovereign, is metaphorically analogous. The
witches produce a 'put-together job', an edible potion which is at odds with
the norms of time and nature – the norms of slow and measured development; it is a cannibal feast, situated outside time, composed of organic and
vegetable bits and pieces torn from living organisms – which are themselves

associated with evil.[28] In a similar fashion, Macbeth's power is abstracted from time, reproduction and continuity – since the couple is sterile – and is founded upon violence. This theme of mutilation, cannibalism and sterility, which is deeply implanted in the innermost fabric of the work, provides an explanation, on other than a purely psychological level, for Macduff's having avoided the banquet offered by Macbeth. It explains what it is that, literally, prevented any exchange taking place between the sailor's wife and the witch, or between Macbeth and the community.

From the above remarks it might be supposed that there are no more than two poles to the play: the one constituted by all that seeks to reestablish norms that are natural and organic, the other by all that seeks to found the order of this world upon laws regulated by some evil mysterious will. It might be supposed that this polarity can be found at every level of the action.

Yet the agents of actions which seem to be related exclusively to the natural order use methods which closely resemble those that the witches have set up as a system. Macbeth, feudal vassal to Duncan, disembowelled Macdonwald before beheading him. The traitor Cawdor has been executed. The blood shed in the initial fighting is the same as that shed by the troops in alliance against Macbeth – and old Siward, in his own way, makes that point:

> *Siward*: Had I as many sons as I have hairs,
> I would not wish them to a fairer death:
> And so, his knell is knoll'd.
> *Malcolm*:   He's worth more sorrow . . .   (V, ix, 14–16)

Whether for order or for disorder, bloodshed must feed whatever is on the increase. The major theme may remain the reestablishment of order, but there is a minor one too: the suggestion that the neutral order must constantly be upheld by the will of men. As Macbeth says:

> Blood hath been shed ere now, i'th'olden time,
> Ere humane statute purg'd the gentle weal . . .   (III, iv, 74–5)

It is human law that has imposed civilisation on the state which, initially, was in no way 'gentle'.[29] King Duncan is amazed at Cawdor's treachery:

> There's no art
> To find the mind's construction in the face:
> He was a gentleman on whom I built
> An absolute trust.   (I, iv, 11–14)

The future King Malcolm has a different attitude: he plays a double game with Macduff, for he can trust nobody:

> . . . Devilish Macbeth
> By many of these trains hath sought to win me
> Into his power, and modest wisdom plucks me
> From over-credulous haste.   (IV, iii, 117–20)

The point is that between the two, the reign of Macbeth has been interposed. The restoration of order or rather the establishment of a new order pre-supposes the political and metaphysical experience derived from the events that have taken place in the course of the play. A new possibility has been presented: that of a kingdom exclusively founded upon violence, a new, crazy kind of temporality, a chaos. All that separates the two orders is the consent and will of the hierarchical community, a community that belongs to civilisation, as is indicated by the creation of a new rank of nobility, the earls. *Macbeth* can be seen as a weakened form of myth in which the necessity for the foundation of order and law is stressed. It implies that the latter are aligned with civilisation and will. In order to avoid the cannibal meal of chaos, it is necessary for the new order to be founded upon a violence which involves another meal: one that bears all the signs of legitimacy and general consensus and in which the departing expiatory victim carries away all the evil in which society might otherwise have been submerged.

3. The image of blood

Caroline Spurgeon has drawn attention to the opposition between night and day and the images relating to clothing, reflections, sickness and horses.[30] G. Wilson Knight's study[31] focussed upon the opposition between the recur-ring themes of life and death, waking and sleeping, meals eaten and meals interrupted, growth and sterility, conduct that is honourable and conduct that is dishonourable. Later, scholars have attempted to link all these images into significant networks. The opposition between nature and what is unnatural and between order and disorder has been tackled by L. C. Knights;[32] while various themes such as the image of the new-born babe and concepts relating to time and to virility have been studied by Cleanth Brooks, Stephen Spender, Eugene Waith and others.[33]

Paradoxically enough, the image of blood has been the subject only of brief studies. Critics have generally been content to cite a few passages in which the word 'blood' appears, to point out, as do Jan Kott, Kenneth Muir and others,[34] that in this play blood is obsessively present, following, in that line, the powerful intuition of A. C. Bradley. Claude Lévi-Strauss once observed that Frazer's mistake, in analysing the role of fire in ethnological literature, lay in assuming that the word applied to one single category.[35] The same mistake seems to have been made where the word 'blood' in *Macbeth* is concerned.

The signified 'blood' in the play is indicated by five different lexical forms: 'blood', 'to bleed', 'bloody', 'gore' (twice) and 'gory', which altogether appear about sixty times. It is evoked metaphorically in a number of ways – there is an allusion to Golgotha, one to dashed out brains, etc. – and visually in every act, the visual signifiers naturally making a longer-lasting impact than the verbal ones which are abolished as the sound of the words dies away. I will now attempt to show that blood falls into a number of different categories in the course of the play, and that in two of them the theme of sacrifice is clearly of importance.

As early as in the second scene of the play, a 'bleeding captain' meets King Duncan and his followers:

> *Duncan*: What bloody man is that? He can report,
> As seemeth by his plight, of the revolt
> The newest state.
> *Malcolm*:   This is the Sergeant,
> Who, like a good and hardy soldier, fought
> 'Gainst my captivity.   (I, ii, 1–5)

The man is thus credited with attributes that specify the particular quality of the blood in which he is covered: this is blood spilt during combat – which qualifies the man as a reliable witness and messenger – and Malcolm's additional comment further gives him a heroic quality.

Having given an account of part of the battle, the sergeant collapses, unable to continue. Duncan thereupon declares:

> So well thy words become thee, as thy wounds:
> They smack of honour both. – Go, get him surgeons.   (I, ii, 44–5)

This blood and these wounds are placed in a favourable context, associated with honour. The only possible follow-up to them is the cure that they call for and that ought to remedy them.

The sergeant has given an account of Macbeth's exploits:

> For brave Macbeth (well he deserves that name),
> Disdaining Fortune, with his brandish'd steel,
> Which smok'd with bloody execution,
> Like Valour's minion, carv'd out his passage,
> Till he faced the slave; [the pitiless Macdonwald]
> Which n'er shook hands, nor bade farewell to him,
> Till he unseam'd him from the nave to th' chops,
> And fix'd his head upon our battlements.
> *Duncan*: O, valiant cousin! worthy gentleman!   (I, ii, 16–23)

After this passage, where blood is both named and forcefully evoked, there is a second which introduces it with a powerful metaphor:

> So they
> Doubly redoubled strokes upon the foe:
> Except they meant to bathe in reeking wounds,
> Or memorize another Golgotha,
> I cannot tell –
> But I am faint, my gashes cry for help.   (I, ii, 38–43)

Note the judgement passed on the actions described – the restriction introduced by 'except' (i.e. did they want to),[36] the implicit comparison between these two warriors and Christ's executioners. Despite all this, however, shedding blood – and the blood shed – remain signifiers of personal valour. Macbeth will be rewarded for the blood that he has spilt: as saviour of the realm, he receives the title of Cawdor.

Blood shed in battle calls for no retribution; on the contrary, it stores up credit for the one who shed it. In scene iv, Duncan declares:

> I have begun to plant thee, and will labour
> To make thee full of growing.   (I, iv, 28–9)

So the blood is endowed with fertilising powers. In the last act, the Scottish lords leading their troops have to meet the army of retribution of Malcolm, Siward and Macduff, in the neighbourhood of the forest of Birnam. As they learn that revolt has broken out in Macbeth's camp, two of the lords exchange the following words:

> *Cathness*: Meet we the med'cine of the sickly weal;
> And with him pour we, in our country's purge,
> Each drop of us.
> *Lennox*:   Or so much as it needs
> To dew the sovereign flower, and drown the weeds.   (V, ii, 27–30)

The medicine for the sickly community is Malcolm. Lennox and Cathness speak, first, of shedding their blood ('each drop of us') so that it may act as a purge or revulsive agent with a two-fold action: first, it would water, and thus make fertile, the sovereign flower; secondly, it would drown the harmful weeds. To its fertile qualities, purificatory virtues are added. Furthermore, the dialogue follows immediately upon the scene in which Lady Macbeth's doctor confesses himself unable to cure her, given that her complaints are 'against nature'.[37] Characteristically enough, purificatory blood is opposed, within the same context, to blood which defiles. Angus says of Macbeth:

> Now does he feel
> His secret murthers sticking on his hands   (V, ii, 16–17)

It is the term 'gore' that is used to refer to defilement when Macbeth tells of how he killed Duncan's guards:

> . . . there, the murtherers,
> Steep'd in the colours of their trade, their daggers
> Unmannerly breech'd with gore . . .   (II, iii, 112–14)

It is used again when he sees the ghost of Banquo, whose blood accuses and, as it were, besmirches him:

> Thou canst not say, I did it: never shake
> Thy gory locks at me   (III, iv, 49–50)

This is defilement, and an unspeakable kind of strangeness, making a break with the past – a 'natural' past in which the dead did not return but disappeared, in conformity with the natural order of things – and the present.

> . . . the time has been,
> That, when the brains were out, the man would die,
> And there an end; but now, they rise again,
> With twenty mortal murthers on their crowns,
> And push us from our stools. This is more strange
> Than such a murther is.   (III, iv, 77–82)

That was the order upset by Duncan's murder. Crime establishes a temporality in which: 'There's nothing serious in mortality', in which: 'All is but toys', in which: 'renown, and grace, is dead' (II, iii, 90–2).

Blood that has been shed, which on the hands of the tyrant signifies defilement, is a sign of suffering and misfortune when the great body from which it has flowed is evoked. Thus, in the dialogue between Malcolm and Macduff, the country's wounds cry out for sympathy:

> *Macduff*:   Bleed, bleed, pour country!
> Great tyranny, lay thou thy basis sure,
> For goodness dare not check thee . . .
> *Malcolm*: I think our country sinks beneath the yoke;
> It weeps, it bleeds; and each new day a gash
> Is added to her wounds   (IV, iii, 31–3; 39–41)

So much for blood that is shed. But there is another kind. Determined to assassinate Duncan, Lady Macbeth invokes the spirits:

> . . . make thick my blood,
> Stop up th' access and passage to remorse
> That no compunctious visitings of Nature
> Shake my fell purpose, nor keep peace between
> Th' effect and it! Come to my woman's breasts,
> And take my milk for gall, you murth'ring ministers . . .   (I, v, 43–8)

Between the two phrases: 'make thick my blood' and 'Come to my woman's breasts, / And take my milk for gall', the analogy is clear. Making fluid blood thick is equivalent to changing milk into gall. Blood in circulation (i.e. not thickened) and milk are set in opposition to blood no longer flowing (thickened) and gall. It is an opposition which spells out the constantly evoked contrast between the natural and the unnatural, order and chaos, nurture and poison. In this same passage Lady Macbeth makes it clear that she desires this metamorphosis which will be like passing from day to night wherein the 'keen knife' sees not 'the wound it makes'. The spilling of sacrilegious blood presupposes such a metamorphosis. Lady Macbeth also says to Macbeth:

> . . . I have given suck, and know
> How tender 'tis to love the babe that milks me:

I would, while it was smiling in my face,
Have pluck'd my nipple from its boneless gums,
And dash'd the brains out, had I so sworn
As you have done to this.   (I, vii, 54–9)

Here the staunched milk prefigures spilled blood; it is a brutal negation of life. Sterility – an important theme in the play, since Macbeth has no posterity whereas Banquo and Duncan both have sons – is thus incorporated into the murder plot right from the very first act. It stands in opposition to the natural, and fertile, course of existence. Blood in circulation, analogous to milk, is described as 'the wine of life' after Duncan's murder. In that same speech Macbeth hides his guilt yet, as if despite himself, reveals his own moral and metaphysical situation:

Had I but died an hour before this chance,
I had liv'd a blessed time; for, from this instant,
There's nothing serious in mortality;
All is but toys: renown, and grace, is dead;
The wine of life is drawn, and the mere lees
Is left this vault to brag of.   (II, iii, 89–94)

'The wine of life' is an image of blood in circulation. All that is left now is the dregs. The catastrophe that this event represents extends beyond the person of the man assassinated:

Donalbain: What is amiss?
Macbeth: You are, and do not know't:
The spring, the head, the fountain of your blood
Is stopp'd; the very source of it is stopp'd. (II, iii, 94–7)

There is thus a double opposition: on the one hand between blood shed and blood not shed; on the other, within the first term of the opposition, between blood shed in a context that renders it honourable and blood shed in a sacrilegious manner. To put it another way:
A. Blood not shed (life's principle; milk, 'wine of life'; natural, ordered elements)
is opposed to:
B. Honourable blood shed.
C. Sacrilegious blood shed.
There is a strong relationship between A and B, for blood shed in an honourable context is fertile, restorative, and life-giving. Between B and C the relationship is weak, although blood shed in an honourable context is not without sacrilegious connotations, as we have seen from the account of the bloodied sergeant (with his allusion to Golgotha).
The properties of C make it possible to specify certain properties of B. Thus, the sacrilegious nature of Duncan's assassination is underlined by Macbeth himself while the action he eventually takes is still no more than a

project. In Macbeth's description of the dead king, the sacrilegious nature of the act is transferred to the blood of the victim:

> . . . Here lay Duncan,
> His silver skin lac'd with his golden blood;
> And his gash'd stabs look'd like a breach in nature
> For ruin's wasteful entrance: there, the murtherers,
> Steep'd in the colours of their trade, their daggers
> Unmannerly breach'd with gore.   (II, iii, 109–14)

On the victim, the blood is 'his golden blood'.[38] On those said to be his murderers, the blood is 'gore': the difference between the terms used as sig-nifiers indicates the distance between defilement and the final shedding of the principle of life.[39] In contrast to blood shed on the field of battle, sacrilegious blood comes to be amplified: 'Most bloody piece of work', says Banquo (II, iii, 126). 'This more than bloody deed', says Ross (II, iv, 22). In act II, scene iv, Ross and the old man are discussing the darkness that has fallen over the land, the horses that are devouring one another, the owls that are attacking falcons:

> Tis unnatural,
> Even like the deed that's done,

says the old man, underlining the aberrant nature of the murder; and the blood that has been shed spills over the entire scene, over the whole country – that is, wherever men live, all over the universe:

> Thou seest the heavens, as troubled with man's act,
> Threatens his bloody stage,   (II, iv, 5–6)

declares Ross. It is not long before the assassin comes to see blood as an element with which he is familiar, within which he moves freely:

> . . . I am in blood
> Stepp'd in so far, that, should I wade no more,
> Returning were as tedious as go o'er.   (III, iv, 135–7)

That is because the blood that stains his hand colours 'the multitudinous seas incarnadine' (II, ii, 61). This metaphorical amplification is reinforced by a series of criminal actions that Macbeth commits. Various allusions suggest that it is a sign of the overturning of the natural order. Take, for example, Donalbain's rejoinder: 'the near in blood, / The nearer bloody' (II, iii, 138–9), which indicates a rupture and inversion in the normal relationships between men, genetic proximity now becoming a source of danger or a pre-text for murder.

Blood shed sacrilegiously becomes impure. It reaches the ultimate in impurity when it is poured into the witches' cauldron – as the blood of a sow that has devoured its own young.

Shakespeare has expressed this division of blood into pure, and impure, categories elsewhere. In 'The Rape of Lucrece' (1593–4), he makes a distinction between the two streams of blood that flow from Lucrece's breast.[40]

> And bubbling from her breast, it doth divide
> Into two slow rivers, that the crimson blood
> Circles her body in on every side,
> Who like a late-sack'd island vastly stood
> Bare and unpeopled in this fearful flood.
> > Some of her blood still pure and red remain'd
> > And some look'd black, and that false Tarquin stain'd.
>
> About the mourning and congealed face
> Of that black blood a watery rigor goes,
> Which seems to weep upon the tainted place;
> And ever since, as pitying Lucrece' woes,
> Corrupted blood some watery token shows,
> > And blood untainted still doth red abide,
> > Blushing at that which is so putrified.   (1737–50)

Blood shed in sacrilege makes whoever shed it impure; it is indelible:

> Will all great Neptune's ocean wash this blood
> Clean from my hand? No, this my hand will rather
> The multitudinous seas incarnadine,
> Making the green one red.   (II, ii, 59–62)

As for Lady Macbeth, she believes that water cannot only wash away the material traces of blood:

> . . . Go, get some water,
> And wash this filthy witness from your hand   (II, ii, 45–6)

but that it will be able to efface the act itself:

> . . . Retire we to our chamber:
> A little water clears us of this deed.
> How easy is it then!   (II, ii, 65–7)

Yet it is Lady Macbeth who, in the sleep-walking scene in act V, tries in vain to wash away an indelible stain:

Doctor: What is it she does now?   Look, how she rubs her hands.
Gentlewoman: It is an accustom'd action within her, to seem thus washing her hands. I have known her continue in this a quarter of an hour. (V, i, 25–9)

Lady Macbeth: Out damned spot! out, I say! – One; two: why, then, 'tis time to do't . . . Yet who would have thought the old man to have had so much blood in him? (33–8)

> . . . What, will these hands n'er be clean?   (41)

. . . Here's the smell of the blood still: all the perfumes of Arabia will not sweeten this little hand. (47–8)

. . . Wash your hands, put on your nightgown; look not so pale. – I tell you again, Banquo's buried: he cannot come out on's grave. (58–60)

Sacrilegious blood can only be purified by other blood. That accounts for the magical quality of what happens in *Macbeth*. Sacrilege and expiatory sacrifice – on the completion of which Macbeth's severed head will recall the severed head of Macdonwald – form an indissociable pair: Macbeth is not simply a tyrant executed, he is also a victim, a *pharmakos*, whose mutilated corpse is consumed, at the end of the play, by Macduff, the supporters of Malcolm and also by the public.

In contrast to blood shed on the field of battle – shed once and for all and calling for no further bloodshed – sacrilegious blood sets up a series, belongs within a system of revenge. Macduff is an avenger figure, the whole community of Scotland seeks vengeance:

> It will have blood, they say: blood will have blood:
> Stones have been known to move, and trees to speak;
> Augures, and understood relations, have
> By magot-pies, and choughs, and rooks, brought forth
> The secret'st man of blood . . .   (III, iv, 121–5)

Finally, sacrilegious blood signifies guilt. Lady Macbeth declares that she will smear Duncan's two servants with blood:

> Why did you bring these daggers from the place?
> They must lie there: go, carry them, and smear
> The sleepy grooms with blood.   (II, ii, 47–9)

>   . . . If he do bleed,
> I'll gild the faces of the grooms withal,
> For it must seem their guilt.   (II, ii, 54–6)

Here the blood is explicitly used as a sign; the play on words, between 'gild' and 'guilt', underlies the transference of the signs of culpability.

The various features of the different categories that we have analysed may be set out in the list.

Blood shed

Honourable	*Sacrilegious*
(Generally shed in battle. Clothing: armour)	(Generally shed not in battle. Clothing: not armour)
– once only	– repeatedly
– unamplified	– amplified
– signifies valour	– signifies guilt
– within the natural order	– unnatural
– can be healed by doctors	– not purifiable by water but by blood
– establishes credit	– establishes a process of retribution
– fertile	– sterile in the natural order
– agent of purification	– agent of impurity
– provides nurture	– poisoned

Blood not shed

analogous to milk – 'the wine of life'
belongs to the ordered elements
the natural principle of life
a supernatural liquid

In this last category a hierarchy is discernible. Macduff expresses it when he describes the death of Duncan whose blood is implicitly compared to that of saints:

> Confusion now hath made his masterpiece!
> Most sacrilegious Murther hath broke ope
> The Lord's anointed Temple, and stole thence
> The life o'th'building! (II, iii, 65–8)

So Duncan's blood is more than simply the natural principle of life; it is a supernatural liquid:

> . . . Here lay Duncan,
> His silver skin lac'd with his golden blood. (II, iii, 109–10)

His wounds are 'a breach in nature'. As W. A. Murray notes,[41] there is a link between Duncan and Edward the Confessor who is invested with magical powers which are possessed neither by Macbeth nor Lady Macbeth nor Lady Macbeth's doctor. The supernatural nature of royal blood is recognised by Macbeth when he sees it colouring the seas, that is to say undergoing a transmutation of substance. As Paracelsus wrote: 'Those who lack faith in the Resurrection cannot understand that the *blood is held in the hand of God*, and kept for the time appointed, unless, should there be need meanwhile, it may appear and flow.'[42]

The various categories under discussion are not semantically impermeable to one another: there is a concrete logic to them but it is conveyed by symbols that are often quite opaque. In fact, given that the same symbol may be used to signify polarised concepts, the antithesis between 'honourable blood' and 'sacrilegious blood' cannot be an absolute one. We have already made this point in connection with the wounded soldier's account of the battle; and the analogies between Macbeth cutting off Macdonwald's head and Macduff cutting off Macbeth's are too strong to be ignored. Blood signifies itself even before it signifies anything else. The opaque nature of Shakespeare's signifiers enables him to overcome the polarisation of antagonistic forces. Good and evil are not opposed in any simple way.

4. Tyrant and victim

In medieval play cycles, certain antagonistic figures have to pursue the evil that they do right to the very end so that the designs of providence can unfold. Thus, in the *York Plays*,[43] there is a scene in which Satan appears in a dream to Pilate's wife, causing her to intervene to save the life of Jesus.[44] There is a similar scene in the *Ludus Coventriae* of N. Town plays. A demon from Hell warns Satan of the dangers involved if Jesus is dragged down to Hell:

> ffor And he onys in helle be
> he xal oure power brest.[45]

Satan then realises that he has gone 'to ferre' (too far) and sends a dream to Pilate's wife so that she should convince her husband not to have Jesus killed. In the words of Claude Gauvin:[46]

A stage direction shows us *Uxor Pilati* tearing aside the curtains of her *schaffald*, leaping out of bed in much distress and running to plead with her husband, 'deme not jhesu but be his frende' (Do not condemn Jesus, but be his friend).[47] The dream of *Uxor Pilati* has its origins in Saint Matthew (XXVII, 10) and attracted the attention of the Fathers of the Church on many occasions. They provide two interpretations; 1. the dream is sent by God to proclaim Jesus' innocence or 2. it is inspired by the devil to arrest the course of the Redemption. The author of the present work chooses the second solution . . . [48]

There are thus two possible views on Judas' betrayal: as an individual he is the worst of traitors, but as the unconscious agent of the designs of providence, his betrayal is an action that is necessary for the salvation of humanity. In the *York Plays* Satan actually says, speaking of Jesus:

> And he be slone, oure solace will sese.
> He will save man saule fro oure wonde.[49]

If we apply this observation to *Macbeth*, it becomes possible to replace the protagonist within a wider framework of interpretation than a social, moral or psychological analysis.

Other commentators have arrived at similar conclusions by other routes. Jean Jacquot analyses the function of the witches as follows:

The witches in *Macbeth*, who are the instruments of the temptation and damnation of the protagonist, that is to say the Devil's assistants, are also spokesmen for an official truth held, whenever the line of the Stuarts is mentioned, to be in conformity with the designs of providence. And once one realises that, from the work's point of view, Macbeth's crime, his usurpation of the throne and his tyranny are the necessary means for the realisation of a providential plan, one already recognises the limits within which the problem of the hero's liberty is posed in the play, and the terms in which the nature of evil is formulated.[50]

In the last analysis, Macbeth uses the terms of Christian theology to pose the problem of the co-existence of evil and divine omnipotence and the problem of the limits of human freedom. From a theological point of view only one answer is possible: evil is the consequence of an original disobedience that itself results from a free choice the effects of which the human race has been feeling ever since. But each man remains free to obey the voice of God or to be won over by the Devil. In the play, Macbeth is free to choose between good and evil but, if one wants to avoid interpreting the work as a struggle for a long time unresolved between two cosmic principles of equal power, one cannot but admit that the forces of darkness must operate within the limits and to the ends permitted by a superior power and that the crimes, tyranny and death of Macbeth are necessary for the accomplishment of history's providential plan.[51]

These suggestions made by Jean Jacquot may be supplemented with another point of view expressed by Northrop Frye in his *Anatomy of Criticism*. In most known tragedies, the polar opposition between the tyrant and the *pharmakos*, which is so important at a theoretical level, is not expressed in a pure form: the tragic protagonist may combine features of both these figures. When this is the case the hero undergoes pain and humiliation too great to allow him to stand simply as a hero; it is easier to make him a villainous hero. 'We reach a point of demonic epiphany . . . Its chief symbols . . . are the instruments of a torturing death . . . A strong element of demonic ritual in public punishments and similar mob amusements is exploited by tragic and ironic myth. Breaking on the wheel becomes Lear's wheel of fire; bear-baiting is an image for Gloucester and Macbeth.'[52]

Frye distinguishes six forms or kinds of tragedy and *Macbeth* belongs to the sixth, in which the central images are 'images of *sparagmos*, that is cannibalism, mutilation and torture'.[53]

John Holloway also stresses the importance of the idea of sacrifice in Shakespeare's tragedies.[54] He notes that Macbeth, the saviour of the state, is also an ambivalent figure, the very image of death. Endowed with a double nature, he delivers himself to the powers of Evil. His rebellion becomes a curse laid upon the whole of Nature and going right back to the roots of time:

> Though you untie the winds, and let them fight
> Against the Churches; though the yesty waves
> Confound and swallow navigation up;
> Though bladed corn be lodg'd, and trees blown down;
> Though castles topple on their warders' heads;
> Though palaces, and pyramids, do slope
> Their heads to their foundations; though the treasure
> Of Nature's germens tumble all together,
> Even till destruction sicken, answer me
> To what I ask you. (IV, i, 52–61)

The image of the horse and the horseman, which in medieval iconography often represented war and destruction, is added to that of the man of blood. Thus Duncan's horses devouring one another like monsters (II, iv, 14–18),[55] Macbeth's gallop that Duncan could not catch up with (I, iv, 20–5) and the horses ridden by cherubim in his first monologue are all compared by Holloway to the four horsemen of the Apocalypse.[56]

The infraction to the order of nature is counteracted by the march of the forest of Birnam, 'a dumb show of nature, overturning anti-nature at the climax of the play'.[57] Holloway sees it as a May ritual in which processions of men and women dressed in green would chase winter away. Thus Macbeth becomes 'a lord of Misrule', the image of revolt becomes the ritualistic victim of the salutary life forces. In his invocation to the witches, Macbeth was ready to see:

> . . . the treasure
> Of Nature's germens tumble all together,
> Even till destruction sicken.   (IV, i, 59–60)

Holloway suggests that, once it has reached that point of excess, nature, which is an art of God, will in a mysterious way follow along His serpentine path or, as Sir Thomas Browne puts it in his *Religio Medici*: 'The lives, not only of men, but of Commonwealths, and the whole World run not upon an Helix that still enlargeth, but on a Circle, where, arriving to their Meridian, they decline in obscurity and fall under the Horizon again.'[58]

Sin must abound so that grace can 'much more abound' (Rom. V, 20). This evangelical maxim can be translated to a political level: it is only when disorder reaches intolerable proportions that order is vehemently and mercilessly sought after.

In the perspective of the play's opening scenes, where order and chaos were confused, the appearance of a figure around whom chaos can be organised gives that figure greater stature than an ordinary individual or simply a wicked tyrant. That is why the spectator cannot remain altogether detached from the protagonist at the end of the tragedy. Quite apart from the fascination everyone feels in a character who assumes to the ultimate limit the consequences of his actions, Macbeth allows us to sense that, at a point where good and evil, and order and disorder, reach an unacceptable level of instability, some formidable social, moral, historical and metaphysical necessity throws up an individual who can tip the scales and who, through his outrageous life, makes it possible for all to become united so that at last, beholding 'where stands / Th'usurper's cursed head' they may proclaim: 'the time is free' (V, ix, 20–1).

5. The near and the far: the Calvin affair and the status of foreigners under James I of England

Foreword

James VI of Scotland became king of England in 1603 with the title James I. One of his chief preoccupations was to promote the union of the two kingdoms. He came up against Parliament's refusal, however. In order to get round this, he tried to establish that all his Scottish subjects born after his accession to the throne of England should be considered in England as English subjects, by a simple court decision.

During the autumn of 1607 a plot of land was bought in the name of Robert Colvill, a child born in Edinburgh in 1605, grandson of Lord Colvill of Culross (whose family name was sometimes spelled Colvin), and a case was brought against two persons who were accused of having dispossessed the child of his property. Before the case could be judged, it was necessary to decide whether the child was an English subject. The question was debated in the Chamber of the Exchequer. Out of the twelve judges, only two judged that Robert Colvill – or Calvin, as he subsequently came to be called in the legal annals – was an alien born. All the rest held him to be English. James I of England had won on that point, but on that point only for he was unsuccessful in bringing about an effective union of the two kingdoms.

Let us study the way in which the judges justified their decision.

1. The writ

Robert Calvin, represented by his guardians, issued a writ before the Middlesex assizes against two individuals, namely Richard and Nicholas Smith who, he claimed, had 'disseised him of one messuage with the appartenances' situated at Haggard (or Haggerston or Aggerston) in the parish of Saint-Leonard in Shoreditch.

The defendants produced an objection: according to them, the said

Robert was not to be answered to his writ, because

the said Robert is an alien born on the fifth day of November in the third year of the reign of the king that now is, of England, France and Ireland, and of Scotland the thirty-ninth,[1] at Edinburgh, within his kingdom of Scotland aforesaid, and within the allegiance of the said lord the King, of the said kingdoms of Scotland, and out of the allegiance of the said lord the King of his kingdom of England; and at the time of the birth of the said Robert Calvin, and long before, and continually afterwards, the aforesaid kingdom of Scotland, by the proper rights, laws and statutes of the same kingdom and not by the rights, laws or statutes of this kingdom of England, was and yet is ruled and governed.[2]

Since foreigners could not inherit land in England or plead in any case involving an inheritance of land, if Robert Calvin, born in Scotland after the unification of the two kingdoms, under the sceptre of James I, was considered to be an alien born, his plea could not be received. And no Scot born in Scotland following the unification of the two kingdoms could be a beneficiary of the liberties and rights of England.

The Middlesex court brought the case before the court of the King's Bench. The judges of this court, conscious of 'the weight and importance' of the affair, submitted it to the Chamber of the Exchequer, where it was heard in three sessions. The most eminent jurists of the realm – among them Sir Francis Bacon, the Lord Chancellor Sir Thomas Egerton and Sir Edward Coke – were able to debate the matter at length. For this was a major constitutional affair and they were all aware that the consequence of the judgement would be to determine who was an English subject and who was alien born, and why. In stating their opinion about this case, the jurists would be circumscribing the territorial and symbolic space occupied by the body politic whose head was the Crown of England, after due examination of its principles, coherence, functioning and origins. They would be taking up a position in a debate that had started in the fourteenth century and that related to allegiance, to the king's two bodies and the right of his subjects, on the strength of that allegiance based on their loyalty to the Crown, to constrain by force any king who failed in his duties. Finally, in a move which, emanating from so high an authority, seems to have been unique in Europe for the period, they would be situating the position of England in relation to the other nations of the world and English subjects in relation to the rest of humanity. It was within this framework that Edward Coke formulated the concept of the 'perpetual enemy'. It is a concept of capital importance in the view of humanity that he puts forward, and one without which the Elizabethan symbolic system is hardly comprehensible.

As can be seen, the scope of the judgement was far wider than the circumstances that prompted it. Nevertheless, the latter are not negligible either and should first be described.

2. The Calvin affair and its historical context

No sooner had he summoned his first Parliament than James I expressed his desire that the union, through his person, of the two kingdoms of England and Scotland should become an effective union, that is – as he was later to specify[3] – that it should be characterised by uniformity in its religion, government and laws. This perspective provoked an explosion of chauvinism in the Commons. Statements such as the following were to be heard: 'that the Scots were pedlars, not merchants'; 'they have not suffered above two kings to die in their beds these two hundred years'; and that England was 'a rich pasture threatened by the irruption of a herd of famished cattle'.[4]

In 1604, English and Scottish commissioners were appointed to draft a proposal for organic union, but their proposal was rejected at the session of 1606, when the Commons refused to naturalise the *ante-nati*, that is to say Scots born before James I's accession to the throne, and also to declare the *post-nati*, those born after that accession, to be natural subjects according to the common law of the realm. All that James I could obtain, in 1607 and 1610, was a vote on two Acts of limited scope, the one abolishing hostilities between the two countries, the other making a number of provisions for a better administration of justice both north and south of the border.

There is nothing particularly surprising about the Commons' reluctance. James I inclined towards absolutism and tended to want the rules of civil society and those of the government to coincide. But in England, the real nation and the legal nation were strongly united. The body politic was regarded as a historically constituted organism (or organic whole) and the increase in the population that would be occasioned by the proposal for an organic union was seen as profoundly upsetting: a threat to the laws and customs, a violation of the physical integrity of the realm. In this first conflict between James I and the Commons, there was a clash between two different concepts of state, government, civil society and tradition.

However, other interpretations of the conflict are possible, for the conflict itself does not emerge clearly from the larger, somewhat confused historical framework. That framework deeply affected the various protagonists and it may account for their actions more immediately than the clash between on the one hand the demands of a royal power that strove to model the body politic into a system subject to the control of the nation-state and, on the other, a society in which the constituted bodies, classes, ranks and different interests were all defending and promoting their own liberties. The distrust felt towards the foreigner was thus fuelled by three different groups of facts and collective representations.

In the first place, the English felt themselves surrounded and threatened by catholic powers. It will be remembered that in 1570 Pope Pius V had excommunicated Elizabeth. In 1586, Sixtus Quintus offered to pay Philip of

Spain one million crowns if he would invade the island. The following year he declared a crusade against England. The Spanish Armada was defeated in 1588 but Spanish ships made another attempt in 1597, and in 1599 they tried to come to the aid of the Irish uprising of Tyrone: a storm – sent by providence, according to the protestants – caused them to fail. In England, to which a number of Jesuit missions had secretly been sent, a series of plots had been discovered: Throckmorton's in 1583, Babington's in 1586, Roderigo Lopez' in 1594. Lopez, who was the queen's doctor, was accused of attempting to poison her at the instigation of the king of Spain: royal propaganda took over the whole affair and exploited it. Finally, in 1605, there was the Gunpowder plot. Threats from within were thus added to threats from without and papists, puritans and foreigners were clearly execrated or suspect. Legislation on treason and religious observance[5] became increasingly specific and inflexible. All this was in no way conducive to the Commons integrating within the body politic just about the entire Scottish population which, not so long before, had constituted such a threat along the northern border.

Politics, religion and patriotism also permeated a second series of factors relating to the social and economic order. For half a century foreigners – of whom there were many in the land – had been introducing and exploiting various new techniques and deriving considerable profit from them.

The extent of England's technical backwardness is illustrated by the fact that, in 1566, when Thomas Gresham was building the London Royal Exchange, he had to employ a Flemish architect and Flemish masons and import glass, flagstones, wooden panelling and almost all the other materials. French Huguenots were setting up the glass industry; Germans, granted exclusive rights, were exploiting the copper mines; the Dutch and the French controlled iron-works and were developing the cutlery trade. Flemish engineers were consulted in the construction of the port of Dover and Elizabeth gave a monopoly over the manufacture of paper to a German. In a period of inflation all this once again aroused the resentment of English artisans and wholesalers: already, under Edward VI (1547–53), five or six hundred men, demonstrating before the mayor of London, had threatened to kill all the foreigners in the kingdom since, according to them, it was they who were responsible for the prevailing penury.[6] In 1571, the citizens of the capital appealed to the city customs to challenge the right of residence for any foreigners who were not burghers of the town. In 1588, 1593 and 1595 rioting against foreigners took place; after the last of the riots, in 1595, five artisans were hanged on Tower Hill. In 1592, the artisans' complaints resulted in an enquiry into the number and activities of foreigners domiciled in London. And a play entitled *Sir Thomas More*, written between 1593 and 1600,[7] includes a scene representing the day in 1517 known as 'Evil May

Day', when the common people of London rose up, attacking all foreigners and burning their homes.

In 1575 the government reacted by expelling the Flemish refugees who had come to England in 1571. The discontent found an echo in Parliament: in 1581 a bill was proposed to prevent the children of foreigners born in England from becoming English subjects. In 1593, another bill was proposed, and was this time supported by the City, to prohibit foreigners from selling imported merchandise on the retail market.[8] Both proposals were rejected but the fact that they were put forward at all is indicative of a significant state of mind: with domestic security under threat, it was felt necessary to take demographic and economic measures as well as exercise political and religious vigilance. Attempts were made to exploit the sense of unease, economically. In every domain, the foreigner was suspect. The body politic hardened against him and that suited the cause of nationalism very well: the theme of unity was exalted. No man should be divided: 'Divide a man's heart and you lose both parts of it and make no heart at all; so he that is not an intire subject, but half-faced, is no subject at all'[9] declared Chancellor Egerton in the course of the debates on the Calvin affair. Every division, every incoherence constituted a danger.

All the same, this sought-for coherence did not cause the English to cower within their beleaguered or encircled citadel. The play of ideological and political affinities led England to intervene in both Flanders and France, on the pretext of defending the true religion. On 31 October 1601, the Speaker of the House of Commons thanked the queen for having defended the true faith, eradicated superstition, sects and schisms and assured internal peace. Before the highest court in the realm, he denounced the pope, 'that man of sin and Belial or Beast of Rome' who sent Jesuits 'or rather Jebusites and priests of Baal' to seduce the people, and he stigmatised Spain as 'bewitched with that cup of the whore of Babylon'.[10]

Thus, threats from both within and without served to strengthen ideological and political convictions. So it is not contradictory that, while closing in on itself in some respects, England was at the same time seeking to expand. This brings us to the third series of factors. During the last quarter of the century, the English in their turn became explorers and colonisers. In 1582, Richard Hakluyt judged that the moment had come for England to enter into competition with Spain and Portugal: it was necessary for her to gain a foothold in America and in other regions yet to be discovered.[11] And in 1585 his cousin set out thirty-one reasons why it seemed to him desirable to undertake a voyage of colonisation to Virginia, the objectives of the voyage being: the implantation of the true Christian religion, commerce and conquest.[12] The wars in Ireland had already provided a model for colonisation and taught the English that an entire community could be considered as a group of savage, ignorant enemies, no better than animals. Ireland had been temporarily pacified by the time of Elizabeth's death and remained a conquered land while some of its conquerors went on to sail to America.[13]

It was in these circumstances that James I presented to his first Parliament his proposal for union between England and Scotland. It was characteristic that he should exalt the theme of unity: he declared himself to be the direct descendant of Henry VII and this lineage to reunite in his person the two princely houses of York and Lancaster that had for so long been enemies. And yet even that union could not compare with the union of the two ancient and glorious kingdoms of England and Scotland, one that in his blood was the emblem of that 'second great blessing that God hath with my person sent unto you', that is, 'peace within'.[14]

But Parliament did not take the same view. While perfectly prepared to conquer distant peoples, open up new markets and assure external and internal peace, it was against opening up England to others. To the members of the House of Commons it seemed shocking that foreigners should be able to benefit from English rights and liberties. On the question of naturalisation, James I's judges preferred to obtain a favourable decision for the *post-nati* by passing judgements of their own. That is why they promoted the Calvin affair. Replaced in its context, the affair makes it possible to appreciate not only the power of common law within the kingdom, but also how even men with, in comparison to the Commons, the least narrow of views regarding national identity, conceived the organic nature of the body politic and the extent to which it could receive foreigners into its midst.

3. The founding act of Edward Coke

Now we can examine the content of the arguments put forward by Sir Edward Coke according to his own account of the affair, published in the seventh part of his *Reports*. The great Jacobean jurist is conscious that he is being faithful to the doctrine shared by his colleagues, that his is at the same time a personal undertaking and that he is formulating a precedent of fundamental importance. He declares that, having decided to set out the arguments presented to the court 'as truly, fully and sincerely as I possibly can',[15] and having noticed that every or almost every judge used his own particular individual method, he will take it upon himself to reduce 'the sum and effect of all to such a method as . . . the reporter himself thinketh to be fittest and clearest for the right understanding of the true reasons and causes of the judgement and resolution of the case in question'.[16] He does indeed accompany the arguments put forward by the other judges with his own personal observations and remarks based upon his own incomparable knowledge of the common law of the realm, conscious as he does so that the arguments in the case are as important as the judgement itself. Following his customary method, he gives his account of the judgement appealing to the spirit of 'Common Law' as manifested in the texts and in reading between the lines in the texts, spurred on by his conviction that this is a unique case, a case, he says, such as

the eye of the law (our books and bookcases) never saw, as the ears of the law (our reporters)[17] never heard of nor the mouth of the law (for *judex est lex loquens*), the Judges our forefathers of the law, never tasted . . . In a word, this little plea is a great stranger to the laws of England.[18]

His account of the case will thus constitute a founding act, for the affair

was one of the shortest and least that ever we argued in this court, yet was it the longest and weightiest that ever was argued in any court, the shortest in syllables, and the longest in substance; the least for the value . . . but the weightiest for the consequent, both for the present and for all posterity.[19]

Edward Coke was quite right both about the political importance of the judgement and about its juridical and symbolic scope. The judges had undertaken to define what a foreigner was and at the same time to circumscribe the characteristics and essence of a subject. The definitions proposed were to establish the juridical space and the nature of the bonds within which an individual could enjoy to the full the rights (or, as they were called at that time, the 'liberties') recognised to belong to every member of the national community: they were rights the fundamental principles of which were unassailable, any secondary limitations being the result of such accidents of nature, misguided behaviour or forms of tenure that could affect any individual within the very system that recognised his status as a subject.

Edward Coke chose to examine the case under four headings: allegiance, laws, kingdoms and foreigners. The four categories are interdependent and all are necessary to establish the distance and frontier that both legally and symbolically separated the foreigner from the subject. The distance between the two is, in point of fact, not absolute, except in the case of foreigners defined as 'perpetual enemies' who provide an absolute antithesis to the subject and who, for that reason, are essential to his nature and definition.

The most important consideration was the coherence of the system and the exhaustiveness of the exposition: the foreigner is such only in relation and contrast to the subject, and the latter, in his turn, only exists by virtue of his relation to the king, the laws and the kingdom. So we must examine Coke's arguments step by step for they bear upon the Elizabethan and Jacobean symbolic world at the most profound level.

4. Allegiance

The defence maintained that two quite distinct allegiances existed: first, the allegiance of the Scots to James I in his capacity as king of Scotland; second, the allegiance of the English to James I in his capacity as king of England. Anybody born out of allegiance to James I, king of England, was a foreigner in England.[20]

To refute this thesis, Edward Coke proceeded to examine decisions and precedents that established the nature, forms and limits of allegiance, the status of the royal person to whom allegiance was due and the different kinds of duties that it involved. This entailed examining the theory known as that of 'the king's two bodies'[21] and situating allegiance within the domain of relations governed by natural law.

Allegiance is the obedience that a subject owes his sovereign. Coke declares that it is stronger than the link binding the lord and the vassal who has paid him homage. It is a form of liege homage exalted to the absolute: 'between the sovereign and the subject there is without comparison a higher and greater connexion: for as the subject oweth to the king his true and faithful ligeance and obedience, so the sovereign is to govern and protect his subjects'.[22]

There exists between them 'a double and reciprocal bond' (*duplex et reciprocum ligamen*).[23] But although Coke magnifies the relation of the vassal to the overlord and refers it to the bond that exists between the subject and the king, he denies that the oath is the origin, source or principle of allegiance: 'Ligeance does not begin by the oath in a leet.'[24]

Chancellor Egerton, in his account of the affair, insists upon the same point: the oath

is not *alta ligeantia* by birth right; it is but *legalis ligeantia* by policie; and Fitzherbert calleth it 'swearing to the lawe'. And if that were the onely bond and mark of allegeance, many are out of it, and so at libertie. As children under twelve years; yet sometimes they may commit treason and felony; where *malitia supplet aetatem*.[25] So women of all sortes . . . also noblemen of all sortes, who are neither bound to attend the leete, nor to take that oath.[26]

Edward Coke shows that the common law of the realm distinguishes between four kinds of allegiance. The first is called 'natural' (*ligeantia naturalis, absolute, pura et indefinita*). It 'originally is due by nature and birth-right'.[27] This is *alta ligeantia*. He who owes it is called *subditus natus*. Characteristically enough, Coke does not explain this by using any positive definition of common law; he deduces it from the expressions used to refer to the king ('natural liege lord') and his subjects ('natural liege subjects')[28] and from the formulae used in the indictments of treason.[29] What he is doing is attempting to represent the quality of a subject as a property that does not stem from positive law but precedes that law, having its source and foundation in natural law. In this view, allegiance is a relationship as indissoluble as the bonds of marriage, a relationship that is both organic and sacred. It incorporates notions (or feelings) covered by terms such as 'faith', 'ligealty' (or bond) and 'obedience'.[30] On these grounds it cannot be limited either in space or in time.

The second kind of allegiance is called 'acquired' (*ligeantia acquisita*). It stems neither from nature nor from birth but obtains its full authority by decision of Parliament: strictly speaking, it is a matter of naturalisation. It can also be obtained by letters of denization from the king.[31] In that case, it is more limited than the first form mentioned and carries with it no right to pass land on to one's heirs. Finally, it can be obtained by conquest: all subjects of the king who have either fought or stood guard in the land on those grounds become 'denizens' of the kingdom or of the conquered territory. Coke does not specify what the status of the conquered people becomes nor whether, in England, they acquire the rights and liberties of the English people. This seems a *lacuna* of some significance to the extent that, according to Coke, conquest does not imply 'naturalisation' for the conquered people.

The third kind of allegiance is called 'local'. It is owed by a foreigner whose sovereign has friendly relations with the king of England and who finds himself within the territories of the latter. If he conspires against the king of England having received a safe-conduct, he will be accused of treason since the law considers that he owes 'local allegiance' to the king. Coke cites the case of Stephano Ferraro de Gama and Emmanuel Lewis Tinoco, two Portuguese who came to England with safe-conducts from Queen Elizabeth. They were accused of conspiring to assassinate Elizabeth, together with Roderigo Lopez, the queen's doctor. The judges (among them Edward Coke), decided that they had plotted *contra dominam Reginam*, that the term *naturalem dominam suam* should be omitted but that the terms *contra ligeant[iae] suae debitum* should be retained.[32] This means that they owed allegiance to the queen despite the fact that she was not their natural sovereign, and they could thus be accused of treason. In contrast, if a foreigner hostile to the king invaded the kingdom, he could not be accused of treason since he never had owed allegiance to the sovereign. He would be put to death, says Coke, in accordance with martial law.[33]

It will have been noticed that 'local' allegiance is geographically circumscribed. It might be thought that the criterion is English 'soil'. Coke emphasises that, however weak, precarious and provisional this local allegiance may be, it is nevertheless strong enough 'to make a natural subject, for if he hath issue here, that issue is a natural born subject'.[34] Yet, in effect, what is important really is not the place of birth, the relationship to territory, but allegiance. Edward Coke says so quite specifically:

It is to be observed that it is *nec coelum, nec solum*, neither the climate nor the soil, but *ligeantia* and *obedientia* that make the subject born; for if enemies should come into the realm and possess town or fort and have issue there, that issue is no subject to the king of England.[35]

The last kind of allegiance is called 'legal' (*ligeantia legalis*), the conse-

quence of an oath sworn by the subject. This was a feudal practice. However, Coke makes it clear that only the form of the oath and the manner of
swearing it were devised by men (*ex provisione hominis*) and stem from
positive law. The substance and effect of the oath stem from natural law (*ex
institutionae naturae*).[36]

Clearly then, the quality of 'subject', stemming as it does from allegiance,
and allegiance alone, is a quality that, in default of a better word, must be
called mystical, for it is, as it were, incorporate in man himself:

Ligeance, and faith and truth which are her members and parts, are qualities of the
mind and soul of man, and cannot be circumscribed within the predicament of *ubi*,
for that were to confound predicaments, and to go about to drive (an absurd and
impossible thing) the predicament of quality into the predicament of *ubi*. *Non
respondetur ad hanc quaestionem, ubi est?* to say: *Verus et fidelis subditus est, sed ad
hanc quaestionem, qualis est? Recte et apte respondetur, verus et fidelis ligeus est* (to
the question, where is he? one does not reply: he is a faithful and sincere subject. But
to the question, what is he?, it is right and pertinent to reply: he is a faithful and sincere subject (liegeman)).[37]

That was how Coke was to justify one of the outcomes of the judgement
in the Calvin affair: natural allegiance can be limited by no boundary,
frontier or confine.[38]

5. The king's two bodies

Having thus determined the nature, forms and frontiers of allegiance –
thereby simultaneously establishing the quality, or rather substance, of the
subject – Coke turns his attention to the figure to whom allegiance is due.
This being is double: the king has within him two capacities, he exists as two
species merged in one. He has 'one a natural body, being descended of the
blood royal of the realm; and this body is of the creation of Almighty God
and is subject to death, infirmity and such like'. But he also has 'a politic
body or capacity, so called because it is framed by the policy of man (and, in
21 E.4.39.b is called a mysticall body) and in this capacity the king is
esteemed to be immortal, invisible, not subject to death, infirmity, infancy
etc.'.[39]

To which of these two natures of his is allegiance due? It is due to 'the
natural person of the king (which is ever accompanied with the politic
capacity); and the politic capacity as it were appropriated to the natural
capacity'. It is not due 'to the politic capacity only, that is to his crown or
kingdom distinct from his natural capacity'.[40]

This formulation is essential: the king is not a 'politic body' incarnate, but
a natural body in which is invested the political body or capacity. Coke produces six reasons for this:

  1. The law presumes that each subject has sworn an oath to the king, just

as the king has sworn an oath to his subjects. And this oath can only be sworn by his natural person, 'for the politic capacity is invisible and immortal; nay, the politic body hath no soul, for it is framed by the policy of man'.[41] If it has no soul, it cannot swear an oath.

2. In all accusations of treason brought against anyone who has sought the death of his lord the king (and this must be understood to mean the death of his natural body, since his political body is immortal), the charge concludes with the words: *contra ligeantiae suae debitum* which, Coke says, shows plainly that allegiance is due to the natural body.[42]

3. The king *in genere* does not die. But it is clear that he does die *in individuo*.

4. A political body as such, being invisible, can neither give nor receive homage.

5. In matters of faith and allegiance, nothing must be simulated; everything must be *ex fide non ficta*.

6. The king holds the kingdom of England by right of birth, through heredity, through transmission of the royal blood. The succession is an attribute of the right of heredity. That is why the formula generally used is 'to the king, his heirs and successors'.[43]

Thus, at the death of Queen Elizabeth, the Crown and kingdom passed by descent to His Majesty the king and by that fact he became king entirely and absolutely without any ceremony being necessary. The coronation is no more than an ornament of royalty: a solemn and external confirmation of the royal succession, but not an essential part of the title.[44]

The king's crown is a 'hieroglyph' (that is to say an emblem) of the laws: it makes it possible for justice to be done. Now, if one removes what is signified by the crown – that is to say: judgement and the administration of justice, the preservation of peace in the realm, the separation of good from evil and truth from error – all that belongs to the king's natural capacity is removed: for it is in a quite concrete fashion (*in rei veritate*) that the king is endowed with bodily and spiritual qualities that render him capable of administering justice; but whatever belongs to his invisible and immortal capacity is not removed since it does not have the same qualities, having in itself neither body nor soul.[45]

It is remarkable that the preeminence of the concrete person over the function, indicated by the emphasis laid upon the right of blood, is a popular idea as well as an erudite one. It is connected with the belief in the sovereign's magical healing powers, a belief which is attested during the reign of Elizabeth.[46] Coke provides a precise legal formulation for the notion and in so doing places the succession within a system that puts it beyond contestation. It is not the coronation that makes the king, but the royal blood transmitted by heredity ever since Noah.[47] Coronation would interpose between successive monarchs a human act which would make royalty if not

contractual at least dependent upon a ceremony – of consecration or anoint-
ing – and that would make the choice of person contingent or arbitrary, for
the ritual would be attributed with the power of raising that person to the
place of sovereign and changing an ordinary individual into a monarch.
Indeed, in a work published in 1594 the Jesuit Robert Parsons, under the
pseudonym of Doleman, maintained that 'succession by Nearness of Blood
is not [determined] by Law of Nature, or Divine; but onely by Humane and
Positive Laws of every particular Common wealth',[48] and such laws may be
altered. Ideas such as these could not be tolerated, for they might lead to a
change of monarchy.[49]

The same goes for allegiance: the whole of Coke's argument tends to
present it as independent of the legal system which, nevertheless, may in
some cases determine the forms homage should take: but then, homage is no
more than the visible and symbolic manifestation of a relationship that precedes it and it is that relationship that makes a subject.

In the second part of his thesis, where he considers the laws, Coke goes
on to confirm and justify all this. He shows that the allegiance due to the king
stems from natural law; that natural law is an intrinsic part of the positive
laws of the realm; that it pre-existed those laws; and that it is immutable and
cannot be abolished or broken. And so it is with allegiance.[50]

6. The laws

To establish – or recall – the fact that God infused natural law into the heart
of man at the moment of creation,[51] Coke makes use of a series of quotations
borrowed from the Scriptures, Aristotle, Justinian, Bracton, Fortescue and
others. He is thus in line with a current of ideas well established in the
Elizabethan period, the principal spokesmen for which were Christopher
Saint-Germain, Heinrich Bullinger, Wolfgang Musculus, John Hayward,
William Fulbecke and above all Richard Hooker.[52]

Natural law is the law that governed God's people before Moses – the first
law-giver in the world – established the commandments. For God and
nature, divine and natural law, are one. According to that supreme law,
allegiance and obedience from the subject are due to his sovereign or
superior. Before positive laws had been created, kings passed judgement in
accordance with equity: so allegiance, faith and obedience existed before
any body of laws 'for that it had been vain to have presented laws to any but
to such as owed obedience, faith and ligeance'. It was by virtue of this primary subordination that they observed and obeyed the laws.[53]

With remarkable ingenuity, by analysing a number of the provisions of
common law, Coke shows that natural law is anterior, superior and intrinsic
to positive law. If a man accused of treason gives himself up and is killed
without mandate, his son cannot appeal to the law because, given that he

could only do so as the man's heir (and that quality is a provision of positive law), he too is affected by the disqualification of his father. The man's wife, on the other hand, can appeal for she remains his wife despite her husband's disqualification: the point is that the relationship between man and wife is *de jure naturae*. Natural law is paramount.[54]

Even more striking is the case of the outlaw who, if he is a fugitive, is placed beyond the protection of positive law. Bracton compares him to a wolf, a wild beast. His blood is corrupt: his son can inherit neither from him nor anyone else. According to feudal law, anybody could put him to death. However, if he was taken, nobody but the sheriff could execute him, so that, Coke says, 'he is not out either of his natural ligeance, or of the king's natural protection'.[55]

This distinction between a disqualification that resulted from a provision of positive law and a natural disqualification was not Coke's personal invention. In a case pleaded in 1658 we find the following argument:

. . . you may see that a disability natural is worse than that which is but accidental, and that it is more base to be born an Alien than to become a Traytor, for a Traytor is but a sudden Enemy of an old Friend, but an Alien is a sudden Friend of an original Enemy.[56]

Coke has often been accused of manipulating the texts to support his own argument. But he does not appear to be doing so here. In England the king is not only a mediator between God and men, endowed with a double nature: both human and divine, secular and priestly – a point that Francis Bacon also makes in his analysis of the Calvin affair, maintaining that *Rex est persona mixta cum sacerdote*;[57] he also belongs to both the civilised and the wild domains. He is the legal and natural protector of wild animals, whom he alone has the right to hunt and kill in his forests, just as he alone has the power to 'inlaw the outlaw'. As a result of that action, the outlaw returns to the world as if new-born (*quasimodo genitus*),[58] able to acquire or receive new rights but not to reassume immediately all those that he possessed before he was outlawed; he is not the person he used to be now restored to the legal order, but a new person, as it were arisen from the natural order to enter, quite naked, into positive law.

This relationship of the sovereign to wildness and violence is not one often commented upon. Nevertheless it becomes quite apparent when he is leader in times of war. Francis Bacon makes the point clearly:

That allegiance is in vigour and force where the power of law hath a cessation, appeareth notably in time of wars. For *silent leges inter arma*. And yet the sovereignty and imperial power of the king is so far from being then extinguished or suspended, as contrariwise it is raised and made more absolute; for then he may proceed by his supreme authority, and martial law, without observing formalities of the laws of his kingdom. And therefore, whosoever speaks of laws, and the king's power by laws, and the subject's obedience or allegiance to laws, speaks but of one half of the crown.

For Bracton, out of Justinian, doth truly define the crown to consist of laws and arms, power civil and martial.[59]

In this role, as war leader, acting beyond all civil law (and even, in some cases, beyond the laws of war), the king is close to the wild beast. Shakespeare was well aware of this redoubtable and relatively secret aspect of the Crown and was quite explicit about it in connection with the most 'positive' of his kings, Henry V:

> Then should the warlike Harry, like himself,
> Assume the port of Mars; and, at his heels,
> Leash'd in like hounds, should famine, sword, and fire
> Crouch for employment.[60]

> But when the blast of war blows in our ears,
> Then imitate the action of the tiger;
> Stiffen the sinews, conjure up the blood,
> Disguise fair nature with hard-favour'd rage.[61]

The king is a 'hieroglyph', a microcosm of the entire natural order in all its aspects – the sacred and the profane, the domesticated and the wild. The protection that the king can afford the outlaw – the most total case of exclusion envisaged in positive law – certainly indicates that the outlaw, who is clearly entirely wild and for whom civility is in abeyance, is nevertheless not situated outside the natural order nor beyond royal protection. This was not to be the case where certain foreigners were concerned.

7. The kingdoms

The fact that natural law is an intrinsic part of the positive laws of England, as it is of the laws of all nations, has one important consequence with regard to the relationship between the English and Scottish kingdoms: the subjects of both are united by birth under natural law in a common allegiance to James I, despite the differences in the positive laws by which the two groups are governed.[62]

Coke specifies in four points what it is that unites the two kingdoms and what it is that divides them:[63] (1) they are united under a natural sovereign despite the fact that they remain two distinct kingdoms; (2) the subjects of the two kingdoms are 'united at heart' in their allegiance to the king despite the fact that the positive laws that govern them are different; (3) they are the beneficiaries of the same royal protection despite the fact that they have different Parliaments; (4) the three lions of England and the lion of Scotland are brought together on a single escutcheon although the respective nobilities of the two countries remain distinct; for the allegiance of the Scottish noble to the king of England does not make him a noble in England: allegiance is ruled by natural law whereas nobility is a royal creation and stems from positive law.

This last point is one that Coke insists upon. For obvious political reasons, in the first place: Scottish nobles are not to sit in the Upper House in England. What he is doing is offering reassurance to the English nobility. But by so doing he is also entering into a debate with which the nobility was much preoccupied and which concerned its nature and 'ontological' status: was it the right of heredity, blood, education, virtue, fortune or courage that made it what it was? The basis of the debate manifests the familiar – and, in the Renaissance, commonplace – opposition between 'nature' and 'nurture'. Coke rules that the ultimate basis of the nobility stems from civilisation (nurture): barons, viscounts, counts, marquesses and dukes are only what they are if their quality is legally recognised in that they are qualified to sit in the Upper Chamber of England. He claims that only the highest rank, that of the king, and the lowest, that of the knight, are considered to be universal: a king may retain his title of king if judged in England but if a foreign duke brings a case, he will be referred to as 'knight', for he is foreign to the nobility of the realm.[64]

8. Foreigners

After studying allegiance, the monarch and the relationship between England and Scotland, Coke can at last examine the status of foreigners. Who is a foreigner? Any individual born out of allegiance to the king and in an allegiance to some other figure.[65] The most general incapacity that affects foreigners is that they cannot go to law in any affair concerning land. In a case where they brought such an action, the defence could plead that the plaintiffs were born under allegiance to another sovereign and they could insist that they brought proof to the contrary.[66]

Coke then divides humanity into a number of different categories which can be expressed as shown in the diagram.[67]

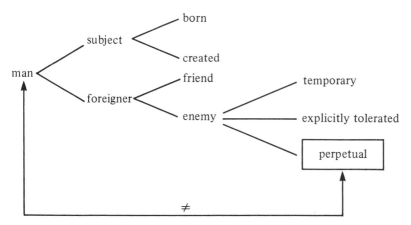

The foreigner who is a 'friend', whose sovereign is linked by treaty to the king of England, can settle in the island, acquire movable goods of every kind and take legal proceedings in connection with any of these possessions. But he cannot acquire land or immovable property, nor can he plead in any affair concerning the inheritance of land. If the foreigner who is a friend becomes an 'enemy', he loses all rights to legal representation.

For the foreigner explicitly tolerated (*specialiter permissus*) the same applies as to foreigners who owe the king 'local' allegiance.

In contrast, the case of foreigners who are 'perpetual enemies' is quite different. A perpetual enemy can bring no legal action nor can he acquire any possessions in the realm. According to the law all infidels are perpetual enemies for it

presumes not that they will be converted, that being *remota potentia* [a remote possibility], for between them, as with the devils, whose subjects they be, and the Christian, there is perpetual hostility, and can be no peace; for, as the apostle saith: 'What concern hath Christ with Belial or what part hath he that believeth with an infidel?' (2 *Cor.* 6.1); and the law saith *Judaeo Christianum nullum serviat mancipium, nefas enim est quem Christus redemit blasphemum Christi* [No Christian shall be servant to a Jew, for it is sacrilege and blasphemy towards Christ to keep in servitude whomsoever Christ has saved] (*Register* 282). *Infidelis sunt Christi et Christianorum inimici* [Infidels are enemies to Christ and Christians]. And herewith agreeth the book in 12 H. 8. fol. 4. where it is holden that a Pagan cannot have or maintain any action at all.[68]

The consequences of this perpetual hostility are not simply domestic. Coke notes that there is a fundamental difference between a Christian king's conquest of a Christian kingdom and his conquest of an infidel one. To be sure, in both cases the conqueror has power over life and death. But in the first, although he may make such alterations as he will to the existing laws, the laws nevertheless remain as they were until he does so. In the second case, in contrast, the laws of the infidel kingdom are abrogated at the moment, and as a consequence, of the conquest,

for that they be not only against Christianity, but against the law of God and of nature, contained in the decalogue; and in that case, until certain laws be established amongst them, the king by himself and such judges as he shall appoint shall judge them and their causes according to natural equity, in such sort as kings in ancient times did with their kingdoms, before any certain municipal laws were given.[69]

In 1578, Humphrey Gilbert received from the queen a charter according to the terms of which he could set off to discover 'such remote, heathen and barbarous lands, countrys and territories not actually possessed of any Christian prince or people'.[70] In 1606 the same terms can, in part, be found in the charter authorising Thomas Gates, George Somers and Richard Hakluyt to settle in Virginia. The king gives encouragement to their desires to undertake such a noble enterprise which may by the providence of Almighty God, hereafter tend to the glory of his divine Majesty, in propagating of Christian religion to such people as yet live in darkness and miserable ignorance of the true knowledge and worship of God, and may in time bring the infidels and savages living in those parts to humane civility and to a settled and quiet government.[71]

The classification Coke uses certainly concerns the whole of humanity on both an individual and a collective or national level. It will have been noted that the 'perpetual' enemy is the only one placed beyond God's and natural law. This exclusion is absolute. Coke underlines the fact when he establishes a homology between what separates the Christian from the infidel and Christ from Belial and, more explicitly, when he reminds the reader that the laws of an infidel kingdom are abolished the minute it has been conquered: for it is the conquest that makes it possible once more to situate within the rule of nature the human group which has hitherto lived in contradiction to that law; the conquest thus redresses an unnatural aberration and makes it possible for the conquering king to judge 'with equity' until such time as positive laws in accordance with natural law can be imposed. All those individuals whom the common law of the realm had, ever since the Middle Ages, placed beyond positive law – whether that exclusion was partial or total, as in the cases of the outlaw and the man pursued 'with hue and cry'[72] – were nevertheless not considered to be beyond natural law: whether they were lepers, lunatics, idiots, excommunicated, in religious orders (and therefore out of civic life), serfs, women, foreigners with rights to residence or enemy foreigners,[73] their exclusion and the disqualifications that stemmed from it were always relative and limited in time.

This limitation in time is of capital importance. In effect, the situation of an 'enemy' foreigner is considered to be temporary, as is the state of war by virtue of which he is an enemy. The legal disqualification of married women is temporary: widowhood is not considered by law to be 'a remote possibility' but rather as both possible and probable. In law, the disqualifications which affect a woman result from her status, not her nature, although her supposed nature does subordinate her first to her father and then to her husband. Nevertheless, upon the death of her husband, a woman does acquire substantial liberties, and the inheritance (in the sense according to the common law, that is to say the fief) becomes hers if there is no male descendant of the same degree.[74] Although a leper cannot inherit or bring legal action or underwrite contracts, and although he is excluded from the human community, he remains in possession of whatever belonged to him before his segregation. His blood is not 'corrupt' as is that of the felon, and the inheritance passes naturally to his descendance. Thus, time is not seen just within the span of an individual existence but also from the point of view of a lineage – in other words several generations.

As for a monk, he is only considered 'civilly dead' so long as he remains a monk. If he is unfrocked he, unlike the felon, reacquires the status that was his before he left the world. The serf has no rights before his lord but is invested with the same rights as any other subject in his relations with other men. Furthermore, his serfdom is not eternal and there are various ways in which he can be freed from it.

In all these questions relating to being set apart and otherness, time is an essential factor. Francis Bacon underlines the fact: 'For it seemeth admirable unto me to consider with what a measured hand and with how true proportions our law doth impart and confer the several degrees of this benefit [i.e. naturalisation].'[75]

There are four of these 'degrees':

1. The enemy foreigner has no protection, for the law considers him, in accordance with the Scriptures, as a spy who comes to spy out the country's weak points. But if he comes with a safe-conduct, he cannot be touched. For such time as he holds a safe-conduct justice can only be done to him, should the need arise, in the highest court of all: none of the king's courts are open to him. He must appear before the Privy Council: there he will be the beneficiary of a 'summary procedure forthwith' and 'will be judged in equity'.[76]

2. The foreigner who is a friend enjoys only 'temporary' benefit from the law, since, given that he may become an enemy, he is only 'temporarily' subject to it.[77]

3. The foreigner who has received from the king letters of 'denization' is by law given 'an ability and capacity abridged not in matter but in time. And as there was a time when he was no subject, so the law doth not acknowledge him before that time.'[78]

4. The last degree is that of birth; it is a quality which can only be acquired by filiation or by decision of Parliament.

Bacon makes no mention of perpetual enemies. Coke unearthed them in an extremely ancient royal ordinance and in a case judged under Henry VIII. It is, nevertheless, they who provide the cornerstone for the entire system. Between the enemy and the subject there are a number of graduated degrees. But the perpetual enemy is a logical conception that stands in opposition to the entire graduated system and it is what confers upon Coke's classification its universality and absolute rigour. The adjective 'perpetual' provides food for thought. It implies an unchangeable quality of being, and hence the impossibility of ever passing through the various degrees or grades ranged between exclusion and proximity and between precarious ownership of possessions that nothing guarantees (for, in common law, he who inherits movable goods only is not the heir) and lasting tenure by the right of heredity, that is transferable and potentially eternal. 'Only God can make an heir',[79] as the English saying goes.

The perpetual enemy who is on the side not of nature but of the devil, must not be able either to inherit or to have recourse to the law; for the law is 'in nature' and it does not protect anything that is set up against it. The perpetual enemy must thus forever remain a perpetual foreigner. He can never be redeemed, for there is no redemption for Satan.

9. On the transmission of human qualities

Could it be said that there is a more or less close relationship between the concept of the perpetual enemy – which presupposes the presence in that enemy of a specific, hereditary quality that renders him incapable of ever becoming a 'friend' or a 'subject' – and the more general idea that some personal properties are genetically, and therefore irrevocably, transmitted from one generation to the next?

The answer must be a qualified one. F. W. Maitland pointed out that, ever since the medieval period, the common law attached more importance to tenure than to personal status. Status is derived from tenure and even the distinction between a serf and a free man appears 'rather as a distinction between tenures than as a distinction between persons'.[80] Even if the serf has no rights in relation to his lord, in his relations with all other men he must be treated as a free man. So it would appear that serfdom is not hereditary and that status is not connected with blood.[81] Marc Bloch sees this as a legal artifice, for one may also be a serf by birth:[82] that is the case if both parents are serfs. According to the principle that 'the bad is stronger than the good', one may also be a serf when only one parent is a serf.[83] A bastard derives his status from his mother. The child born of a serf mother and a free father will be free if he is born on a free holding, but serf if born on a serf holding. Later on, it was the condition of the father that determined that of the son so that a bastard, given that he had no father, would always be born free. As can be seen, the law hesitates: the criterion is sometimes hereditary, sometimes tenure.

More importance was attached to tenure in the Elizabethan period. By then all men were presumed to be free.[84] However, certain qualities or rights were still transmitted by heredity, that is to say, through blood. First and foremost, the Crown. Coke and all the jurists attached to James I lay emphasis on the rights of blood; and royal blood has particular properties of its own.[85] Secondly, inheritance (in the common law sense).[86] Finally, the status of subject. At this point we must venture to disagree with Maitland who, in connection with the distinction between subject and foreigner, says: 'The place of birth is all-important. A child born within any territory that is subject to the king of England is a natural-born subject of the king of England and is no alien in England . . . On the other hand every child born elsewhere is an alien.'[87] But in 1343 and 1350, under Edward III, there was, precisely, disagreement over the question of children born 'elsewhere'. The king was concerned that the succession to the throne might be affected. Reassurance was forthcoming: the children of the king would succeed him, wherever they were born. As for other cases, their fate would be decided by Parliament: this was the famous statute *De nati ultra mare* (25 Ed. III), which stipulated that 'children born beyond allegiance to the king, whose fathers and mothers, at the moment of birth, are and remain within faith and allegiance to the king' would be subjects. Maitland maintains that the expression 'allegiance to the king' referred to territorial location.

However, James I's jurists were not of that opinion. For Coke, as we have seen, the place matters not at all: the only matter of importance is allegiance. Francis Bacon is less categorical: sometimes it is the place that matters, sometimes it is lineage: born abroad of English parents, the child will be English but be considered to be *ex officio* naturalised 'as the law of England must favour naturalization as a branch of the law of nature'.[88] And Francis Bacon also writes: 'if divers families of English men and women plant them- selves at . . . Roan or at Lisbon, and have issue, and their descendants do inter-marry amongst themselves, *without any intermixture of foreign blood*, such descendants are naturalised to all generations',[89] and he adds: 'which indeed sheweth the wisdom and excellent composition of our law, and that it is the law of a warlike and a magnanimous nation fit for empire'.[90] As can be seen, the status of subjects and foreigners can hardly be separated from the imminent colonial enterprise. The law of blood wins out.

Even more remarkable in this respect is the doctrine of 'the corruption of the blood' as a consequence of treason. It is, to be sure, above all a juridical concept: in an Act of Elizabeth we find the formula: 'This Act . . . can under no circumstances involve a corruption of the blood' (Act 5, Eliz. C.3–1563). All the same, the metaphor is a significant one and in 1769 Blackstone, in his *Commentaries*, writes: 'It is to be hoped that this corruption of the blood, with all its connected consequences not only of present escheat but of future incapacities of inheritance, even to the twentieth generation, may be abolished by act of parliament.'[91] The idea that the blood may transmit virtues or imperfections, rights or disqualifications, cannot be separated from this legal concept. It is hard to see why perpetual enemies should not be affected by faults just as deeply rooted.

10. On the virtues and vices attached to certain nations

One corollary of the mystical definition and hereditary transmission of allegiance – from which stems the concept of hereditary transmission of the quality of a subject, still detectable in many codes of nationality, even today – is the hereditary transmission of mystical and permanent qualities attached to certain categories of foreigners.

In the sixteenth century, there were many works on the variety of human behaviour and customs which attributed specific qualities to various nations.[92] Furthermore, the great division between Christians, pagans and infidels persisted. In England, Jews and Turks were classed together: their closeness finds classic expression in Christopher Marlowe's *Jew of Malta*, where Barabas says to Ithamore, the Turkish slave:

> . . . make account of me
> As of thy fellow; we are villaines both,
> Both circumcised, we hate christians both.[93]

Even a man as tolerant as Thomas Browne writes in his *Religio Medici* (1635) that the accomplishment of 'the promise of Christ to make us all one flock' is as problematic and obscure as the last Judgement.[94] Of the four religions (pagan, Muslim, Jewish and Christian) the Christian religion has the fewest followers. And whereas pagans deny Christ because they do not know him,

the religion of the Jew is expressly against the Christian, and the Mahometan against both; for the Turk, in the bulke he now stands, is beyond all hope of conversion; if hee fall asunder, there may be conceived hopes but not without strong improbabilities. The Jew is obstinate in all fortunes; the persecution of fifteene hundred yeares hath but confirmed them in their errour: they have already endured whatsoever may be inflicted, and have suffered in a bad cause, even to the condemnation of their enemies.[95]

So, as Coke points out, conversion is no more than a remote possibility and, as Sir Thomas Browne observes, an event it would be vain to hope for. Of course, individual conversions may occur. But in the eyes of the English, during the Elizabethan period, the convert seemed as it were to retain the kernel of his former allegiance. This can be clearly seen in a play such as *Othello*, in which the protagonist is a quasi-convert but one whose conversion is incapable of resisting Iago's quasi-demoniacal projects, so that in the end he acts exactly as he is expected to. Another example is the Lopez affair, which resuscitates the idea of the fragility of conversions. For the Elizabethans, conversion was a mystery or source of perplexity if not of indignation.

Neither Coke nor Sir Thomas Browne confuse the individual with the collective group. Infidels are 'perpetual enemies' in a collective sense, even if individual conversions do occur and are known, even if the deep-seated reason for this eternal difference, this perpetual otherness, can hardly be explained except by reference to the devil. Coke does not explicitly attribute it to a property believed to be inherent in particular nations. As for Sir Thomas Browne, he discusses the point in a fashion so modern and in his analysis refutes prejudices that were so widespread that he deserves to be quoted at length. The passage is taken from a chapter from his *Pseudodoxia*

Epidemica (1646) entitled 'That Jews stink', where he is concerned to refute the legend of the famous *foetor judaicus*.

. . . that an unsavoury odour is gentilitious or national unto the Jews . . . we cannot well concede, nor will the information of reason or sense induce it. For first, upon consult of reason, there will be found no easy assurance to fasten a material or temperamental propriety upon any nation; there being scarce any condition (but what depends upon clime) which is not exhausted or obscured from the commixture of introvenient nations either by commerce or conquest; much more will it be difficult to make out this affection in the Jews; whose race, however pretended to be pure, must needs have suffered inseparable commixtures with nations of all sorts.[96]

It is remarkable that 'enlightened' opinion should manifest such scepti cism over the possibility of attaching physical or humoral particularities to specific nations, and no less so that it should seem necessary to deny the possibility. Sir Thomas Browne goes on to observe that, given their dietary and sexual rules, the Jews are even less likely to give off a 'national stench' than other groups are; and he goes on, humorously, to quip: 'And lastly, were this true, yet our opinion is not impartial; for unto converted Jews, who are of the same seed, no man imputeth this unsavoury odour; as though aromatized by their conversion, they lost their scent with their religion, and smelt no longer than they savoured of the Jew.'[97]

More remarkable still, Sir Thomas Browne blames language – or, to be more precise, the use of metaphor – as the cause of the superstitious absurdities that are commonly rife. His analysis could easily be transposed to the domain of the 'corruption of the blood' mentioned above or, more generally, to many areas in which contemporary thought, through its use of concepts or images, suggested altogether fanciful beliefs:

Now, the ground that begat or propagated this assertion might be the distasteful averseness of the Christian from the Jew, upon the villainy of that fact, which made them abominable and stink in the nostrils of all men. Which real practice and metaphorical expression did after proceed into a literal construction; but was a fraudulent illation; for such an evil savour their father Jacob acknowledged in himself when he said his sons had made him stink in the land, that is to be abominable to the inhabitants thereof (*Gen.* XXXIV). Now, how dangerous it is in sensible things to use metaphorical expressions unto the people, and what absurd conceits they will swallow in their literals, an impatient example we have in our own profession; who, having called an eating ulcer by the name of a wolf,[98] common apprehension conceives a reality therein and against ourselves [doctors] ocular affirmations are pretended to confirm it.[99]

11. Exclusion and its duration

Sir Thomas Browne makes a striking distinction between the particular characteristics of nations which stem from their 'seed' and those that result from their rules, that is to say from their culture. He is clearly a believer in monogenism: for him the human race is one genus and he writes: 'Neither doth herein my zeale so farre make me forget the generall charitie I owe unto humanity, as rather to hate than pity Turkes, Infidels and (what is more) the Jewes.'[100] But the fact that he includes them within humanity does not prevent him from considering their pitiful aberration as virtually eternal. And 'eternal' is virtually the same as 'essential', for it is will that transforms being. His insistence on duration is also discernible in the text to the extent that he sees no hope of conversion for the Jews and Turks until the day of the last Judgement, a view that is, in the strongest sense of the term, utterly despairing.

Nowadays, our reflections on the subject of discrimination tend to use spatial or geographical metaphors more often than temporal ones: we speak of distance, of exclusion, of being shut in or shut off, of ghettoes, of enclosures, of expulsion or segregation, etc. Such expressions suggest horizontal barriers, surface compartmentalisation. There are others which evoke hierarchical gradations on a vertical axis: dominant/dominated, oppression, superior/inferior, etc. W. D. Jordan has written a book entitled *White over Black*. Reading certain contemporary studies, one gets an impression of histological sections, maps frozen at a particular moment in time, as if the territorial nature of the various nations, the permanence of hierarchies and the geographical limits for the application of laws were reinforcing the fashion for generalised synchronism and so directing reflection to the subject of the frontiers between different groups, as if those frontiers were always and everywhere independent of the passing of time; and also as if the groups involved had simply one univocal character and one limitative definition. But in hierarchical societies which assign multiple roles to individuals and which respond to the gathering momentum of history, is it really possible to argue as if each individual had only one role and that role were eternal or immutable until such time as the social structures be overturned?

Earlier generations did not believe that an individual lives only for the short term, and alone. There was a kind of eternity attached to the succession of the generations, a social, and a family, temporality. The isolated individual lived in the present, that is to say in despair. This explains the importance that was attached to lineage and the hereditary fief. In England, the term 'estate' signified both class or social rank and, from a legal point of view, 'that title or interest which a man hath in lands or tenements'.[101] Thus, a man's 'estate' could only be understood in terms of time, since he would hold his land either inalienably ('in fee simple') and by perpetual right[102] for himself and his heirs forever, or else in a temporary fashion ('in tails', 'in fee taile') for himself and the heirs of his own body only, the land returning to its feudal owner in default of direct descendants. But as the term 'estate' could mean both the condition of the man and that of his land, the very status of the individual was, as it were, stamped with a temporal mark, inscribed within a period of time. That is evident from the way in which Bacon speaks of the various classes of foreigners and also from the quasi-eternity attached to the 'corruption of the blood'. The fact is that family time and land time combined to situate the individual unequivocally in-between a past and a future. Even at the beginning of our twentieth century, people were still killing themselves with overwork in order 'to change class' through their posterity, to ensure for their descendants what they had never had for themselves.

In those days, living in family time or lineage time was common enough, so that the loss or alienation of a patrimony was considered as a wound done to honour and to continuity. John Norden, who deplored the instability of patrimonies, thus wrote:

Patrimonies are like unto the famed wheel of fortune, resembling also the waves of the sea, driven now to the shore and forthwith to the channel as the tide and the windes: so are possessions passed from one to another, more in these latter daies than ever before. Mindes become inconstant breede estates inconstant. In former ages an inheritance continued many generations, never altring either the line or the name of the owner: men had a kinde of religious regard to preserve the inheritance of their ancestors: and in these dayes, they think it a superstitious ceremony to keepe it . . . the father buyes in hope to better his sonne, and the sonne sels to dishonour himselfe.[103]

Given the importance attached to the duration of alienations, rights and disqualifications, it seems clear that the concept of the perpetual enemy is to a certain extent analogous to what the notion of race (inferior or accursed) has meant during the twentieth century. To understand the 'gaps' which separated men in the Elizabethan period, it is not enough simply to refer to that 'hierarchical geography' which assigned a predetermined place to each group, each man. Each individual was placed in a particular pigeon-hole or on a particular scale; but just as important as the social or symbolic placing was the period of time for which one was assigned to it. That is why it is not legitimate indiscriminately to class among the 'excluded' categories and groups that differ as widely from one another as do women, madmen, lunatics, melancholics, lepers, Jews, Turks, foreigners, etc. The levels of hope and despair in each case varied according to whether they were determined by time or by place.

12. The domesticated, the wild and natural law

It is generally believed that there is a discontinuity between what is domesticated and what is wild, between the wild and the civilised. Within the system that we have just described we must make more subtle distinctions. The domain of nature covers both what is civilised and what is wild. The king, by reason of his sovereignty over the space ruled by positive law and also over areas where positive law is suspended, stands for social relations – and, more generally, human relations – in the fields of both the civilised and the wild. The case of the outlaw is significant: he is not beyond allegiance although he is beyond what is civilised. Allegiance, understood as a relationship established prior to positive law, binds together all those who are part of the natural order, whether they belong to or are beyond the civilised. To be sure, in practice, the man who has 'become a wolf' is like a wild animal, at the mercy of the hunter. But the hunter does not enjoy total liberty: for example, royal prerogative returns to the king any swans which may escape from their owner's domain. Coke makes this quite clear:

If they have gained their natural liberty and are swimming in open and common rivers, the King's officer may seize them in the open and common river for the King: for one white swan, without such pursuit as aforesaid, cannot be known from another; and when the property of a swan cannot be known, the same being of its nature a fowl royal doth belong to the King.[104]

Furthermore, hunting in royal forests, naturally reserved for the king by reason of his prerogative (which also includes the right to declare war and to pardon those condemned), was governed by laws that were totally unaffected by the common law of the realm.

This is why relations between the domesticated and the wild were bound to be equivocal: first, for symbolic and logical reasons. The civilised can only be defined by opposition to what it is not, that is to say the wild. Outside the terms of that opposition it ceases to know itself, so can no longer call itself civilised. Its identity and being depend upon the opposition that it discovers or creates. And to this an ontological necessity is added.

But there is another reason for the equivocacy of these relations: the origin of what is civilised is what is wild. Even the pastoral works which postulated a Golden Age at the beginning of time were not unaware that in actual day to day existence the wild is the creative origin of being and, more generally, of life. In a case upon which he pronounced during the reign of Henry VIII, Judge Brooke made the following remarks:

In the beginning of the World all the beasts showed obedience to our . . . father Adam, and all the four elements showed obedience to him: but after his transgression of our Lord God's commandment, all the beasts began to rebell and to become wild, and that was a punishment for his crimes. And now they are common to all, *et occupante conceduntur*, like fowls in the air, fish in the sea and beasts on the earth. And when I have captured a fowl and made it tame through my industry, by curbing its liberty, I have then a special property in it, in so far as it became obedient because of my own labour; nobody then can rightly take it: like a deer in my park, or fish in my pond, though the case is altered if they are in the river. The same applies to a tame beast which I use in my home. The case is altered if they are at large: for if I have a singing bird, though it brings me no profit, yet it refreshes my spirits and that gives a great well-being to my body, which is a greater treasure than all possible riches.[105]

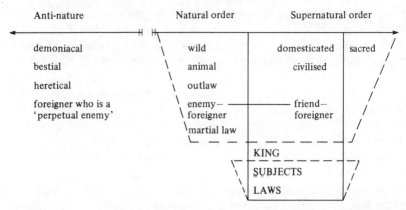

As can be seen, Judge Brooke takes 'tame' to mean now a wild animal in one's possession, now a domesticated animal. This confusion is remarkable. Possession of a singing bird is good for the 'valetude' of one's body – just as the king's privilege to hunt in the forests reserved for him alone is connected with the idea of the refreshment that stems from contact with wildness.

Shakespeare was not indifferent to this particular function of wildness. The difficulties of interpretation that critics face in connection with the plays in which Falstaff appears – or 'outlaws' such as the inhabitants of the forest of Arden – stem from the fact that a positive evaluation of the characters linked with wild nature or torn from a civilised state is contradicted by the weight of the offences they have committed. The offences drag them towards evil, out of the domain of the natural order, while their sustaining and creative vitality draws them towards an unsophisticated way of being and an order of law.

To return to the case of foreigners, their position within the framework of this opposition may be represented in the diagram above. A state of conflict and open warfare exists between the natural order and the order of anti-nature – unnatural man is 'worse than the wild beasts' – but the supernatural order has dominion over the anti-natural forces and these can only exert their evil with express licence from God.[106]

13. Modifications

Being anxious to provide a solid foundation for his concept of the perpetual enemy, Coke cites two legal precedents one of which is borrowed from the *Registrum Omnium Brevium*,[107] cited above.[108] The other comes from an opinion expressed by Judge Brooke on the occasion of a case brought under Henry VIII. The judge declares that: 'If a lord beat his villein, or a husband his wife, or a man beat an outlaw or a traitor or a pagan, they shall hove no action because they are not able to sue an action.'[109]

Insubstantial though these precedents seem, Edward Coke's opinion was repeated by Michael Dalton and twice quoted in a legal work published in 1658.[110] Towards the end of the century attempts were made to modify the legislation. Reporting the case in 1697, Salkeld does not even take the trouble further to justify his disagreement with Coke:

Turks and infidels are not *perpetui inimici*, nor is there a particular enmity between them and us; but this is a common error founded on a groundless opinion of Justice Brooke; for though there be a difference between our religion and theirs, that does not oblige us to be enemies to their persons; they are the creatures of God and of the same kind that we are, and it would be a sin in us to hurt their person.[111]

However, the notion reappeared in a slightly different form in the courts and it proved necessary to kill it a second time in 1744, on the occasion of a case in which the right of a plaintiff of Hindu origin to take the oath was challenged on the grounds that he was not Christian but pagan.[112]

As for the distant origins of the notion, apart from its theological bases, it does appear that – despite the opinion of the enlightened judge who opposed it – it was not without precedent in English law. At least, that is what is suggested by a jurist writing at the beginning of the twentieth century who quotes a judgement delivered by Judge Stowell in 1817:

With professed pirates, there is no state of peace. They are the enemies of every country, and at all times; and therefore are universally subject to the extreme rights of war. An ancient authority, the laws of Oleron, composed at the time of the Crusades, and as supposed by an eminent leader of those expeditions, our own Richard I, represents infidels as equally subject to those rights [i.e. laws applicable to pirates] but this rests partly upon the ground of notions long ago exploded, that such persons could have no fellowship, no peaceful communion with the faithful.[113]

Judge Stowell was not mistaken. The laws of Oleron were familiar to the English Admiralty: Holdsworth considers them to be one of the bases of English maritime law. They contain the following passage on the subject of everybody's obligation to restore wrecks to the legitimate owners:

Likewise, the thynges preceding ought to be understood yf the said shyp was not engaged in the practice of pillage, that the crew of her were not pirates or sea-rovers or enemies of our Holy Catholic Faith. For in that case yf they be pirates, pillagers or sea-rovers, or Turks, or others opposed to and enemies of our Holy Catholic Faith, every one may take from suche manner of men as from dogs, and may strip them and despoil them of theyr goodes without any punishment. This is the judgement.[114]

6. Othello, or the husband from afar

Qui de nous deux inventa l'autre?
[Which of the two of us invented the other?]

Paul Eluard

Foreword

There is, as we have seen, a kind of paradox in the view of foreigners held
by the Elizabethans and Jacobeans. An abundant literature of travel told
them of the extreme variety of the inhabitants of the world, a variety
supported by both the marvels of fable and attested evidence, where the
accounts of contemporary travellers juxtaposed or complemented collections of tales that drew upon Herodotus, the Bible, Pliny and Mandeville.[1]
However, this considerable variety was ideologically reduced and restricted
by categorisations which divided up the known peoples of the world according to their political regime (monarchic, aristocratic or democratic), their
religious persuasions (Christian, pagan or infidel), their supposed degree of
civilisation (savage, barbarian or civilised) and their distribution in the
various climatic zones of the world (hot, cold or temperate).[2] In England,
where distrust of foreigners had a long tradition,[3] we have already seen how,
in the course of the polemic which shook Parliament over the naturalisation
of the Scots, arguments of a religious or legal nature were supplemented by
purely ethnic considerations, the Scots being regarded as a nation naturally
deprived. This violent and popular rejection was, we should point out,
directed against a Christian, nay, protestant people.[4] Pagans or infidels
would have been even more deeply execrated.

Thus, the abundance of information available on the East, Africa and
America must have given rise to a certain unease: at a moment when
England was still under the threat of Catholicism, it became aware of a
plurality of customs and religions – a plurality which must have occasioned

a feeling of despair. For, to thinking minds, the conversion of pagans and infidels – that is to say the accomplishment of the divine promise – must have seemed a most improbable eventuality.[5]

This improbability gave rise to anxiety, if not to doubt. And the reaction to this was an excess of distrust. Threats appeared to be pressing in from a concentric network. Protestant England was worried at being surrounded by Catholics. Furthermore, Christianity itself was surrounded by antagonistic, or simply pagan, religions. Thus, far away, on the frontiers of Christendom foreigners were looming on every side. They could be assigned physical locations: the increasing diffusion of atlases was making such new perceptions possible. But closer at hand, the presence of the foreigner undermined certain spiritual beliefs and, whether openly or in some more mysterious manner, was subversive to the familiar symbolic universe. As for the political order, it was, or was believed to be, threatened from within by Jesuit missions and agents from abroad. Conspiracy was a constant obsession.

When Sir Edward Coke divides foreigners into four classes he no doubt does so in conformity with a classification that stems from tradition and common law. But he systematises and arranges the legal data in such a way that medieval concepts are given a practical significance and his system becomes politically and symbolically operational: 'friendly foreigners', 'temporary enemies', 'enemies with safe-conducts' and 'perpetual enemies' are, so to speak, localised according to their respective distance from English subjects and from the king. Absolute separateness and antagonism is attributed to the 'perpetual enemies', whom Coke places beyond God's or natural law. It is a way of 'demonising'[6] the perpetual enemy, the demonisation being a consequence of the fact that the devil himself may operate even within Christian society. And even if the dominant ideology, for which Coke's text provides elaborate expression, situates the essential menace at the outermost limits of Christianity and the body politic (and here the frequent assimilation of Catholics to pagans and those demoniacally possessed is significant), the fact remains that the threat also lies extremely close at hand. The famous 'An Homily Against Disobedience and Wilfull Rebellion' expressly associates domestic troubles with foreign invasion and attacks those who 'make their country, thus by their wicked mischief, threatened, ready to be a prey and spoil to all outward enemies that will invade it'.[7] A relationship between the nearest and the farthest is clearly established.

Othello is a play in which the man whom the general opinion of the city labels as a bestial being and a sorcerer, on the grounds that he is a being from far away, is driven to destroy two individuals who, each within their own order, are the incarnation of perfect virtue: himself and Desdemona. And he does this under the influence of a source of evil, a quasi-devil, lodged at the very heart of the city. Thus, Shakespeare, to some extent distancing himself from the accepted view of foreigners, changes its character and significance while yet not entirely freeing himself from it. The multiple interpretations that can be given to this tragedy are testimony to this.[8]

1. Being and discourse

The first act of *Othello* takes place in Venice, at night, as if to suggest the equivocal and illicit character of some of the events to which it refers on stage. Two contrasting images of the protagonist emerge. The one, which is unfavourable, stems from Roderigo's conversation with Iago and from Brabantio's insults. The other, which is positive and exalted, is the image that Othello presents of himself, an image borne out by his behaviour, his words, the high esteem in which he is held by the Duke and the love and declarations of Desdemona. Right from the start, it could be said, the bestial savage and the noble hero both exist. But in this case the one is a being created by discourse, the other is apprehended by the audience as truly existing. Even before the end of the first act, the second image ousts the first in the mind of the spectator. Othello appears in all his nobility, Iago in all his baseness.

However, the speeches of envy, jealousy and xenophobic hatred indicate that the play begins after the Moor has carried off the consenting Desdemona, after their meeting and mutual rapture, after the great exploits and voyages of the protagonist who is already 'declin'd / Into the vale of years' (III, iii, 269–70).[9] In other words, the play opens *in medias res*, in the middle of a life about whose earlier stages it is impossible not to speculate. So the initial interpretation is challenged; what the play presents is a dramatic interrogation into the nature of man. If we believe the evil is already there even before it manifests itself, we will reconstruct an Othello whose origins are barbarous and who has ever been guilty on the grounds that he proves capable of crime later on. If we believe that man creates himself through his actions, we will seize upon Iago's exclamation: 'He is much chang'd' (IV, i, 264) and pay attention to the way Lodovico speaks of Othello when the whole action has almost run its course:

> O thou Othello, that wert once so good,
> Fall'n in the practice of a damned slave,
> What should be said to thee?   (V, ii, 292–4)

Thus, in the first act all that remains of Othello's past are its consequences and what is said about it. The spectator is invited to form his opinion of these speeches by comparing them with the behaviour, words and personality of the characters who speak. As Montaigne observed: 'The true mirror of our discourse is the course of our lives.'[10]

'Mere prattle without practice / Is all his soldiership',[11] says Iago of Cassio who has been promoted to the rank of lieutenant over his own head. Shakespeare in this way indicates, right from the beginning, how precarious is the relationship between the past and the present, given that it is at the mercy of discourse which either establishes or destroys it. Two ontological axes are suggested: a human being's relationship to the past is fundamental to him but the past is indissociable from the present and from social or community relationships which at times introduce the past into the present and perpetuate it there, at others negate, change or annul it.

Iago's first grudge against Othello is that 'his Mooreship'[12] has not recognised his, Iago's, merit and has denied him the promotion to which his seniority gave him the right in accordance with 'the old gradation, where each second / Stood heir to the first'.[13] The genetic metaphor[14] suggests an ordered transition from past to present that Iago judges his master to have transgressed.

> . . . So our virtues
> Lie in th'interpretation of the time

is what Aufidius, in a more general manner, elsewhere remarks.[15] Only love can shelter the past from such fluctuations.

That is what accounts for the notable difference between the social bond and the bond of communion.[16] The first is founded upon utility, profit, the law, conventions, a quasi-commercial exchange of services; it is essentially opportunistic. The second, to use terms familiar at the period, depends upon nature or the supernatural, in other words upon values that are shared, the recognition of another being, love. The stranger, coming from another place, another time, is particularly vulnerable to the way that discourse can affect reality. For the reality of the past may suffer a variety of fortunes, being apprehended sometimes through social discourse, sometimes through discourse sustained by communion: words of falsehood or truth, poison or nurture. Their circulation cannot be arrested and it is they that provide confirmation of the reality of the past, establishing its permanence or, alternatively, losing and destroying it. The true or anterior reality can easily be replaced by a reality created by discourse which diminishes and displaces the former and can then, following some modification or metamorphosis, become the new veritable reality.

2. The noble hero

The flattering image of Othello is that of the 'noble hero', many times described by literary critics.[17] His stature as a warrior is immediately apparent even from the words of one who hates him:

> . . . for their souls,
> Another of his fathom they have not
> To lead their business . . .

(I, i, 151–3)

In the next scene, Othello reminds Iago and informs the audience of the full scope of his services to Venice. He adds that his origins – and therefore his nature – are royal. He had not mentioned that fact, for the vainglorious vaunting of one's quality of birth is not necessarily honourable. Besides, his exploits are such that merit alone is sufficient justification for his receiving fortune's bounties in all fairness:

> My services, which I have done the signiory,
> Shall out-tongue his complaints; 'tis yet to know –
> Which, when I know that boasting is an honour,
> I shall provulgate – I fetch my life and being
> From men of loyal siege, and my demerits
> May speak unbonneted[18] to as proud a fortune
> As this that I have reach'd.   (I, ii, 18–24)

The insistence upon merit, which stems more from education than from nature, is important: for it is by denouncing his barbarian, foreign, animal essence that Iago and Brabantio will attempt to reject as far as they can the foreigner who enters into the heart of the Venetian community by means of a surreptitious marriage:

>   . . . [the Duke] will divorce you,
> Or put upon you what restraints, and grievance,
> The law (with all his might to enforce it on)
> Will give him cable.   (I, ii, 14–17)

Critics have often insisted that Othello already sensed the weakness and incompleteness of his character – or even some essential corruption of his being.[19] The fact is that Othello's psychology is relational. His own discourse stands in opposition to the rumours that are rife in Venice in the first act. Characters of dramas are entirely composed from speech and the first statement made by the protagonist establishes a hierarchy of native and acquired virtues: whatever people say, it cannot be denied that his accomplishments give him certain rights. If Shakespeare has him give first place to merit acquired, that is because the age, while not rejecting lineage, justified the rights of nobility above all on the grounds of a 'personal manifestation of virtues'.[20]

From this point of view Othello cannot be faulted. His discourse is not of a kind to suggest weakness on his part, rather, justified confidence. The Moor places his trust in his image and the substance of his being. When two groups of men, the one under the leadership of Cassio, the other under Brabantio, are seeking him out, he refuses despite Iago's advice to hide:

>   . . . I must be found:
> My parts, my title, and my perfect soul,[21]
> Shall manifest me rightly.   (I, ii, 30–2)

It is at this point impossible to dissociate the parts acquired and the parts that are innate in this character. 'Parts' are merits as well as natural gifts;[22] 'title' may mean name or (hereditary or other) right to possession; 'perfect' sometimes means essentially perfect, sometimes meticulously prepared;[23] and, according to Othello (and also the audience, since we are dealing with what is an almost explicit moral code), these virtues and this title ought to be a clear manifestation of his personality, of his 'self', of his true being, and should consequently lead to his acceptance by others. 'I must be found', says Othello, and that means: 'I am what I am'.[24]

The remainder of the act, and many other speeches in the play, bear out this heroic and aristocratic image. As contemporary manuals of behaviour would have it, Othello is all of a piece, there is no divorce between the secret and the visible parts of his self. Perfect master of himself, as Lodovico and especially Iago remark (IV, i, 260–5; III, i, 131–6), he refuses to draw his sword despite the provocation from Brabantio's men.

When Brabantio accuses him of bewitching his daughter, Othello reminds him of his past and thereby also of the bases upon which his fabulous stature rests: he uses images of exoticism, dangerous voyages, incredible adventures. The style of his account works in favour of its credibility: Othello quite simply enumerates his travels and exploits. He gives an account of his actions – the feats he has accomplished and the vicissitudes he has endured. He is what he has done. His being, constructed from the succession of actions he has accomplished, has gained in stature from each of them. His personality has been built up by time.

In short, his account of himself and also the mission with which the duke entrusts him, namely to fight the Ottoman foe, suggest a situation of righteous warfare in which the warrior will achieve self-accomplishment in obedience to the threatened values of the city that he serves: the situation is powerfully described in act III, in the famous speech in which Othello makes his farewell to arms:

> . . . O now for ever
> Farewell the tranquil mind, farewell content:
> Farewell the plumed troop, and the big wars,
> That makes ambition virtue. (III, iii, 353–6)

It is a nostalgic evocation of a situation in which, to quote the French romance of Jean de Bueil, *Le Jouvencel*, 'there comes a delight such that, unless a man has experienced it, he cannot tell how marvellous it is'.[25]

In short, at the beginning of the play Othello truly is what Lodovico in act IV says he used to be, although by then Lodovico can no longer recognise him as such:

> Is this the noble Moor, whom our full senate
> Call all in all sufficient? This the noble nature
> Whom passion could not shake? Whose solid virtue

> The shot of accident, nor dart of chance,
> Could neither graze, nor pierce?   (IV, i, 260–4)

3. The husband from afar and the perfect wife

And, by the most improbable fairytale and literary chance, Othello meets a woman who falls in love with what he is and what he has been, with the man of both the past and the present, the total person as manifested in discourse, in Othello's own account of himself:

> My story being done,
> She gave me for my pains a world of sighs;
> She swore i' faith, 'twas strange, 'twas passing strange;
> 'Twas pitiful, 'twas wondrous pitiful;
> She wish'd she had not heard it, yet she wish'd
> That heaven had made her such a man: she thank'd me,
> And bade me, if I had a friend that lov'd her,
> I should but teach him how to tell my story,
> And that would woo her.   (I, iii, 158–66)

The audience also learns how she has, despite Venice, secretly married this foreigner, this Black, made him her sovereign, not for the sake of the exoticism of his legend but for his legendary actuality:

> That I did love the Moor, to live with him,
> My downright violence, and scorn of fortunes,
> May trumpet to the world: my heart's subdued
> Even to the utmost pleasure of my lord:[26]
> I saw Othello's visage in his mind,
> And to his honours, and his valiant parts
> Did I my soul and fortunes consecrate:
> So that, dear lords, if I be left behind,
> A moth of peace, and he go to the war,
> The rites for which I love him are bereft me.   (I, iii, 248–57)

Shakespeare makes it clearly understood that, according to the criteria that then applied for feminine virtues, Desdemona is just as exceptional among women as Othello is according to the contemporary criteria for heroic values. There are three women in *Othello* and, besides the other characteristics that distinguish them, they are set at different levels on a moral scale. One of them, Bianca, is easy enough with everyone: 'A housewife that / by selling her desires / Buys herself bread and clothes' (IV, i, 94), but has an insatiable appetite for Cassio. The second is the faithful spouse, Emilia, Iago's wife; but we know, because she says as much in the last scene of act IV, that 'for the whole world', 'a great price', she would be ready to 'make her husband a cuckold'. The third, Desdemona, is so innocent and so chaste (the contemporary word to denote fidelity) that she cannot even conceive of the possibility of infidelity, not for the whole world (IV, ii, 77–8), nor that any woman could exist who would be willing to sell herself in such a way.[27]

These oppositions are established with sufficient force and clarity for us to understand that perfect fidelity here is simply a way of suggesting absolute virtue. In Desdemona, as in Othello, being and seeming, the form and the essence, are one. As Cassio puts it when she arrives in Cyprus:

> . . . He hath achiev'd a maid
> That paragons description, and wild fame:
> One that excels the quirks of blazoning pens,
> And in the essential vesture of creation
> Does tire the ingener.[28]   (II, i, 61–5)

In this way, Shakespeare has established a link between the two characters who are the admiration or envy of all, who exist on a higher plane than those who surround them, who are, for their age, exemplary models: the incarnation of a moral and aristocratic dream. Within the terms of that dream, their union is in conformity with nature and also with their natures. Each has made half the advances (I, iii, 176), each has increased in love for the other (I, iii, 125) and it is a love that has become an imperative law for them, making them defy convention, customs, society. Their marriage at dead of night is a sign that the couple have chosen a relationship of communion as opposed to a social one and that the law of nature[29] has proved stronger than that of custom or convention. It has involved a transgression and Othello admits as much before the Duke:

> That I have ta'en away this old man's daughter,
> It is most true: true, I have married her,
> The very head and front of my offending
> Hath this extent, no more . . .   (I, iii, 78–81)

and the Duke, ineffectually, tries to console Brabantio for it:

> When remedies are past, the griefs are ended
> By seeing the worst, which late on hopes depended.
> To mourn a mischief that is past and gone,
> Is the next way to draw new mischief on.
> What cannot be preserv'd when fortune takes,
> Patience her injury a mockery makes.
> The robb'd that smiles, steals something from the thief,
> He robs himself, that spends a bootless grief.
> *Brabantio*: So let the Turk of Cyprus us beguile,
> We lose not so long as we can smile.   (I, iii, 202–11)

As the Duke sees it, the 'worst' has already happened. Brabantio is faced with what cannot be undone; so he must accept this 'mischief' because if he frets about it he will attract others in its wake. The nature of the calamity is, as Brabantio clearly states, similar to the capture of Cyprus by the Turks: the capture of a possession by an absolute enemy, the capture of a Christian land by infidels. Desdemona has chosen a husband from afar whose place is not within the customary and organic communion of Venice. Othello is socially acceptable, but only insofar as his function is necessary and his sword committed to a military and ideological struggle.

The way in which Venice judges Othello is apparent from the second image of the protagonist, the one that is purveyed by rumour and presented by Iago, Roderigo and Brabantio.

4. The thick lipped barbarian: a digression on poisoned discourse

The play opens with a scene, the tone of which is very strange, in which the protagonist, although not named, is presented as an object of the hatred of Iago who, for his part, expressly rejects the idea that he might not hate him.

> *Roderigo*: Thou told'st me, thou did'st hold him in thy hate.
> *Iago*: Despise me if I do not . . .   (I, i, 7–8)

A creature of dissatisfaction, craving advancement, jealous of love, of beauty, of anything that promotes a yearning towards the infinite, Iago will not rest until he has persuaded Roderigo 'to poison [the] delight' of the Moor. Between Iago and his dupe there is an astonishing measure of agreement, a compound of hatred and xenophobia: Iago resents Cassio, that 'Florentine' (I, i, 20), while Roderigo, jealous of the Moor who has married the woman he himself desires, says:

> What a full fortune does the thicklips owe,
> If he can carry't thus!   (I, i, 66–7)

In the face of the irremediable marriage,[30] they will resort to the remedy of poison, the discourse of calumny[31] and slander, the venom of defamatory falsehood. Contemporary physiology held that poisons and poisoned discourse could act at a distance, in a virtually physical and humoral fashion. Thus, Ambroise Paré writes:

Poisons can kill not only when taken by the mouth but also when applied externally. Similarly, beasts can kill not only by their bites and stings or scratches: but also by their frothing saliva, their *look*, or simply by their touch or their breath or by their blood when this is eaten or drunk, or by *their cry or hiss* or excrement.[32]

Comparisons between the effects of calumny, 'slander' and 'backbiting' and those of poisons are a commonplace of the period. The origins of this commonplace can be traced to the Bible and a rich body of pulpit literature.[33] The influence of words and discourse upon society and individuals was considered so baleful[34] that laws on treason even included the repression of 'treason by words', although Elizabethan laws admittedly tended to impose some limitations upon the scope of earlier legislation in this respect.[35] No doubt at all was felt about the power of the word over the imagination and the power of imagination over human beings. In Iago's poisoning of Othello,[36] the various stages are clearly marked and there is nothing metaphysical about the progress made by the poison. Iago is first called 'slanderer' by Desdemona, by way of a jest, when she arrives in Cyprus (II, i, 113). But he is in very truth determined to slander her and looks forward to the moment when he will 'pour this pestilence' into Othello's ear (II, iii, 347). In the middle of the 'temptation scene' he says to himself:

> The Moor already changes with my poison:
> Dangerous conceits are in their natures poisons . . .   (III, iii, 330–1)

And when Othello falls into a fit under the effect of his passion, Iago comments:

> Work on,
> My medicine, work!   (IV, i, 44–5)

In an Elizabethan context the effect wrought by preconceptions is no metaphor but a medical reality; but at the same time, those preconceptions have quasi-magical connotations. 'Saying' and 'doing' were, to be sure, already recognised as separate, but only just. That is why the first scene of *Othello*, in which almost all the words that refer to the protagonist are aimed at denying or destroying his exceptional qualities, has a ceremonial aspect that is at once magical, social and personal. 'The long knives' of speech with its incantatory powers are out and we witness preparations for a number of 'self-fulfilling prophecies' the very expression of which will entail fulfilment.[37] For, according to scholastic doctrine, the act must accomplish the 'form', the form must be accomplished, come to complete fulfilment in action and movement. Othello, who is a bestial being, must 'accomplish' himself in bestiality. Desdemona, who is 'unnatural', given that she has followed a 'bestial' being, must accomplish herself in deceit and adultery in accordance with Brabantio's prophecy to Othello at the end of act I:

> Look to her Moor, have a quick eye to see:
> She has deceiv'd her father, may do thee.[38]   (I, iii, 292–3)

The interaction between the unfolding of imaginary actions and their real accomplishment is to be one of the determining mechanisms of the plot and establish a graded progression that passes from murderous or lying discourse to the power of that discourse over a man's mind and thence from that quite immaterial action to its irruption into reality. By so doing, it creates an illusion of verisimilitude and sets up the successive stages in an inexorable chain of events.

5. The thick-lipped barbarian: white ewe and black ram

From the very first act, then, we know that Othello is to become the 'being of discourse' who may potentially be substituted for the being of reality. Iago's hatred on its own could not bring this about. What is needed is a conjunction between that hatred and the latent opinion or image of the foreigner, the Black, which Othello's clandestine marriage has prompted, an image which Iago, as he himself says, engenders:

> I ha't, it is engender'd; Hell and night
> Must bring this monstrous birth to the world's light.　　　　(I, iii, 401–2)

The essential theme of this discourse is Othello's bestial nature which stems from his close relations with Barbary – and his bestial nature makes him a partner to the devil. So Othello's quality as an outsider is at the same time, natural, cultural and theological. Up to line 48 of scene iii, the protagonist is not named at all: he is 'the Moor', 'the thick-lipped' one, 'his Mooreship'. The first senator calls him 'the valiant Moor' (I, iii, 47) before the Duke, addressing him, finally says 'valiant Othello' (I, iii, 48). But for Brabantio, who never will address him by name, he is 'the man, this Moor' (I, iii, 71). The expression denotes his ethnic origins, origins with overtones that were by no means neutral. In the literature of the period a Moor was sometimes a magic, malevolent being. Boaistuau writes:

The ancients held extraordinary creatures in such great horror that if by chance they met one on their path it was for them an omen or augury of disaster. For this reason, when the Emperor Hadrian had happened to catch sight of a Moor, he was convinced that he would shortly die. Brutus' soldiers, ready to join battle against those of Octavius Caesar, having met with an Ethiopian in their path, foresaw that they would lose the battle, and so they did.[39]

A royal edict of 1601 ordered that all Negroes and Blackamoors[40] should be expelled from England and provided for measures to exert pressure upon any owners of Blacks who refused to get rid of them. The pretext was that the Blacks were receiving 'relief' which loyal subjects of the queen needed and, above all, that they were 'infidels, having no understanding of Christ or His Gospel'.[41]

Thus, Iago and Roderigo waken Desdemona's father: they present him with an image both implicit and explicit of the man who has carried off his daughter. For Brabantio the image is an obvious and believable one and is immediately applicable to the being of the seducer.

> *Iago*: Awake! What ho, Brabantio! thieves, thieves, thieves!
> Look to your house, your daughter, and your bags
> Thieves, thieves!　　　　(I, i, 79–81)
>
> Zounds, sir you're robb'd . . . .
> Your heart is burst, you have lost half your soul;

Even now, very now, an old black ram
Is tupping your white ewe.   (I, i, 86–9)

The animal metaphors are not symmetrical: Desdemona is not a ewe in the same way as Othello is a black ram. The first comparison denotes virtue; the second establishes an essentially evil quality:

. . . You'll have your daughter cover'd by a Barbary horse; you'll have your nephews neigh to you; you'll have coursers for cousins, and gennets for germans. (I, i, 110–13)

Iago is warning Brabantio that his descendants will be subjected to a metamorphosis. The Moor is as far from a Venetian as a man is from an animal. The union between the woman and the animal is monstrous; it breaks her father's heart; it is the death of him (V, ii, 205–7). Roderigo proceeds to connect the unnatural union with insubordination, disrespect for the hierarchy. The better to indulge in 'the gross clasps of a lascivious Moor' (I, i, 126), Desdemona has run off in the night with no chaperone other than a 'knave of common hire, a gondolier' (I, i, 125) and thereby:

Your daughter (if you have not given her leave,
I say again), hath made a gross revolt,
Tying her duty, beauty, wit, and fortunes,
In an extravagant and wheeling stranger,
Of here, and every where . . .   (I, i, 133–7)

The stranger has no place in the hierarchy, topography or scale of beings; he has been drifting among fixed stars and rolls there like the wheel of Fortune which, Ronsard says, is 'Sans foy, sans loy, sans lieu, vagante sans arrest'[42] (Without faith, without law, without place, ceaselessly wandering). He therefore stands in opposition to the order of nature and negates it. Brabantio's reaction is immediate: the discourse of the outraged father is a subjective echo to Roderigo's words:

O treason of the blood!
Fathers from hence, trust not your daughters' minds
By what you see them act, is there not charms,
By which the property of youth and maidhood
May be abus'd? Have you not read, Roderigo,
Of some such thing?   (I, i, 169–74)

The allusion to 'charms'[43] denotes the incredible nature of the marriage just contracted and the father's absolute need to believe that the will of Dedesmona, that is to say of his own blood, was in no way consenting. Even if he has never seen such spells, such kinds of enchantment must exist – the books say they do – for natural repugnance to marry with a Moor is surely invincible. When Brabantio meets Othello, in the company of his men, he spells out his reactions:

> O thou foul thief, where has thou stow'd my daughter?
> Damn'd as thou art, thou hast enchanted her,
> For I'll refer me to all things of sense,
> (If she in chains of magic were not bound)
> Whether a maid, so tender, fair, and happy,
> So opposite to marriage, that she shunn'd
> The wealthy curled darlings of our nation,
> Would ever have (to incur a general mock)
> Run from her guardage to the sooty bosom[44]
> Of such a thing as thou? to fear, not to delight.   (I, ii, 62–71)

'Damn'd as thou art': possessed by the devil and obedient to him. The enchantment stems from this 'possession' which Desdemona's consent in the elopement indicates. Iago is not the only one to seek to justify[45] his hatred. Brabantio discovers the only possible cause for this unnatural attachment. So it must be condemned at once:

> For if such actions may have passage free,
> Bond-slaves, and pagans, shall our statesmen be.   (I, ii, 98–9)

That is an image of the world turned upside down, in other words, of chaos.

Before the Senate, Brabantio thus pleads that the Moor has bewitched his daughter, corrupting her by witchcraft, spells and drugs. Desdemona proudly admits that she herself made half the advances and this exonerates Othello from the crime of bewitchment. However, it does nothing to change his new character which is now recognised by the whole of Venice – a character so repulsive that no one should go near him. Brabantio's claim presents the image clearly:

> A maiden never bold of spirit,
> So still and quiet that her motion
> Blush'd at herself: and she, in spite of nature,
> Of years, of country, credit, everything,
> To fall in love with what she fear'd to look on?
> It is a judgment maim'd, and most imperfect,
> That will confess perfection so would err
> Against all rules of nature, and must be driven
> To find out practices of cunning hell,
> Why this should be; I therefore vouch again,
> That with some mixtures powerful o'er the blood,
> Or with some dram conjur'd to this effect,
> He wrought upon her.   (I, iii, 94–106)

Now the image is complete, close enough to the one that emerges from Sir Edward Coke's legal text studied in chapter 5: the foreigner has no connections, his rights are those of slaves and pagans – that is to say, none at all. He is linked with animality but that does not mean that he can be classified among the animals on any scale of living creatures since he has a human form. And so he is a monster. The attraction that a Venetian girl can feel towards him is aberrant, contrary to all the laws of nature. If such a union has, despite everything, come to pass, it can only be the work of the devil.[46]

Desdemona's union with the being from afar who has infiltrated the organic community of Venice provokes brutal reactions. The play does not make it clear whether the Senate gives a favourable verdict on Othello simply because it is applying justice or because the city needs him, at that moment, to defend Cyprus. But the condolences that the Duke offers Brabantio suggest that he may well share Brabantio's opinion of the Moor. The fact is that were Othello a man like any other, the union would not be so irremediable. The scandal, amplified and dramatised by Iago, has taken place: the union between Othello and Desdemona is truly an illicit one from the point of view of custom and public opinion. From the very first act, despite the couple's vehement affirmations of the legitimacy of their union, a legitimacy founded upon the values that they embody and also that particular fairytale perfection that each of them in their own way possesses and that is reinforced in the eyes of the public by the mutual love they manifest – despite all this, serious upheavals in the life of the city can clearly be expected.

6. The threatened city: an excess of baseness

Iago's nihilistic self-centredness causes him to attribute to everybody else the fundamental disloyalty that marks *him* out, the unreliability caused by an exclusive constancy to oneself that the Elizabethan age denounced as being ruled either by sexual appetite or greed for money. His desire is to make the world conform to the image he himself has formed of it, and his particular way of doing so is to demonstrate by his own words and deeds that commitments and contracts are worthless; that the only constancy of which man is capable is his submission to his own natural desires, desires whose source is permanent even though their object may change:

It cannot be that Desdemona should long continue her love to the Moor, . . . put money in thy purse, . . . nor he to her; it was a violent commencement, and thou shalt see an answerable sequestration: put but money in thy purse . . . These Moors are changeable in their wills . . . fill thy purse with money. The good that to him now is as luscious as locusts, shall be to him shortly as acerb as the coloquintida. When she is sated with his body, she will find the error of her choice; she must have change, she must . . . If sanctimony, and a frail vow, betwixt an erring barbarian and and a super-subtle Venetian, be not too hard for my wits, and all the tribes of hell, thou shalt enjoy her . . . (I, iii, 342–58).

Of course, Iago is speaking to his dupe; but his argument is remarkably coherent: anything other than desire for pleasure and power is a sham. In nobility all Iago can see is superiority of rank; in valour nothing but vainglory; in love nothing but orgasm. Such ubiquity, such alacrity, such deep-rooted malice used to be considered the attributes of the devil. He, Iago, is the master of double-dealing and deceit, a virtuoso when it comes to juggling with being and seeming:

> It is as sure as you are Roderigo,
> Were I the Moor, I would not be Iago:
> In following him, I follow but myself.
> Heaven is my judge, not I for love and duty,
> But seeming so, for my peculiar end.
> For when my outward action does demonstrate
> The native act, and figure of my heart,
> In complement extern, 'tis not long after,
> But I will wear my heart upon my sleeve,
> For doves to peck at.   (I, i, 56–65)

What is threatening Venice is a breakdown of the chain of being, of men's duty towards obedience and truth; Iago's vital impetus is essentially destructive to social and organic relations. But one already senses other changes in the hierarchies and distances that must be respected if the body politic is to function harmoniously. Thus, the role of an ensign is not to play the go-between, that is to bring together what should remain apart; a woman's role is not to follow her husband to the wars, nor a general's to take his wife along with him. The Turkish threat has maintained a superficial kind of order, which this too perfect union between these two perfect beings has upset. For perfection is a touchstone: it shows up insufficiency.

7. The threatened city: an excess of virtue

> Nothing is extreme that hath its like.
>
> Montaigne, *Essays*, I, xxviii, 'Of Friendship'

There can be no excess of perfection. But perfection itself is an excess, for it appears as a divine gift or divine qualities[47] which stand in opposition to the finite nature of humanity and the imperfections to which man is heir. More than a few commentators have discovered in Othello or in Desdemona[48] some initial imperfection which explains their fall. But it can hardly be denied that these are imaginary beings invested with an essential perfection while yet remaining human beings, for obviously they are not gods. Their imperfection is indeed that very perfection with which Shakespeare has endowed them, that is to say an altogether human perfection, which is a contradiction of the human condition and ties up with the old tradition of *hubris*. The fact is that *hubris* is not always an essential quality or defect stemming from an immutable essence or form. It is not necessarily willed nor necessarily founded upon a lack or failing. It stems from a mismatch between what the City believes it can without danger tolerate in the way of excellence, and the raising of a human being, through his or her excellence, to a quasi-divine stature.[49] Among men there can be no gods. Faced with live heroes or live saints, all the City can do is counter with the 'average' values of equilibrium and moderation. And meanwhile the basest of the human cogs in the machine will, for their part, oppose them with anti-values that justify their own abdication in the face of the challenge to excel oneself and reject the finite and levelling-down processes of life. Paradoxically enough, those critics who are put out by the theory of the 'noble hero' and the 'chaste and pure heroine' in fact adopt Iago's point of view in order to save 'verisimilitude'. As Péguy, denouncing the methods of the 'intellectual party' once said: 'The *task*, as we know, is to prove that saints and heroes do not exist.'[50] But Shakespeare's system 'is a system of order and hierarchy, a system so to speak of reality . . . , that is to say a system that operates on several levels . . . , that admits, recognises saints and heroes, and God at the top of the edifice',[51] a system which also acknowledges that evil and malevolence are always at work and that the blurring of distinctions, the abrasion of virtues, the reduction of everything and everyone to some common mean does not provide any foundation for equality, but merely destroys values and relationships of communion. Now, Shakespeare desired to show up this blurring of distinctions on every level of the world of the play: individual, social, natural and cosmic.

8. The threatened city: the citadel and the hearth

As if to emphasise the importance of distances and distancing, the transition from Venice to Cyprus, between the first and second acts, is one of the fundamental divisions in the tragedy. Othello and his followers spend an unspecified time crossing the sea, separated one from another, and the rupture this involves is underlined by the description of the storm which spares the Venetian vessels but sinks the Turkish fleet. The storm acts as a pivot or hinge that is connected with both the elements that compose this scenic and narrative opposition: it brings to a happy conclusion the episode of the Turkish threat but anticipates disorders yet to come, as is suggested by a number of lines with double meanings. Cassio, for instance, says:

> The great contention of the sea and skies
> Parted our fellowship   (II, i, 92–3)

and Othello, in lines steeped in dramatic irony, greets Desdemona as follows:

> O, my soul's joy,
> If after every tempest come such calmness,
> May the winds blow, till they have waken'd death,
> And let the labouring bark climb hills of seas,

Olympus-high, and duck again as low
As hell's from heaven. If it were now to die,
'Twere now to be most happy, for I fear
My soul hath her content so absolute,
That not another comfort, like to this
Succeeds in unknown fate.   (II, i, 184–93)

Cyprus is situated on the frontiers of civilisation;[52] it is a most suitable place to show the pressures that may be applied to the behaviour of Christians. In Cyprus, Othello stands in for the Prince. But he remains a soldier rather than a governor and his first decision, to reduce the rank of Cassio, whom Iago has slandered, is misjudged. The enemy is within, even if he has been repulsed without. 'Are we turned Turks?' he exclaims, at the spectacle of the quarrel between Montano and Cassio. This is Iago's chance. So long as the distant threat was present the threat close at hand remained without effect. But Cyprus is no longer a citadel under immediate threat; it is now neither at peace nor at war – just a citadel governed by a general with nothing to do.

The internal threat now becomes dramatic. In symbolic terms, it manifests a situation which Péguy – not without anachronism – described as follows:

There is no longer any such thing as a christian at peace. Those crusades that our forefathers used to seek out in the lands of the Infidels . . . have now sought us out, and we have them at home. Our faith is a citadel . . . No longer do we sally forth to fight the Infidels. The battle has been brought home to us by the scattered, formal, formless *or* formal infidels to be found everywhere, common-law infidels or – even more, infidelities. The least one of us is a soldier. The least one is quite literally a crusader. Our forefathers, like a human wave, an army wave, used to invade the infidel continents. Now, in contrast, it is the wave of infidelity [i.e. unbelief: translator's note] . . . that dominates the sea and the high seas and assails us from every side, without respite. Each one of our houses is a fortress *in periculo maris*, in peril from the sea. The holy war is everywhere. It is eternal.[53]

In one sense, Othello is a domestic tragedy: the aggression that is rife in the world has overtaken hearth and home, love and sexuality. And having struck the domain of what is private and intimate, the 'wave of infidelity' rebounds upon the public scene. However, it is not a domestic play in the generally accepted sense of literary criticism, that is to say the dramatisation of a conflict that only concerns individuals.[54] 'My life upon her faith' (I, iii, 294) is Othello's retort to Brabantio who warns that, having deceived her father, Desdemona might well deceive her husband. 'Faith': sworn faith, fidelity, loyalty, obligation that stems from allegiance and tenure just as it does from the bonds of matrimony.[55] There could be no clearer way to indicate from the start that a mistake on Othello's part where Desdemona is concerned may cost him his life. Literally, but symbolically too: Northrop Frye notes that Shakespearean heroes live in an 'ecstatic' society, that the centre of their life and personality lies outside themselves. 'In the "ecstatic" heroic society one's life is in one's loyalties: to die bravely in battle is still, in a very real sense, to preserve one's essential life.'[56] Conversely, one way or another, to destroy a relationship of loyalty or fidelity is to destroy oneself. For, while it necessarily involves people, the bond of dependence or obligation has no meaning unless God is at its origin and end.[57] That is why treachery and infidelity still have such profound symbolic meaning in the sixteenth century: they reveal that man's obligation towards God may be broken, that it is not necessarily the basis of existence. In these circumstances, it matters little whether one betrays oneself or is betrayed by the person that one loves:

> But there, where I have garner'd up my heart,
> Where either I must live, or bear no life,
> The fountain, from the which my current runs,
> Or else dries up, to be discarded thence . . .   (IV, ii, 58–61)

> Excellent wretch, perdition catch my soul,
> But I do love thee, and when I love thee not,
> Chaos is come again.   (III, iii, 91–3)

The breaking of the personal bond involves one's relationship with the creator and invites chaos to 'come again'. The difference between the foreign enemy and the domestic one now becomes clear: the former manifests himself without a mask; he is what he seems. The latter comes in disguise. Othello is well equipped to fight the external enemy but is unfailingly mistaken when it comes to Iago. Ideally, the city should survive through heroism manifested on its frontiers and through the love (or faith) that exists at its centre. In the last analysis, Iago's 'destructive power' is aimed at the heart of the City.

But there is another aspect to the personal bond. The loved one that it presupposes is fallible and ephemeral. In contrast to the love of God, love for his creatures is essentially transitory, fragile and hopeless. It is in thrall to time. That is why Iago is not simply a villain at a particular point in time: his destructive achievements symbolise the instability of things under the moon. If he 'is not what he is', it is not just because of the perversity of his particular character but by reason of the very nature of the human condition which causes us at times to deny that eternity is a delusion, and at others to deny that denial. Thus, Iago gives the lie to those who deny that everything changes and declines. The fascination that he exerts stems from this double negation, one that is only possible in a period of doubt and one that gives him a secret and daunting positive power.

9. The metamorphosis of Othello: custom and reason

It is by playing upon the relationship between Othello and Desdemona – that is to say, by altering the distance that exists between them – that Iago achieves his ends: to divide what is united in love, to transform the husband, *par excellence* the one who is closest, into an implacable, blinded and mortally alien enemy. For this to happen, it is enough that Othello should become for Desdemona what he is already held to be in general Venetian opinion, or that he should believe that this is what he has become for her, and that Desdemona should become in his eyes an object that he must destroy in order to purify himself. As Iago says:

> . . . for whiles this honest fool [Cassio]
> Plies Desdemona to repair his fortunes,
> And she for him pleads strongly to the Moor,
> I'll pour this pestilence into his ear,
> That she repeals him for her body's lust;
> And by how much she strives to do him good,
> She shall undo her credit with the Moor;
> So I will turn her virtue into pitch,
> And out of her own goodness make the net
> That shall enmesh 'em all.   (II, iii, 344–53)

An entire metamorphosis of Othello takes place in the 'temptation scene'. Here, he himself repeats what Venice said about foreigners. Brabantio had expressed doubt that perfection could, without witchcraft, be led away and made to deny the laws of nature. This is what Othello now does:

> *Othello*: I do not think but Desdemona's honest.
> *Iago*: Long live she so, and long live you to think so!
> *Othello*: And yet how nature erring from itself –   (III, iii, 229–31)

The subtle inversion that governs the metamorphosis of Othello depends upon the equivocal meaning of the word 'nature' in common contemporary opinion.[58] In Montaigne's words:

The lawes of conscience, which we say to proceed from nature, rise and proceed of custome: every man holding in special regard and inward veneration the opinions approved and the customes received about him cannot without remorse leave them nor without applause applie himselfe unto them . . . And the common imaginations we finde in credit about us, and by our fathers seed infused in our soule, seeme to be the generall and naturall. Whereupon it followeth, that whatsoever is beyond the compasse of custom, we deeme likewise to be beyond the compasse of reason.[59]

Before Montaigne, customs were held to reflect natural law, and one's consciousness of those customs was seen as reason based upon that law. But now a rift develops between the laws of nature and those of custom. What is natural for some is custom for others. It is in conformity with nature, but not with custom, that a Venetian girl should marry a Moor: that is how the married couple regard it. Desdemona makes that point forcefully in her reply to her father before the senators:

> *Brabantio*: Do you perceive in all this noble company,
> Where most you owe obedience?

> *Desdemona*:   My noble father,
> I do perceive here a divided duty:
> To you I am bound for life and education,
> My life and education both do learn me
> How to respect you, you are lord of all my duty:
> I am hitherto your daughter: but here's my husband:
> And so much duty as my mother show'd
> To you, preferring you before her father,
> So much I challenge, that I may profess,
> Due to the Moor my lord.   (I, iii, 179–80)

In fact, the entire debate before the Senate is aimed at determining whether Desdemona's love for Othello is natural or whether it has been aroused by unnatural means.

> Did you by indirect and forced courses
> Subdue and poison this young maid's affections?
> Or came it by request, and such fair question,
> As soul to soul affordeth?   (I, iii, 111–14)

In Brabantio's opinion, the fact that Desdemona can yield to Othello is contrary both to nature and to custom. Being 'out of hinge of custom', she is 'unhinged from reason'.

10. The metamorphosis of Othello: the postulates of Iago

Shakespeare makes Iago the mouthpiece of a view according to which nature is governed by secondary causes alone[60] and which interprets all human activity in 'realistic' and reductive terms: it always boils down to man's appetite for sex and money. Like Edmund in *King Lear*, Iago dismisses as 'opinions' or stuff and nonsense anything in man's 'nurture' or birth which might distinguish him from the baboon. Where Iago is so clever is that he imposes this view upon Othello in a series of relentless generalisations. The movement of his argument is both logical and emotional and its plausibility rests upon three postulates:

 1. Othello is an aristocrat; he will not tolerate the slightest aspersion upon his honour.[61]

> Good name in man and woman's dear, my lord;
> Is the immediate jewel of our souls:
> Who steals my purse, steals trash, 'tis something, nothing,
> 'Twas mine, 'tis his, and has been slave to thousands:
> But he that filches from me my good name
> Robs me of that which not enriches him
> And makes me poor indeed.   (III, iii, 159–65)

 2. Othello is a man: he will accept the traditional account of women, particularly in respect of their inconstancy and insatiable appetite:[62]

> O curse of marriage,
> That we can call these delicate creatures ours,
> And not their appetites! (III, iii, 272–4)

He is all the more disposed to accept it given that the love he bears Desdemona is an absolute love, analogous to the love usually borne to God.[63] It is, as Iago points out, an infinite love invested in a finite and fallible object:

> His soul is so infetter'd to her love,
> That she may make, unmake, do what she list,
> Even as her appetite shall play the god
> With his weak function (II, iii, 336–9)

In contrast to Desdemona who has openly proclaimed that she desires all the 'rites' of love, Othello, in the presence of the senators, denies that it is his desire that prompts him to wish Desdemona to accompany him to Cyprus.[64] This suggests that he underestimates sexuality in marriage. His idealistic exaltation of love will not be proof against Iago's third postulate.

3. Othello is a foreigner. He is not familiar with the customs of Venice, in other words with the true nature of Venetian women, about which Iago is quick to inform him:

> *Iago*: I know our country disposition well;
> In Venice they do let God see the pranks
> They dare not show their husbands: their best conscience
> Is not to leave undone, but keep unknown.
> *Othello*: Dost thou say so?
> *Iago*: She did deceive her father, marrying you. (III, iii, 205–10)

Marriage with the husband from afar can therefore be seen in two different lights: first, as an act of exalted love ('That I did love the Moor, to live with him, / My downright violence, and scorn of fortunes, / May trumpet to the world'), a love which makes the lover prefer nature to custom, which raises him or her beyond custom and ordinary passions. This is how Othello and Desdemona, and Cassio too, present their love during the first two acts. They are as it were surrounded by hyperbolic declarations of love in which the hyperbole reflects no exaggeration in their words but is on the contrary the exact verbal translation of the feelings involved.

On the other hand, this marriage can also be presented from the conventional view. Brabantio cannot resign himself to this 'betrayal of his blood' that is the result not of a magic bewitchment but of a voluntary action: it must then follow that the will itself is unnatural.

11. The metamorphosis of Othello: a Rabelaisian digression

No one has described better than Rabelais the scandal provoked by the canonical ruling that marriage could rest solely upon the will of those joined together, expressed in the presence of a priest – regardless of the wills of their 'fathers, mothers and nearest kindred', for 'All legislators have taken this Liberty from Children and have reserved it for Parents.'[65] It is worth noting that Erasmus and the members of the reformed church were of the same opinion and that Richard Hooker approved of the ancient custom of a woman being led to her marriage by her father or some other guardian.[66] But let us see what Rabelais says:

> For there never was Law in the World which gave to Children the Liberty to marry without the Knowledge, Acknowledgement, and Consent of their Fathers.
> By means of the Law of which I speak, there is no Whoremonger, Imposter, Scoundrel, Gallows-bird, stinking, measly, leprous Ruffian, Brigand, Robber, Miscreant, in their Countries, who may not violently snatch away any Maiden he shall have a Mind to choose, be she as noble, beautiful, rich, honourable, modest as you can tell, from the House of her Father, from the Arms of her Mother, in spite of all her Kindred . . . Could a worse or more cruel Act be done by the Goths, the Scythians, the Massagetae in a hostile Town, after a long siege, beleguered at great Cost and taken by Storm? And so the grieving Fathers and Mothers behold carried and drawn away from their Houses by an unknown Man, a Stranger, a Barbarian, a vile Cur, a rotten, botchy, scraggy, poor, miserable Creature, their beautiful, delicate, rich, healthful Daughters, whom they had nurtured so tenderly and in all virtuous Exercise, and whom they had disciplined in all honourable conduct, hoping in fitting time to bestow them in Marriage on the Children of their Neighbours and ancient Friends, who had been nurtured and brought up in the same Care, so as to attain to the Felicity of Marriage, that from them they might see born a Progeny representing and inheriting as much the Breeding of their Fathers and Mothers as their Estate, their Property and Inheritance.[67]

With ever-increasing vehemence, the worthy Gargantua compares the anguish (*déconfort*) of the family to that of the Lacedaemonians when Helen was carried off or that of Ceres when Proserpine was ravished. Deprived of their beloved daughter, the parents 'in Tears and Lamentations end their Life', and some of them 'have become so much out of their Minds and like Maniacs, that with Mourning and Regret they have drowned, hanged or killed themselved, being unable to endure that Indignity'. It is natural and reasonable, says Gargantua, that at the news of the rape of his daughter, a virtuous man should feel as much despair as at her death. And just as any man, catching his daughter's murderer red-handed,'by the Sanction of Reason can, by the Dictates of Nature ought, to slay him out of Hand', similarly, if he surprises some 'ruffian', encouraged by a priest, 'corrupting and stealing his Daughter out of his House, however much she may have been consenting to it, he both can and ought to put them ignominiously to Death and fling their Carcasses to be torn to pieces by brute Beasts'.[68]

It is not possible to tell from the syntax whether this multiple killing is supposed to involve the seducer, the priest and the girl as well, or just two of the three. At all events, those with parental authority wish to punish the guilty and wash away the defilement they have produced by destroying their bodies: that is exactly the kind of destruction that, when his metamorphosis is complete, Othello desires Desdemona to undergo.

A debate similar to that reflected in Rabelais was taking place in England at the end of the century. In 1589, John Stockwood published in London *A Bartholomew Fairing for Parentes, to Bestow upon their Sonnes and Daughters . . . : Shewing that children are not to marie without the consent of their parentes . . .* In this little work of a hundred pages or so, the author reviews dozens of reasons – biblical, evangelical or borrowed from various theologians (Luther and Calvin among them) – which argue against marriage contracted without the 'seal, recognition and consent' of the parents. He notes (p. 91) that the consent of the daughter was an aggravating circum stance since it broke the bond of obedience between her and her father.

12. The metamorphosis of Othello: the unnatural man

Seen from the point of view of custom, as understood in the light of the above remarks, Othello and Desdemona are equally at fault. That is why Iago's first attack – after Cassio, shamefaced, has furtively left the scene so as not to encounter his general – is aimed at the period before the marriage had taken place, when Cassio was secretly acting as a go-between for the lovers, and meeting with Desdemona. Iago pretends to be suppressing a number of lying statements, in such a way that, as they gradually come to light, they are the more easily accepted as the truth.[69] Thus, seeming not to wish to put what he is thinking into words – since the thoughts assailing him may be impure – he suggests that the pure and the impure co-exist in everyone:

> Though I am bound to every act of duty,
> I am not bound to that all slaves are free to;
> Utter my thoughts? Why, say they are vile and false:
> As where's that palace, whereinto foul things
> Sometimes intrude not? who has a breast so pure,
> But some uncleanly apprehensions
> Keep leets and law-days, and in session sit
> With meditations lawful?   (III, iii, 138–45)

Setting himself up as an example of average humanity, he manages to suggest that he is thereby exemplary. The implication of his words is: why should Desdemona not also belong to this humanity into whose palace it is normal for foul things to intrude?

That suggestion links Iago's remarks to his next speech in which he declares that one's good name – honour – is the 'immediate jewel' of men's souls (having earlier maintained quite the opposite to Cassio) (II, iii, 200–63): if one's good name is 'filched' (and through the fault of a woman, is the implication), the theft does not enrich the thief,[70] yet nonetheless ruins the victim. And he describes (and thereby suggests and provokes) the torment of uncertainty caused by jealousy, the monster that 'doth mock / That meat it feeds on':

> *Iago*: . . . that cuckold lives in bliss,
> Who, certain of his fate, loves not his wronger:
> But O, what damned minutes tells he o'er
> Who dotes, yet doubts, suspects, yet strongly loves!
> *Othello*: O misery!
> *Iago*: Poor and content is rich, and rich enough,
> But riches, fineless, is as poor as winter
> To him that ever fears he shall be poor . . . (III, iii, 171–8)

Of course, the remarks do not apply to Othello, since Desdemona's fidelity is absolute, but they might concern any other husband whose wife was not endowed with the fairytale and improbable perfection with which Shakespeare has invested his heroine. Through foolishness and lack of trust,[71] Othello steps out of the fairy-story that was his marriage and into the intolerable world where all love is relative, the world where partners are interchangeable, where

love is nothing else but an insatiate thirst of enjoying a greedily desired subject. Nor Venus, that good huswife, other than a tickling delight of emptying one's seminary vessels: as is the pleasure which nature giveth us to discharge other parts: which becommeth faulty by immoderation, and defective by indiscretion . . . I beleeve that which Plato saies to be true, that man was made by the Gods for them to toy and play withall:

> *quaenam ista jocandi*

Soevitia! (what cruelty is this, so set on jesting is?) And that Nature in mockery left us the most troublesome of our actions, the most common: thereby to equall us and without distinction to set the foolish and the wise, us and the beastes all in one ranke.[72]

In this way Othello is brought to the state of agonising uncertainty which, in a century when belief in the divine absolute, though undermined, was not obliterated, appeared as a threat to the wholeness of all human relationships. Thus, the first stage in the metamorphosis of Othello is his loss of confidence in the unique nature of the one he loves. The undermining of his trust is closely linked with the transgression of customs which the clandestine marriage with a being from afar has rendered necessary. The following words of Iago clearly allude to that connection:

> *Iago*: She did deceive her father, marrying you;
> And when she seem'd to shake and fear your looks,
> She lov'd them most.
> *Othello*: And so she did.
> *Iago*: Why, go to then,
> She that so young could give out such a seeming,
> To seal her father's eyes up, close as oak,[73]
> He thought 'twas witchcraft . . . (III, iii, 210–15)

'When she seem'd to shake and fear your looks' echoes the words of the father. The rumours against the foreigner[74] are rebounding, rebounding against the Black whom it would not be possible to marry without fear and disgust – unless witchcraft were involved. The shift in the meaning, despite the similarity in the words used, is remarkable: Desdemona now stands as the principal figure accused, even if the accusation is couched in the very same terms as the rumours; in Othello's eyes Desdemona is becoming more distant, becoming once more part of the common human condition, whilst he himself is settling into the exceptional position of the dreaded foreigner. The end of this first stage is marked by the following lines:

> *Iago*: I humbly do beseech you of your pardon,
> For too much loving you.
> *Othello*:   I am bound to thee for ever.   (III, iii, 216–17)

Othello turns away from true love, to embrace 'the love' of Iago.

But the poisoned word continues on its course. It is in the form of a double negative that Othello now expresses his trust – and at the same time his distrust – in Desdemona's honesty and then, still hesitant, goes on to adopt Brabantio's earlier discourse:[75]

> *Othello*: I do not think but Desdemona's honest.
> *Iago*: Long live she so, and long live you to think so!
> *Othello*: And yet how nature erring from itself –   (III, iii, 229–31)

The word 'nature' is used in a dangerously equivocal way, for, with his unfinished phrase, Othello may mean either that it is unnatural (although possible) to deceive one's husband or that it is unnatural (although possible) to marry a man such as he, a Black, a foreigner. Iago seizes upon the second meaning, repeating and magnifying the common talk:

> Ay, there's the point: as, to be bold with you,
> Not to affect many proposed matches,
> Of her own clime, complexion, and degree,
> Whereto we see in all things nature tends;
> Fie, we may smell in such a will most rank,[76]
> Foul disproportion; thoughts unnatural.
> But pardon me: I do not in position
> Distinctly speak of her, though I may fear
> Her will, recoiling to her better judgement,
> May fall to match you with her country forms,
> And happily repent.   (III, iii, 232–42)

Even as he claims not to be speaking explicitly of Desdemona, Iago goes one step further. But his disclaimer is just a stylistic device and is, one senses, taken to be such by his listener, so astonishingly present in the speaker's words: he is present there in that he is not of the same country, the same colour, the same rank; in that he has been the object of too strong or too perverse a desire provoked by the very foreignness of his appearance or nature; and, above all, in that he henceforth believes Venetian corrupt customs to be a fact of nature, and the erstwhile incomparable Desdemona to be an unnatural being for having chosen him, Othello.

So Othello accepts the smear attached to Desdemona. 'Why did I marry?' he says (III, iii, 246). The monologue he then delivers is sometimes interpreted as a revulsion of man in general against the traditional defects of women. Nevertheless, it makes a clear evaluation of the ideas it sets out. If Desdemona is unfaithful, he will turn her away, even if it tears his heart asunder; for fidelity must be mutual. The curse of marriage is that it binds to you the being, not its appetites. Just as it is impossible to love both God and an idol, it is intolerable not to be loved as a jealous God is loved. He has made the intolerable discovery of the possible relativity of love. And – what is even harder to bear for this character generally taken to be beyond vulnerability and who believed himself to be so 'all in all sufficient' (IV, i, 261) – he has discovered the extent of his own fragility now that he has totally committed himself to another. 'True, perfect liberty is for one to be able to doe and work all things upon himselfe.'[77]

> . . . if I do prove her haggard,
> Though that her jesses were my dear heart-strings,
> I'ld whistle her off, and let her down the wind,
> To prey at fortune. Haply, for I am black,
> And have not those soft parts of conversation
> That chamberers have, or for I am declin'd
> Into the vale of years, – yet that's not much –
> She's gone, I am abused, and my relief
> Must be to loathe her: O curse of marriage,
> That we can call these delicate creatures ours,
> And not their appetites! I had rather be a toad
> And live upon the vapour in a dungeon,
> Than keep a corner in a thing I love,
> For others' uses: yet, 'tis the plague of great ones,[78]
> Prerogativ'd are they less than the base,
> 'Tis destiny, unshunnable, like death:
> Even then this forked plague is fated to us,
> When we do quicken: Desdemona comes,
> If she be false, O, then heaven mocks itself,
> I'll not believe it.   (III, iii, 264–83)

Wanting to find causes for the supposed infidelity of Desdemona, Othello seeks them now in himself, now in the nature of women in general. Is the infidelity caused by the fact that he is Black, lacks the polish of a courtier, is declining into the vale of years? Is it a curse that is attached to marriage? – an inevitable destiny that affects the mighty more than others? The assertiveness of his words should not mislead us: there are no certainties in this questioning of the loved one and himself, where the deprecatory animal

comparison, with the toad, marks a new stage in the protagonist's acceptance of the poisoned language of Iago.

The third stage is reached when Emilia gives Iago the handkerchief lost by
Desdemona. Othello reappears, in a frantic state, beseeching Iago to provide him with visible proof (III, iii, 365)[79] of his wife's infidelity. The uncertainty is unbearable, contradictory declarations follow one upon the other in
a tirade in which, eventually, his belief in treachery wins the day:

> I think my wife be honest, and think she is not,
> I think thou art just, and think thou art not;
> I'll have some proof: her name, that was as fresh
> As Dian's visage, is now begrim'd, and black
> As mine own face.[80]   (III, iii, 390–4)

Blackness becomes an obsessive theme: it is the colour of his skin and of
defilement, the opposite to the purity of Diana. That there is defilement
between Othello and Desdemona is now taken as established and becomes
so intolerable that in the following lines he contemplates suicide if he does
not obtain the 'satisfaction' of proof, the term 'satisfied' signifying either
'satisfaction' or 'conviction'. Iago proceeds to subject the word to a veritable
syntactical torture: a grammatical image of the torture he is inflicting upon
the protagonist:

> *Iago*: You would be satisfied.
> *Othello*:   Would, nay, I will.
> *Iago*: And may, but how, how satisfied, my lord?
> Would you, the supervisor, grossly gape on,
> Behold her topp'd?[81]   (III, iii, 399–402)

The desire for certainty thus veers towards a conviction which is no longer
based upon anything tangible – since the action itself cannot be witnessed –
but which will continue to seek for 'circumstantial' proof. While he is about
it, Iago implicates Desdemona in bestiality, by describing her as 'topp'd'.
Then, after pointing out that that kind of 'satisfaction' is not obtainable, he
goes on to complete the identification with bestiality:

> *Iago*:   . . . Where's satisfaction?
> It is impossible you should see this,
> Were they as prime as goats, as hot as monkeys,
> As salt as wolves, in pride; and fools as gross
> As ignorance made drunk: but yet I say,
> If imputation and strong circumstances,
> Which lead directly to the door of truth,
> Will give you satisfaction, you may ha't.   (III, iii, 407–14)

Iago now only has to recount a supposed dream of Cassio's (in which
Cassio is in bed with Desdemona) to provoke Othello into exclaiming 'I'll
tear her all to pieces' (III, iii, 438). He goes on to swear he will be avenged
and Iago promises to assist him. Desdemona has now become a 'lewd minx',

a 'fair devil' (III, iii, 482 and 485). Iago is promoted to lieutenant and exclaims, 'I am your own for ever' (III, iii, 486). Totally separated from Desdemona, whom he desired to tear to shreds, Othello is now united with Iago as if in marriage – he has *become* Iago. Essentially, the metamorphosis is now complete. 'My lord is not my lord', Desdemona cries (III, iv, 121). Othello attributes to her the mixture of animality and devilishness that common talk had attributed to himself. At the beginning of the next act, his epileptic fit suggests he is possessed.

This scene may be interpreted in a number of different ways: as a progressive infection of Good by Evil,[82] a retreat of a superior rationality founded upon trust in the face of an inferior rationality founded upon proof.[83] The means employed to bring about the metamorphosis are rhetorical. But the most convincing analogy is that of a poisoning.

13. The metamorphosis of Othello: words and poison

According to F. R. Leavis, the remarkable thing about Iago's success is not so much the diabolical intellect that enables him to accomplish his ends, but: 'Othello's readiness to respond. Iago's power, in fact, in the temptation scene is that he represents something that is in Othello – in Othello, the husband of Desdemona: the essential traitor is within the gates'[84] – the idea being that, if a character changes, it is because right from the start he was bound to be what he becomes,[85] or that in each one of us there is always a little self inside the bigger one, the smaller being the real one while the bigger is just a mask that conceals the other until it grows. Such an idea does not seem very Shakespearean: the conventions of the Shakespearean theatre were, rather, that any character who dissembled in the presence of others revealed himself in his true light to the audience in the course of his soliloquies.

Let us consider an episode in the play which presents a narrative analogy anticipating this change. It is in the scene in which Cassio, led on by Iago, gets drunk and thereby loses his honour. Although we should not lose a sense of proportion, it is fair to describe the role of this scene in *Othello* as similar to that of the blinding of Gloucester in relation to the madness of the king, in *King Lear*. The drink that makes Cassio lose control is certainly real; nevertheless, what he exclaims is: 'O thou invisible spirit of wine,[86] if thou hast no name to be known by, let us call thee devil!' (II, iii, 273–5), and he goes on to say, 'It hath pleas'd the devil drunkenness to give place to the devil wrath; one unperfectness shows me another, to make me frankly despise myself' (II, iii, 287–9). It is also during this episode that Iago makes his first pronouncement on the subject of reputation (II, iii, 258–64). It is a speech that he later repeats, in an inverted form, for Othello (III, iii, 161–5). According to Cassio, the effect of wine – all the more radical if one's toler-

ance of it is low and one is not a habitual drinker (II, iii, 30–3) – is to transform with remarkable speed the one who drinks it:[87] 'to be now a sensible
man, by and by a fool, and presently a beast!' (II, iii, 296); and 'I drunk!' he
exclaims, wonderingly (II, iii, 303).[88]

As for the change that Othello undergoes, that is caused by discourse, but
its effects are physical as well as moral: despair, epilepsy and murderous
insanity. The effects of slander are those of a poison and all the more violent
when the words employed are the very ones used by the slanderer or enemy
himself. The danger that lies in using the words of malevolent beings is discussed in a number of treatises of the period. Thus, Léonard Vair writes:

And I believe one should be particularly careful not to use words which come from
Moors, Turks and all other infidels for, because they are possessed by devils, one
must also take it that their words are pacts and agreements that they have with the
devils, so that if we ourselves use them we are obliged to be in agreement with the
Demons.[89]

Shakespeare reverses the traditional ideas: instead of the Moor poisoning
the Venetian, the Venetian poisons the Moor. The traitor is essentially
within the gates but is not, essentially, Othello. As for 'agreements' reached
with devils, the play provides an example of this at the end of the temptation
scene.

On the subject of the reasons for the behaviour of malevolent beings,[90]
the verbal poison that they use and the cunning ploys they use, Léonard Vair
explains that:

Just as rhetoricians declare that the greatest perfection there is in the art of oratory
is to palliate and disguise it so well that it does not appear to be an art at all, so the
supreme cunning of Demons lies in the fact that their tricks and deceptions are not
at all recognised and that one may never discover that the power of bewitching and
casting spells comes from them . . .
    And so, in order to conceal and keep hidden the wish and desire they have to harm
us, they always try to deceive us beneath a mask and disguise of honesty and
rectitude . . . [91]

As for the way in which poison permeates the body and how it utterly
changes it into a substance like itself, Ambroise Paré describes it thus:

And first we will say that venom or poison is a thing which, once it has entered or
been applied to the human body, has the power of fighting against it and overcoming
it, just as the body is victorious over nourishment that it daily takes in: which is done
either by its manifest qualities or else by properties that are hidden and secret. The
Conciliator,[92] in the book he has produced on *Venoms*, says that all venom taken into
the body is entirely different in all properties from the meat upon which we feed. For
just as meat is changed into blood and makes all the parts similar to the limbs which
it principally nourishes, taking the place of all that is continually escaping from our
bodies and being resolved and consumed: thus venom, in just the opposite way,
changes the body and limbs that it touches into a particular, venomous nature. And
so, neither more nor less than all the animals and fruits that the earth produces,
which can be changed into food if we eat them, similarly, but in the opposite way,
poisonous things taken into the body make all the limbs of our body poisonous.[93]

To be sure, Jacques Grevin, in his *Deux livres des Venins*, denies that words can have the same effect as poison, even though he recognises the efficacy of poetic discourse,[94] and partially believes in the effects of fascination,[95] just as John Baptista Porta does: 'So when Envy bends her fierce and flaming eyes, and the desire of mischief bursts thereout, a vehement heat proceedeth from them which infecteth those that stand nigh, especially the beautiful; they strike them through as with a sword, set their entrails on fire.'[96] On the continent, in a work on legal practices and criminal procedures in Flanders, J. H. de Damhoudere included a chapter entitled 'On killing or slaughtering by the tongue' (chap. LXX). This is what it says:

There are four ways of committing murder and killing by the tongue: by bearing witness, by advice, by accusation or command and by judgement. False witness that anyone bears with the tongue or which leads to death should be punished as falsehood, perjury or murder. False witness does harm to and damages three persons: first God, for whose presence it shows contempt. Then, the judge whom it deceives by falsehood and lies. Thirdly and lastly, the innocent party to whom it does damage, is a grievance and whom it wounds by its false witness; and because it is a grievance against and damages three persons, it can be punished in three ways, as being falsehood, perjury and murder, and this way of killing is detestable . . .
    And whoever has given advice to kill anybody (so that the deed would never have been committed if he had not given that advice) is punishable as if he was the principal offender, and here it is apparent how dangerously wrong are those who say and believe that the only murderers are those who perform the murder or killing with their own hands and not those by whose advice, fraudulence, urging or provoking, men are slaughtered and killed, such as the jews, who in no way killed our Lord with their own hands and delivered him over to death, yet the death of our Lord is certainly and publicly imputed to them and ascribed to them because by false witness, advice, whispering and instigation they delivered him up to death, braying with their tongues and shouting and saying, 'Crucify him, crucify him!' as the Gospel stories clearly attest.[97]

In England, the common law provided a number of ways of gaining legal redress for slander. Edward Coke enumerates some of them. The rule seemed to be that there was no redress against 'moral' defamation (insults such as 'whore', 'heretic', etc.). On the other hand, if the slander or insult had practical consequences (as for an affianced girl said to be pregnant and who thereby had to give up her marriage), it was punishable by law.[98] The importance attached to the poison of slander during this period was such that, in order to explain the metamorphosis of Othello, it does not seem necessary to postulate that he was sick even before contracting the sickness.

14. The metamorphosis of Othello: a digression on the werewolf

Othello has absorbed a poison which makes him believe that he is changed into a beast (IV, i, 62) but also which does indeed transform him into a wild being frothing at the mouth, as Iago explains during the epileptic fit:

> The lethargy must have his quiet course,
> If not, he foams at mouth, and by and by
> Breaks out to savage madness.   (IV, i, 53–5)

Desdemona can no longer recognise him. As for her, she has become a whore in his eyes, a woman who cannot keep her distance. Close to all men, she is on the contrary set apart from him. New distances are established. Shakespeare has created a gap between visible signs and what they manifest so that what is and what seems, things and their meanings no longer correspond. This is the principle on which Iago himself works:

> I must show out a flag, and sign of love,
> Which is indeed but sign.   (I, i, 156 7)

In the scene in which Othello calls Desdemona a prostitute and Emilia a procuress, what is happening is understood in quite different ways by each of the characters and by the spectators. The faithful wife finds herself trapped in a role which she does not understand, in such a way that the whore of Othello's imagination and the true Desdemona to whose denials he is deaf end up by becoming superimposed one upon the other in the mind of the spectator. The truth and its deformation – which to Othello is the truth – become a single reality, in a perfectly unified dramatic image. Thus, beings and things can perhaps only be understood within the framework of a vision that can give them meaning: and in these circumstances that meaning is not, as it were, tacked on to reality but is incorporated in it.

Faced with his prostitute-wife, Othello discovers that he is in a position that is both as far away from her as possible, since he believes her to belong to everybody, and at the same time as close as possible to her, since she is his wife though belonging to everyone, so that she can for him only be an object that is defiled and defiles him. The idea of offering her up as an expiatory sacrifice is a natural consequence of the situation, a measure of his former love and of his present alienated trust. He wants to 'tear her all to pieces' (III, iii, 438), to 'chop her into messes' (IV, i, 196); he is obsessed by visions of lacerated bodies: 'Noses, ears and lips' (IV, i, 42). Defilement calls for the dispersal of the body at fault, its return to the elements: it should not be forgotten that the bodies of traitors were quartered and the limbs dispersed. For Othello, the whole of nature is revolted by Desdemona:

> *Desdemona*: I hope my noble lord esteems me honest.
> *Othello*: Oh, ay, as summer's flies, are in the shambles,
> That quicken even with blowing:
> O thou black weed, why art so lovely fair?
> Thou smell'st so sweet, that the sense aches at thee,
> Would thou hadst ne'er been born!
> *Desdemona*: Alas, what ignorant sin have I committed?
> *Othello*: Was this fair paper, this most goodly book
> Made to write 'whore' on? . . . What, committed?

Committed! O thou public commoner!
I should make very forges of my cheeks,
That would to cinders burn up modesty,
Did I but speak thy deeds. What committed!
Heaven stops the nose at it, and the moon winks,
The bawdy wind, that kisses all it meets,
Is hush'd within the hollow mine of earth,
And will not hear't: . . . what committed, –
Impudent strumpet! (IV, ii, 66–83)

He assumes the posture and role of a loving sacrificer who dares not shed the blood of the victim that he loves and yet must kill for the sake of justice:

. . . yet I'll not shed her blood,
Nor scar that whiter skin of hers than snow,
And smooth, as monumental alabaster;
Yet she must die, else she'll betray more men. (V, ii, 3–6)

The fact remains, though, right up to the moment of 'sacrifice', that his discourse is marked by images of mutilation and bestiality. If his cause were just, he would certainly be in the right role, that of a purifier. Emilia, one of whose functions is to express the opinions of common sense,[99] exclaims:

Has she forsook so many noble matches,
Her father, and her country, all her friends,
To be call'd whore? (IV, ii, 127–9)

Brutally, the point of view which is both that of common sense and of general rumour imposes itself. By calling Desdemona a whore, Othello reveals himself to be that foreigner for whom she abandoned everything. And the spectator – who knows more about Othello's discourse than Emilia does – can see in the man obsessed with the idea of tearing his wife's body to pieces, not a sacrificer but a wild animal, a man changed into a beast, invested with all the animality that common rumour in Venice attributed to him even when he was still the 'noble hero'.

The sixteenth century was obsessed with the theme of the werewolf. Some believed werewolves were people deluded by a sickness caused by melancholia; others that they were the creations of the devil. A well-known engraving shows a werewolf at large in a village, standing amid the torn limbs of its victims. The victims were often children: innocents.[100] The symbolic force of the metamorphosis of man into wolf lay in the sudden distancing of one hitherto a close intimate. The one who had been close inexplicably became murderous. A 1610 text tells us that when Shakespeare's company presented *Othello* at Oxford, ' . . . Desdemona, though always excellent, moved us especially in her death when, as she lay on her bed, her face itself implored the pity of the audience.'[101] For her the noble hero had become a bestial murderer, killing after producing a torrent of sexual abuse. Desdemona, the perfect wife according to the norms of the period, is subjected to the madness of her husband yet refuses to denounce him. The result is that Othello is seen as a demoniacal murderer:

> *Othello*: She turn'd to folly, and she was a whore.
> *Emilia*: Thou dost belie her, and thou art a devil.   (V, ii, 133–4)

Shakespeare ends the play in such a way that Othello emerges from his blindness to see the enormity of what he has done: destroyed the only pure object there was in the world – acting, paradoxically enough, in accordance with the norm accepted by Iago when he said:

> . . . if Cassio do remain,
> He has a daily beauty in his life,
> That makes me ugly . . .   (V, 1, 18–20)

As for Othello, he accepts damnation for, as G. R. Hibbard notes, the subject of the play concentrates our attention upon 'the wanton destruction of happiness – something so precious and so fragile that its loss is felt as quite irredeemable',[102] and it is to be expected that whatever is inexpiable should be set upon the path to hell:

> . . . Where should Othello go?
> Now: how dost thou look now? O ill-starr'd wench,
> Pale as thy smock, when we shall meet at count,
> This look of thine shall hurl my soul from heaven,
> And fiends will snatch at it: cold, cold, my girl,
> Even like thy chastity; O cursed slave!
> Whip me, you devils,
> From the possession of this heavenly sight,
> Blow me about in winds, roast me in sulphur,
> Wash me in steep-down gulfs of liquid fire!   (V, ii, 272–81)

The whole tragic revelation is encompassed in this moment when Othello's eyes are opened to his folly. The Greek model is probably Euripides' *Bacchae*, in which the women of Thebes, initially benevolent, invoking milk, honey and wine, are changed into Furies. Agave, the priestess of Dionysus, sacrifices her own son in her blinded state, tears his limbs asunder and then discovers that the head of the 'lion cub' tossed on to the *thyrsus* is the head of Pentheus, her son:

> O sorrow unmeasurable and beyond seeing,
> Since murder you have achieved with these poor hands!
> A fine victim you have struck down for the Gods . . . [103]

says Cadmos. In similar fashion, Othello discovers that 'the artificious whore of Venice' is the chaste and pure Desdemona.

Othello's suicide is designed not so much to 'save face' or show that Iago has been entirely successful in taking possession of his soul,[104] rather to enable him to do himself justice with a Venetian hand, by killing the 'circumcised dog' that is within him:

And say besides, that in Aleppo once,
Where a malignant and turban'd Turk
Beat a Venetian, and traduced the state,
I took by the throat the circumcised dog,
And smote him thus. (*Stabs himself*)   (V, ii, 353–7)

For he is a man

           . . . whose hand
Like the base Indian, threw a pearl away,
Richer than all his tribe . . .   (V, ii, 347–9)

In the two Quarto editions, the word that appears here is 'Indian'. But in the Folio, it is 'Judean', that is 'Jew'. Shakespearean scholars have argued endlessly as to which version is right.[105] The doubt itself is significant: what Othello kills at the end of the play for having discarded the unique pearl, the source of life, is the Indian, the Jew, the Turk, all at once, that is to say those beings whom the dominant ideology situated beyond the pale of natural law and whose proximity represented a threat to the values of the City. But Shakespeare situates the essential menace within the City. Condemned to slow torture, Iago, the traitor, opaque, indecipherable, is an image of the principal enemy who uses the threat from outside to gain his own ends. The deep purpose of his machinations is not to destroy a marriage but to thwart the accomplishment of an exceptional and exemplary love, the norms of which go far beyond the demands of convention, in defiance of the hatred accumulated against foreigners. The suggestion here is that belonging to humanity cannot be defined by one's belonging to a particular territory, nation or religion: it is defined by the rejection of a rejection.

No one can say who has the right to live and love upon this earth and who may be refused that right. Iago's crime, in the first place, was the generalised rejection that he stirred up by starting the rumours against Othello in Venice, for by so doing he was taking up a stand against mankind in general.

Shakespeare made use of England's awareness of other civilisations[106] to show that the worst enemy is not always the most obvious one.[107] Man need not look far ahead for what is destroying him: he may be sure of finding it on the spot, and love, upon which communions are founded, is, *par excellence*, the favourite haunt for crime.[108]

7. Elizabethan travel literature and Shakespeare's *The Tempest*

1. The reality and the gloss

'Our world hath of late discovered another (and who can warrant us whether it be the last of his brethren, since both the Daemons, the Sibylls, and all we have hitherto been ignorant of this?)'[1] The edition of the *Essays* in which this remark of Montaigne's appears was published in 1588, almost a century after the discovery of the New World, and it shows that the event had provoked a lasting perplexity and that the novelty of it had not yet worn off. During this same period, the English show a comparable curiosity respecting the New World, other possible worlds and everything to do with exploration. The wealthy, and the less wealthy too, were travelling in every conceivable manner, in England, in Europe, in the known world, for 'the nature of man, by an inward inclination, is alwaies inquisitive of forraine news'.[2] Already considerable in the Middle Ages, when 'the motives of pilgrim, ecclesiastic, scholar, business man, diplomat, soldier and mere tourist to surmount the difficulties and dangers of foreign travel'[3] were strong, the stream of travellers increased during the Renaissance, and the English protestant of the sixteenth and seventeenth centuries found that 'the political and commercial conditions of Europe, combined with the ideals of Renaissance humanism, gave a new importance to the study of the history, policy, language and manners of foreign countries as a preparation for public service and international trade'.[4]

The literature of the Elizabethan and Jacobean periods reflects, stimulates and crystallises this interest: Great Britain is described in minute detail in the works of William Camden,[5] William Harrison,[6] John Stow[7] and Michael Drayton.[8] But it was the far-away lands particularly that were all the rage, as is shown by, among other texts, the vast compilations of Richard Hakluyt[9] and Samuel Purchas,[10] the translation of foreign tales and a number of descriptions extolling the marvels of America. It was the birth of the English passion for colonisation.

These new 'tales' took their place alongside more ancient accounts, biblical, Homeric or Virgilian voyages, the stories of the Golden Legend, printed by Caxton in 1483, real or metaphorical pilgrimages like that of Saint Brandan, the edifying voyages of Brandt's *Ship of Fools*, translated in 1509 and – of course – the travels of Sir John Mandeville which were translated in 1377, printed in 1496 and repeatedly reprinted right up to the eighteenth century.[11]

There was thus a kind of synthesis or co-existence between the real and the imaginary, truth and fantasy, literal reality and metaphor, while at the same time the need for exact information required that the truth be distinguished from the false. Navigators of the period were a long way from reckoning all these texts to be of equal worth, as texts. When seeking a haven or a land-fall, they certainly distinguished between accounts that would strand them on the reefs and those that would help them to reach the shore. Nevertheless, considerable tension remained between the constraints of exactitude – or, to put it another way, realism – and men's appetite for marvels. Montaigne is aware of this when he writes:

Subtile people may indeed marke more curiously and observe things more exactly, but they amplify and glose them . . . We had need of Topographers to make us particular narrations of the places they have beene in. For some of them, if they have the advantage of us that have seen Palestine, will challenge a privilege to tell us newes of all the world besides. I would have everie man write what he knowes, and no more.[12]

Shakespeare himself enters the debate when he opposes the excessive scepticism of Antonio and Sebastian, upon discovering the island (*The Tempest*, III, i), and their sudden and no less excessive credulity after the 'strange shapes' have served the banquet:

> *Sebastian*:   . . . Now I will believe
> That there are unicorns; that in Arabia
> There is one tree, the phoenix' throne; one phoenix
> At this hour reigning there.
> *Antonio*:   I'll believe both;
> And what does else want credit, come to me,
> And I'll be sworn 'tis true: travellers ne'er did lie,
> Though fools at home condemn 'em.   (III, iii, 21–7)

The literature thus reflects a world of equivocal status in which the boundaries between the fabulous and the real are not clearly defined,[13] in which reality is elusive and, while the fantastic seems about to become real, reality is on the point of becoming fantastic. As has often been pointed out, this is one of the most disorientating aspects of *The Tempest*.

2. Warding off excessive closeness

Elizabethan literature describes close places, as well as far-away ones, in accordance with a double axis: one both spatial and temporal. Thus, a geo-

graphical description of Great Britain is accompanied by a history of the
land and its monuments. And in the case of distant lands that can be indicated on maps or portulans, the old dreams are also recorded, introduced to
lend material actuality to what the collective imagination had hitherto
situated in the past: the Golden Age, Earthly Paradise, the Isles of the
Blessed, lands of everlasting spring-time, the Fountain of Youth. Furthermore, the 'barbarians' found in these new lands are perceived not to be men,
at least not yet men. Take, for instance, the following description of the
inhabitants of a region of Cuba, who live as 'in the golden world', in the
Decades by Peter Martyr of Angleria (Pietro Martire d'Anghiera), translated into English by Richard Eden in 1555.

> For it is certeyne, that amonge them the lande is as common as the sonne and water.
> And that Myne and Thyne (the seedes of all myscheefe) have no place with them . . .
> They seeme to lyve in the goulden world, without toyle, lyving in open gardens, not
> intrenched with dykes, dyvyded with hedges, or defended with waulles. They deale
> trewely one with another without lawes, without bookes and without Judges.[14]

These men have not yet experienced the evils of civilisation; since we can
now reach them physically, we are no longer separated from them by space,
but we are by time. They have a past that we can now perceive as the present,
in the manner of a spectacle. And the same goes for the millions of inhabitants of the Americas still not acquainted with the Good News of the Gospel,
yet beseeching the English to bring it to them: ' . . . the people of America
crye out unto us, their nexte neighboures, to come and help them [against
the Spaniards] and bringe unto them the gladd tidings of the gospell.'[15]

   Travel to different locations in space, which made possible the discovery
of human beings who were leading lives that belonged to earlier times, but
were nevertheless contemporary, tore a rent in the fabric of the traveller's
symbolic world. The existence of these beings was a threat and a challenge.
Once discovered, they had to be fitted into the space and time of the
Christian world in order not to upset the traditional chronology. So these
newly discovered beings were judged according to the criteria that were
familiar to 'civilised' people. Montaigne, to be sure, wrote: 'Men call that
barbarism which is not common to them. As indeed we have no other ayme
of truth and reason than the example and Idea of the opinions and customes
of the countrie we live in. There is ever perfect religion, perfect policie, perfect and compleat use of all things.'[16] But Captain John Smith, for his part,
could not see that the beliefs of the Indians of Virginia were quite different
from his own. He considered them to be the same but inverted:

> But their chief God they worship is the Devill. Him they call *Okee* and serve him
> more of feare than love . . . In their temples they have his image evill-favouredly
> carved, and then painted and adorned with chaines of copper, and beads, and
> covered with a skin, in such manner as the deformitie may well suit with such a God.[17]

From the fifteenth century up until the mid-seventeenth most travellers manifested indifference or hostility toward the cultures of primitive peoples. Their descriptions of the latter are dictated not so much by what they could perceive of the native culture itself but rather by what they had heard said of it in their own country of origin.[18] Favourable descriptions draw analogies with the Golden Age, unfavourable ones with the reign of the devil or with animals. Furthermore, travellers project their own European social hierarchies upon these primitive societies, attributing to them their own type of monarchs, aristocrats and popular classes. But this does not do away with the simplistic oppositions with which they organise their accounts: civilisation and barbarity (an opposition inherited from Aristotle), good and evil, natural goodness and fallen nature (oppositions superimposed upon the first by Christianity). These oppositions are at once moral, social, geographical and historical. They are also genetic since Blacks are the sons of Shem, the accursed one.

What is discovered at the end of the voyage is not really other worlds: rather, different moments of our own. The voyage brings together places formerly far apart, the far becomes the near, indeed becomes so dangerously near that it invariably proves necessary to recreate familiar distances to separate the far-off world from the world of Christian civilisation. Some savages are potential converts. These can become citizens of the contemporary world. Even so a natural inferiority is attributed to them; they are assigned the most humble position of all in the hierarchy of the civilised. As for cannibals and rebels (those who attack the colonisers), they are assimilated to what the Christian civilisation situates beyond the protection of divine or human laws. Samuel Purchas writes of the Indian uprising of 1633 in Virginia, and goes on to say:

The very prosperity and pregnant hopes of that Plantation made the Devil and his lims to envy, feare and hate it. Hence that bloudy Massacre which caused almost a sudden Chaos . . . whereof yet we hope not only a recovery but greater advantage, the greatest danger from the Savages growing out of our mens' confidence, which that terrible stroke (except a stupid Devill possesse us) hath cut off; which likewise requires that servile natures be servily used; *that future dangers be prevented by the extirpation of the more dangerous, and commodities also raised out of the servilenesse and serviceablenesse of the rest.*[19]

Their wide diversity notwithstanding, natives are all classed in one of two categories: wild animality, or domesticated or domesticatable animality. But perhaps we should introduce a number of qualifications at this point and note in particular that Samuel Purchas' puritanism leads him to describe that animality as diabolical whereas others use that sort of term much more sparingly. However, it is above all worth noting that what has thus been brought closer thanks to the conquest of space and the manipulation of time is subsequently once more set at a distance but this time in familiar terms.

The recently discovered human groups docilely take their place within the cultural system of the explorers, right at the bottom of the hierarchy of human beings, in a far-away region that is compatible with the symbolic universe of the narrator.

3. A proliferation of forms

But if the diversity of the new human groups was thus easily reduced, the same cannot be said of the goods, riches, plants, marvels and prodigies that such distant lands might proffer. all these were enumerated with a wealth of detail and remarkable precision. The intention was often, no doubt, to encourage the enterprise of colonisation. That was certainly the case with the enthusiastic descriptions to be found in so many accounts, for instance in that – among others – of the mathematician Thomas Harriot who in 1588 published *A Brief and True Report of the New-found Land of Virginia*, where he listed the commercialisable products, edible plants, game and fish and all the materials that could be used for construction.[20] Samuel Purchas is another who devotes nearly thirty pages to these same riches.[21] But in some cases the accounts simply reflect a need to believe in wonders. Sir Walter Raleigh, in his *Discovery of Guiana*, gives a description of a city built entirely of gold. Henry Hawkes goes into ecstasies over the riches of New Spain. John Frampton, an English merchant working in Spain, translated a treatise on the herbal remedies of the New World and expressed his belief that miraculous medicines were there to be had for the taking. Simon Forman, the Elizabethan 'magus', is passionately interested in the *flora* and *fauna* of Virginia and copies into his journals all the information provided by William Strachey's description.[22]

Why such an abundance of details, such a proliferation of natural products? Because the first thing to strike men seeking temptation was the multiplicity of the forms and colours of all these items. V. Jankélévitch writes:

If, then, man is tempted first and foremost by what is perceptible to him through his senses, this is because what is 'sensible' is legion . . . There is an infinite multiplicity of qualities. And it is not by chance that this is so: were there only one quality, there would be no quality at all. There are qualities because quality implies an infinite pluralism, a picturesque heterogeneity, an inexhaustible polymorphism which is the irridescent fabric of the sensible world itself.[23]

The descriptions of travellers mention not only the riches that might be enjoyed but also the monsters that nature, departing from its order, presents as a spectacle to mankind: images of frighteningly composite creatures made up of all kinds of limbs, bodies and elements borrowed from familiar and 'normal' things and creatures (Hieronymus Bosch's imagery springs to mind). The various collections of monsters and prodigies that were in circulation during the Renaissance, those of Boaistuau and Ambroise Paré, not to mention Mandeville's *Voyages*, also represent one aspect of the complex of desire and censure, covetousness and repression, for these images of temptation which were recognised at the same time to be forbidden necessarily generated teratological doubles or counterparts. Thus, according to popular tradition, monstrous births were the fruit of illicit copulations between humans and devils, incubuses or succubuses. Whoever succumbed to temptation engendered monsters and, in the last analysis, whether these took material form or remained internalised was of little importance. Thus, in his *Histoires prodigieuses* (1560), Boaistuau, while concerned to refute popular belief in monstrous births, at the same time recognises the role played by devils in the awakening of desires:

What absurdity, repugnance and confusion there would be on nature's part if it allowed the devil, succubuses and incubuses to conceive from men and men from them! And since the creation of the world down to our own times, how many Monsters the devils would have produced throughout the human race, projecting their seed into the vessels of beasts and in this way, through the confusion of seed, creating an infinity of monsters and prodigies. But we certainly confess (as even Saint Augustine did not deny) that devils may sometimes be transformed into the shape of men or women and perform the works of nature and have dealings with women and men to tempt them into lasciviousness and to mislead and deceive them.[24]

So it is not surprising that the men of the Renaissance should have repeatedly returned to the themes of desire, temptation and covetousness at a juncture in time when, as V. Jankélévitch again writes:

all recognised values appear fluid and once more questionable. After the disappearance of the theocratic Europe of the Middle Ages, everything is *on the point of changing*. Just as tempted man himself is *on the point of* mutating . . . The discovery of distant lands and also of contingency, the transformation of forms, the fact that man feels himself to be changing, – all this inclines him towards metamorphosis. And temptation itself represents an imminent metamorphosis . . . Tempted man is tempted by multiform forms, by teratological polymorphism, by monsters which appear in various shapes and also by woman . . . who is the vehicle of otherness.[25]

We can see how it was that travellers felt bound to deny the plurality of cultures even as they seized upon the proliferation of natural forms: it was a ploy to counter the sense of contingency, the destructive instability that was impressing itself upon society and people's minds: the changes in religion, the fluctuations in currencies, the transformations taking place in systems of production, the discovery of new lands and civilisations. It was better to maintain that unknown societies – just like the monsters, marvels and riches – were the products of nature alone, nature which the devil sometimes leads into error. Better that than to accept that *usage* (conventions), in the sense that Montaigne gives the word, would appear to be contingent, that faith is but one faith in a thousand, that the unshakeable truth might become simply one dubious pronouncement in the ever wide-open field of pronouncements possible.

4. Contingency and necessity

When man travels, he exposes himself to the unpredictable, is at the mercy of accidents, the hazards of chance, the interplay of circumstances; he lays his symbolical universe open to the test of fortune. In this respect, the literature of travel is profoundly attuned to the age's anxieties which, in turn, it both fosters and assuages. It fosters them in that it reveals the multiplicity of life in abundance, comes to the assistance of the devil of temptation and even provokes doubt in his existence – and all this lays the traditional symbolical universe open to question once more. It also assuages them in that it gives meaning to the description of accidents, events and adventures that any man may experience empirically, meaning which makes it possible once more to fit everything into the old familiar history of Judeo-Christian humanity. Nothing could be more illuminating in this respect than the accounts of the adventures that befell Sir Thomas Gates and Sir George Summers (or Somers) in the Bermudas. They are known to be among the sources of *The Tempest*:[26] caught in a storm, their ship was separated from the eight others sailing to Virginia; cast on the reefs, it was stranded there but not destroyed. It was a lucky misfortune, a false contingency, since the hand of providence could be read into it. If the accounts of the voyages had been no more than factual, the event might have seemed accidental. However, it became part of another account superimposed upon the previous ones yet an integral part of them, an account of the obscure but always significant ways of providence. And in that account there is no room for contingency. Each event falls into place within the order and meaning of the divine will which tolerates no accident and never operates capriciously.[27]

5. Single and multiple meanings

We have indicated a number of different themes: the opposition between the near and the far, a layering within the dimension of time of microcosms discovered to be scattered through space – microcosms which the traveller, after approaching them, is at pains to set at a distance; the tension between the one and the many, that is to say between the relatively coordinated whole comprising what one is and what one possesses and the proliferation of images of what it is forbidden to be or to possess, which arouse desires and censures; and, finally, the opposition between the contingent and the necessary. They are themes that cannot all be apprehended on the same narrative level. One of the characteristics of travellers' tales during this period is the way in which events follow one upon another as if along the different layers in flaky pastry, changing in meaning depending on whether they are situated at one level or another. It is not simply a matter of the semantic depth or relative capacity that characterises any narrative signifier, any event described and integrated into a tale, but rather of a process similar to that of the biblical exegesis much favoured in the Middle Ages which consists, for example, in regarding the episodes of the Old Testament as a prefiguration of the stories that make up the New Testament or in reinterpreting them in an allegorical fashion, setting aside the so-called 'literal' meaning. Erich Auerbach has made a study of this process[28] and Tzvetan Todorov points out that each of the events in the *Quête du Graal* is recounted through two types of alternating episodes, the first being the earthly account, the second interpreting the events as manifest signs of the divine will. 'The two types of episode resemble one another (without ever being identical), having the following in common: both the signs and their interpretations are simply *stories*. The story of adventure signifies another story; the spatio-temporal coordinates of the episode change, not its intrinsic nature.'[29]

Despite its apparent novelty, the contemporary tale took the form of a reproduction, or repetition, of a more ancient one – or of a reference source – which appeared to have a definite mythical function since it organised the new tale, giving it a meaning – a meaning the sense of which was immediately evident and convincing only to the human group which had used the reference source as an essential element in the machinery of its own vision of the world.

We can recognise this procedure in the travel tales of a number of puritans. Thus, for William Bradford, the arrival of the puritans in Plymouth is homologous to the arrival of the Jews in the promised land,[30] while for Edward Johnson, who took part in the 'Great Migration' of 1630, Jesus Christ – the latter-day Moses – had in 1628 called upon his people to assemble and depart from an England which had become a place of oppression, and here too there was an obvious homology with the exodus from Egypt.[31]

In *Hakluytus Posthumus or, Purchas His Pilgrimes*, Samuel Purchas systematised the process and theorised about it. The work is a vast collection of travellers' tales in which the compiler sets out to present 'the world to the world' through the accounts of all those who have explored it, ranging from the peregrinations of the kings, patriarchs, apostles, philosophers and others of antiquity right down to contemporary explorations. In it, accounts of imaginary, fabulous or symbolic voyages precede more real or better attested ones as if the latter would acquire meaning thanks to the former and thus make it possible for the world to discover, through the inexhaustible variety of its concrete spaces, the complexity and at the same time homogeneity of its symbolic vistas.

As an introduction, Samuel Purchas offers the reader the voyage of King Solomon's fleet to Ophir.[32] After transcribing the relevant passages from the Bible which provide a literal meaning (I Kings IX, 26–8; X, 11–15, 21; II Chron. IX, 21–7), he adopts the medieval manner and suggests allegorical, anagogical (or mystical) and tropological (or moral) interpretations.

In the literal sense, King Solomon sends his fleet to Ophir, under the leadership of Hiram, in order to obtain gold and other precious substances; and a great abundance of these are brought back to him. But Purchas' commentary is interpretative right from the start: he maintains that the purpose of the voyage is 'to fetch from Ophir Materialls for the Temples structure, and to edifie Christ's Church' (p. 2), and he goes on to justify the inclusion of this story as follows: 'Salomon was first in time, and shall be first here: the first in all things which usually are accounted first, Royaltie, Sanctitie, Wisdome, Wealth, Magnificance, Munificence, Politie, Exploits, Renowne' (p. 3). Note the strong element of historicism in this declaration (temporal precedence explains both the position of the story in the collection and its significance in relation to the collected tales that follow it). Note also the way in which moral qualities are organised with an implicit series in which only the first term is declared; a historical and causal series being, as it were, superimposed upon what follows.

Purchas goes on to say that, according to the allegorical interpretation, Christ sent his Church to journey over the ever-changing seas of this world in order to bring back treasures of wisdom and knowledge. Hiram is the natural man who has always stayed at home – in other words inside himself – and who must leave the shores of earthly wisdom and set forth upon the sea, allowing his sails to fill with the winds, which represent enlightenment for the mind.

According to the anagogical interpretation, the frail craft of Solomon's fleet are the Christians. They cross a stormy sea and reach Ophir which represents the communion of Saints in the universal Holy Church. There, thanks to the water of baptism and repentance, they accede to Faith. They seek for hidden treasures as one seeks for gold and precious stones – but also for straw and hay, for they are unable to purify themselves completely. The straw and hay will be burned when they return to Solomon but they themselves will live to build the Temple in the Holy City, the new Jerusalem. Their journey will thus have contributed towards a metamorphosis.

As for the tropological interpretation, Purchas develops this in a series of rather confused passages on the subject of the legitimacy of voyages of discovery, international trade and conquest in distant lands. The point of departure for his long digression (pp. 9–45) is the following question: did King Solomon have the right to send his fleet to Ophir? Purchas uses the biblical story to condemn expeditions of conquest in the name of tolerance, natural law and the Old and New Testaments. Even proselytism should not be used as a pretext for violence: 'The Gospell is not a sword to take away earth' (p. 39); 'To usher religion by the sword is scarcely approved amongst Mahumetans, which permit men liberty of soule, though not of body' (p. 42). On the other hand, given that the gold used by Solomon was indirectly useful to Hiram, Purchas produces a long *apologia* for commerce and trade, the imperfect means for a return to a primitive human commodity (p. 10):

There is an universall tenure in the Universe, by the Lawes of God and Nature, still remaining to each man as hee is a Man . . . He that hath made all Nations of one blood would . . . that there should still remain mutual Necessitie, the Mother of mutuall Commerce, that one should not bee hungry and another drunken but the superfluitie of one countrey should supply the necessities of another.

These different interpretations are important less for their content than by reason of the very fact of their juxtaposition. During the Elizabethan period all travel tales were more than *just* travel tales since the reader immediately placed them in a category constituted by other accounts of a similar type and they conveyed far more than they described literally, given the prevalence of the habit of interpreting them allegorically. Purchas devotes a long passage to the theme of human life seen as a pilgrimage or as a peregrination, motivated by original sin; the account he refers back to being, in this instance, the descriptions of the peregrinations of Christ and his apostles, 'the first planters of the Gospell' (p. 135).

The various 'levels' of meaning, the various stories contained within the discourse are not really integrated with one another and the narrative is constantly punctuated by heavily discursive passages as Purchas operates both as narrator and at the same time his own critical interpreter. However, the multiplicity of interpretations modulates and reinforces a single ideological system. The same can certainly not be said of the dramatic narrative constituted by *The Tempest*.

6. An equivocal world

The spectator discovers the world that *The Tempest* represents very much as the jester and the butler discover Caliban. At first Trinculo judges him to be fish rather than flesh, then flesh rather than fish since his fins look like arms. Stephano counts his four legs and his two voices and pronounces him 'a most delicate monster' (II, ii, 91) and throughout the play the 'moon-calf' thus discovered retains his, so to speak, dubious ontological status which the oxymoron that Stephano uses serves to underline.[33] This figure, who can be seen either as a complete and irreducible contradiction or, alternatively, as having two positive but separate natures, each stemming from a different scale of values,[34] gives the reader a feeling of instability that remains with him through to the end of the play.

Right from the opening scenes, in fact, *The Tempest* makes us constantly change our minds about the events shown and the nature of the illusion that the play presents. We see the storm (I, i) as a real storm and the shipwreck as a real shipwreck. But then we learn that the storm has been conjured up by a character in the play. Its reality is of the first degree for some of the characters but only of the second degree for others and also for us, the spectators. We are therefore bound to accept it as both real and an illusion and, on top of that, as real even while it is illusory. The author manifestly situates it in a zone where rain is wet and hulls are holed on reefs, but at the same time also in a place where 'wished-for' storms can be made to materialise and where the thunderbolt that falls from the sky is immediately invested with more significance than simply that of fire.

Whether accepted or not, this plurality of viewpoints is maintained at a number of different levels in the dramatic discourse. Shakespeare has Prospero perform the five magic actions in such a way that 'the formal and symbolic qualities of the masque emphasise the structurally important episodes in the action'.[35] These actions are the enchantment of Ferdinand (I, ii), the bewitching of the conspirators, Antonio and Sebastian (II, i), the disappearance of the banquet which Prospero, from his superior position, has organised in order to cast a spell over his enemies (III, iii), the masque of Iris, Ceres and Juno through which he celebrates the betrothal of Miranda and Ferdinand (IV, i) and, finally, after Caliban, Trinculo and Stephano have been hunted down by 'divers spirits in the shape of dogs and hounds', the discovery of Miranda and Ferdinand 'playing at chess' (V, i).[36] But on top of this integration of the masque in the play, by means of which Shakespeare creates or reinforces the supernatural atmosphere of the work, the influence of the masque can be detected in the general organisation of the play, even if – as Kermode maintains – the work is deliberately constructed in accordance with the rules of classical dramatic structure.[37] What we are given is a synthesis which allows us to recognise that, as in a masque, the subject of the play is 'metamorphosis' and it ends 'with the thought not of eternity but of the swift flight of time and of the inevitable end of beauty and delight',[38] even as it simultaneously offers a promise or hope of eternal spring. Better still, this synthesis explains the play's double temporal structure which is contradictory and also leads to a bitter-sweet ending.[39]

This plurality is made much more evident by the disparity between what the various characters in the play know, or between what some characters know on the one hand and what the spectators know on the other – what Bertrand Evans calls 'discrepant awarenesses' or 'the gap between awarenesses'.[40] It is a stratagem that is often exploited in the theatre, especially in comedy, and it is particularly striking in *The Tempest* where Prospero always knows more than anyone else. This has the effect of making the spectator see and judge events from his point of view – even though it is not possible, in the conflict between him and Caliban, for example, entirely to eliminate or discredit the reasoning of the latter. The tension thus created contributes in its turn towards preventing the spectator from passing unequivocal judgement upon the conduct of most of the characters.

The themes conveyed through the images or metaphors all combine to produce the same effect, namely to create the feeling of a fleeting, changing universe in which reality is elusive and all creatures and things are involved in a constant metamorphosis. According to Brower, the terms that point to this pattern or explain this effect are 'strange-wondrous', 'sleep-and-dream', 'sea-tempest', 'music-and-noise', 'slavery-freedom', and 'sovereignty-conspiracy'.[41]

Shakespeare uses this plurality of viewpoints to show how the castaways discover their state to be as uncertain as Caliban's. Time and again he has them argue about the nature of what they see and hear, and wonder about the destiny of those whom they love: 'Where should this music be? I' th'air or th'earth?', Ferdinand wonders as he wanders about the island, alone (I, ii, 390). Is the grass before Gonzalo and Sebastian green or brown? Is the air fragrant or foul? Have their clothes been stained by the sea-water or not (II, i)? Is the island inhabited by wild beasts or not (II, i, 305–20)? At the point when the 'strange shapes' set out a banquet before the group of aristocrats, Alonso exclaims: 'I cannot too much muse. / Such shapes, such gesture and such sound . . . ' (III, iii, 36–7), but even as he speaks the shapes fade away, leaving the dishes behind. It is then that Antonio and Sebastian declare themselves ready to believe the fables of travellers, and Gonzalo replies to the king who fears to taste the food before them:

> Faith, sir, you need not fear. When we were boys,
> Who would believe that there were mountaineers
> Dew-lapp'd like bulls, whose throats had hanging at 'em
> Wallets of flesh? Or that there were such men
> Whose heads stood in their breasts? Which now we find
> Each putter-out of five for one will bring us
> Good warrant of. (III, iii, 43–9)

Gonzalo urges the king to eat. The dishes are no more dangerous than the tales of those adventurers are false. It is all in perfect conformity with the natural order. But then, alas, all the food suddenly disappears and a harpy materialises. None of it was natural after all: and who is to be believed now? Were the adventurers lying? And what was the Elizabethan spectator supposed to believe? That 'mountaineers dewlapp'd like bulls' do not exist but harpies do? That neither harpies nor that kind of 'mountaineer' exist? That the whole world represented in the play was pure fantasy? Quite apart from its most explicit theme, namely retribution for sins, and quite apart from its relation to the question of desire and censure, this scene is the most ironical commentary on the veracity of travellers' tales that could be imagined.

But Shakespeare carries his poetic meditation upon the relationship between language, reality and truth even further. First, we have Prospero's famous speech in which, speaking of the elusive actors in his masque and, by implication, of the actors in the Globe theatre, of the Globe itself and yet beyond that of the living creatures and world that surrounds the theatre, he declares that all this will dissolve and totally pass away. Then there are all the expressions of the incredulity that assails the castaways at the moment of the comic catastrophe. 'This is as strange a maze as e'er men trod' (V, i, 242), says Alonso: for his labyrinth exists not only in space, a testing place where these erring aristocrats must blindly wander about; it also exists in-between illusion and truth, between what has substance and what has none – a specifically human location where the symbolic world and the incomprehensible manifestations of reality interact.

Thus, the world of *The Tempest* is presented to us with all the uncertainties that might arise in the mind of an Elizabethan reading some traveller's tale. Shakespeare uses these uncertainties as one of his themes, projecting them on to the entire dramatic work which thus becomes a discourse on both the world at large and itself. Neither true nor false but at the same time both true and false; stemming from what is imaginary yet destined to affect real human beings; now reality expressed through imagery, now a discourse expressed in actions and tableaux, now imagery loaded or overlaid with meaning. In the end, the play offers illusory certainty and uncertain reality so that, when Gonzalo rediscovers Prospero whom he had believed dead, he says:

> Whether this be
> Or be not, I'll not swear

and Prospero replies:

> You do yet taste
> Some subtleties o' the isle, that will not let you
> Believe things certain.   (V, i, 122–5)

7. The near and the far, or Caliban

The opposition between the near and the far remains a powerful one even in our own day. It is a theme taken up by proverbs (never trust a stranger; no man is prophet in his own land; out of sight, out of mind)[42] and many other expressions. It has to do with space, time and kinship relations. It makes it possible to bestow some unity upon different places, periods and human behaviour patterns. Thus, in most societies it is forbidden to marry one who is too close (prohibition of incest or endogamy) and also one who is too distant (outside the zone within which exchanges are made). The marriage between Othello and Desdemona is a transgression, bound to be attended by misfortune. In *The Tempest* the shipwrecked aristocrats are returning from Tunis where Alonso has married his daughter 'to an African'. This distant marriage is presented as the cause of the misfortunes that have befallen the king of Naples and his train. Despite their quarrel, Alonso and his brother Sebastian are certainly in agreement at least on this point. There is a connection between the distant marriage, misfortune and death.

> *Alonso*: . . . Would I had never
> Married my daughter there! for, coming thence,
> My son is lost, and, in my rate, she too,
> Who is so far from Italy removed
> I ne'er again shall see her. O thou mine heir
> Of Naples and Milan, what strange fish
> Hath made his meal on thee? (II, i, 103–9)

> *Sebastian*: Sire, you may thank yourself for this great loss,
> That would not bless our Europe with your daughter,
> But rather loose her to an African; (II, i, 119–21)

> . . . the fair soul herself
> Weigh'd between loathness and obedience, at
> Which end o'th'beam should bow. (II, i, 126–8)

Far away is where idyllic lands are to be found, improbable societies laden with symbolic meaning and regions half-way between heaven and earth. Take, for example, the Phaeacia of the *Odyssey*, where men are as other men are but where:

Alcinous' garden is a magic garden, unaffected by the passing of the seasons; an eternal Zephyr blows through it, the vine displays its flowers, its green grapes and its ripened grapes all at the same time. In short, although only one orchard is involved, it forms a proper little golden age enclave in the heart of Phaeacia.[43]

In *The Tempest*, what is peculiar about the land is that nobody cultivates it, it seems possible to live off it simply by picking and gathering its produce. The Golden Age and Utopia are present here, but in the form of desires, dreams and promises: the world of fruitful cultivation and overflowing abundance in the masque of Ceres, Iris and Juno (IV, i); the world of the Utopian community in Gonzalo's day-dream.[44] The island itself, situated somewhere between Tunisia and Italy, is an intermediate spot, neither near nor far, yet both near and far, beyond the city and as far away from cultivated fields as those blessed isles where everything is produced in such profusion that there is no call for servants.

As in other travellers' tales, we can also discern a critical image of the society from which these characters originate. The many conspiracies convey this theme. As Kermode has shown,[45] both Caliban and his accomplices on the one hand and the group of aristocrats on the other make it possible to suggest the formidable superiority of the civilised world and equally its formidable corruption.

Finally, in far-away lands one comes across creatures which are either more or less than human. In Circe, Odysseus discovers a being who possesses the faculty of speech, to be sure, but who is in reality the terrible goddess with a human voice; at another stage in his journey, he 'wonders among "what eaters of bread" he is living, that is, among what kind of men; but the point is that he is not among bread-eaters at all, he is among Lotus-eaters of Laestrygonians (eaters of men)',[46] who are inferior to men. Shakespeare, for his part, presents us with Prospero who, by reason of his magical powers, is practically an equal of the gods, a Caliban whose position on the scale of living creatures is extremely low, and an Ariel who is a powerful sprite. And distance – or, to put it another way, closeness in a far-away place – causes Ferdinand to take Miranda for a goddess and her to take him for a god. Meanwhile, Caliban magnifies a poor drunkard and sets him in his Pantheon while that drunkard sees Caliban as more bestial than he really is. As for the marvellous New World, Miranda mistakenly identifies it with the old one when she sees the aristocrats appear in their varying degrees of repentance. Her vision magnifies what she sees (V, i, 181).

Distancing is a fundamental element in such bypassing of the ordinary human scale. Through its presentation of what is more and what is less than human, the work defines what is ideally human, what man must or should be in his own near and familiar universe. Barely sixty years after *The Tempest*, Milton's nephew, Edward Phillips, wrote as follows: 'Those who have either of these qualifications singly [i.e. *melior natura* and education] may justly be termed *Men*; those who have both united in a happy conjunction, *more* than *Men*, those who have neither of them in any competent measure . . . *less* than *Men* . . . '.[47]

However, it is possible for the two terms of the opposition to come together or exist one within the other. What one would like to conjure up in the immediate world can be projected on to a distant one. Caliban, who inherits the island, has most of the characteristics of a savage. He is a kind of Indian, a fabulous being, half-man, half-beast, who needs to be educated but proves ineducable. He is a bastard without a father, one whose nature is suspect from the start, in contrast to Miranda who is certain of her paternal descent. In the list of *dramatis personae*, Caliban is described as a 'salvage and deformed slave', the first term indicating his bestiality, the second the ugliness of both his physical and his moral aspect. As for the third, 'slave', it may refer either to the social situation or to his natural disposition or to both at once. It is possible to become a slave through an accident of fortune or as a result of war; but one may also be a slave by nature, as when one's disposition is to subject oneself to unworthy or despotic masters. That is a Platonic idea echoed by Aristotle and to be found, for example, in Etienne de la Boetie's *Discours de la servitude volontaire*. It is true that Shakespeare gives Caliban excellent reasons for feeling animosity towards Prospero, so that we might take him to be a slave simply through an accident of fortune:

> The island's mine, by Sycorax my mother,
> Which thou tak'st from me. When thou cam'st first,
> Thou strok'st me, and made much of me . . .
> . . . I am all the subjects that you have,
> Which first was mine own King: and here you sty me
> In this hard rock . . .   (I, iii, 333–5; 343–5)

But we soon discover that he rushes into servitude even when striving for freedom. When Stephano, the drunken butler, appears, Caliban immediately casts him in the role of master, his new master, his God: 'I will kiss thy foot: I prithee, be my god' (II, ii, 149) and at the end of this scene he exclaims:

> *'Ban, 'Ban, Cacaliban*
> *Has a new master: – get a new man.*
> Freedom, high-day! high-day, freedom! freedom,
> High-day, freedom!   (II, ii, 184–7)

This is certainly not an image of the 'good savage', dwelling in the Isles of the Blessed. In fact, one of the play's themes is that man's *melior natura* cannot develop in the savage state, and so it is impossible to discover it in far-off places. Nature provides certain potentialities, good or evil, which only the appropriate nurture can, in certain cases, bring to fruition. Liberal though it might appear, this is in truth a remarkably conservative view for it significantly restricts the possibilities of successful fruition: for a fully accomplished being to emerge, a Miranda, for example, there must be a combination of favourable genetic circumstances (a choice line of aristocratic forefathers), together with an education that satisfies a series of strict norms. It is thus not possible for those with some defect of birth or education to belong to the clan of human beings worthy of admiration nor, *a fortiori*, for those who fall short on both these counts. The 'creature of a distant land' who is discovered on the island was planning to pervert a pure lineage by violating Miranda:

> O ho, O ho! would't had been done!
> Thou didst prevent me; I had peopled else
> This isle with Calibans.   (I, ii, 351–3)

Education can gain no purchase on him; on the contrary:

> A devil, a born devil, on whose nature
> Nurture can never stick; on whom my pains,
> Humanely taken, all, all lost, quite lost;

> And as with age his body uglier grows,
> So his mind cankers.   (IV, i, 188–92)

It is the view that was later to encompass those far-away creatures, the Indians and the Blacks of North America.[48]

Meanwhile, through his portrayal of a being situated outside his own cultural universe, Shakespeare suggests a number of the features of that universe itself. The being who is most far away is also the nearest of all, for it is first and foremost the internal being who threatens to shatter the norms that Elizabethan culture imposed upon the English of the period. And the English defended that culture even as they defended themselves against it. Caliban is a representation of what the Elizabethans saw in the passions or in instinct: a principle of anarchy and destruction, of violence and danger, that threatened the established order and also the personal order that each individual must compose within himself in order to control and overcome a 'nature' that was conceived to be a chaos of greedy impulses. When Spenser's witch sees her son consumed with passion for Florimell, she despatches in her pursuit a hideous beast, the embodiment of desire for whoever holds desire in horror:

> Eftsoones out of her hidden caue she cald
> An hideous beast, of horrible aspect,
> That could the stoutest courage haue appald;
> Monstrous, misshapt, and all his back was spect
> With thousand spots of colours queint elect,
> Thereto so swift, that it all beasts did pass:
> Like neuer yet did liuing eye detect;
> But likest it to a *Hyena* was,
> That feeds on womens flesh, as others feede on gras.
>   (*The Faerie Queene*, III, vii, 22)

Caliban has tried to violate Miranda and that represents a triple transgression: it is wrong for desire to satisfy itself in defiance of the rules, wrong for an inferior creature to be united with the daughter of a duke, wrong for a guest to betray the trust of one who offers him asylum. Furthermore, in a remarkable amplification of the image of violation, he then seeks to assassinate Prospero (III, ii, 85).

The Elizabethans had already devised figures to represent characteristics such as these, in particular the *homo ferus*, the wild man or man of the woods. Substantial iconographical evidence for this figure exists and, as Kermode notes, 'portraits' of him appear in the pastorals of the period: the witch's son mentioned above, Bremo in *Mucedorus*, and a number of others in court entertainments.[49] Shakespeare, for his part, assigns the characteristics in question to a creature in a far-away land. This confusion between the bestiality of a creature near at hand and a creature from far away was to appear even more clearly in Aurelian Townshend's antimasques of the

Tempe Restored (1631): 'Indians and Barbarians, who naturally are bestiall, and others which are voluntaries and but halfe transformed into beastes.' His last antimasque incorporated the following significant list of characters: '2 Indians, 2 Hounds, 2 Apes, 1 Asse, 2 Lyons, 2 Barbarians, 2 Hogges.'[50]

We should also note that Caliban, the son of Sycorax, the fruit of fornication between a witch and an incubus, is affiliated to the sorcerers and witches who were hunted down under James I (and it was of witchcraft that the puritans were to accuse the Indians of America).

But Caliban is more than simply a counter-type which makes it possible to convey the contrast between fallen nature and Christian, aristocratic civilisation. He also represents the counter-type of the social being who in all circumstances owes obedience to the authorities. The two themes are linked since those authorities and the social order that they guarantee derive their legitimacy from the natural order. The revolt of the wild, colonised Caliban against his White master can be associated with the various movements of defiance or rebellion that periodically agitated England under the Tudors and Stuarts. Whether the origin of these movements were catholic or puritan, aristocratic or popular was of little importance. They were conspiracies, just as Caliban's revolt was, and conspiracy was a word and a practice that the average Elizabethan held in horror. Thus, in an abortive attempt made by Caliban and his acolytes, what is being condemned and ridiculed is the idea that the populace, always given an unfortunate image in Shakespeare's work, has any right to rebel.

The savage who revolts is thus assimilated to the rebellious, the factious, the defiant. Even grumbling is forbidden him. By the same token, the rebel is attributed all the unfavourable characteristics that are associated with the savage. The conjunction of these two figures who mutually reinforce each other's worst characteristics shows the extent to which political intolerance and cultural intolerance are linked: for the foreigner, the allogene, the 'deviant' exist at the heart of society as well as on its periphery. If destructive constraints are exercised within the familiar universe, they will sooner or later also be exercised on its frontiers. Whatever resists will be destroyed. The outside is treated the same as the inside. The far is trampled underfoot just as the near is.

Caliban passes through three stages: at first taken in as a human being by Prospero, he is soon reduced to the position of a servant – or a domesticated animal – who is shut up in his den. That is what his status remains so long as he is obedient, whether he likes it or no. After the failure of his conspiracy, he is no longer a domesticated animal: now he is treated as a wild beast, hunted by a pack of dogs. The distinction was to have a prosperous future.[51] In America the first colonisers were soon to be involved with two categories of 'savages': Indians and Blacks. Attitudes to the two groups and the treatment meted out to them were to be very different: the Indian was assimilated to wild nature, untamed nature that must be dominated and overcome; for him there was no quarter given. The Black, on the other hand, was seen as a domestic animal, one necessary to the exploitation of the continent and the domination of nature by the White man. In Caliban we find a combination of these two categories which were to become differentiated in the process of colonising the continent. From the Whites' point of view, Indians and Blacks both had features of animality but the former were like wild beasts, the latter like tamed ones. They tried to exterminate the Indians and to get the Blacks to reproduce themselves, making sure that they were prevented from elaborating their own cultural world. This policy was justified by declaring them to be ineducable. For one group, then, genocide; for the other, ethnocide and perpetual servitude.

8. Desire and censure, or Ariel

Prospero's island is a place where desires are aroused to be satisfied only selectively, according to whether or not they are presented as legitimate. One could also reverse the argument and say that we are here in a dramatic world where the legitimacy of a desire is manifested by the fact that it is permitted to be satisfied. The provocation of desires is one of the features of travel literature and it is also a feature of *The Tempest*, where the theme is elaborated with particular care: first and foremost through the figure of Ariel, the *agent provocateur* as Jan Kott would have it: Ariel is the tempter, but he is also the one who prevents illegitimate desires from being satisfied. First, he conjures up the titillating vision, then its monstrous shape. He himself is polymorphous and changeable, just like the reality that is perceptible through the senses, whose qualities are legion: the character whom critical tradition holds to be the most impalpable and ethereal serves to embody the irridescent quality of things to which our desires reach out.

In the form, first, of Saint-Elmo's fire, he directly counters the desire for power of the great in this world, humiliating them by unleashing the elements against it. Transformed into a nymph, he draws Ferdinand towards Miranda and, since he is invisible (except to Prospero and the audience), when Ferdinand discovers Miranda he thinks she is the nymph or goddess who is accompanied by Ariel's music: 'Most sure the goddess / On whom these airs attend' (I, ii, 424–5). As for Ariel's song, it tells of metamorphosis, the journey across the seas with their transforming power, mutation beyond the death of the mortal being that was Alonso.

By means of solemn music, Ariel sends Alonso and his train to sleep, all except for Antonio and Sebastian, and this gives them their chance to plot the assassination of the king of Naples – but he rouses Gonzalo in time to thwart their plans. Then his music distracts Caliban's new friends just as they are reaching an agreement to take over the island between them. At the banquet – which is both a real temptation for the castaways, who have had nothing to eat, and at the same time a traditional image for everything that attracts the senses[52] – he substitutes for it the monstrous figure of the harpy, and their frustrated desire now leads the sinners into a purifying madness. Similarly, having cast a spell upon the other three conspirators and lured them into a stinking bog, he brings them glittering, tawdry finery and this distracts them from their murderous schemes by arousing in them another desire that sidetracks them. Finally, it is also he, together with Prospero, who sets the hounds on the three conspirators. He is thus the most multiple of characters, one who implies an infinite plurality: Saint-Elmo's fire, nymph, harpy, hunter, music sad or gay, ready to respond to the 'good pleasure' of a master whose desires are legitimate and just, able to fly, to swim, to plunge into fire, to ride the clouds: such is 'Ariel and all his quality' (I, ii, 193).[53] In this respect he is related to the 'trickster' who appears in certain myths. But his presence and function at Prospero's side will certainly seem less strange if one considers that it is only to be expected that Prospero, so skilled in theurgy, should have at his side a figure analogous to the diabolical servant of Doctor Faustus, who is so skilled in sorcery. The two pairs, Prospero/Ariel and Faustus/Mephistopheles are symmetrical, homologous and opposite. With a schematic comparison, sequence by sequence,[54] it is easy to indicate their similar and opposite features. However, while Prospero's 'desires' are legitimate, those of Faustus are not. Mephistopheles must make the sinner succumb to wicked temptation in order to destroy him and extend the dominion of evil, whereas Ariel is the agent of a design in which temptation tries the soul and punishment is a means of redemption: the purpose is to save those who err and extend the dominion of the good. Just as Prospero practises a kind of Machiavellianism for the good, Ariel is a tempter for the good, just the opposite from Faustus and Mephistopheles. The themes of desire, temptation and censure thus lie at the heart of both dramatic works. Mephistopheles, like Ariel, is a creature of metamorphoses. His changes of form and the marvels that he conjures up underline the relation between desire and the plurality of the perceptible – or the temptations which one resists, repulses or shuns.

However, Ariel is but one of the inhabitants of this island where all the characters come together, and the place itself is the object of covetous desire. Prospero has seized it. Caliban lays claim to it and, together with Stephano and Trinculo, wishes to make himself master of it. Even the worthy Gonzalo sketches out a contradictory plan of domination in which he sees himself as the king of an egalitarian, 'communist' society. Furthermore, to the extent that in this play dreams of sovereignty are echoes one of another, the object of Antonio's and Sebastian's desires is analogous to that of Caliban's and also to what Antonio, in the play's prehistory, has already made his own.

And if Ariel's special role is to meet Prospero's desires, to provoke attempts at satisfaction and then conjure up obstacles, most of the other characters also play the role of tempter or temptress, either deliberately or involuntarily. Miranda arouses the desires of Caliban, Caliban leads his acolytes into temptation just as Antonio does Sebastian, and Prospero engineers the meeting between Ferdinand and Miranda. Hardly a single character avoids some temptation or other: in Alonso's case it is despair, in that of Prospero himself, vengeance. The temptation that assails each one reveals his character and defines him. Thus, the island is a revealer of truth.

It is also significant that for all these human beings the visit to the island is, in both a literal and a metaphorical sense, a detour. The deviation by way of the island from the direct route from Tunis to Naples makes it possible to put straight what had been warped out of true form and to restore to the rectitude of the norm these characters whose desires have been changed, frustrated or fulfilled. For no society can tolerate the fulfilment of all desires, nor even that those considered legitimate should be immediately satisfied. Between desire and satisfaction stand rules and obstacles and it is by these that social beings are preserved, or believe themselves preserved, from animality. Thus, even legitimate desire must make a detour which consists in the individual coming to terms with the norms of the collectivity. It is not seemly that Ferdinand should possess Miranda before the appropriate rites have been celebrated. And for Ferdinand, the detour by way of the island, which was the prelude to the arousal of his desire, is complicated by other detours, namely the trials of waiting that Prospero imposes upon him:

> If thou dost break her virgin-knot before
> All sanctimonious ceremonies may
> With full and holy rite be minister'd,
> No sweet aspersion shall the heavens let fall
> To make this contract grow; but barren hate,
> Sour-ey'd disdain and discord shall bestrew
> The union of your bed with weeds so loathly
> That you shall hate it both.   (IV, i, 15–22)

As for illegitimate desire, it is punished, in the play, by frustration. Sebastian, Alonso and Antonio, who have satisfied or tried to satisfy their illegitimate desires, have to undergo the trial of the conjured-up Banquet whose effect, in *The Tempest*, is that of an anticipatory metaphor: the object which they have illegitimately seized will – just like the feast – be taken from them and their illicit ambition will be frustrated just as their appetite is. Punishment is proportionate to the wildness of the character's dreams: some are driven mad, others changed into the quarry just when they believed themselves the hunters. Led astray by Ariel, all of them pass through the labyrinth with all its multiple detours, which the island is. And after temptation comes the moral detour – to which Antonio will submit only under duress – by way of a qualifying and transforming trial which renders them capable of taking part in the final comic catastrophe and reconciliation.

9. Union and separation, or marriage

A traveller goes away from what is near to journey to what he is far away from. Shakespeare's last plays tell the story of families 'whose various members are for many years scattered, in the end to be miraculously reunited'.[55] Although less obvious than in *Pericles* or in *The Winter's Tale*, this is a theme that is also present in *The Tempest*, and, through the oppositions that it sets up, it makes it possible to seize upon numerous homologies.

In the first place, *The Tempest* presents a collection of characters who have been separated, in scandalous circumstances, from their proper functions, from the place where their roots are or where they were in their element. Prospero has been separated from his dukedom and from the people who owed him allegiance: his brother is 'the ivy which had hid my princely trunk' (I, ii, 86). Miranda has been ejected from Milan along with him. Caliban has been separated from his island: 'And here you sty me / In this hard rock, whiles you do keep from me / The rest o'th'island' (I, ii, 344–6). Even Ariel, who was first imprisoned in an oak tree, is prevented by Prospero from rejoining the elements.

The play also presents characters who have illegitimately united together or become allies, or who have attempted illicit unions or assumed roles to which they had no right. Antonio forced Prospero away 'To have no screen between this part he played / And him he played it for' (I, ii, 107–8). He then contracted a sinister alliance with the king of Naples who made the dukedom subject to his kingdom. On the island he enters into alliance with Sebastian, with the intention of assassinating Alonso. Caliban acquires Stephano and Trinculo as allies with equally criminal intent: he attempts to violate Miranda. And this attempt at rape could be interpreted as a reference to Prospero's incestuous desire for his daughter: it thus evokes the possibility of another sinister union, a consequence of previous separations, for the island is devoid of any men worthy of Miranda.

In accordance with a system of homologies often adopted by Shakespeare, these illegitimate unions and separations are matched one against another on a number of levels – individual, social and cosmic. Thus the storm itself is a sign of the disorder of the elements as well as being the instrument of a subsequent return to order. The consequence of earlier misdeeds is the presence of all these people upon the island where nothing is cultivated, where visions of happiness, fertility and normal rhythms of cultivation can only be perceived in the imagination or in a distant past. The moment when the situation begins to be rectified is when there is a favourable conjunction of the stars which must be seized upon immediately. The marriage between Prospero, his star and his fortunes prefigures the reunions that are effected at the end of the play:

> . . . my zenith doth depend upon
> A most auspicious star, whose influence
> If now I court not, but omit, my fortunes,
> Will ever after droop.   (I, ii, 181–4)

But that conjunction no longer exists by the time that Antonio tries to persuade Sebastian that this is his chance (II, i, 202) and that he is letting fortune sleep (II, i, 211). Now it is the disoriented travellers, deprived of their ship, their homes and their hopes, who must wander about the island and undergo what Prospero has undergone. The theme of families separated is also present. Alonso bewails the loss of his son and of his daughter Claribel whose distant marriage is interpreted as a sinister disjunction; Ferdinand believes his father dead; Sebastian agrees to assassinate his own brother.

The trials that the miscreants are to undergo will separate them one from another, revealing to each his own true moral situation so that each will be able to rediscover himself as well as his companions. And it is through a legitimate union, the future marriage of the son of the king of Naples and the daughter of the duke of Milan, that the final reunion is accomplished. At that point everything changes in significance and meaning, or at least appears to. The villains become 'goodly creatures' in Miranda's eyes; the old world becomes the new. Following up the marvels that the travellers have experienced on the island comes Gonzalo's swan-song which retraces the principal events in the story and lends them an interpretation which ascribes much to the hand of providence and thereby magnifies the part played by the miraculous:

> Was Milan thrust from Milan, that his issue
> Should become Kings of Naples? O, rejoice
> Beyond a common joy! . . .

The duke's separation from his dukedom of Milan, and the new union – to be a fruitful one this time – between Milan and Naples, are noted in such a way as to establish a link of causality between them, and Gonzalo then goes on to say:

> . . . and set it down
> With gold on lasting pillars: in one voyage
> Did Claribel her husband find at Tunis.

Instead of being considered as a separation from those near to her, this far-away marriage is now seen as a favourable union.

> And Ferdinand, her brother, found a wife
> Where he himself was lost, Prospero his dukedom
> In a poor isle, and all of us ourselves
> When no man was his own.   (V, i, 205–13)

Now the island becomes no more than 'a poor isle' where all these redis-coveries of one another and of themselves happen to have taken place. Before returning to the City Prospero must divest himself of a power which, like that of the Pythia, can only be exercised outside the City. Perhaps Caliban will regain his island and Ariel return to the elements. Once again, the moral, social and natural orders are at one.[56] Only unity of this kind can hold out a promise of fertility for the young couple, for the two States and for nature itself, as could be shown by an analysis of the masque of Iris, Ceres and Juno. Ceres even expresses her hope of an impossible union – between autumn and spring:

> *Spring come to you at the farthest,*
> *In the very end of harvest!* (IV, i, 114–15)

It is a hope that accompanies the newly wed couple as they return to the Old World. For, for Shakespeare, the Golden Age is not to be found on the Isles of the Blessed, but in the discoveries, visions and hopes of men. It is an ideal that only the human will can bring into being, on condition that men agree upon what the natural order is, make the effort to control their appetites, discipline their desires and promote harmony. That is what accounts for the overwhelming impression of sadness that the play transmits through its happy ending.

10. The monopoly of discourse, or Prospero

In *The Tempest* any particular event is liable to be given a number of dif-ferent interpretations by the agents of the action or by the audience. There is, however, a fundamental difference between this play and, say, a bible story, to which any of the four traditional interpretations may be applied: Shakespeare makes this possibility of multiple readings one of the very themes of his work. The critique of the tale is integrated within the tale itself, as a meta-tale which, incidentally, may quite well become or re-become, the tale itself.

I have attempted elsewhere[57] to show how Prospero engineers the final reconciliation, leaving the role of commentator to Gonzalo so that he may encourage a belief in the version of providential intervention, but also how all this is presented with sufficient perspective for the perplexities of the attentive spectator to remain unresolved even when the play is over. The dis-tant voyage of Claribel changes in meaning depending on when it is reported and who reports it: to some it represents a misfortune, to others an oppor-tunity (notably to Antonio, when he is trying to win over Sebastian (II, i, 250–55)), to others still a piece of good fortune. In similar fashion, the general significance of what happens changes depending upon whether one is of the opinion that the comic catastrophe is directly engineered by providence or, on the contrary, by an agent in the action who disguises himself as providence. The difference between *The Tempest* and the other comedies of the last period stems from the fact that the triumph of good is here brought about by violence disguised as magic and here there is no question of restoring a natural order postulated by the play as existing in its own right and outside the framework of the play itself.

At this point in time, at the end of the Renaissance, when men's shaken convictions were being crystallised in a multitude of philosophic statements regarding the place and role of man in the world, Shakespeare creates a dramatic system within which uncertainty is the rule and certainty an illusion produced by naivety or imposed by force. He creates a character who acts as the master of discourse and of events and who 'forces the convictions' of the other agents of the action. Prospero's pronouncements are given weight less by the truth than by a disguised violence. The master of discourse and events is therefore the master of meaning. In this way Shakespeare makes us sense that no discourse may enjoy a monopoly, that where human matters are concerned there is never a single, undivided truth, that meaning is never fixed unless imposed by violence.[58]

APPENDIX I
A schematic comparison between a number of sequences from
The Tragic Story of Doctor Faustus **and**
The Tempest

1. Ariel's liberty before his imprisonment by Sycorax. – Mephistopheles' bondage before his meeting with Faustus.
2. Prospero's alienation at the moment of his meeting with Ariel. – Faustus' liberty at the moment of his meeting with Mephistopheles.
3. In accordance with a contract for services rendered (Prospero having liberated Ariel from the oak tree in which he has been held prisoner for twelve years), Prospero acquires the services of Ariel. – In accordance with a contract that stipulates a service to be rendered (Faustus will deliver up his soul), Faustus acquires the services of Mephistopheles.
4. Ariel is subject to Prospero for twelve years. The total period of his alienation is thus twenty four years – Mephistopheles is subject to Faustus for twenty-four years.
5. Prospero sets Ariel free. Both characters find freedom once more. – Mephistopheles makes Faustus his prisoner. Continued state of alienation for Mephistopheles, perpetual bondage for Faustus.

APPENDIX II
Metamorphoses and apparitions

1. The devil changes himself into an old Franciscan friar. Mephistopheles makes Helen appear. – Ariel changes himself into a nymph and then into a harpy. He makes Miranda appear.
2. Mephistopheles lays on a parade of the seven deadly sins. – Ariel engineers the masque of his own figures.
3. Mephistopheles sends the cardinals to sleep. – Ariel sends Alonso and his train to sleep.
4. An invisible Faustus has the pope listen to his voice, in a comic scene. – An invisible Ariel has Caliban listen to his voice, in a comic scene.
5. Faustus removes dishes in the course of a banquet. – Ariel makes banquet dishes disappear.
6. Faustus changes Benvolio into a stag and conjures up a pack of hounds. Benvolio and Martino are dragged, the one through brambles, the other through a lake of mud and filth, as a punishment for having plotted against Faustus. – Prospero and Ariel set the dogs on Caliban and his accomplices. Caliban, Trinculo and Stephano are dragged through brambles and dumped in a stinking bog to punish them for having plotted against Prospero.
7. Faustus dumbfounds the carter and the horsedealer. – Prospero paralyses Ferdinand.
8. Mephistopheles brings grapes in winter to the Duchess of Vanholt. Faustus dreams of dividing the world into two circles, one for winter, the other for summer. He proves himself capable of proffering the fruits of the summer even during the winter. – Ceres expresses a wish for an eternal spring and the eternal banishment of winter.

8. Incest and social relations in *'Tis Pity She's a Whore* by John Ford

1. Incest, morality and corruption

Critics generally interpret the incest between Giovanni and his sister Annabella as a sin, a prohibition transgressed – even if transgressed in the name of a love that is entirely pure or, as S. P. Sherman at the beginning of the century held, a love that the author 'crowns with roses'.[1] That is an idea that H. J. Oliver[2] attacks when he points out that nobody believes that just because Shakespeare endowed Othello with remarkable virtues, that means that he approved of husbands who murder their wives.

In Elizabethan theatre, which includes a number of plays about incest,[3] Ford's drama is the only one where the subject is followed right through, where the incest is consummated almost before the very eyes of the spectators and is situated within a network of complex relations that involve at times amorous pursuits, at times machinations that are motivated by vengeance. Nevertheless, critics generally regard the incest as quasi-autonomous and independent in relation to the other intrigues, although occasionally it is viewed as symbolic of the moral corruption by which the society of Parma is tainted. Thus, for Mark Stavig,[4] Giovanni has substituted for the love of God love for an idol, to wit his sister. By delivering himself up to this idolatry, he has inverted the natural order. He has perverted platonic teaching – or the neo-platonic versions of it current at the time in the court of Charles I[5] – in order to justify his lust and egocentricity.

At the beginning of the play, Annabella and Giovanni are morally pure but by committing incest they betray the values they formerly shared and lower themselves to the same level as the rest of the characters. The quality of Giovanni's love becomes debased, as is shown by the obsessive jealousy that he manifests when his sister has to marry Soranzo and by his reaction when Annabella repents in the last act (V, v): she wants him to flee from the danger threatening him but he accuses her of preferring Soranzo's love-play to his own. Lust and jealousy are now inseparable for him. In defiance of natural, divine and human law, Giovanni adopts the code of honour of a perverted society while nevertheless retaining a sense of sin. Revenge can be his only law: he stabs his sister, unable to tell her why he is killing her; he tears out her heart and presents it, bleeding, to the dinner guests gathered at the final banquet where he publicly reveals the incest. True, in this way he foils the trap Soranzo has prepared for him but, for Stavig, that is just a way of seeming to justify himself, of saving face. Nothing counts any more, except himself. He has become insane in his egocentricity. As for Annabella, she is not sincere in her repentance when Friar Bonaventura threatens her with hell-fire and advises her to marry Soranzo (III, vi). She is not honest with Soranzo when she marries him without revealing she is pregnant. She still loves her incestuous lover: she sings his praises before Soranzo whom she defies; she calls for death and reckons divine grace to be of little account. Only at the beginning of act V does she declare:

> Now I confess
> Beauty that clothes the outside of the face
> Is cursèd if it be not clothed with grace.   (V, i, 11–13)

According to Stavig, what counts is the profound truth of the sin she has committed and the sincerity of her repentance. A similar view is conveyed by Ford's use of the final comment from the infamous cardinal:

> Of one so young, so rich in nature's store,
> Who could not say, 'tis pity she's a whore.   (V, vi, 159–60)

– a phrase that he adopted as the title for his play. It is a phrase that invites the audience not to share the view of these characters who set themselves up as the agents of providence and applaud the various manifestations of what they call divine justice. Somewhere along the line the question of the love between brother and sister has been forgotten by the commentator; as too has Annabella's desire for Giovanni to make his escape from Soranzo, a desire that involved her forgetting all about herself. The incest and the moral corruption of Parma are thus described from a moral, even moralising point of view.

To be sure, it would be wrong not to respond to the invitation that this play – like all the rest of this period – proffers to our need to pass judgement upon men and the affairs of the City. But other relations, too, exist between the incestuous couple and those who surround them, and also between the world of the play and ourselves.

2. Elizabethan attitudes to incest

At the end of the sixteenth century and the beginning of the seventeenth, the prohibition of incest was most frequently explained as a ban against an unnatural relationship. The monstrosity of it was made quite clear by the allegation that such unions produced monsters and this related them to copulation with animals.[6] In addition, incestuous behaviour led to crime, as could be seen from the medieval play entitled *Dux Moraud*.[7] The daughter of the protagonist, who commits incest with her father, kills her mother when the latter threatens to denounce them and, at the instigation of her father, also kills the child that she has conceived by him. Similar ideas can be found in Shakespeare's *Pericles*, Massinger's *The Unnatural Combat* and – although in a more veiled form – in Webster's *The Duchess of Malfi*. In *'Tis Pity She's a Whore*, the mythological allusions to Jupiter and Juno[8] and later to Leda and the Swan[9] testify to similar preoccupations.

Meanwhile, in his *Anatomy of Melancholy* (1621), Robert Burton declares that the prohibition of incest safeguards men against the sinister effects that may result from consanguineous marriages.[10] He notes that a hereditary defect may spare the father but strike the son and may sometimes not reappear until the third generation. He goes on to say: 'For these reasons, belike, the Church and commonwealth, human and divine laws, have conspired to avoid hereditary diseases, forbidding such marriages as are any whit allied.' He advises every family to choose as partners persons who, so far as possible, differ in temperament from themselves, 'if they love their own and respect the common good'. Finally, he writes that, 'it hath been ordered by God's especial providence that, in all ages, there should be (as there usually is) once in six hundred years, a transmigration of nations to amend and purifie their blood, as we alter seed upon our land'. He thus takes a positive view of the barbarian invasions such as those of the Goths and Vandals who, like a flood, swept most of Europe and Africa so as to 'alter (for our good) our complexions, which were much defaced with hereditary infirmities, which by our lust and intemperance we had contracted'.[11] This genetic and hygienic theory was to be readopted in the nineteenth century by L. H. Morgan and H. S. Maine.[12] What is important here is that Burton approves of a union between the near and the far. Presented in a somewhat different form, the same approval is to be found in John Ford's *Love's Sacrifice*. The duke of Pavia revolts against the grey-beards of the Senate who:

> Would tie the limits of our free affects
> (Like superstitious jews), to match with none
> But in a tribe of princes like ourselves;
> Gross nurtur'd slaves, who force their wretched souls
> To crouch to profit; nay, for trash and wealth
> Dote on some crooked or misshapen form,
> Hugging wise nature's lame deformity,
> Begetting creatures ugly as themselves: –
> But why should princes do so, that command
> The storehouse of the earth's hid minerals?[13]

The duke desires to marry Bianca, which, in the eyes of the Senate, constitutes a mismatch. The interest of the passage lies in the fact that in it Ford makes a comparison between marriage within a single class and endogamous marriage within a tribe, the term 'tribe' here being applied to princes instead of to the Jews, as was more usual. *A contrario*, marriage outside one's own class holds out the promise of a posterity that will be neither crippled nor deformed. So why should princes, who are in a position to choose and who have at their disposal all the precious reserves that the earth conceals within it, restrict themselves to the limitations imposed by class prejudices?

In a more general fashion, ever since Saint Thomas Aquinas, Christian tradition had justified the prohibition of incest on three grounds,[14] regarding it as an aggravated form of the sin of lust. Saint Thomas notes a combination of three drawbacks to physical union between blood relatives or between people otherwise related within the degrees prohibited by the Church. The first is that the respect due to parents suffers from this movement of sensuality. It seems repugnant (Lev. XVIII.6–18) that blood relatives of the same flesh should have sexual relations with one another or with one and the same person, becoming one flesh with that person. This could be interpreted by saying that the one should not fornicate with the one, that is to say with oneself. It is an explanation that Giovanni alludes to in the play where he exalts what the Church prohibits:

> Shall a peevish sound,
> A customary form, from man to man,
> Of brother and of sister, be a bar
> 'Twixt my perpetual happiness and me?
> Say that we had one father, say one womb
> (Curse to my joys) – gave us both life and birth;
> Are we not therefore each to the other bound
> So much the more by nature? by the links
> Of blood, of reason? nay, if you will have't,
> Even of religion, to be ever one,
> One soul, one flesh, one love, one heart, one all?   (I, i, 24–34)

The same can be said of the following passage, where Giovanni confesses his love to Annabella and, to win her over, maintains that right from the start nature, in her wisdom, has willed Annabella to be his:

> . . . else't had been sin and foul
> To share one beauty to a double soul.
> Nearness in birth or blood doth but persuade
> A nearer nearness in affection.   (I, ii, 233–6)

The monstrous character – here inverted and exalted – of the one uniting with himself and the fact that Giovanni considers his nearest of kin in the way that one ought to consider one's neighbour bear out the unsuitability that Saint Thomas Aquinas mentions. The emphasis that Ford lays upon 'nearness of birth' which, according to Giovanni, ought to lead to an ever 'nearer nearness in affection', shows that the author is fully conscious of the complex relations that marriage determines between individuals and society, between nature and culture.

The repetition of the term 'one' in Giovanni's first speech implies, in the first place, that only God can create on his own. Ever since the fall, the human condition has been such that generation is the business of a conjunction of man and woman – creatures separated ever since their births – not of some phoenix, some auto-reproduction or mysterious androgyny that neoplatonism might have rediscovered. A recent study[15] has shown how, of the three double beings (male, female and hermaphrodite) into which human nature was divided in ancient times in the myth of Aristophanes that Plato records, only the third of these (the hermaphrodite) has been retained in modern culture, in particular by Freud (who uses it to account for homosexuality). Giovanni, in a fairly obvious platonic echo, certainly appears to be alluding to the hermaphrodite when he speaks of that unique beauty divided into two souls whose incestuous reunion is, he claims, legitimate and in conformity with the laws of nature. Certain commentators of the Talmud had suggested that Genesis I.27 ('Male and female created He them') should be read as referring to the creation of a hermaphrodite.[16] Saint Augustine (*De Genesi ad Litteram*, 3, 22) had gone to the trouble of refuting this interpretation which postulates an original unity of the sexes, attributes their later separation to God and makes it possible to interpret sexual union (or reunion) as a return to origins – that is to say to the eternally voluptuous sterility of indistinction.

The second interpretation that Saint Thomas Aquinas provides is that a life led in one another's close company would encourage blood relatives to indulge too easily in lust. That is the kind of prenatal unity of beauty that Giovanni suggests. Putana's remark, which comes at the point when the incest has just been consummated, is an allusion to this theme: 'I say still, if a young wench feel the fit upon her, let her take any body, father or brother, all is one' (II, i, 44–5).

Similarly, in one of the sources of the play, a story entitled 'Des amours incestueuses d'un frère et d'une soeur et de leur fin malheureuse et tragique'[17] (On the incestuous love of a brother and a sister and their unhappy and tragic death), the author François de Rosset notes that when they were children Doralice and Lizeran 'usually slept together and perhaps this went on for too long'.[18] He then declares 'I am of the firm opinion that the harm resulted from this over-long intimacy which proceeded from one day to the next.'[19] The love between Doralice and Lizeran, who, the author tells us, are both very beautiful and also very intelligent, stems from what might be called an elective affinity reinforced by their resemblance to each other and the life they lead in each other's company.

The third explanation provided by Saint Thomas Aquinas is borrowed from Saint Augustine. In *The City of God*, the latter explains why it is that the incestuous union between the children of Adam and Eve is not to be condemned: 'This was, of course, a completely decent procedure under the pressure of necessity', for all Adam and Eve's children were brothers and sisters. But as soon as it became possible for men to take wives who were not their sisters,

such unions henceforth were banned. For if the grandchildren of the first human beings who by then could have taken their cousins as wives, were joined in marriage to their sisters, then there would no longer be two but three relationships comprised in one person; and those relationships ought to have been separated and distributed among different individuals . . . Thus the social tie would not be confined to a small group but would extend more widely to connect a large number with the multiplying links of kinship.[20]

The doctrine according to Saint Augustine on this matter is summarised as follows by B. Alves Pereira:

Union and concord are the greatest blessings of human society . . . Therefore charity stipulates that links of friendship should be widened as much as possible by all the means at men's disposal. Marriage is one of the most effective of those means. It links in kinship those who are friendly only by reason of a resemblance in their natures. Now, if one contracts marriage with individuals already united by the same blood, one is clearly thereby forgetting the precept of charity since one is limiting conjugal society to one's own relatives, whereas one ought to be extending it to the most distant persons.[21]

This is an extremely modern doctrine. It in no way contradicts, indeed confirms, explanations offered by our anthropologists. Margaret Mead, for instance, records the following reflections collected in the field among the Arapesh (New Guinea) in the Sepik region:

What, you would like to marry your sister? What is the matter with you anyway? Don't you want a brother-in-law? Don't you realise that if you marry another man's sister and another man marries your sister, you will have at least two brothers-in-law while if you marry your own sister, you will have none? With whom will you hunt? With whom will you garden? Whom will you go to visit?[22]

A specialist would say that the only concern of modern ethnological theory is to follow native theory and make it explicit. The prohibition of incest is understood here as the other side to the need for exchange. Even before it establishes a prohibition against this or that person, it first and foremost operates as a prescription relating to a quite other category of persons: it is aimed not so much at the wife who is proscribed, rather at the husband who is prescribed.[23]

After the Reformation, the influence of Saint Augustine remained strong in England. A monumental edition of *The City of God*,[24] with notes by the humanist Luis Vives, was published in 1610 and a second edition followed in 1620. The Augustinian concept according to which the prohibition stems from the horror inspired by incest[25] and is, as it were, the other side to the obligation to sociability and charity immediately makes one infer that, in *'Tis Pity She's a Whore*, the love between Annabella and Giovanni is not unrelated to the hatred that develops between the other various characters in the drama, in a world entirely devoid of charity.

3. An elective affinity and the rejection of exchange

Affinity – an 'elective affinity' – plays an important role in the incestuous relationship. The play begins at the point when Giovanni's feelings are clear enough to himself for him to disclose them to Friar Bonaventura in the hope, he claims, that the latter will be able to deliver him from them. Giovanni already regards the prohibition of incest as 'a customary form', not a natural or divine law.[26] The love for which he begs licence from his mentor is right from the first a carnal one:

> Shall then, for that I am her brother born,
> My joys be ever banished from her bed?   (I, i, 36–7)

The friar immediately interprets this as an impulse that will lead to lust and perdition, 'For death waits on thy lust' (I, i, 59).

The desire that impels Giovanni towards his sister, which Friar Bonaventura calls 'madness', is invested with a remarkable natural force. The inversion or confusion between nature and custom is quite clear right from the very first scene:

> It were more ease to stop the ocean
> From floats and ebbs than to dissuade my vows.   (I, i, 64–6)

It is an inversion for which we are, moreover, prepared as soon as Giovanni declares that because 'we had one father . . . , one womb (. . .) gave both us life and birth', he and Annabella are thereby all the more closely united by nature. But Giovanni's passion also belongs to the category of arbitrary things: admittedly, this is not fully explained by the term used by Giovanni himself because Ford does not have him pursue his explanation right through to the end. The contradictory ideas about necessity and free will with which Giovanni juggles so facilely seem to act as a pointer to the profound irrationality of all major passions and also to the fact that, once they have been committed, it is easier to analyse irremediable transgressions in terms of fatality than in terms of freedom. To accept the irremediable is to use one's freedom in order to subject oneself to one's destiny. To provoke the irremediable is to forfeit one's freedom in order to give oneself a destiny. It is thus quite legitimate to wonder about or hesitate over the content of this

passion, and either to identify oneself with it or draw away from it completely. It may have been conceived without cause – like the jealousy of the
jealous men that Emilia speaks of and that possesses Iago[27] – it may stem
from simple carnal desire,[28] from the idealisation of such a desire or from a
love that is as egocentric as it is absolute. At all events, while there may be
disagreement as to its nature, there can be none where its force is concerned,
and that is the justification for speaking of it in terms of fatality: it is a passion
placed right from the start under the sign of prohibition and death. And
passing from feeling to action is, in the full sense of the word, fatal.

The following scene, in contrast, provides a description of social
relations. In the course of it, nearly all the characters in the drama are
paraded before the audience. First, there is an exchange of insults between
Grimaldi (who wishes to marry Annabella) and Vasques, the servant of
Soranzo who has also asked for her hand. Following a brief duel in which
Grimaldi fares the worse, a semblance of civic decency is introduced by the
entrance of Florio, a city worthy and father to Annabella, Donado – a rich
bourgeois who wishes to see his nephew, Bergetto, wed the girl – and
Soranzo who, for his part, is a nobleman. All this while Annabella and her
duenna, Putana, positioned on a higher level, look on silently without being
seen. Quarrelling flares up again, this time between Soranzo and Grimaldi.
It is over Annabella. She is the cause of all these arguments and insults. We
learn that Florio has promised his daughter to Soranzo. He assures the latter
that he has won Annabella's heart and so there is no need to fight over something that is his already. Love for his daughter must not cause a single drop
of bloodshed, he says. Later on he contradicts himself and declares that his
daughter may marry whoever she pleases, instead of following his own
wishes in this respect. And it is in the name of love for Annabella that most
of the murders in the play are committed. As soon as he has left, Putana
says: 'How like you this, child? Here's threatening, challenging, quarrelling,
and fighting, on every side, and all is for your sake' (I, ii, 63–4).

So this is a hunt, a rather special kind of hunt in which the prize can only
be won at the price of a fight between the hunters. Putana appears to relish
the prospect of a competition is which her mistress is to be at stake. She tells

Although situated in Parma, in a catholic country, this opening scene is
quite cut off from any social context. We see Giovanni's soul and passion
addressing themselves to some form of moral and religious conscience and
yet it is impossible for any real dialogue to take place. There can be no
appeal against the condemnation, for it is as irresistible in the imperiousness
with which it refuses Giovanni's desires as are those desires in the passion
with which they are held. Friar Bonaventura is as incapable of approaching
an understanding of the passion of his disciple as he seems out of place later
on in the hate-ridden world of Parma. The bridges between religion, passion
and social relations are broken.

Annabella the choice is up to her. But she makes short work of discrediting Grimaldi: he is a spurious hero who might just as well be castrated. She recommends Soranzo for his virility on the basis of his success with Hippolita while her husband (whom she believes to be dead) was still alive. The previously committed adultery is thus presented as an argument that should be decisive despite the fact that, from a moral point of view, it discredits Soranzo. At this point Bergetto, a silly imbecile, makes his appearance together with his servant Poggio. Their conversation reveals the infantilism of Bergetto, the third suitor, so he in his turn is also discredited. When Annabella catches sight of him, she calls him an 'idiot'. Finally, Giovanni appears. She does not recognise him:

> But see, Putana, see: what blessed shape
> Of some celestial creature now appears?
> What man is he, that with such sad aspect
> Walks careless of himself?   (I, ii, 126–9)

Putana tells her that the melancholy fellow is her brother. As they make their way down to speak to him, Giovanni, in a soliloquy, tells of the fatality that pursues him, the sin he has in mind, his anxiety and his decision to declare his love to his sister. After that, his affinity, love, passion or desire find ways to express themselves. There are five stages in the progression towards his confession and her consent, a progression that finds fulfilment in a remarkable improvised ritual[29] in which the two characters, on their knees, pronounce apparently symmetrical vows, swearing either to love or to kill each other. They then go off to 'learn to court in smiles, to kiss, and sleep'.

Annabella's consent is thus given after the parading of her suitors. There is no question of any marriage in the offing for Giovanni but three possibilities are presented to his sister, all of which she rejects. In effect, the choices offered simply emphasise the absence of choice with which she is, in reality, faced. In François de Rosset's story, the author notes that Doralice's father forces her to marry Timandre, 'a gentleman who is his neighbour, very wealthy but already a greybeard'[30] despite other, more appropriate offers of marriage. The incest is consummated only after the marriage which is rendered inevitable by the absolute power of fathers over their children.[31] François de Rosset condemns the lovers but also disapproves of the constraint exercised by the father.

In Ford's play, there is no suitable husband for Annabella for there are at least five conditions implicitly required if a marriage is to be acceptable according to nature, custom and the law: the husband should be neither too near nor too far; his social rank should be acceptable; it should have the consent of the father; also that of the daughter; the husband should possess certain physical and moral qualities such as fidelity, virtue, beauty of both body and mind and devotion to his loved one. Ford's lovers transgress three rules:

they are closely related; they are not married;[32] and they deceive their father. The fact remains that the absence of any acceptable choice for Annabella does to some extent act as a constraint. The role that, in François de Rosset's tale, is played by the father is here played by the society as a whole which treats women as objects of exchange or pleasure. The context thus justifies the observation that the measure of affinity or passionate resolution that moves Annabella towards Giovanni is less strong than the impulse that carries him towards her. The play makes all these motivations quite clear. Nevertheless, a number of conjectures may also be in line. If it is true that the prohibition of an incestuous union may be seen as the other side to an obligation, Ford, in default of a more precise ruling, clearly defines what that obligation is, namely to ensure the continuity of the family. Florio says to Donado:

> You see I have but two, a son and her;
> And he is so devoted to his book,
> As I must tell you true, I doubt his health:
> Should he miscarry, all my hopes rely
> Upon my girl. (I, iii, 4–8)

The father's survival thus depends upon the daughter's marriage since, in the Restoration period, time was gauged in terms not only of the existence of one individual but also of a whole line. The incest, followed by the assassination of Annabella, is a means of killing the father. Ford has Giovanni express this when Florio has been struck down dead at the news of Annabella's murder, 'Now survives / None of our house but I . . . ' (V, vi, 67–8). As for Giovanni himself, he has joined the funeral feast, there to die. This is an interpretation that is confirmed by the lack of symmetry in the oath sworn by the two characters at the beginning of the play:

> *Annabella*:   On my knees,
> Brother, even by our mother's dust, I charge you,
> Do not betray me to your mirth or hate,
> Love me, or kill me, brother.
> *Giovanni*:   On my knees,
> Sister, even by my mother's dust, I charge you,
> Do not betray me to your mirth or hate,
> Love me, or kill me, sister. (I, ii, 249–55)

Whereas Annabella speaks of '*our* mother's dust', Giovanni refers to '*my* mother's dust'. His egocentricity places him in explicit competition with his father: even with Annabella he will not share his mother.

The incest thus seems to be provoked by a number of things: the affinity between brother and sister, Giovanni's refusal to share anything, the relative impossibility of a marriage outside the family or a love that is acceptable, Giovanni's desire to kill his father and to dominate his sister and, through this real domination, to strike symbolically at a corrupt society: love cannot find fulfilment because of the very fact of that corruption; the choice of an unacceptable relationship is at once an indication of the corruption, its consequence and also a sign that Giovanni wants to put an end to it by means of the totally destructive quality of the absolute power he seeks. And his search for that power is characterised by his rejection of exchange in a context in which the normal exchanges are impossible.

4. Near kin and near neighbours

Considerations of rank, fortune, honour and power are much in evidence. Thus, the foolish Bergetto thinks he can buy not just intelligence but women too and, in particular, Annabella. His suit is encouraged by his uncle Donado who promises Florio that this 'big baby' will have three thousand florins a year and all his lands when he himself is dead. But Annabella's father's preference goes to Soranzo:

> . . . the hope
> Of your still rising honours have prevailed
> Above all other jointures.   (III, ii, 3–5)

He later thrusts Annabella into Soranzo's arms at a moment when she, knowing herself to be pregnant, sees it as a way to conceal this consequence of her relations with her brother. The cardinal uses his rank and position to extricate Grimaldi from the arms of the law following the assassination of Bergetto on the grounds that Grimaldi is no man of the common run and is not a native of Parma but of Rome – which prompts Florio to remark that justice has flown away to the heavens never to return. At the end of the play this same cardinal orders that Putana be burned at the stake – even though she was no more than an accomplice to the incest – and that the lands of those now dead be seized. Hippolita, whom Soranzo, after promising to marry her, never wishes to see again, with all her hatred expresses the scorn she feels for Annabella, 'your goodly madam-merchant' (II, ii, 48).

However, the general climate of the drama is above all determined by the fact that all its amorous intrigues turn into revengeful machinations when, that is, they are not destroyed by bad faith or the unfolding of some other plot. There are seven love intrigues in all (one of which is recounted, having taken place before the play begins, namely Soranzo's seduction of Hippolita). Annabella is pursued by four suitors, Grimaldi, Soranzo, Bergetto and Giovanni. She gives herself to Giovanni, then marries Soranzo. Bergetto, in his disappointment, turns to Philotis (the niece of Hippolita's husband who has secretly returned to Parma to avenge the infidelity of his wife). None of these intrigues is crowned with success. Hippolita tries to have Soranzo poisoned by Vasques but the latter, whom she has promised to marry in return for his help (this is the seventh intrigue), makes her scheme recoil against her. Richardetto, disguised as a doctor, provides Grimaldi with a poison with which to kill Soranzo, but it is Bergetto who takes it and dies. Finally, Soranzo prepares a dramatic vengeance against Giovanni and Annabella, but Giovanni cheats him of his revenge by killing his sister and then having Soranzo killed before being, himself, struck down by Vasques and his henchmen. The 'accidental' murder of Bergetto – the one moment of emotion in the comic intrigue in which he is involved – and the impunity enjoyed by the assassin Grimaldi are tokens of the formidable disproportion that Ford creates between the actions of men and the punishments for those actions. It is the fool, the idiot, the 'baby' who is thus struck down by accident – an example of innocence, real, albeit unattractive, destroyed as it were on the rebound. Moreover, no character is innocent or morally pure. Yet not one of the deaths is presented in such a way that the audience can see it as an expression of that divine justice with the effects of which Friar Bonaventura was threatening Giovanni at the beginning of the drama: it is as if even divine justice can only be retributive, incapable of purifying Parma from its festering corruption.

What is particularly revolting in this respect is the position in which women are placed. In his other plays Ford often attributes his female characters with many scruples, nobility and depth of character. In *'Tis Pity She's a Whore* their fates are finely in the balance. The men judge them by double standards. Hippolita who is out to get her revenge against Soranzo sees her scheme miscarry to the satisfaction of all. Whereas, in the case of Soranzo, adultery was seen as a proof of virility, where she is concerned it is deemed a sign of degeneracy. When a man seduces and a woman is seduced the blame always falls upon the woman, as is indicated, moreover, by the very title of the play. Soranzo's invectives against Annabella, when he learns she is already pregnant, are unbelievably violent and stem as much from the wound to his own self-esteem as from his distress. Even more horrible is Putana's fate: the cardinal rules that she should be burned at the stake, after Vasques has put her eyes out. Philotis, it is true, fares better, as in the end Richardetto manages to withdraw her from the world, that is to say from the current system of exchange, by dispatching her to a convent where she agrees to go with the same docile obedience that earlier prompted her to 'fashion her heart' to love Bergetto.[33] The impossibility of marriage within the framework of reference of the play and the only alternatives that appear open to a woman – to be an object of exchange, called a whore or dispatched to a convent – points to the theme of sterility. It is as if this world was characterised by the impossibility of procreation and consequently of passing on from one generation to another. But it is not only a world without a future that these schemes of vengeance betray. They are also the mark of one from which love and charity have fled. It is a place where the powerful are pardoned and the weak mutilated, a place where justice is no more than retribution, unjust in all its applications.

From time to time John Ford indirectly suggests what would be the humane and desirable way to behave. Thus, when Hippolita comes to see Soranzo, Vasques intervenes to temper his master's violence: 'Sir, I beseech you, do not perplex her; griefs, alas, will have a vent' (II, ii, 63). Soranzo then declares that the vows he made to Hippolita were perverted: it would be a greater sin to honour than to break them. It is Vasques, the most villainous character in the whole play, who stresses the falseness and unworthiness of the part his master is playing. Similarly, in the course of the banquet to celebrate the marriage between Soranzo and Annabella (IV, i), Hippolita joins together the hands of the married couple and her deceitful ploy is accepted at its face value by Soranzo. If a feigned pardon can pass for a true one then a true one must be a possibility. Finally, when Soranzo, at Vasques' instigation, pretends to forgive Annabella whom he now knows to be pregnant, Annabella, who is touched and upset, wants to kneel before him (IV, iii). Here again a charitable mode of conduct is suggested by the dramatic and psychological form taken by Soranzo's cunning trick. In John Ford's play the norm is provided not only by Friar Bonaventura but also by suggested modes of conduct which are based upon the principle of charity.

In this world devoid of charity in which, as Saint Augustine indicated, love *could* be spread by means of marriages, in the same way that Giovanni and Annabella behave towards each other as if they were not near kin, the rest of the characters in the drama treat one another as though they were not near neighbours. When the play is read the confusion that exists between near and distant relations comes over most strongly: the terrifying distance between these neighbours, the unnatural nearness of these relatives makes the incest homologous to the social and spiritual alienation of each individual. There is a simple inversion between the two relationships: forbidden love and excessive hatred mutually complement and shed light upon one another.[34]

It is sometimes claimed that the Italian setting of a number of plays written under James I or Charles I allowed their audiences to distance themselves almost entirely from these dramas and regard them simply as spectacles of other, exotic *mores*. But there are grounds for doubt here. Upon his accession to the throne, Charles I immediately blocked the social mobility that the sale of posts and titles had accelerated during his father's reign. With the support of Archbishop Laud, he took steps to favour the most ancient titles and brutally curb the hopes for social promotion on the part of the lesser nobility and bourgeoisie. Lawrence Stone[35] describes the social fragmentation that had affected the ancient body politic of England: not only were the classes becoming increasingly separated one from another but increasingly acute rivalries were cutting through the upper strata of society. England was entering upon a period of individualism but it was an individualism both outraged and outrageous because it arose against the background of what had been a belief in the City as an organic whole, and what was often no mere belief but a reality. Ford's play thus truly seems in tune with a historical turning point when a religious, political and social reaction was taking place and public respect for authority in all its forms throughout the realm was faltering.

5. 'A feast they made of her for the baron and the princes', or the sacrificed doe

Thus, what we have here is not simply a work in which melodrama, moralising and irony provide a framework, so to speak, for the tragedy of two beings 'caught in a situation that they cannot handle'.[36] As Northrop Frye remarks, tragedy almost always includes irony but is in no way constituted by it.[37] Kaufmann appears closer to the truth when he writes:

> without being baroquely overdrawn, the world of the play is made to act (in its negations of beauty) as a foil to the desperate choices of Giovanni and his sister. This is not, of course, because Ford approves of incest but it is done to put the unthinkable within access of thought. Not the least of the functions of tragedy is to enlarge our imaginative tolerance.[38]

The particular tension of this drama, the unease it arouses in the reader or spectator stem from the fact that the response it provokes is a double rejection. The relations within society are unacceptable; incest is unacceptable. However, the two reactions are not symmetrical because the spectator's involvement with the incestuous couple is quite different from his involvement with the rest of the characters. It is the couple who, to the detriment of the rest, monopolise all the force and passion and the ability to act and suffer for an absolute cause. The blindness that unites the couple and that subsequently separates Giovanni from Annabella is not something alien to us, for we are all liable to make choices and undergo constraints whenever love, or even egocentric madness, dons the mask of legitimacy. But we are then forced, by ourselves as well as by the world, to tear off the mask and with it the face. And sometimes that face is our own, sometimes that of a victim both innocent and guilty. Annabella tries to sacrifice herself for Giovanni, urging him to flee while she remains behind, waiting to be killed. And Giovanni does not become so alien to Annabella that in killing her he fails to kill himself, in a dizzying climax of isolation. As he proffers Annabella's bleeding heart to the city notables, he says:

> You came to feast, my lords, with dainty fare;
> I came to feast too, but I digged for food
> In a much richer mine than gold or stone
> Of any value balanced; 'tis a heart,
> A heart, my lords, in which is mine entombed.
> Look well upon't; d'ee know't?   (V, vi, 24–9)

Because of its very horror, this unnamable banquet repulses and fascinates us. Giovanni has come alone to feast there, his meal is an inestimable expiatory victim. But it is a sacrifice for which there can be no consummation: it does not bring men closer to God or God closer to men. It cannot be the foundation for any communion. It is a metaphor for a cannibal feast, rejected by all but which nevertheless establishes a striking symbolic relation between itself and both what society does to the characters in the play and also what they do to one another.

It is a metaphor that refers beyond the social context and draws the strength of its impact from more distant origins. Custom demanded that after the hunt the choicest morsels should be offered to the greatest figures present. There is an ancient song, discovered in the Vendée district, about a girl who becomes a doe and is hunted and killed by her own brother. Now, incestuous relationships have often been felt to represent a return to animality. That is an explicit Ovidian theme; Myrrha, who is in love with her father, speaks as follows:

To what is my purpose tending? What am I planning? O Gods, I pray you, and piety and the sacred rights of parents, keep this sin from me and fight off my crime, if indeed it is a crime. But I am not sure, for piety refuses to condemn such love as this. Other animals mate as they will, nor is it thought base for a heffer to endure her sire, nor for his own offspring to be a horse's mate, the goat goes in among the flocks which he has fathered and the very birds conceive from those from whom they were conceived. Happy they who have such privilege.[39]

In the song, which we give below, the theme of metamorphosis, the incestuous hunt, murder and the cannibal meal are set out in clear, compact sequences. Marguerite 'dare[s] not tell' her mother that she is a ' . . . maid by day, / White doe by night', as if this illicit metamorphosis was a voluntary action by which the sister made herself into a creature to be pursued, reserved for princes and, above all, for her brother Renaud, who is presented as the most important personage in the hunt. And it is in the course of the dinner that – hacked into quarters in the forest, but drained of blood in the kitchen and now served up, head, limbs and heart, at the table of the noblemen – she reveals her identity to the cannibal community of diners, while her 'poor bones' 'do grill', as if in some unnatural sacrifice.

The White Doe

To the woods
Go mother and daughter.

The mother sings,
The daughter sighs.

Why do you sigh,
Marguerite, my daughter?

I am full of trouble
And dare not tell you.

I am maid by day,
White doe by night.

The hunt pursues me,
Barons and Princes all.

And my brother Renaud too
And that is even worse.

Go, mother, hurry
Away to tell him

To stop his hounds,
Hold back 'til the morrow.

Where, Oh Renaud, are your hounds,
Where your noble hunt?

They are deep in the woods,
Off coursing the white doe.

Stop, Oh Renaud, stop them,
I do beg of you.

Three times did he call to them
With his copper horn.

But at the horn's third blast
The white doe was seized.

Let's send for the flayer
To flay the doe.

The one who flays her
Says: What can I say?

She had the golden tresses
And fair breast of a maid.

His knife he did draw out
And cut her into quarters.

A feast they made of her
For the baron and the princes.

Now that all are present,
We need my sister Marguerite.

All you need do is eat now,
I am the first one seated.

The platter holds my heart
And all from heart to ankles

And all my blood is spilt
And lies there in the kitchen,

While upon your black coals
My poor bones do grill.[40]

Notes

Introduction

1 Douglas, 1966 (VII). On the hunt and the hunt for love in Shakespeare, see Madden (1897), 1907 (VI); Henn, 1972 (VI); Marienstras, 1972 (VI); White, 1976 (VI). The bracketed Roman numerals refer to the bibliography, where the work in question can be found.

2 Lévi-Strauss (1973), 1978 (VII), p. 275.

3 Lévi-Strauss, in Bellour and Clément, 1979, p. 195 (VII).

4 Lévi-Strauss, *ibid.*, p. 195.

5 Fuzier, 1970, pp. 97–111 (VI).

6 Elton (1966), 1968 (VI): see the index of terms 'Beast', 'Custom', 'Law', '*Natura naturans et naturata*', 'Natural Law', 'Nature', 'Opinion', etc.

7 *The Tempest*, ed. Frank Kermode (1954), 1958: preface, in particular pp. xxxiv–lix (IV).

8 *King Lear*, ed. K. Muir (1952), 1959: I, ii, 1–3 (IV).

9 *Othello*, ed. M. R. Ridley (1958), 1962: I, ii, 30–2 (IV).

10 *All's Well That Ends Well*, ed. G. K. Hunter (1959), 1962: II, iii, 118 and 127 (IV).

11 Haydn (1950), 1960, pp. 461–8 (III).

12 See Bloch (1924), 1961 (III); and Thomas, 1971, pp. 192–206 (III).

13 This is the role of Edward the Confessor in *Macbeth*, IV, iii. The magical and prophetic powers of Edward are contrasted with the sickness of Scotland and its usurper-king.

14 Janson, 1952 (III).

15 See Kantorowicz, 1957 (III); and Axton, 1977 (III).

16 James I, 1918, p. 63 (V), cited in Lamont and Oldfield, 1975 (III).

17 See Skinner, 1965 (III), and also the commentary by Lamont and Oldfield, 1975, p. 4 (III).

18 *The Works of Christopher Marlowe*, ed. C. F. Tucker Brooke (1910), 1953 (IV).

19 *The Ruler* (trans. Peter Rodd), Bodley Head, London, 1954, Chapter XVIII, p. 91. See Wyndham Lewis (1927), 1966 (VI).

20 Tillyard, 1943, pp. 6, 8, 28, 32, etc., and (1944), 1969, pp. 149, 207–9, etc. (VI). Theodore Spencer, 1942, in particular pp. 86–95 (VI). An adverse criticism of these views may be found in Howarth, 1961, pp. 165–91 (VI). The fullest brief study on Elizabethan ideology is that of Elton, 1971 (VI).

21 Pocock (1957), 1974, pp. 30–5 (III).

22 Coke, 1644, p. 301 (V).
23 Girard, 1972 and 1978 (VII). I do not subscribe to the views of Girard who, to
    adopt M. Detienne's description, inscribes all human history within the limits of
    an original act of lynching and the sacrifice of Jesus Christ. R. Girard's sociology
    and symbolism continue and make explicit Judeo-Christian (or, to be more pre-
    cise, Christian) thought, by offering 'a key to our past and our future'. Neverthe-
    less, his formulations are useful for an understanding of the Christian civilis-
    ation's attitude to sacrifice. See Detienne and Vernant, 1979, pp. 7–35 (VII).
24 Antonin Artaud sees in this play 'the absolute of revolt': 1964, p. 40 (VIII).
25 *Macbeth*, ed. Kenneth Muir (1951), 1977 (IV). Anon., *The Life and Death of
    Jack Straw*, ed. Kenneth Muir and F. P. Wilson, 1957 (IV). I owe this quotation
    to an unpublished thesis by Mrs D. Goy-Blanquet, 'Récit historique et structure
    dramatique dans la trilogie des "Henry VI" de Shakespeare', Université Paris
    VII, Paris, 1984.
26 *Hamlet*, ed. J. Dover Wilson (1934), 1936 (IV).
27 Hooker (1907), vol. 2, 1960, Book V, chap. LXXIII, 4, pp. 392–3 (V).
28 See Gorfain, 1976 (VI).
29 Douglas, 1966, p. 150 (VII).
30 Howell (1809–28), vol. 2, 1816, col. 184 (III). The sequence of the execution
    took place according to the law: Coke is simply giving his own interpretation of
    it.
31 The relations between Shakespeare and the law have been the subject of many
    studies exploring direct influences. It is not necessary to list them all. For a
    recent survey, see Richard J. Schoek, 'Shakespeare and the Law', *Shakespeare
    Research and Opportunities*, no. 7–8, ed. W. R. Elton, New York, 1972–4, pp.
    61–7.
32 Bacon, 1857–74, vol. 7, 1859, pp. 31–2 (V).
33 See Sahel, 1978 (VI).
34 On certain problems concerning the legality of legitimacy of Mary Stuart's
    claims to succeed Elizabeth I, see Axton, 1977, pp. 18–25 (III). On the problems
    of succession since Henry IV and the legal validity of Henry VIII's will, see
    Levine, 1973 (III), and Axton, 1977, p. 35 (III).
35 Levin, 1970, p. 187 (VI).

**1. The forest, the wild and the sacred: a study of *A Treatise and Discourse of the Lawes
of the Forest* by John Manwood**

1   Quite apart from the role played by the bear in popular English spectacles ever
    since at least the reign of Henry II, during the Middle Ages this creature rep-
    resented concupiscence or lust. In European folklore it was a symbol of male
    sexuality: in some stories, bears violate women or fornicate with others who are
    consenting. The bear also symbolises brute force, cunning and anger. It is con-
    nected with rituals associated with the end of winter. (On animal symbolism, see
    Klingender, 1971 (VIII); Rowland, 1974 (VIII); and n. 66 below.) A list of
    medieval romances and Renaissance novels containing adventures with wild
    animals is given by Bullough, 1957–75, vol. 8, 1975, pp. 125–8 (II).
2   On the man of the woods or the wild man see in particular Bernheimer, 1952
    (VI); and Janson, 1952 (III). Apart from the information to be found in the
    article by Le Goff and Vidal-Naquet, 1974 (VII), the following may also be con-
    sulted: Harrison, 1940 (VI); Goldsmith, 1958 (VI); Foltinek, 1961 (VI);
    Cheney, 1966 (VI); Bergeron, 1971 (VI); Dudley and Novak, 1972 (III); Doob,

1974 (VI); Wells, 1975 (VI); Neaman, 1978 (III). An efficient synthesis and important bibliography can be found in Sheehan, 1980 (III).

3 The text of *Mucedorus* is that of C. F. Tucker Brooke, published in *The Shakespeare Apocrypha* (1908), 1967 (IV). Note that Bremo is one of the rare 'wild men' of the sixteenth century who belongs to the species that is hostile to men and living creatures, a species which, according to Bernheimer, 1952 (VI), descends from Orcus. Most of the wild men we find represented are rather of the 'Silvanus' type; they often figure in pageants. The interchangeability of the wild man and the bear is noted by Bernheimer. If their death occurs in January or February it is not followed by resurrection and represents a destruction, or purification, of winter (pp. 55–6).

4 For example, Caliban who is carried away by music.

5 IV, iii, 36.

6 V, i, 27.

7 Boccaccio, 1930, vol. 1, Fourth Day, Novel II, pp. 243–51 (V).

8 The polarity – and contiguity – of the wild man and the hermit comes out clearly in the legend of Merlin, the origins of which can be found in Nennius' *Historia Britonum* popularised by Geoffrey de Monmouth in his *Vita Merlini* even before Mallory made it famous in England. Driven insane by the spectacle of the battle between the Gauls and the Celts of Scotland and the massacre at Ardderyd that resulted from it (574), he became a 'man of the woods', feeding upon berries and roots. It was in the woods that he began his career as a seer and diviner. Shakespeare alludes twice to Merlin. We should again emphasise that the contiguity of contraries or opposites is a frequent theme in literature, sometimes taking the form of a contrast between appearance and reality; thus in the case of Spenser's 'Savage man', the wildness is all exterior. As Serena realises (*Faerie Queene*, VI, v, 29ff), 'Savage man' is endowed with a chivalrous soul. Cheney, 1966, p. 210 (VI), has commented on this point.

9 Le Goff and Vidal-Naquet, 1974 (VII). This article, with additions, has been reprinted in Bellour and Clément, 1979 (VII). Despite the differences between *Mucedorus* and *Yvain*, note the contiguity between the wild man, the knight and the hermit.

10 Cited in Le Goff and Vidal-Naquet, 1974, p. 557 (VII).

11 On the forest as a place of refuge, trials and meetings, see Marianne Stauffer, 1958 (VI). See also in the bibliography of Keen (1961), 1977 (VI) the considerable body of literature connected with Robin Hood and the notes to the article already cited by Le Goff and Vidal-Naquet.

12 See Hill, 1972 (III), chap. 3. Hill notes that the number of masterless men in 1569 was 13,000 (mostly in the north) while in 1602, according to a less reliable estimate, it was 30,000 'in London alone' (pp. 35–6). Clearly, Hill's remark, 'London was for the sixteenth century vagabond what the greenwood had been for the medieval outlaw' is pertinent here. It suggests that there must be strong doubts as to whether the *banditi* in Massinger's *The Guardian* (performed in 1633) were really related to the 'courteous English thieves', as Hill calls them (p. 39). The space for wildness has moved from forest to town. The men now installing themselves in the forests were seeking land (see Thirsk, 1967, pp. 37, 95–6 (III)) or pasturage. They also built cottages there illegally (pp. 96–7, 411–12).

13 The parallelism between these two stories is noted by Cheney, 1966, pp. 108–9 (VI).

14 Carrive, 1975, p. 16 (VI).

15 The dates of publication were as follows, according to W. W. Greg, cited by Brooke (1908), 1967, pp. xxiv and 444: 1598, 1606, 1610, 1611, 1613, 1615, 1618, 1619, 1621, 1626, 1631, 1634, 1639, 1663, 1668 (IV). There is also an undated edition in existence and one other, the only copy of which is without a title page. The possible influence of *Mucedorus* on Shakespeare has been noted by Kermode. The play is mentioned in the induction to *The Knight of the Burning Pestle*. It was performed in Whitehall at the beginning of James I's reign as well as several times in Oxfordshire in 1652. Reynolds, 1959 (VI), is puzzled by the popularity it enjoyed and attributes this possibly to the presence of a live bear on stage.

16 See Rowse (1950), 1964, p. 67 (III); Tawney and Power, 1924, vol. 1, pp. 231, 241, 284; vol. 2, pp. 105, 107; vol. 3, pp. 3, 135, 144 (III); Camden (1586), 1610, pp. 212, 241 (V); Thirsk, 1967, p. 271 (III), who writes that such complaints may have been exaggerated as the situation varied greatly from one region to another. However, she does note the increase in the cost of wood and the fact that there was a severe shortage of fire-wood in the East Midlands and the Eastern counties. She remarks that the sale of wood remained an important source of revenue if not for the Crown at least for the nobility (pp. 477–8) and that land was being put under cultivation to the detriment of the forest (p. 607). In 1651, R. Child (*Samuel Hartlib His Legacie*) criticised the destruction of woodlands caused by rights to gather wood for heating and for building in a forest. The glassworks of the south, the salt marshes of Cheshire and the forges of Sussex, Surrey and elsewhere were all responsible for the state of affairs (Ernle (1912), 1961, p. 110 (III)).

17 M. Drayton, 'Polyalbian' (in *Works*, IV, I, ed. J.W. Hebel, 5 vols., 1931–41), quoted by Rowse (1950), 1964, p. 67 (III).

18 Holinshed, Harrison *et al.*, 1807–8, vol. 1, bk ii, chap. xix, p. 346 (V). Harrison was not mistaken: according to Saxton's maps (1575–80), there were more than seven hundred parks in England and twenty-one in Wales (Shaw, 1956, p. 1 (III)).

19 Lines 6393–8, cited by Le Goff and Vidal-Naquet, 1974, p. 569 (VII).

20 There are several editions: 1592, 1598, 1599, 1615. The references in the present chapter relate to *A Treatise of the Laws of the Forest, Wherein is declared not onely those Laws, as they are now in force but also the Original and beginning of Forests . . . Also a Treatise of the Pourallee . . .* , 1665 edn (V).

21 *Ibid.*, dedication to Lord Howard, sig. [a–8ᵛ].

22 See, for example, Fisher, 1887 (III): on 24 June 1594, a Sunday, during the hour of the church service, several men killed a stag in a purlieu (p. 210); there is mention of a charge brought against Richard Muffet who had killed a fallow buck with a rifle, and against six men who used bows in the forest on 23 July 1591 (p. 214); a charge against James Atkin who hired a butcher to kill a stag with a crossbow and cut it up in his kitchen (p. 216). Fisher notes that illegal hunting often took place at night or 'between the dog and the wolf' (p. 216). Nocturnal poaching was traditional: the poacher would disguise himself or wear a hood so as not to be recognised (pp. 208–9). Fisher adds that Turbervile, the author of *The Noble Art of Venery*, was very keen on hunting at night (p. 209).

23 See Thompson, 1975 (III).

24 Harrison, in Holinshed, Harrison *et al.*, 1807–8, vol. 1, bk ii, chap. xix, p. 344 (V).

25 This treatise, dated 27 April 1609, is reproduced in [John Saint John] *Observations on the Land Revenue of the Crown*, London, 1787, Appendix I. The

biographical details for Manwood are borrowed from *Dictionary of National Biography* (*D.N.B.*).

26 Turner, 1901 (III).

27 In Stubbs, 1913, vol. 2, pp. 747–849 (III).

28 Holdsworth, 1903, vol. 1, pp. 340–52 (III).

29 There were sanctuaries at Westminster, Wells, Norwich, York, etc., and in London, in the locality of Savoy and Whitefriars. John Stow (1598), 1956 (V), describes the privileges of Westminster as follows: 'This church hath had great priviledge of Sanctuary within the precinct thereof, to wit, the church, churchyard and close . . . from whence it hath not beene lawfull for any prince or other to take any person that fled thether for any cause' (p. 410). On this question: De Mazzinghi, 1887 (III); Trenholme, 1903 (III); Cox, 1911 (III); Watson, 1924 (III).

30 Bracton writes that in such a case, the said person 'ought to choose some port by which he may pass to another land beyond the realm of England . . . And there ought to be computed for him his reasonable travelling expenses as far as that port, and he ought to be interdicted from going out of the king's highway, and from delaying anywhere for two nights, and from entertaining himself anywhere, and from turning aside from the high road except from great necessity or for the sake of lodging for the night, but let him always continue along the straight road to the port, so that he shall always be there on the appointed day, and that he shall cross the sea as soon as he shall find a ship, unless he shall be impeded by the weather; but if he does otherwise, he shall be in Peril.' *De legibus et consuetudinibus Angliae*, ed. and trans. by Sir Travers Twiss, London, 1879, vol. 2, II, xvi, 1, p. 393. Kiralfy reproduces a 1302 text which reports the case of a man who strayed from his route and was hanged: 1957, p. 7 (III).

31 The right of asylum was limited by the following statutes: 26 Hen. VIII, c. 13 (1534); 27 Hen. VIII, c. 19 (1535); 33 Hen. VIII, c. 15 (1541); and abolished by the statute 21 Jac. I, c. 8 (1624).

32 Walter R. Davis, 1965, p. 35 (VI). Shakespeare uses the term 'purlieu' in *As You Like It*: it certainly refers to a territory intermediary between the political world and the 'sanctuary' of the forest. See also, in Cowell, 1607 (V), the terms 'purlue' and 'purlie man'.

33 Manwood refers to the severity of these punishments, chap. IV, ii.

34 'It is also in the forests that places of retreat are found for kings who there find their greatest joy': Fitz Nigel, 1711, p. 29 (III). There is a more recent edition, with a translation by C. Johnson, 1950, pp. 59–60 (III). The best text appears to be that of Arthur Hughes *et al.*, 1902 (III). Manwood cites this treatise at greater length in chap. XXV, i, p. 486.

35 Henry de Bracton (*d.* 1268), an ecclesiastic and a judge, was the first jurist who attempted to clarify and classify the English common law. His *De legibus et consuetudinibus Angliae* (written between 1235 and 1259) was 'the crown and flower of English medieval jurisprudence', Pollock and Maitland (1895), 1968, vol. 1, p. 206 (III).

36 John Cowell, *The Interpreter*, 1607 (V), article 'Praerogatiue of the King'. In Manwood's cited text, the disputable passage, which Edward Coke indeed disputes, runs as follows: 'The laws do allow unto the King, among many other priviledges, this prerogative, to have his places of recreation and pastime, wheresoever he will appoint.'

37 This question shortly afterwards became the subject of a long analysis by Hugo Grotius in his *On the Law of War and Peace* (published in Latin in 1525). He

writes that the possession of objects that belong to nobody – in particular, wild beasts – is decided by rules which are not 'so bound up with the law of nature that they cannot be changed. They are not a part of the law of nature absolutely, but are such only under a certain condition, that is, if no provision has otherwise been made. Thus the peoples of Germany, since properties had to be assigned to their kings and princes for the maintenance of the proper rank, wisely considered that a beginning ought to be made with those things which could be assigned without loss to anyone. To this class belong all things which have not become the property of any one' (bk 2, chap. viii, para. v): Grotius (1625), 1925, vol. 2, p. 297 (V). He goes on to remark that this is now common law, and as it were a people's right. Grotius also speaks of the various ways of possessing wild beasts whether shut up, in flight or at liberty. What Grotius considers to stem from the particular disposition of things according to the law (bk 2, chap. viii, para. v) Manwood considers to be purely and simply natural. Bracton, whom Manwood cites, had established the same kind of order as Grotius. Devèze, 1961, vol. 1, p. 104 (III), for his part, notes that although the right to hunt may have been an attribute of property ownership under Roman law, in the Middle Ages it was essentially feudal. Like fleecing (there was a complex assortment of rights for this in the 'vert') and pasturage, hunting belonged to whoever wielded the right of justice. He notes also, however, that Bouteiller (1479), 1621, bk 2, chap. xxxvi, pp. 250–1 (V), writes: 'By natural law, the wild beasts which flourish in the sky and also those which flourish on common land belong to whosoever is able to catch them, without distinction as to whether whoever seizes them does so on his own land or on that of another.' Manwood, who is not unfamiliar with the right of 'finders keepers' where wild beasts are concerned, nevertheless founds the king's hunting rights upon a kind of primitive natural right which predates any other.

38 Petit-Dutaillis, 1913, p. 62 (III). Devèze, 1961, vol. 2, Annexe I (III), discusses this etymology at length. He notes that in France (as in Germany with the word *Forst*) the 'forest' had lost its meaning of 'royal hunting territory' and become totally synonymous with *silva*, which accounted for the disappearance of the word *silve* from modern French. The situation was quite different in England, where the eminent status of the king ensured that the institution of the 'forest' retained all its meaning right into the fifteenth century (pp. 345–6).

39 On allegiance and natural law, see below, Chapter 5.

40 In Jowitt, 1959 (II), a 'corporation sole' is defined as a collectivity which contains only one member at a time, 'the corporate character being kept up by a succession of solitary members' over a long period of time. Under feudal law a corporation could neither swear an oath nor give homage, for both these acts required the physical presence of the person involved. Constituted bodies – religious ones for example – were known as corporations. This concept remained valid in the sixteenth century. Thus, Judge Brooke writes: 'Nota in Scaccario que Deane & chapter, & auters corps politike ne fra homage, car ceo serr[a] fait in p[er]so[n], et corporation ne poet apere in p[er]so[n] mes p[er] Attorney, Et hommage ne poet estre fait per Attorney, mes solem[en]t in p[er]son' (Note in Exchequer that Dean and Chapter, and other political bodies, cannot pay homage, for this is to be done in person and corporations cannot appear in person, only through an Attorney, and homage cannot be made through an Attorney, but only in person): Brook[e], 1578, p. 329 (V). On this idea see Maitland, 'The Corporation Sole' and 'The Crown as Corporation', in *Collected Papers*, 1911, vol. 3, pp. 210–43 and 244–70 (III).

41 Markham (1615), 1649, p. 4 (V).
42 This information is provided by Hill (1958), 1968, p. 68 (III). Hill cites Adam Blackwood, *Opera omnia*, Paris, 1644, pp. 42–3. In that work Blackwood is replying to *De Jure Regni apud Scotos dialogus* (1579) by George Buchanan. Cowell cites him in his *Interpreter*. Arthur Hall's attack against the Commons is reported by Neale (1949), 1963, pp. 353, 377–8 (III).
43 In James I, 1918, p. 62 (V), cited by Allen (1928), 1960, p. 253 (III).
44 James I, 1918, p. 62 (V), cited by Lamont and Oldfield, 1975, p. 4 (III). The editors point out that such views were less rare than is generally believed.
45 Cited by Hill (1958), 1968, p. 69 (III). He points out in a note that in 1608 Bacon wrote that 'the ancient laws and customs of this kingdom' were 'practised long before the conquest'.
46 Allen (1928), 1960, pp. 253–4 (III).
47 The state of the dispute over whether there was really a fundamental constitutional conflict under James I is described clearly by Smith, 1973, pp. 160–9 (III). Kenyon, 1966, p. 8 (III), for his part, points out that James I's absolutism was mainly theoretical: in his speech to Parliament delivered on 21 March 1610, he makes a distinction between original kings with limitless powers and the kings of established nations who, even if not strictly obliged to respect the laws and customs of their subjects, are nevertheless accountable to God if they transgress them.
48 See Eccleshall, 1978 (III).
49 Vernant and Vidal-Naquet, 1972, p. 138 (VII).
50 On the hierarchy of forest authorities, see Petit-Dutaillis, 1913, p. 60 (III).
51 Turner, 1901, introd., p. xxx (III).
52 Coke, 1644, p. 294 (V).
53 *Quia a tempore ut lagatus est, caput gerit lupinum*: Cowell, 1607, 'Outlawry', 'Woolferthfod' (corrected to 'Wolferhefod' in the emendations) (V). The quotation is from Bracton.
54 This practice was still current in contemporary times: the Sheriff's Act of 1887 confirms the statute of 1275, 3 Edw. I, c. 9. See Jowitt, 1959, 'Hue and Cry' (II). Coke comments on the law, 1644, p. 294 (V).
55 See Petit-Dutaillis' major study cited above. As Shaw, 1956 (III), notes, if the king alienated all or part of a forest, this became a chase. On the other hand, parks (which were enclosed), belonging to subjects, could be located within the confines of the forest – or in its purlieus – but were not subject to the constraints that affected the forest (p. 4).
56 Turner, 1901, pp. cxiv–cxv (III). His argument is taken up by Cox, 1905, pp. 25–40 (III).
57 It is, in effect, remarkable to note that in a collection produced in 1622, dedicated to Sir Thomas Posthumus Hobbie Knight, and entitled 'A looke of all the oulde Customes used in Pickeringlithe time oute of memorie . . . ', there is a similar classification to Manwood's: this document is reproduced in Turton, 1894–7, vol. 2, p. 2 (III).
58 Here Coke provides various references to legal and historical works, as well as to hunting treatises.
59 Psalm 104.
60 This 'pseudo-Canute' appeared at the end of the twelfth century. See Petit-Dutaillis, 1913, p. 62 (III), which is based upon Liebermann, 1894 (III). An English translation of this charter is to be found in Lewis, 1811, pp. 141–6 (III).

Also in the same work, *La Carta de Foresta* (9 Hen. III) and the *Assiza et Consuetudines Forestae* (6 Edw. I).

61 Cox, 1905 (III). He is referring to the best manuscript of *The Master of Game* (translated from the famous *Livre de Chasse* by Gaston de Foix (alias Gaston Phoebus)) preceded by *Le Art de Vénerie* by Guillaume Twici, chief huntsman of Edward II (Cottonian MS Vespasian B. XII). For more recent editions of the principal books on hunting, see the reference list in the appendix to this chapter.

62 'To encroach royal power or prerogative' was the principal transgression that made a subject a traitor. This concept is the basis for the laws on treason.

63 He mentions this explicitly on pp. 61 and 62 (II, 2); he declares that a forest can be created by Act of Parliament, see 31 Hen. VIII, c. 5. It was by reason of his 'princely clemency, to show his most gracious benignity towards the owners of the same ground' that the king granted them certain privileges to compensate for the wrong they had suffered. Edward Coke expresses his disagreement in no uncertain terms. He claims that, according to the *Carta de Foresta* (9 Hen. III), the king has no right to establish a forest on the domains of his subjects (1644, p. 300 (V)). He cites the case of Henry VIII who wanted to create a forest around Hampton Court but realised that he could not do so without the consent of his free tenants and of those occupants in possession of the customary tenure. 'It hereby plainly appeareth . . . that the king could neither erect any Chase or Forest over any man's grounds without their consent and agreement. And yet King Henry VIII did stand as much upon his prerogative as any king of England ever did' (p. 301).

64 Aged one year, the stag is a 'hind calf' or a 'calf'; aged two it is a 'broker' (or 'brocket' or 'picket' – a *daguet* in French); aged three it is a 'spayad'; aged four a 'staggard'; aged five, a 'stag'; aged six a 'hart'.

65 Or sometimes a 'stag' at four, a 'halt' at five, and a 'great stag' at six.

66 On the boar and the texts – literary and otherwise – that describe it, see Thiébaux, 1969 (VI).

67 Voragine, 1967, vol. 2, pp. 192–8 (VIII).

68 On the stag and its symbolism, see Thiébaux, 1974 (VI). On the iconographical and literary traditions relating to animals, see Klingender, 1971 (VIII). For an overall view of animal symbolism, see Rowland, 1974 (VIII). On the conventional beliefs about animals during the Tudor period, see Carroll, 1954 (VI).

69 Turbervil[l]e (1575) (1611), 1908, p. 128 (V). See also the lesson Tristan gives to the huntsman of King Marc, in Joseph Bédier's reconstitution of the episode (1946), 1958, pp. 6–8 (VIII). On the meaning of this episode and other hunting rituals, see Klingender, 1971, pp. 468–75 (VIII).

70 Cited in Strutt, 1876 (according to Nichol's *Progresses*, vol. 2), p. 71 (III).

71 Cited by Strutt, 1876, pp. 112–13 (III).

72 Cited in *ibid.*, pp. 68–9. See *The Squyr of lowe degre*, London, 1550 (?), sig. D. ii. verso. Critical edition by William E. Mead, Athenaeum Press, Boston, 1904.

73 William Harrison, 'The Description of England' (1586) in Holinshed, Harrison *et al.*, 1807–8, vol. 1, bk ii, chap. xix, p. 343 (V).

74 Coke, 1644, p. 301 (V).

75 Grotius (1625), 1925, vol. 2 (V); see bk 2, chap. viii, 'On acquisitions commonly said to be peoples' rights' (para. v, 'On wild beasts belonging to the king . . . '; para. vii, 'To whom does treasure naturally belong?').

76 Tawney (1926), 1948, chap. 3, p. 40 (III): 'The new economic realities came into sharp collision with the social theory inherited from the Middle Ages. The result

210 *Notes to pp. 37–42*

was a reassertion of the traditional doctrines with an almost tragic intensity of emotion, their gradual retreat before the advance of new conceptions, both of economic organization and of the province of religion.' Morris (1953), 1965, p. 73 (III): 'The hysterical note can be heard most clearly in the Homilies or set sermons which the government ordered to be read in Churches.'
77 Cox, 1911, pp. 126–7(III).
78 Just as the French edition of this book was going to press, I came across the important article by Le Goff, 1980 (VII), which elaborates on a number of themes discussed in this chapter.

2. The forest, hunting and sacrifice in *Titus Andronicus*

1 The edition used is that of J. C. Maxwell (1953), amended edn 1968 (IV).
2 A Rome that, if we are to believe Terence J.-B. Spencer, 1957 (VI), would have seemed altogether believable to the cultivated Elizabethan public which had read Edward Hellowes, *A Chronicle, conteyning the lives of tenne Emperours of Rome* (1577), a translation of the *Decada* of Antonio de Guevara. Both the institutions and the *mores* of Rome depicted in the play represent a kind of summary of Roman politics as if the author had been eager to include, in the words of Spencer, '*all* the political institutions that Rome ever had' (p. 32).
3 The Ghost that appears in *Hamlet* and the one in *The Spanish Tragedy* show that there was still belief in the anger of the dead. Keith Thomas notes that medieval ghosts would appear in order that some sin committed be confessed and absolved. In the Reformation period, the view was rather that ghosts appeared for the purpose of denouncing some misdeed (Thomas, 1971, p. 597 (III)). George K. Hunter, 1974 (VI), says that the sacrifice in *Titus Andronicus* was seen as a legitimate religious act, made necessary by the cult of the family, and would not have been seen critically by the audience. He claims that the importance of the cult of the family can be seen from the reiteration of the theme of burial.
4 Brockbank, 1976, pp. 9–10 (VI).
5 *The Spanish Tragedy* is a striking example. Bowers (1940), 1966, p. 38 (VI), notes that in his treatise against Machiavelli, I. Gentillet maintains that Roman law disinherited the son who refused to avenge his father. A similar declaration, dated 1612, can be found in a manuscript that Bowers attributes to the count of Northampton. On revenge, see the points made by Fuzier, 1965 and 1968 (VI).
6 Lopez de Gomara (1578), 1596, p. 398 (V).
7 Scot (1584), 1972, XI, i, p. 108 (V).
8 For example, J. Dover Wilson, in his edition of the play, 1948, pp. xi–xii (IV). For Bradbrook, the decorous and decorative imagery is there to mask the tragedy, which is 'an exercise in the manner of Seneca': (1935), 1960, pp. 98–9 (VI). This is an idea that she develops in her introduction to the play, where she describes the various characters as emblems or badges, who make up 'tableaux' or 'moral emblems'. Waith, 1957 (VI), for his part, remarks that in the interpretative tradition of the Renaissance, Ovid was seen as a teller of tales who took as his theme the moral transformation of man into beast, the passing from order to chaos. He stresses that the 'metamorphosis' of the characters in *Titus Andronicus* comes about under the effects of passion, pain or despair. The ornate narrative style reinforces the impact of horror. The play is a contribution to a particular tragic mode: it is a spectacle 'both horrible and pathetic, but above all extraordinary' (p. 48). See also Reese, 1970 (VI).

9 The quotations from *Henry VI*, Part III are taken from A. S. Cairncross' edition, London, 1964. On the opposition between the civilised and the barbarous, see Zeeveld, 1974, pp. 207–10 (VI), who stresses the bond of barbarity shared by Goths and Moors. For a different view of the Goths, see Broude, 1972 (VI).

10 Sommers, 1960, p. 277 (VI).

11 *Ibid.*, p. 283.

12 According to J. C. Maxwell's gloss in this edition of the play: 'solemn', here, means 'ceremonial'.

13 Artaud, 1964, p. 42 (VIII).

14 *Ibid.*, p. 35. Kurosawa made use of the opposition between the forest and the ritual in *The Spider's Castle*. See Marienstras, 1979b (VI).

15 The word was later used by Giovanni in a murderous (and sexual) context in *'Tis Pity She's a Whore*, at the point when he is proferring Annabella's bleeding heart: 'You come to the feast, my lords, with dainty fare' (V, vi, 26). Neither Colman nor Partridge comment upon it. Alfred Harbage (1947), 1961, p. 14 (VI), notes 'the presence of episodes habitually eliminated from all other plays of the dramatist . . . : a rape attempted and accomplished, an adulterous relationship entered into with thoughtless alacrity, a mother disposed toward infanticide', etc.

16 From this point of view, Sommers' contrastive analysis of the speeches of Saturninus and Bassianus is convincing (1960, n. 10 (VI)). I also found Nicholas Brooke (1968), 1973 (VI), and Tricomi, 1974 (VI) useful in writing this chapter.

3. Some reflections on sacrifice

1 The Thirty-nine articles, article 28.

2 Jewel, 1847, vol. 2, pp. 708 and 734 (V).

3 *Ibid.*, pp. 719 and 734.

4 Hooper, 1852, p. 32 (V). The text is taken from 'A briefe and clear Confession of the Christian faith . . . ', originally published in 1550 and reprinted in 1581 and 1584.

5 Bullinger (1587), 1849, vol. 1, p. viii (V).

6 Auerbach, 1959, pp. 11–76 (VII).

7 Bullinger (1587), 1850, vol. 3, p. 194 (V).

8 *Ibid.*, pp. 194–5.

9 *Ibid.*, p. 196.

10 *Ibid.*, p. 197.

11 *Ibid.*, p. 198.

12 Sandys, 'A sermon preached at Paul's Cross, at what time a Main Treason was Discovered', in 1841 (V), following the text of: *Sermons made by the most reverende Father in God, Edwin, Archbishop of Yorke, Primate of England and Metropolitane*, London, 1585.

13 *Ibid.*, p. 405.

14 *Ibid.*, p. 408.

15 *Ibid.*, p. 410.

16 *Ibid.*, p. 410.

17 *Ibid.*, p. 411.

18 Relating the murder of Caesar, William Fulbecke remarks that he 'fell as a sacrifice' at the foot of Pompey's statue (p. 169).

19 Hakluyt (1907), 1967, vol. 1, pp. 353–6: sacrifice among the Samoyedes; vol. 6,

p. 296: cannibalism among the Samboses on the island of Sambula, etc. (V). According to the O.E.D. the word 'cannibal' was used for the first time in an English translation of Sebastian Muenster (Richard Eden, *A Treatyse of the newe India*, 1553, a translation of the *Cosmographia*). As early as 1522, however, an English translation of the letters of Vespucci refers to a man eating his own wife and children in 'Armenique' (cited by Sheehan, 1980, p. 67 (III)). Two illustrations from the letters of Vespucci can be found in Hugh Honour's album, 1976, pp. 8–9 (III). See also *Mandeville's Travels*, 1967, chap. 19 (V), which mentions children being sacrificed. The first English mention of Indian cannibals is in 1511: see Hodgen, 1964, p. 409 (VII).

20 Reproduced in Hodgen, 1964, p. 147 (VII).
21 Mentioned by Jones (1964), 1968, p. 53 (III).
22 López de Gomara (1570), 1596, pp. 398 and 392–3 (V).
23 Burton (1621), 1964, vol. 3, pt 3, sec. 4, memb. 2, subs. 3, p. 360 (V).
24 As Burton does over several pages, just before the passage cited. The feeling of horror could be caused by the intuition that 'a sacrifice . . . cannot but be a murder and is apt to be an atrocity, in which the cruelty of the crime is an element in its motivation', as Philip Brockbank forcefully puts it (1976, p. 10 (VI)).
25 Roland Mushat Frye (1963), 1967, p. 168 (VI).
26 *King Lear*, ed. K. Muir (1952), 1959 (IV).
27 Cited by Roland Mushat Frye (1963), 1967, pp. 168–9 (VI).
28 *Ibid.*, p. 170.
29 *Ibid.*, p. 172.
30 Elton (1966), 1968, p. 37 (VI). His discussion of such attitudes in relation to *King Lear* takes up more than 200 pages.
31 Scot (1584), 1972, XI, i–xii, pp. 108–15 (V).
32 Simmons, 1973, pp. 1–17 (VI).
33 *Ibid.*, p. 7.
34 North, in Plutarch (1579), 1595 (V). Barroll, 1958 (VI), cited by Simmons, 1973, p. 8 (VI), notes that North's remarks echo those of Saint Augustine, *The City of God*, V, xviii.
35 Simmons, 1973, p. 8 (VI).
36 See Marienstras, 1979a (VI).
37 The references are to *Julius Caesar*, ed. T. S. Dorsch, 1955 (IV).
38 Zeeveld, 1974, p. 89 (VI), suggests that this type of oath is reminiscent of the 'Bond of Association' contracted between staunch partisans of Elizabeth against Mary Stuart; but the reference he gives offers very little convincing evidence for this. See, rather, the idea expressed by Edward Coke, that allegiance came before the swearing of an oath (see below, chapter 5, on the Calvin affair). Brutus separates the body politic from its head and considers himself to owe allegiance to Rome. His point of view is also that of the Spencers, condemned under Edward II for having made a distinction between the body politic and the physical body of the king, between the Crown and the realm, that is to say between the head and the body. The idea that Caesar was emperor appears to have been one widely held by Elizabethans. See the references in Simmons, 1973, p. 79 (VI). See also Shirley, 1979, p. 77 (VI).
39 Noted by various commentators: Traversi, 1963, pp. 25–7 (VI); Palmer, 1965, pp. 5–6 (VI).
40 There is an interesting commentary in Simmons, 1973, pp. 80–4 (VI): even those who defended a hierarchical society recognised the existence of a time prior to

the fall, when the reign of a Caesar would have been an anomaly. The Anabaptists cited the *Epistle to the Galatians*, V, i, 12–13, which refers to the 'liberty' that Christ gave to men. Simmons also cites remarks credited to Robert Kett in 1549 and mentions the puritan reformists who were fighting against the episcopal hierarchy. The ideal behind Brutus' assassination of Caesar is one that the dominant ideology had not stifled (p. 84). On nostalgia for the Golden Age, see Levin, 1970 (VI).

41 Eccleshall, 1978 (III) has shown how, throughout the century, there was conflict between the alternative theories of 'limited' and absolute monarchy. The former theory maintained that 'Englishmen had discovered in Parliament institutional procedures for co-operating with one another in the rational order of the universe' (p. 100).

42 Stirling, 1951 (VI); revised version, 1956 (VI). See also Kirschbaum, 1949 (VI). These two texts are reproduced in Ure, 1969 (VI). Schanzer (1963), 1965 (VI), has used ethnological ideas in his discussion of the play.

43 Lévi-Strauss, 1962 (VII). This definition of sacrifice, based on that produced by Hubert and Mauss (1899), 1968 (VII), rests upon a distinction between the sacred and the profane. Now, as Philippe Ariès writes, 'the mental frontier between the sacred and the profane remained more or less imprecise up until the reforms of the sixteenth and seventeenth centuries: the profane was steeped in the supernatural and the sacred was penetrated by naturalism' (Ariès, 1977, p. 57 (III)). But the very nature of the arguments about the transubstantiation show that a frontier was in the process of being established. It was homologous to the frontier between morals and politics, between *virtù* and virtue, between the time of the city and the time of the church, between human and divine or 'natural' law. That is why Lévi-Strauss' definition seems pertinent here. For a brief history of western interpretations of sacrifice, see the article 'Sacrifice' by R. Bastide in the *Encyclopaedia Universalis*, vol. 14, 1968 (II). See also the works of Girard, 1972 and 1978 (VII).

44 On the rite of communion as practised by the Jews, note, in the company of the authors of the article 'Sacrifice' in the *Dictionnaire de théologie catholique*, vol. 14, 1, col. 674, 1941 (II), that 'in the ancient texts, immolation is not considered as an act reserved for the priest so it is not strictly speaking sacerdotal. The essential role of the priest begins with the oblation of blood and the burning of flesh.'

45 Simmons notes his need for an 'absolute moral purity' (1973, p. 102 (VI)).

46 Knight (1931), 1965, p. 48 (VI).

47 Stirling, 1951, *passim* (VI).

48 Knight (1931), 1965, p. 51 (VI).

49 Brents Stirling, in Ure, 1969, p. 167 (VI).

50 See above, chapter 2, on the forest.

51 Charney, 1963, p. 57 (VI).

52 *Ibid.*

53 *Ibid.*

54 Despite the contrary view held by some commentators, this ideal is strongly stressed by Zeeveld, 1974, p. 92 (VI).

55 In Ure, 1969, p. 170 (VI). Knight (1931), 1965, p. 33 (VI), produced a similar commentary.

56 For a more complex study, see Bacquet, 1974, pp. 123–4 (VI). See also Carson, 1965 (VI). Proser, 1965, pp. 12–13 (VI), points out that the blood of Pompey's statue is mentioned by Plutarch in connection with the idea of revenge on the

part of Pompey. Plutarch (1579), 1595, p. 794 (V), writes: 'Caesar . . . was driven either casually, or purposedly, by the Counsell of the conspirators, against the base whereupon Pompey's image stood, which ran all of a goare bloude, till he was slaine. Thus it seemed that the image tooke iust revenge of Pompeys ennemie.'

57 Simmons, 1973 (VI).

58 *Ibid.*, p. 107: 'Those qualities in Caesar that had caused Brutus to kill him – the attempted isolation from humanity, the presumptuousness, the potentiality for evil – are in Brutus.' And as he is incapable of knowing himself, being a Roman, he has to continue to see himself solely through the eyes of Rome.

59 This is McCallum's expression (1910), 1967, p. 266 (VI). The fact that the 'Caesarian principle of authority has been established within the frame of the conspiracy' (Simmons, 1973, p. 105 (VI)) is also noted by other writers: Mark Hunter, 1931, p. 132 (VI); Goddard, 1960, vol. 1, pp. 312–321 (VI); Gordon Ross Smith, 1959 (VI); Rabkin, 1964 (VI). Simmons, however, insists: 'Brutus consciously plays no role but rather acts in accord with his mistaken knowledge of himself. *The true self, which remains like a norm*, will not deny Cassius' appeal to love' (1973, p. 104 (VI), my italics). Nicholas Brooke (1968), 1973, p. 159 (VI), on the other hand, takes a more straightforward view: the source of values, in the play, is provided by the unstable populace, so it is impossible for Brutus' honour to flourish fully in reality. In other words, self-knowledge has nothing to do with the matter.

60 Pocock, 1971 (III), writes: 'Civic humanism denotes a style of thought . . . in which it is contended that the development of the individual towards self-fulfillment is possible only when the individual acts as a citizen, that is as a conscious and autonomous participant in an autonomous decision-taking political community, the *polis* or republic. Now, the republic – unlike the hierarchised cosmos of medieval imperial or monarchical thought – had to be conceived of as finite and localised in time, and therefore as presenting all the problems of particularity. The individual's prospect of fulfilling his moral and rational nature consequently depended on his ability to partake in political decisions within a particularised and secular framework; to be fully human, he must master the politics of time. Civic humanist thought strongly implied that the republic and its citizens were somehow capable of this mastery, but did not of itself offer an epistemological formula which could emancipate cognition of the particular from the medieval conceptual scheme. And if the individual as citizen should fail to master time through participation in political decision, he would find himself in the world of time neither understood, legitimised nor controlled' (pp. 85–6). He goes on: 'Only as a partnership in virtue among all citizens could the republic persist; if virtue were less than universal, its failure at one point must in time corrode its existence at all others' (p. 87). 'The theory of classical republicanism [derived from Aristotle, Polybius, and subsequently from Machiavelli and Guicciardini] required an ethos of extreme personal autonomy – a requirement, it is interesting to note, which a feudal ethos of honour and a Puritan ethos of self-respect seem to have been equally capable of meeting' (p. 90).

To consider, as Phillips does (1940), 1972 (VI), that the Rome in *Julius Caesar* is a monarchy *de facto*, attacked by a group of aristocrats (p. 184) and the spirit of Caesar as the 'concept of a unitary sovereignty' (p. 188) seems excessive.

61 Roland Mushat Frye (1963), 1967, p. 170 (VI).

62 Simmons, 1973, pp. 107–8 (VI).

63 For a study that lays emphasis upon the blindness of Brutus, see for example

Rabkin, 1967, pp. 117–19 (VI). According to Heilman, 1964 (VI), the equanimity shown by Brutus before his death (which indicates that he is not questioning himself) stems from the fact that 'Shakespeare's imagination is not yet carrying him into the inner puzzles of tragic character' (p. 43); it could be objected that Richard II and Henry IV are not without their introspective moments. A work that particularly stresses self-knowledge in the tragic hero is that of Jorgenson, 1967 (VI). For a finer distinction drawn between consciousness of self and consciousness of one's errors, see Ellrodt, 1975 (VI), in particular pp. 42 and 47, n. 3.

4. Macbeth or the tyrant sacrificed

1 Bradley (1904), 1958 (VI).
2 Knights (1933) 1946 (VI).
3 At this point Macbeth adds that his 'fears in Banquo / Stick deep'. The quotations refer to *Macbeth* ed. Kenneth Muir (1951) 1977 (IV). The fact that Macbeth cannot commit the definitive action that will make him king is emphasised by Eagleton (1967) 1970, pp. 131–3 (VI).
4 Many commentators have emphasised this exclusion: Hawkes, 1973 (VI) and Mack, 1973 (VI), are among the most recent to do so.
5 *De officio regis*, eds. A. W. Pollard and C. Sayle, London, 1887, p. 18, l. 28.
6 A number of emendations have been proposed for this line. The Cambridge edition gives 'Each way and none'. Kenneth Muir adopts Samuel Johnson's version.
7 As Muir notes, there are three possible senses to 'hereafter': (1) the one adopted by Pierre Leyris, ed. Aubier, Paris, 1977, in his French translation: 'Il aurait bien fallu qu'elle vienne à mourir', i.e. she would have had to die eventually; (2) the idea that 'she should have died at a better moment' (Johnson); (3) the meaning suggested by Murry (1936), 1955, p. 335 (VI) which I myself favour: 'hereafter', I think, is purposely vague. It does not mean 'later'; but in a different mode of time from that in which Macbeth is imprisoned now. 'Hereafter' in the not-Now. Deviant beings are outside natural and social time, ordered time, and enter a time of their own.
8 'Recorded time' could have a number of meanings: (1) 'the record of time' (Hudson); (2) 'the time fixed in the decrees of Heaven for the period of life' (Johnson); (3) 'till the last judgement' (Elwin). (Muir's note.)
9 Kott (1962), 1965, pp. 102–3 (VI).
10 Sanders and Jacobson, 1978, p. 63 (VI).
11 *Ibid.*, p. 67.
12 *Ibid.*, p. 72.
13 *Ibid.*, p. 81.
14 A familiar idea. On the subject of the king of France leading his army into Flanders to punish the murderers of Count Charles, Suger writes: 'Through various kinds of vengeance and through much bloodshed, Flanders was purified (*blanchi*) and, as it were, rebaptised': *Vie de Louis VI* (twelfth century), cited by Duby, 1978 (III).
15 Delumeau, 1978 (III), using a number of texts from the period, shows the importance and wide diffusion of the various kinds of fear evoked in *Macbeth*. I will not give an exhaustive list, but, for instance: the sea, the far and the near, the new and the old, curses, the night, ghosts, sedition, etc. His work brings up to date the study by Campbell (1930), 1961 (VI), in which chapter XV is entitled

'*Macbeth*, a study in fear'. This psychological study in no way invalidates Merchant, 1966 (VI): Lady Macbeth, who deliberately submits to demoniacal powers, forms 'a contrast' that 'could scarcely be pointed more strongly' with 'Macbeth's extended casuistic attitude'. On the relations between fear and remorse, see Milward, 1973, pp. 47–8 and 132 (VI), and Farnham (1950), 1963, pp. 112–19 (VI).

16 Heilman, 1966 (VI). The same problem is discussed in psychological terms by Wayne Booth (1951), reprinted by Lerner, 1963 (VI).

17 Heilman, 1966, p. 23 (VI).

18 Before revealing that he was 'not born of woman', Macduff says: 'I have no words; / My voice is in my sword' (V, viii, 6–7). Historical violence is unleashed without words before the establishment of order or a return to nature. For Muir, 1972, p. 155 (VI), however, the spectator is unable to identify with Macbeth beyond act IV.

19 Holinshed (1927), 1963, p. 211 (V).

20 The fact that agents of evil can exceed their power is a theme not unknown in the writings of the Fathers of the Church: 'In the conflict in which he is in opposition to God, Satan is all-powerful over man by reason of the sins of the latter. But, by provoking the martyrdom and death of Christ, Satan abuses his power and thus prepares his own downfall' (Gauvin, 1973, p. 162 (VI)). The development of this theory in the Church Fathers has been described by Fry, 1951 (VI). Gauvin notes that the source of the interpretation is to be found in the Apocrypha, particularly in the *Gospel of Nicodemus*. He discusses this theory on pp. 215–20.

21 Bradley (1904), 1958 (VI).

22 Tillyard (1944), 1969, pp. 316–17 (VI). In support of his thesis, Tillyard cites the following words of Malcolm: 'Macbeth / Is ripe for shaking, and the Powers above / Put on their instruments' (IV, iii, 237–9).

23 Curry (1937), 1968 (VI).

24 Sanders, 1968 (VI). The role of the witches has given rise to many studies. Of these I would cite those of Farnham (1950), 1963 (VI); Rossiter, 1961 (VI); Jacquot, 1957 (VI); McGee, 1966 (VI); Anthony Harris, 1980 (VI).

25 Barthes, 1966, p. 10 (VII).

26 *Ibid.*

27 Stewart, 1949 (VI).

28 On the symbolic meaning of the animals named, see the notes to the Furness edition (1873), 1903 (IV), and the work by Rowland, 1974 (VIII).

29 Spender, 1941, p. 124 (VI), notes in connection with these lines that Macbeth 'looks back on a time when the past was really past and the present present', whereas now 'the present disgorges the past'.

30 Spurgeon, 1935 (VI).

31 Knight (1931), 1965 (VI).

32 Knights (1933), 1946 (VI).

33 Cleanth Brooks (1947), 1968 (VI); Spender, 1941 (VI); Waith, 1950 (VI). On duplicity and the practice of equivocation, see also Rogers, 1964 (VI); Edward A. Armstrong (1946), 1963 (VI).

34 Kott (1962), 1965 (VI); Muir, 1966 (VI).

35 See Sir J. G. Frazer, *The Golden Bough*, abridged edn, Macmillan, London, 1923, Index, article 'Fire'.

36 Sanders, 1968 (VI), draws attention to these implicit restrictions.

37 This theme, tackled by Robert Burton, is a medical and theological common-

place; see (1621), 1964, vol. 1, pt 1, sec. 2, memb. 1, subs. 1: 'Paracelsus is of opinion that such spiritual diseases (for so he calls them) are spiritually to be cured, and not otherwise' (p. 179) (V).

38 Murray, 1966 (VI), cites Paracelsus to show that, thanks to some mystic alchemy, the blood of a saintly king turns to gold just as, according to John Donne, Christ can transform the flesh of a sinner, making it eternally perfect, like gold.

39 In the Bible, blood is something sacred. 'The blood is the life', Deut. XII, 23. 'For the life of the flesh is in the blood; and I have given it to you upon the altar to make an atonement for your souls', Lev. XVII, 10–11. 'The voice of thy brother's blood crieth unto me from the ground', Gen. IV, 10. The principle of life is in the blood, but we know that this principle, which has been given by God, belongs to Him only: see the *Dictionnaire de théologie catholique*, article 'Sacrifice', vol. 14, 1, col. 665, 1941 (II). According to William Harvey, ' . . . Blood it self, without *spirit* and *heat*, is no longer to be called *Blood*, but *Gore*' (*Anatomical Exercitations concerning the generation of Living Creatures*, London, 1653, p. 447).

40 'The Rape of Lucrece' in *The Poems*, 1960 (V).

41 Murray, 1966, pp. 40–1 (VI).

42 Cited *ibid.*, p. 41. The passage is taken from a treatise by Paracelsus entitled *De Sanguine Ultra Mortem* (About the Blood beyond Death), in *Opera Omnia*, vol. 2, pp. 465ff.

43 Anon., *The York Plays*, 1885 (IV).

44 Play 30 (First trial before Pilate and dream of Pilate's wife).

45 Anon., *Ludus Coventriae or the Plaie called Corpus Christi*, ed. K. S. Block, London (1922), 1960, p. 288, lines 505 and 506.

46 Gauvin, 1973, p. 182 (VI).

47 Anon., *Ludus Coventriae*, l. 524.

48 Gauvin, 1973, p. 182 (VI).

49 Anon., *The York Plays*, 1885, xxx, 163–4 (IV).

50 Jacquot, 1957, p. 186 (VI).

51 *Ibid.*, p. 191.

52 Northrop Frye (1957), 1967, p. 223 (VI).

53 *Ibid.*, pp. 222–3.

54 Holloway (1961), 1966 (VI).

55 *Ibid.*, p. 64.

56 *Ibid.*, p. 65.

57 *Ibid.*

58 Cited *ibid.*, p. 72 (Browne, 1928, vol. 1, p. 24 (V)).

5. The near and the far: the Calvin affair and the status of foreigners under James I of England

1 James VI of Scotland was crowned on 29 July 1567 at Stirling. He was thirteen months old.

2 Coke (1600–59), 1826 (V). The Calvin affair is reported in part vii (1608), vol. 2, pp. 1–48 (hereafter cited in this chapter simply as Coke). The citation occurs at 1a. On Edward Coke, see Johnson, 1837 (III); Thorne (1952), 1957 (III); Bowen, 1957 (III); Hill, 1965, chap. 5 (III); Beauté, 1975 (III).

3 On 19 March 1604, James I, in his first speech to Parliament, laid emphasis upon the domestic peace with which, through his own person, God had blessed

England. The king put forward his proposal for organic union on 31 March 1607. See James I, 1616, pp. 485–97 and 509–25 (V). The text of these speeches is reproduced in Tanner (1930), 1961, pp. 24–30 and 35–7 (III). On the political projects of James I, see Willson, 1960 (III).

4 Cobbett, 1806–20, vol. 1, 1806, pp. 1082 and 1086 (III), cited by Tanner (1930), 1961, p. 23 (III). The various fortunes of the proposals for union and for naturalisation are discussed in Gardiner, 1883–4, vol. 1, pp. 324–39 and 355–7 (III).

5 Legislation against treason was modified in 1558, 1563, 1571, 1572, 1581 and 1585; see Bellamy, 1979, pp. 47–82 (III). In 1585, 1593, 1604 and 1606, Acts were passed against Jesuits, papists and non-conformists. On the Elizabethans' anti-catholic obsession, see Wiener, 1971 (III).

6 See Lipson, 1961–2 (III), and Tawney and Power, 1924 (III). See also George K. Hunter, 1964 (VI).

7 This play which for a long time remained in manuscript form was published for the first time in 1844. It is not certain that it was ever performed, although the name of an actor, Thomas Goodale, appears in the manuscript. It was censored, then revised. Specialists think it was composed by Anthony Munday, Henry Chettle and Thomas Heywood (?) and revised by Shakespeare and Thomas Dekker. Three pages of the manuscript may be in Shakespeare's hand. On the attribution of the text and handwriting to Shakespeare, see the symposium, *Shakespeare's Hand in 'The Play of Sir Thomas More'*, 1923 (VI). The history of the attribution is summarised by Schoenbaum, 1966, pp. 104–7 (VI). There is a description of Evil (or Ill) May Day in Hall's *Chronicle*, conveniently reproduced in Tawney and Power, 1924, vol. 3, pp. 82–90 (III).

8 On these two bills, see Neale (1949), 1963, p. 385 (III), and (1953), 1965, vol. 1, pp. 411–12 (III).

9 Egerton, Viscount Brackley, 1609, p. 103 (V).

10 Neale (1957), 1965, vol. 2, p. 373 (III).

11 In the dedicatory epistle to Sir Philip Sidney of his first collection of voyage accounts, *Diverse Voyages touching the Discovery of America*, 1582. The text of the epistle may be found in Wright, 1965, pp. 21–36 (V).

12 Richard Hakluyt the Elder (jurist, and cousin of the other Richard Hakluyt), 'Inducements to the Liking of the Voyage intended towards Virginia . . . ', written in 1585 and published in 1602 by John Brereton, *Discovery of the North Part of Virginia*. The text can be found in Wright, 1965, pp. 26–36 (V).

13 The literature on this question is extensive. See, for example, Quinn, 1966 (III). An overall view, together with a basic bibliography, can be found in O'Farrell, 1971 (III). On the views of Edmund Spenser and William Camden on the Irish, see Hodgen, 1964, pp. 364–6 (VII).

14 In Tanner (1930), 1961, p. 25 (III).

15 Coke, 4a.

16 *Ibid.*

17 These 'reporters' are not exactly clerks, but jurists noting the course taken by the debates, with a view to their publication. Coke was really operating as a reporter as he described and commented upon the arguments exchanged during the course of the Calvin affair.

18 Coke, 4a.

19 *Ibid.*, 3b.

20 *Ibid.*, 2b.

21 First studied by Kantorowicz, 1957 (III), and by Axton, 1977 (III), who provides

a commentary for a recently discovered and identified manuscript treatise by Edmund Plowden (p. 18).

22 Coke, 4b. The vassalage relationship was originally a contractual one. The vassal owed his 'faith' rather than his obedience to the 'suzerain'. The homage tacitly implied the right to disobey if the suzerain failed in his obligations. The alteration was made towards the middle of the thirteenth century: henceforth, any disobedience might be regarded as treason and the king now tended to consider himself as a 'natural' sovereign. See Bellamy, 1970, pp. 10–11 (III). Maitland, who situates the change around the mid-fourteenth century, underlines the difference between the link of vassalage and allegiance: see Pollock and Maitland (1895), 1968, vol. 2, p. 505 (III).

23 Coke, 5a.

24 *Ibid.*

25 Egerton is here referring to a case pleaded during the Middle Ages in which a child of less than twelve years was condemned for murder: because he had gone into hiding after committing the murder, the judge ruled that he was capable of discerning between good and evil and that his 'malignity' made up for his tender years.

26 Egerton, Viscount Brackley, 1609, p. 78 (V). The speech can also be found in Howell, 1809–28, vol. 2, 1816, cols. 560ff (III). It has been freshly edited and discussed by Knafla, 1977 (III).

27 Coke, 5b.

28 *Ibid.*

29 *Ibid.* When she acceded to the throne, Mary Tudor was in no doubt that her subjects would obey her 'according to the duties of their allegiance' since she was 'their natural and liege sovereign and queen': Hughes and Larkin, 1969, vol. 3, p. 3 (III).

30 Coke, 5b.

31 See nn. 78 and 79.

32 Coke, 6b.

33 *Ibid.*

34 *Ibid.*

35 *Ibid.*

36 *Ibid.*, 6b

37 *Ibid.*, 7b.

38 *Ibid.*, 10a: *Quod ligeantia naturalis claustris coercetur, nullis metis refraenatur, nullis finibus premitur.*

39 *Ibid.*

40 *Ibid.* This formulation differs from that of Plowden, cited by Kantorowicz, 1957 (III), and Axton, 1977 (III). There are, in fact, four ways of conceiving the relationship between the body politic and the natural body.

41 *Ibid.*, 10b.

42 *Ibid.*

43 *Ibid.* Jurists of common law (common lawyers) call heir whoever succeeds by right of birth, whereas jurists of Roman law (civilians) call heir whoever is designated as such in the will. In English common law, the heir is whoever had the right to the fief: see Cowell, 1607, article, 'Heire' (V). In the oath as set out in the Act 'for the better discovering and repressing of Popish Recusants' (3 and 4 Jac. I, c. 4), the accused must swear as follows: 'I will bear faith and true allegiance to his Majesty, heirs and successors.' The text may be found in Prothero (1894), 1954, p. 259 (III).

44 Coke, 10b.
45 *Ibid.*, 11b.
46 See Thomas, 1971, pp. 192–204 (III).
47 *Ibid.*, p. 206.
48 Doleman (1594), 1972 (V). The phrase cited is the title of the first chapter. Doleman does not challenge the validity of hereditary successions, but he subordinates the rules for that procedure to positive law: 'The examples before alleaged . . . of a madd or furious heyre apparent, or of one that were by education a Turke or Moore in religion, or by nature deprived of his witt, or senses, do playnely prove that propinquity of birth or blood alone, without other circumstances, is not sufficient to be preferred to a crowne: for that no reason or law, religion or wisdom in the world, can admit such persons to the government of a common wealth by whom, no good, but distruction may be expected to the same, seeing that government was ordeyned for the benefit of the weale publique and not otherwise . . . thes condicions and circumstances of succeding by birth, are divers or different in different countryes, as also they are subject to changes according to the diversity of kingdomes, realmes, and people . . . wherby we are forced to conclude that every particular countrey and commonwealth hath prescribed thes condicions to it selfe and hath authority to do the same' (pp. 1–2).
49 Coke, 10b–11a, mentions the conspiracy of William Watson, a Catholic priest who in 1603 maintained that the king was not truly king until he had been crowned.
50 *Ibid.*, 12b.
51 See Phillips (1940), 1972, p. 39 (VI); Herndl, 1970, pp. 13–109 (VI); see also Gierke, 1934 and 1939 (III).
52 Coke, 12b.
53 *Ibid.*, 13b.
54 *Mari et foeminae conjunctio* is *de jure naturae* (*ibid.*, 13b). In support of this argument, Coke cites Bracton and Christopher Saint Germain.
55 Coke, 14a.
56 'Foster versus Ramsey', Siderfin, 1689, p. 27 (V).
57 Bacon, 1857–74, vol. 2, 1859, p. 645 (V). Cowell defines martial law as the law that 'dependeth upon the voice of the king' whereas 'the king . . . doe not in time of peace make any lawes but by the consent of the three estates in Parlament yet in warres by reason of great daungers rising of small occasions, he useth absolute power in so much as his word goeth for law' (Cowell, 1607, article 'Martiall lawe' (V)). On the medieval view according to which the king is a *bellator*, a mysterious receptacle of power, mentioned by Suger in the twelfth century in his *Vie de Louis VI*, see Duby, 1978, pp. 278–9 (III).
58 See Pollock and Maitland (1895), 1968, vol. 1, pp. 476–7 (III).
59 Bacon, 1857–74, vol. 7, 1859, p. 666 (V). On the use of martial law in peace time, see Holdsworth, 1903, vol. 1, pp. 337–8 (III).
60 *King Henry V*, ed. J. H. Walter (1954), 1960, Prologue, 5–8 (IV).
61 *Ibid.*, III, i, 5–8.
62 Coke, 14a–b.
63 *Ibid.*, 15a.
64 *Ibid.*, 15b–16a.
65 *Ibid.*, 16a.
66 *Ibid.*, 16b.
67 *Ibid.*, 17a.

68 *Ibid.*, 17a–b.
69 *Ibid.*, 17b.
70 'The Letters Patents graunted by her Majestie to Sir Humfrey Gilbert, knight, for the inhabiting and planting of our people in America', 1578, in Hakluyt (1907), 1967, vol. 5, pp. 349–55 (V). The quotation comes from p. 350.
71 'Charter to the Virginian Colonies, April 10, 1606', in Prothero (1894), 1954, pp. 456–7 (III).
72 See Pollock and Maitland (1895), 1968, vol. 2, pp. 378–80 (III), and Thomas Smith, 1583, book II, chap. 20 (V).
73 The disqualifications affecting these categories of people are analysed in Pollock and Maitland (1895), 1968, vol. 1, pp. 412–85 (III).
74 'But by the common lawe, if hee that dieth hath no sonnes but daughters, the land is equally divided among them': Thomas Smith, 1583, book III, chap 7, p. 107 (V).
75 Bacon, 1857–74, vol. 7, 1859, pp. 647–8 (V).
76 *Ibid.*, p. 648.
77 *Ibid.*
78 *Ibid.*, p. 649. There is an important consequence to this: if he had children before his 'denization', those children could not inherit any land he might acquire after it. The old French word *denzein* means 'within', 'interior'.
79 'Only God can make an heir (*heres*), not man', Glanvill (*Tractus de Legibus*, ed. 1604), quoted by Pollock and Maitland (1895), 1968, vol. 2, p. 254 (III).
80 Pollock and Maitland, 1895 (1968), vol. 1, pp. 407–8 (III).
81 *Ibid.*, p. 419.
82 Bloch (1939), 1968, p. 379 (III). Marc Bloch opposes royal justice (which he calls 'public') with feudal justice, for 'the idea had probably never quite disappeared that to be free meant above all having a right to public justice, a slave being liable only to correction from his master'. Thomas Smith distinguishes between the servile condition and serf tenure but does not oppose the two absolutely.
83 Pollock and Maitland (1895), 1968, vol. 1, pp. 422–3 (III).
84 However, on this point see the embarrassment of Thomas Smith who has to admit that the constraints attached to certain tenures reduce the 'owners and possessors thereof into a certaine servitude or rather *libertinitie* [the condition of freedmen]': 1583, book 3, chap 8, p. 113 (V). It is Thomas Smith himself who treats the condition of persons, that of tenures, hereditary rights and the status of foreigners as a continuum. In the same chapter he describes how the status of freeman has progressively spread to all Christian kingdoms by virtue of the very fact of Christianisation but that it is a status still refused to Jews who are 'amongst all people [. . .] holden as it were in a common servitude, and have no rule nor dominion as their own prophecies doe tell that they should not have after that Christ was promised to them, was of them refused for . . . they would not acknowledge him, obstinately forsaking their helpe in soule for the life to come and honour in this worlde for the time present not taking the good tidinges, newes, and evangill brought to them for their disobedience by the great grace of God, and by the promise of the Prophets fructified in us which be Gentile and [which] brought forth this humanitie, gentlenes, honour and godly knowledge which is seene at this present' (p. 110). Smith considers the servile condition to be not unsuitable for Turks and barbarians.
85 On royal blood, Coke writes: 'The Kingly dignity is an inherent inseparable to the royal blood of the King and descendible to the next blood of the King, and

cannot be transferred to another': (1600–59), part xii (1656), 1826, vol. 6, p. 230 (V). On the other hand, in his speech to Parliament on 19 March 1604, James I refers to the 'benefits that do arise of that union which is made in my blood', a union which prefigures that of the whole island: 'I am the husband, the whole isle is my lawful wife; I am the head and it is my body', Tanner (1930), 1961, pp. 26–7 (III).

86 See above, n. 43.
87 Pollock and Maitland (1895), 1968, vol. 2, p. 458 (III). See the qualified opinion of Holdsworth, 1926, vol. 9, pp. 75–86 (III). Cowell, for his part, writes that the term ligeance sometimes means 'the dominions or territorie of the Liege Lord': 1607, article 'Ligeance' (V).
88 Bacon, 1857–74, vol. 7, 1859, p. 664 (V).
89 *Ibid.*, p. 652, my italics. In the above mentioned case of 'Foster versus Ramsey', one of the lawyers pleaded as follows: 'Any descent either lineal or collateral must be derived from Natural Blood. And for natural blood to be inheritable, it must be 1. Untainted blood; 2. Full blood (hence half blood is barred); 3. Loyal blood. But an alien has no Loyal blood although he can have Natural blood. Full blood and Untainted blood: but all those, without Loyal blood, can obtain no benefit nor advantage in our present case': Siderfin, 1689, p. 52 (V).
90 Bacon, 1857–74, vol. 7, 1859, p. 665 (V).
91 Cited in *The Compact Edition of the Oxford English Dictionary* (hereafter *O.E.D.*), 1971, article 'Corruption', 2, b (II). On the rules of succession, the exclusion of ascendants and 'half-breeds', see Coke (1600–59), part iii (1602), 1826, vol. 2, pp. 99–117 (V).
92 The already existing works (Isidorus' *Etymologies*, Bartholomaeus Anglicus' *De proprietatibus rerum*, the works of Vincent de Beauvais, Mandeville's *Voyages*) were joined by others imitating or expanding the *Omnium gentium mores* . . . (1520) by Johann Boemus which was translated into five languages and appeared in England in 1555 with the title *The fardle of façions*, and in 1611 with that of *The Manners, Lawes and Customes of all Nations*. In England alone this literature included the *Enquiries touching the diversity of languages and religions in the chief parts of the world* by Edward Brerewood and the collections of voyages by Hakluyt and Purchas, as well as a number of geographies or cosmographies in the style of the *Cosmographia* by Sebastien Muenster (1544) and the *Theatrum orbis terrarum* by Ortelius (1570) – consulted by Marlowe and possibly by Shakespeare – composed between 1559 and 1625 by William Cunningham, George Abbot, Peter Heylyn, Robert Stafford, Nathanael Carpenter and Samuel Clarke.
93 *The Works of Christopher Marlowe*, ed. C. F. Tucker Brooke (1910), 1953, *The Jew of Malta*, lines 974–81 (IV). For other quotations, see George K. Hunter, 1964, p. 49 (VI).
94 Thomas Browne (1906), 1959, p. 30 (V). Jean Bodin has Octavius – a converted muslim – declare that 'the whole of Asia, most of Africa and much of Europe' doubt the truth of Christianity: *Heptaplomeres*, book IV, cited by Don Cameron Allen, 1964 (III).
95 Thomas Browne (1906), 1959, p. 30 (V). These are ideas that already appear in Edward Brerewood (cf. n. 92).
96 Thomas Browne, 1835, vol. 3, pp. 36–7 (V).
97 *Ibid.*, pp. 39–40.
98 See Littré (1863–72), vol. 4, 1957, article 'Loup', 9 (II), and *O.E.D.*, 1971, articles 'Wolf', 6, and 'Lupus', 4 (II).

99 Thomas Browne, 1835, vol. 3, p. 41 (V).
100 Thomas Browne (1906), 1959, p. 3 (V).
101 Cowell, 1607, 'Estate' (V).
102 *Ibid.*, 'Fee'. According to Maitland, the most striking feature of English law is that 'Proprietary rights in land are, we may say, projected upon the plane of time. The category of quantity, of duration, is applied to them. The life-tenant's rights are a finite quantity; the fee-tenant's rights are an infinite, or potentially infinite, quantity': 1911, vol. 2, p. 10 (III).
103 Norden (1607), 1618, p. 252 (V).
104 Coke (1600–59), 1826, part vii (1608), 'The Case of Swans', 16b (V).
105 Brook[e], 1679, 12 Henry VIII, p. 4 (V).
106 For example, in relation to witchcraft, the commonly held idea was that the devil, through the mediation of wizards and witches, could only act as the instrument of God, with the licence of God; this was the thesis supported by Gifford, 1587 (V); by James I (1597), 1603 (V); by Holland, 1590 (V). In another domain, the image of the Turk, usually a negative, 'bloody and cruel' one, went hand in hand with the idea that his misdeeds were occasioned by the sins of Christians: the Turk is the scourge of God. On this image and various conceptions of it, see Chew (1937), 1965 (III); Daniel, 1958 (III); Southern, 1962 (III); Patrides, 1963, pp. 126–35 (III); and Schwoebel, 1967 (III).
107 Several editions in the sixteenth century.
108 See above, section 8, on 'Foreigners'.
109 Brook[e], 1679, 12 Henry VII, p. 4 (V). I should like to express my thanks to Ian Willison, curator of Rare Books in the British Library, London, who procured me a photocopy of this document and a number of others. This passage is quoted (in the English translation) by Henriques, 1908, p. 189 (III).
110 Wingate, 1658, maxim 7, 4, p. 10, and maxim 89, 16, pp. 346–7 (V). Dalton (1655), 1677, chap. 117, p. 270 (V).
111 Salkeld, 1795, vol. 1, p. 46, 'Wells *versus* Williams', 9 William III (V), quoted by Henriques, 1908, p. 189 (III).
112 Atkyns, 1765, vol. 1, 'Ramkissenseat versus Barker' (V). In 1739 a commission was despatched to India to obtain the oath of a Hindu plaintiff. The Lord Chancellor was of the opinion that any person who believed in a god was capable of swearing an oath (p. 20). In response to the advocate for the prosecution who was pleading that if a Jew may be a witness so may an infidel, the advocate for the defence replied that Jews do believe in God and, following Bracton, said that since a foreigner by birth could not be a witness, no more could an infidel foreigner (pp. 23 and 26). The advocate general pointed out that if the plaintiff had not 'bodily' sworn an oath on the Gospel, he had nevertheless used another symbol: he had taken the foot of the priest in his right hand. Judgement was pronounced in favour of accepting the oath on 10 November 1744.
113 Henriques, 1908, p. 191, n. 1 (III). Henriques cites or mentions a number of the works mentioned above, the titles of which also appear in the marginal notes of the 1826 edition of Coke's *Reports* (V). See also Henriques, 1908 (III). The study by Robert Kirkpatrick, 'Le Status des étrangers en droit anglais au cours des derniers siècles' in *L'Etranger*, Recueils de la Société Jean-Bodin, vols. 9 and 10, Brussels, 1958 (vol. 10, pp. 451–62), is most succinct on the Calvin affair.
114 'Rolle Dolayron' (published in Poitiers at the end of the fifteenth century, a sixteenth-century reprint can be found in Pierre Garcie, *Le Grand Routier, pillotage et encrage de mer* . . . , printed by J. and E. Marnef, Poitiers, 1542). See the text in Twiss, 1871–6, vol. 2, 1873, pp. 478 and 480 (V).

6. Othello, or the husband from afar

1 And upon many other accounts too. One example, of an extremely encyclopaedic kind, is *The Anatomy of Melancholy* (1621), 1964 (V), where Robert Burton cites dozens of them (vol. 2, pt 2, sec. 2, memb. 3, pp. 35ff).

2 The most complete contemporary examination of these classifications appears to be the study by Bodin (1945), 1969 (V).

3 Thus John Knox, inveighing against 'the monstrous Regiment of women' reproaches the latter for delivering kingdoms and nations over to foreigners: Knox (1558), 1880 (V).

4 '. . . a certain English knight called Pacquet, a man of quality and means, being summoned to the Lower Chamber of Parliament to give his opinion on the matter of the union of the two kingdoms, inveighed in such a way against the Scottish nation, that the most barbaric and evil people in the world could not be more abused'. The words are those of the French ambassador, Antoine le Fevre de la Boderie, *Ambassades de Monsieur de la Boderie en Angleterre Sous le Règne d'Henri IV et la minorité de Louis XIII depuis les années 1606 jusqu'en 1611*, 5 vols., 1750, vol. 2, p. 87.

5 We have seen in chapter 5 what Sir Thomas Browne's opinion was. Robert Burton's was more radical: 'To purge the world of idolatry and superstition will require some monster-taming Hercules, a divine Aesculapius or Christ Himself to come in His own person, to reign a thousand years on earth before the end, as the millenaries will have Him. They are generally so refractory, self-conceited, obstinate, so firmly addicted to that religion in which they have been bred and brought up, that no persuasion, no terror, no persecution can divert them: the consideration of which hath induced many commonwealths to suffer them to enjoy their consciences as they will themselves.' Any remedy would have to be a radical one: 'As Hippocrates said in physic, I may well say in divinity: *Quae ferro non curantur, ignis curat* [What is not cured by the sword is cured by fire]': Burton (1621), 1964, vol. 3, pt 3, sec. 4, memb. 1, subs. 5, pp. 375 and 378 (V).

6 Léon Poliakov's expression: 1980 (III). On the obstacles impeding the development of religious tolerance, see Wilbur Kitchener Jordan, 1932 (III).

7 'An Homily Against Disobedience and Wilfull Rebellion' (1571), in the anon., 1640 edition of *Certaine Sermons or Homilies . . .* , p. 296 (or in the Oxford edition of 1822, p. 529) (V).

8 For an interpretation of Othello as simultaneously noble and savage, see Foakes, 1976 (VI).

9 The references are to the Arden edition of *Othello*, ed. M. R. Ridley (1958), 1962 (IV).

10 Montaigne, 1958, I, xxvi, p. 203 (Florio trans., 1928, I, xxvi, p. 178) (V).

11 I, i, 26–7.

12 Contrary to M. R. Ridley, I am here following the Folio and Q2: 'His Mooreship' (I, i, 33).

13 I, i, 37–8.

14 According to the common law of the realm, inheritance could only be transmitted by filiation i.e. 'the old gradation'. The information the play provides does not make it possible to tell whether Iago has truly been wronged or whether his grievance is an imaginary one: when virtue is recognised it ceases to be a natural property of the being and becomes a matter of opinion.

15 *Coriolanus*, ed. P. Brockbank, 1976, IV, vii, 49–50 (IV). John Donne expresses the idea as follows:

> The golden laws of nature are repealed,
> Which our first Fathers in such reverance held;
> Our liberty's reversed, our charter's gone,
> And we made servants to opinion,
> A monster in no certain shape attired,
> And whose original is much desired . . . Elegy 17, 'Variety', 1, 47–52

Shakespeare, for his part, puts it thus: 'For there is nothing either good or bad, but thinking makes it so' (*Hamlet*, II, ii, 254–5);'What is aught but as 'tis valued?' (*Troilus and Cressida*, II, ii, 52); on the origins and diffusion of the idea, see Elton (1966), 1968, p. 128 and n. 30 (VI).

16 A similar distinction is used, differently, in Auden, 'The Joker in the Pack', in (1962), 1963 (VI).

17 For example, by Bradley (1904), 1958 (VI); Gardner, 1956 (VI); Holloway (1961), 1966 (VI); Rosenberg, 1961 (VI); Marienstras, 1964 (VI).

18 The term 'unbonneted', one of the well-known difficulties in the text, is the subject of a page of commentaries in H. H. Furness' New Variorum, 1886.

19 Following T. S. Eliot's remark that Othello, in his last speech, is adopting an attitude that is more aesthetic than moral, playing a role in order to save face (1934, 'Shakespeare and the Stoicism of Seneca' (VI)), the search for moral and other imperfections in him has been pursued by Leavis, 1937 (VI); Kirschbaum, 1944 (VI); Traversi (1938), 1968 (VI). Heilman, 1956 (VI), and Honigmann, 1976 (VI), can be associated with the same school. Rosenberg, 1961 (VI), notes that the modern origin of this idea (the older one being Rymer) of Othello as an impostor or 'a creature of bad faith' goes back to the study of the German critic J. L. F. Flathe, 1863 (pp. 321–48). A refutation of the school of F. R. Leavis can be found in Holloway (1961), 1966, appendix A, pp. 155–65 (VI).

20 Richard Braithwait, *The English Gentleman*, London, 1630, 3rd edn, 1641, p. 349, cited by Patrides, 1964, p. 64 (III). Patrides shows that, given that the usefulness of nobility was already being questioned by 1560, its *raison d'être* had become the exercise of its acquired virtues. The question of the disparity of social rank at the time of marriage is debated in *All's Well That Ends Well*. The king of France's speech to Bertram, who refuses to marry Helena on the grounds that she is 'a poor physician's daughter', is worth quoting:

> 'Tis only title thou disdain'st in her, the which
> I can build up. Strange is it that our bloods,
> Of colour, weight and heat, pour'd all together,
> Would quite confound distinction, yet stands off
> In differences so mighty. If she be
> All that is virtuous, save what thou dislik'st
> A poor physician's daughter – thou dislik'st
> Of virtue for the name. But do not so.
> From lowest place when virtuous things proceed,
> The place is dignified by th' doer's deed.   (II, iii, 117–26)

G. K. Hunter, in the preface to his edition ((1959), 1962 (IV)) points out that Muriel C. Bradbrook has discussed the question (1950 (VI)). The theme is a commonplace. G. McVogt has reviewed instances where it is expressed, *Journal of English and Germanic Philology*, 24, 1925, pp. 102–24. It is referred to in Ruth Kelso, *Doctrine of the English Gentleman*, Urbana, 1929, and in J. E. Mason, *Gentlefolk in the Making*, Philadelphia, 1935. The opposition between virtue and nobility is one of the forms taken by the opposition between nature and culture.

The fact remains that, from a legal point of view, nobility was an ineffaceable mark. Dalton writes: 'If such a woman, being a Countesse or Baronesse, etc. by marriage onely shall marry againe under the degree of Nobility, she hath thereby lost her name of dignitie; . . . But if she be noble by birth or discent, whomsoever she shall marry, yet she remaineth Noble for birthright *est character indelebilis*' (Dalton (1655), 1677, chap. 117, p. 267 (V)).

21 Ronsard also pleads that fine souls and virtuous actions should come to light and not be hiddeii by ' . . . long cilence endormi; / Monstre qui a de coutume / De couver dessous sa plume / La vertu qui s'est parfaite / En l'honneur d'un acte beau . . . ' (' . . . long sleeping silence: / The broody Monster whose custom it is / To hide beneath its feathers / Virtue that has come to perfect fruition / In the honour of a fine action . . . '): Ronsard (1950), 1958, 'La Victoire de Guy de Chabot', vol. 1, ode IX, antistrophe 4, p. 386 (V).

22 See Onions (1911), 1958, article 'Part' (II).

23 *Othello*, ed. M. R. Ridley (1958), 1962, note to line 31 (IV), and Onions (1911), 1958, article 'Perfect' (II).

24 'I must be found' is implicitly opposed to Iago's ontological definition: 'I am not what I am' (I, i, 65). The two phrases are connected with the metamorphosis of Othello who, as Terence Hawkes points out (1964, p. 176 (VI)), himself comments upon the change that has taken place in him, at the end of the play: 'That's he that was Othello; here I am' (V, ii, 285). For a contrast between the truth of a being and the truth of a judgement passed upon that being, see Shakespeare's sonnet no. 121.

25 De Bueil (end of the fifteenth century), 1887–9, vol. 2, 1889, p. 21 (V).

26 M. R. Ridley prefers 'utmost pleasure' (Q1) to 'very quality' (F and Q2) for the same excellent reasons that cause him to interpret the term 'rites' as he does. See his notes to lines 251 and 257, and his introduction, p. lxv.

27 The fundamental issue in the debate, at this point, concerns the relative or absolute character of values. Emilia would not hesitate to 'make her husband a cuckold to make him a monarch'. Desdemona would not do it 'for the whole world'. But for Emilia 'the wrong is but a wrong i' the world; and having the world for your labour, 'tis a wrong in your own world and you might quickly make it right' (IV, iii, 74–82). Long, 1976, p. 58 (VI), for his part sees Emilia as 'the most complete person in the play'. However, as Bernanos has it: 'Honour is an absolute. What can it have in common with doctors of the Relative?': Bernanos (1938), 1955, p. 75 (VIII).

28 Although M. R. Ridley prints the text of Q1 ('Does bear all excellency', line 65), he prefers the reading from F ('Does tire the ingener'), which I have used.

29 The union between husband and wife, founded upon love, is in conformity with natural law. Richard Hooker, after reminding the reader of a woman's inferiority in comparison to man, goes on to comment upon the exquisite and absolute harmony with which nature has endowed her; this is 'the reason why that kind of love which is the perfectest ground of wedlocke is seldom able to yeeld any reason of itself': (1907), vol. 2, 1960, Book V, chap. LXXII, 2, p. 391 (V).

30 I, iii, 202. It should not be forgotten that marriage was indissoluble.

31 On the effect of persuasion 'entering the soul through speech', Gorgias notes

that, similar to drugs in this respect, 'by means of a harmful kind of persuasion, words can drug and bewitch the soul', *Ancilla to the Presocratic Philosophers*, trans. K. Freeman, Blackwell, Oxford, 1948, p. 133. See Derrida, 1972, p. 133 (VII). On fascination through the soul being 'transfused' by words or by looks, see Craig (1936) 1952, pp. 43–7 (VI). It is Jean Starobinski who speaks of 'the circulation of the poisoned word', an evil ploy 'which consists in listening to a word of death and propagating it in speech in which the poison continues to work': Starobinski, 1967, pp. xx–xxi (VI).

32 'Des venins et morsures des chiens enragés et autres morsures et piqueures de betes veneneuses', chap. i, in Paré, 1954, p. 238 (V), my italics. See also p. 244. The poison works because of its own specific character ('vertu'). It alters the entire organism or affects the body 'with all its substance and occult quality' and 'in open warfare it attacks the form and essence of life, which lies in the vital faculty, which is the heart' (chap. 5, pp. 240–1). For Robert Burton, slander creates 'an incurable wound' (1621), 1964, vol. 1, pt 1, sec. 2, memb. 4, subs. 4, p. 341 (V). Ridley cites Wilson's *Rhetoric*: 'a slanderer is worse than any thief, because a good name is better than all the goods in the world . . . and a thief may restore that again which he hath taken away, but a slanderer cannot give a man his good name which he hath taken from him'. Note to lines 159–65, III, iii.

33 See Owst (1933), 1966, pp. 450–8 (VI). On the verisimilitude of slander, in connection with 'rules of the game' in the theatre, see Stoll, 1953, pp. 440–1 (VI).

34 In the fourth part of the 'Homily Against Disobedience and Wilfull rebellion' we find the following passage: 'Those examples are written to stay us . . . from murmering or speaking once an evil word against our prince, which though any should do never so secretly, yet do the holy scriptures show that the very birds of the air will betray them . . . [and] they shall not escape horrible punishments therefore', anon., 1640 edn of *Certaine Sermons or Homilies* . . . , p. 300 (or in the Oxford edition of 1822, p. 532 (V)).

35 See Elton, 1965, pp. 59–60 (III); Holdsworth, 1903–72, vol. 3, 1929, pp. 287–93, vol. 4, 1945, pp. 492ff (III). There is an exhaustive study of the laws against treason in Bellamy, 1970 and 1979 (III).

36 The metaphors relating to poison have been picked out by Heilman, 1956 (VI).

37 This term, from American sociology, was used by Gavin I angmuir, following Merton, 1949 (VII). See the facsimile no. 13 of the Group d'études d'histoire du racisme, roneotyped by the Maison des sciences de l'homme: Poliakov and Marienstras, 1976, p. 19 (VI).

38 This is the Q1 version. The Folio version, which Ridley finds less idiomatic, is more insulting for Othello: 'if thou hast eyes to see'.

39 Boaistuau (1560), 1961, pp. 27–8 (V). For other statements of a similar kind, see George K. Hunter (1967), 1968 (VI). In the earliest accounts of voyages in Africa, the Blacks are compared to brutish beasts: see Hodgen, 1964, pp. 410–11 (VII). On the existence of prejudice against Blacks in England, see Winthrop D. Jordan, 1968, pp. 239–40 (III), who cites a sermon by William Crashaw.

40 The text of this edict can be found in Hughes and Larkin, 1969, vol. 3, p. 221 (III). The facsimile of the manuscript is reproduced in Eldred D. Jones, 1965, plate 5 (VI). Jones reviews all the opinions expressed on the subject of Africans. As early as 1596, the queen let it be known that there were too many Blacks in the kingdom: Walvin, 1973, p. 8 (III).

41 Hughes and Larkin, 1969, vol. 3, p. 221 (III) ('infidels having no understanding of Christ or his Gospel'). Shyllon, 1974 and 1978 (III) dates the arrival of the first slaves in England to 1555. They were five Blacks brought by John Lok. In the

Times Literary Supplement of 3 March 1978, C. Fyfe notes that, despite Elizabeth's decree, there is evidence that there were Blacks living in England in the seventeenth century. On this question, see also Walvin, 1971 and 1973 (III). On Blacks sold as slaves and what the English knew of them, see Winthrop D. Jordan, 1968, pp. 57–62 (III). 'Blacks' and 'slaves' became closely associated words. The case of a White woman who married a Black in England is reported by George Best[e], a companion of Martin Frobisher's: 'I my selfe have seene an Ethiopian as blacke as a cole brought into England, who taking a faire English woman to wife, begat a sonne in all respects as blacke as the father was, although England were his native countrey, and an English woman his mother: whereby it seemeth this blacknes proceedeth rather of some natural infection of that man, which was so strong, that neither the nature of the Clime, neither the good complexion of the mother concurring, coulde anything alter.' Beste[e], 'A true discourse of the three Voyages of discovery, for the finding of a passage to Cathaya . . . ' (1578), in Hakluyt (1907), 1967, vol. 5, p. 180 (V).

42 Ronsard (1950), 1958, vol. 2, p. 399, 'Discours contre Fortune', line 15 (V).

43 On love philtres and other spells, see Dyer (1883), 1966, pp. 337–8 (VI), and Thomas, 1971, pp. 233–4, 302, 442–3 (III). The 1604 Act made magic for the purpose of inciting love a crime.

44 Although it is sometimes denied, the quasi-racial character of Iago's attacks is noted by commentators, particularly in the United States: see, for example, K. W. Evans, 1969 (VI), who believes that this is the factor underlying Othello's feelings of insecurity and Iago's of inferiority, but that Shakespeare does not accept the racial stereotype; K. W. Evans sees the cause of Othello's fall in his incapacity to accept the physical realities of love. Doris Adler, 1974 (VI), meanwhile, distinguishes five different meanings for the word 'black' (each time opposed to 'white' or 'fair'): (1) the darkest colour; (2) the designation for a Black or a Moor; (3) the dark 'black and witty' as opposed to the blonde 'fair and wise' (II, i, 129 and 133); (4) defilement or dirt; (5) moral degradation, a satanic quality. The word always has an unfavourable connotation. Othello progressively turns against Desdemona the 'blackness' for which he has been criticised. This study is concerned with the semantic field of the play, not with the Elizabethan period for which 'black' could sometimes have a favourable connotation, as Michel Grivelet has pointed out to me in conversation. See the comparison that Bradbrook (1976), 1979, pp. 161–2 (VI), makes between *Othello* and Ben Jonson's *Maske of Blacknesse*.

45 Coleridge's famous comment on Iago: 'The last speech, the motive-hunting of motiveless malignity – how awful! In itself fiendish . . . ' (I, iii, 381–402), while it does not explain everything about Iago, is nevertheless a theological explanation and it is more convincing than, for example, Michael Long's (in 1976 (VI)). Long finds sufficient reason for Iago's malignity in the fact that he is 'a man so degraded in self-image by social rejection that it becomes an imperative for his ego to find somebody who is beneath even him' (p. 56). He brings down everything that belongs to the world of chivalry in order to raise himself up. But that does not explain what it is that impels him to take the extra step, to action. The desire to bring down others may accompany many other situations apart from social frustration: it is also the stamp of certain forms of absolute tyranny. As Melville saw clearly (in *Billy Budd*), 'the mystery of iniquity' is one of the marks that stamps the actions of Claggart (who is modelled on Iago). This religious formulation may be understood as an earlier way of expressing the irrational need to humiliate and debase others. The play gives it to be under-

stood that no redemption is possible for Iago and that, even triumphant and socially esteemed, he would still have acted in the same way. The Elizabethan age, which believed in evil, could not understand it except as the work of the Devil – and would certainly not have explained it in terms of 'social frustration'. The latter simply created a situation that favoured its monstrous flowering. Besides, Shakespeare makes it quite clear in his play that feelings may arise without any natural cause. Thus, on the subject of jealousy:

> *Desdemona*: Alas the day, I never gave him cause!
> *Emilia*: But jealous souls will not be answer'd so;
> They are not ever jealous for the cause,
> But jealous for they are jealous. (III, iv, 159–9)

We should not forget that the principal jealous character in the play is Iago. For a 'pluralist' study of Iago, see Hyman, 1970 (VI).

46 De Damhoudere, 'Councillor and steward for the domains and Finances of the Emperor Charles V', writes that abominable types of sensuality (sodomy, bestiality) should be punishable by death. Similarly, he goes on, 'there is also another kind, which seems to be part of and have affinities with the above-mentioned types and will also be punished although, in truth, it is quite different from the afore-mentioned types. For it is not unnatural but is nevertheless accounted and reputed to be so in the consideration and sight of our faith, and offenders are punished as sodomites, to wit those who have to do with Turks, Sarasins or Jews, for the laws and our holy faith hold them to be no more than beasts (not by nature or by the way they reason or by common vocation) but on account of their obdurate malice by reason of which the Christian faith (without which nobody is promised salvation) prohibits all from conversing or staying with them, and *a fortiori* from sleeping with them and holding carnal converse with them': De Damhoudere, 1555, chap. XCVI, p. 210 (V).

Edward Coke reports on the ancient English ruling that assimilated the union of Christians and Jews to sodomy and bestiality: *Contrahentes cum Judaeis, Judaebus, pecorantes, et sodomitae in terre vivi confodiantur . . .* The text is by Fleta, lib. 1, ca. 35. Coke cites it in 1644, chap. 27, p. 329 (V).

47 'Man, who is mortal, is not worthy to see / the Gods in their essential being, and even less to receive them: / He is a vessel of clay surrounded with weakness. / Humans seek out humans, and the God seeks the Goddess'. (L'Homme qui est mortel, n'est pas digne de voir / Les Dieux en leur essence, et moins les recevoir: / C'est un vaisseau de terre entourré de foiblesse. / L'Humain cherche l'humain, et le Dieu la Déesse): Ronsard (1950), 1958, vol. 1, p. 352, 'L'Amour amoureux', lines 41–4 (V). For Balthazar Castiglione, human nature cannot admit perfection: see (1959), 1975, I, 7 (V). Desdemona says: 'We must think / Men are not Gods' (III, iv, 145–6).

48 On Desdemona interpreted as Iago sees her, see Kott (1962), 1965 (VI). Holloway (1961), 1966, p. 49n (VI), ironically mentions a number of interpretations which make Desdemona out to be an exhibitionist, a potential sadist, a masochist (with infantile regressions), a necrophile, etc.

49 On recent studies relating to *hubris*, see Kaufmann, 1968, chap. 15, pp. 68–79 (VII); Vickers, 1973, pp. 29–30 (VI). See also Vernant and Vidal-Naquet, 1972 (VII). But pride is a concept that was flourishing in the Middle Ages and during the Renaissance: see Payne (1951), 1960 (III).

50 Péguy, 1961, p. 1162, 'L'Argent' (VIII).

51 *Ibid.*, p. 1156. Péguy was not writing about Shakespeare.
52 The remarks which follow were inspired by Emrys Jones, 1968 (VI).
53 Péguy, 1961, pp. 966–7, 'Un nouveau théologien' (VIII).
54 On *Othello* as a domestic drama, see Ridley (1958), 1962, *op. cit.*, pp. xlvii–xlviii (IV); many commentators share the same view: e.g. Whitaker, 1965, p. 259 (VI). But it had been expressed earlier by Bradley.
55 On the relation between the terms *fee* and *fide*, see Thomas Smith, 1583, Book III, chap. 8, pp. 111–12 (V). See also Cowell, 1607, article 'Fealtie' (V). Helen Gardner, who sees the play as a tragedy of sworn faith, develops this point ((1955), 1956 (VI)). On faith or fidelity as the basis of justice, see Elyot (1531), 1962, book 3, chap. vi (V).
56 Northrop Frye, 1967, p. 83 (VI).
57 See John William Allen (1928), 1960, p. 122 (III)
58 See Matthews, 1964, pp. 132–3 (VI). On the concept of nature and its multiple meanings, see Haydn (1950), 1960, pp. 131–75 (III); Danby, 1961 (VI); Elton (1966), 1968 (VI).
59 Montaigne, 1958, I, xxiii, p. 144 (Florio trans., 1928, I, xxiii, p. 114) (V).
60 On the fact that secondary causes are incapable of 'removing God's prerogative', see Sir Walter Raleigh, *History of the World*, I, 2, 11, cited by Tillyard, 1943, p. 52 (VI). For a documented discussion of this theme, see Elton (1966), 1968, pp. 220–3 (VI).
61 Montaigne notes the moral and legal conflict that arises between 'the fourth estate of people handling lawsuits' and the nobility: 'whence double Lawes must follow, those of honour and those of justice; in many things very contrarie do those as rigorously condemne a lie pocketed up, as these a lie revenged: by the law and right of armes he that putteth up an injurie shall be degraded of honour and nobilitie; and he that revengeth himselfe of it, shall by the Civill Lawe incurre a capital punishment. He that shall addresse himselfe to the Lawes to have reason for some offence done unto his honour, dishonoureth himselfe. And doth not so is by the Lawes punished and chastised': Montaigne, 1958, xxiii, p. 147 (Florio trans., 1928, I, xxii (*sic*), p. 117) (V). On Othello and honour, see Klene, 1975 (VI), and his bibliography, p. 150.
62 See Marienstras, 1966, pp. 424–8 (VI). Fiedler (1973), 1974 (VI), sees women, no doubt erroneously, as alienated beings in the same way as Blacks, Moors, Jews and infidels. The disqualifications of women were different from those of 'perpetual enemy foreigners'. On this point, see chapter 5, above.
63 See Whitaker, 1965, pp. 247–51 (VI).
64 I, iii, 262–5. Whitaker, 1965, pp. 244–5 (VI), sees it as one of the keys to the play.
65 Rabelais, 1955, chap. XLVIII, 'Le Tiers Livre', p. 495; English trans. by Smith, 1893, vol. 1, p. 582 (V). On clandestine marriages in the fifteenth century, see Febvre (1942), 1962, pp. 468–9 (VI).
66 On the subject of the custom of 'offering' the wife to the husband and accompanying her to the altar, a duty which fell to 'the father or . . . some other', Hooker notes that 'in ancient times all women which had not husbands nor fathers to governe them had their tutors without whose authoritie there was no act which they did warrantable. And for this cause they were in marriage delivered unto their husbands by others, which custome retained hath still this use that it putteth women in mind of a dutie whereunto the very imbecillitie of their nature and sex doth bind them, namely to be alwaies directed, guided and ordered by others – although our positive laws do not tie them now as pupils':

Hooker (1907), vol. 2, 1960, Book V, chap. LXXII, 5, p. 393 (V). On the opinion of Erasmus and the reformists, see Plattard, 1927 (VI).

67 Rabelais, 1955, chap. XLVIII, 'Le Tiers Livre', pp. 496–8; English transl. by Smith, 1893, vol. 1, pp. 583–4 (V).

68 *Ibid.*, p. 499; Smith, p. 585.

69 Thus, Montaigne writes: 'He that speakes all he knows doth cloy and distaste us. Who feareth to expresse himselfe leadeth our conceit to imagine more than happily he conceiveth. There is treason in this kind of modesty; and chiefly . . . in opening us so faire a path into imagination': Montaigne, 1958, III, v, p. 985 (Florio trans., 1938, III, v, p. 108) (V).

70 The gratuitousness of the action is even noted by Iago.

71 See the article by Gardner, 1956 (VI).

72 Montaigne, 1958, III, v, pp. 981–2 (Florio trans., 1928, III, v, p. 105) (V). The Latin quotation is from Claudius.

73 Q: 'seale'; F: 'seele'. Two different terms (placing a seal, and sewing up the eyes of a hawk). See the commentary of Ridley and that of Henn, 1972, pp. 17 and 25 (VI).

74 I, ii, 63–71. The pertinent terms are: to fear, not to delight. See also I, iii, 94–106, cited above: 'To fall in love with what she fear'd to look on', and I, iii, 293: 'She has deceiv'd her father, may do thee'.

75 I, iii, 96: 'and she, in spite of nature', and I, iii, 100–1: ' . . . perfection so would err / Against all rules of nature', cited above.

76 This is the F and Q2 punctuation; Q1 reads: 'such a will, most rank/Foul disproportion', where 'rank' relates to 'disproportion'. See Ridley's note.

77 Montaigne, 1958, III, xii, p. 1173 (Florio trans., 1928, III, xii, p. 300) (V).

78 Some commentators find a difficulty here: why should the mighty be less favoured than the humble where female fidelity is concerned? At all events, examples of great men deceived by their wives are given by Montaigne, 1958, III, v, p. 966 (Florio trans., 1928, III, v, p. 89) (V). He notes also: 'Nowadays the ordinary entertainments and familiar discourses of meetings and at tables are the boastings of favours received, graces obtained and secret liberalities of ladies' (Florio trans., 1928, III, v, p. 88) (V). Gardner, 1956, n. 9 (VI), mentions a note by Robert Toft inserted into his translation of *The Blazon of Jealousie* (1615) by Benedetto Varchi, where he refers to the great men mentioned by Montaigne. See Ridley's note to this line. Klene, 1975 (VI), appreciates the fact that the great are more vulnerable than the humble with regard to aspersions cast upon their honour.

79 For a discussion concerning the exigencies and the providing of the proof, see Hawkes, 1964, pp. 100–23 (VI).

80 I am following the generally accepted version, namely that of Q2: 'her name', despite Ridley (and Rowe, and Malone, etc.) who prefer F: 'my name'. See Ridley's qualifying note.

81 Q: 'topt'; F: 'top'd'. This crude, brutal term occurs on three occasions in the play: twice in speeches of Iago, here and at I, i, 89; once in a speech of Othello's: 'Cassio did top her' (V, ii, 137). It is not used elsewhere in Shakespeare with this meaning.

82 Whitaker's analysis, 1965, pp. 250 and 257 (VI). See also Hawkes, 1964, p. 106 (VI).

83 As Hawkes shows, 1964, pp. 109–10 (VI).

84 Leavis, 'Diabolic Intellect and the Noble Hero', in Wain, 1971, p. 128 (VI). Refutation in Holloway (1961), 1966, Appendix A, pp. 155–65 (VI).

85 According to Matthews, 1964, pp. 137–8 (VI).
86 Ambroise Paré notes: 'I would say . . . that the best wine is poison, because it removes the senses and understanding and suffocates', 'Des venins et morsures . . . ', chap. ix, in 1954, p. 238 (V). On beliefs about poisons in the Renaissance, see Bowers, 1937 (VI), and Harrison, 1948 (VI).
87 Similarly, if the homology convinces, the more trusting one had been, the more jealous one would become.
88 Compare 'I drunk!' with 'Can he be angry?' (III, iv, 131). The words 'he be angry' are repeated three times by Iago.
89 Vair, 1583, p. 303 (V).
90 Of course, Iago is not a 'devil'. Shakespeare accepts the constraints of realism. But this character is clearly related to the Evil One and there are grounds for a theological interpretation. On the relationship of Iago to the 'Vice' of morality plays, see Spivack, 1958 (VI).
91 Vair, 1583, pp. 441–2 (V).
92 The name given to Petrus Aponensis, an Italian doctor whom Paré mentions in the Preface to his 'Introduction ou entrée pour parvenir à la vraye cognoissance de la chirurgie': see Paré, 1954, p. lv (V).
93 Paré, 'Des venins et morsures . . . ', chap. ix, in 1954, p. 237 (V).
94 Grevin, 1568, pp. 32–3 (V). Grevin, who spent some time in England, dedicated this book to '*La Treshaute, Trespuissante et Tresvertueuse Princesse Madame Elizabeth, Royne d'Angleterre*'.
95 *Ibid.*, pp. 37–9.
96 Porta (1589), 1658, p. 231 (V).
97 De Damhoudere, 1555, pp. 120–1 (V).
98 Coke (1600–59), part iv (1604), 1826, vol. 2, pp. 282–317 (V).
99 However, that does not make her a normative character. Common sense is a wisdom which aims to preserve life, even at the cost of values. In *King Lear*, the Fool's advice is not to follow figures who fall into disfavour; but he follows Lear, notwithstanding.
100 *The Werewolf*, wood-cut by Lucas Granach, the elder, sixteenth century, Bibliothèque Nationale, Réserve, Ca 9a. Reproduced in Bibliothèque Nationale, 1973, facing p. 86 (III). On the diffusion of the belief, see Summers (1966), 1973 (III).
101 Latin letter cited by G. Tillotson, '*Othello* and *The Alchemist* at Oxford', *Times Literary Supplement*, 20 July 1933, p. 494. The quoted text has been published in Rosenberg, 1961, p. 5 (VI).
102 Hibbard, 1968, p. 43 (VI).
103 *The Bacchae*, trans. G. S. Kirk, 1979, lines 1244–6 (IV).
104 As Hawkes, for instance, suggests, 1973, pp. 141–2 (VI).
105 See the notes of Furness and Ridley. Hawkes, 1973, p. 122 (VI), prefers 'Iudean', for 'like Judas, [Othello] has betrayed what he should have loved'. Similarly, Veit, 1975 (VI), and Shaheen, 1980 (VI). Poisson, 1975 (VI), defends 'Indian'.
106 See George K. Hunter (1967), 1968, pp. 139–63 (VI), and 1964 (VI).
107 Robert Burton writes: 'The greatest enemy to man is man, who, by the devil's instigation, is still ready to do mischief – his own executioner, a wolf, a devil to himself and others . . . We can keep our professed enemies from our cities by gates, walls and towers, defend ourselves from thieves and robbers by watchfulness and weapons: but the malice of men, and their pernicious endeavours, no caution can divert, no vigilancy foresee, we have so many secret plots and

devices to mischief one another': Burton (1621), 1964, vol. 1, pt 1, sec. 1, memb. 1, subs. 1, pp. 134–5 (V).

108 This chapter was read as a paper in a symposium held at Cérisy-la-Salle in May 1977. It was published in Poliakov, 1980 (VII).

7. Elizabethan travel literature and Shakespeare's *The Tempest*

1 Montaigne, 1958, III, vi, p. 1018 (Florio trans., 1928, III, vi, p. 141) (V).
2 An Elizabethan traveller cited by Bush, 1952, p. 170 (VI).
3 *Ibid.*, pp. 170–1.
4 *Ibid.* See Howard, 1914 (III), and in Levine, 1968 (I), nn. 985, 1055 and 1057.
5 Camden (1586), 1610 (V).
6 His *Description of England*, preceded by his *Description of Britaine*, appeared in Holinshed's *Chronicle* (1577 and 1586–7). *The Description of England* was edited by F. J. Furnivall (New Shakespeare Society, 4 pts, 1877–1908).
7 Stow (1598), 1956 (V).
8 His huge poem *Polyolbion* . . . was published in 1612–13 and expanded in 1622 (V).
9 Hakluyt (1589), 1598–1600 (V).
10 His third published work was *Hakluytus Posthumus or, Purchas His Pilgrimes*, 1625 (V).
11 Saint Brandan, Brendan or Brenainn (484–577) made a voyage which, according to the *Navigatio Sancti Brendani abbatis*, 1959 (V), took him to a number of islands including the 'Paradise of Birds' which was strewn with precious stones. These islands were for centuries sought for in vain. See Harvey, 1969 (II); Cawley, 1940 (VI); d'Avezac, 1845 (VI). See [Mandeville], 1967 (V); the *Voyages* of Mandeville were included in the first edition of Hakluyt and were accepted as being perfectly true right up until the beginning of the seventeenth century.
12 Montaigne, 1958, I, xxxi, pp. 202–3 (Florio trans., 1928, I, xxxi, p. 218) (V).
13 As Nuttall points out, 1967, pp. 137–9 (VI). All the texts relating to voyages have been minutely examined by Cawley, 1937 (VI) and in the work cited in n. 11. The interpenetration of attested voyages and fabled ones is quite clear. The quotations from *The Tempest* refer to the Arden edition edited and introduced by Frank Kermode (1954), 1958 (IV).
14 Martyr (1555), 1885, the third book of the first decade, p. 78 (V). It is a theme that is even more pronounced in Montaigne, in a passage of his essay 'Des Cannibales': 1958, I, xxxi, p. 203 (V). See Kermode, p. 35, and J. H. P. Pafford, Arden edn of *The Winter's Tale*, 1963, p. 169 (IV).
15 Hakluyt (1584), 1887, vol. 2, p. 11 (V).
16 Montaigne, 1958, I, xxxi, p. 203 (Florio trans., 1928, I, xxxi, p. 219) (V). See also what Montaigne says about voyages at III, ix ('De la vanité'), p. 964, and at II, xii ('Apologie de Raimond Sebond'), p. 443.
17 John Smith (1899), 1910, vol. 1, p. 370 (V).
18 On this problem as a whole, see George, 1958, pp. 62–72 (III), and Pearce, 1953 (III).
19 Purchas (1625), 1906, vol. 19, p. 246 (V), my italics. Indians are unmistakably assimilated to wild beasts by Frobisher: '[they] live in caves of earth, and hunt for their dinners or preye even as the beare or other wild beastes do': Hakluyt, 1904, vol. 7, p. 370 (V). Purchas, for his part, writes that they are 'so bad people, having little of humanitie but shape, ignorant of Civilitie, or Arts, or Religion; more brutish than the beasts they hunt, more wild and unmanly than that

unmanned wild country, which they range rather than inhabite': (1625), 1906, vol. 19, p. 231 (V). Both these quotations are borrowed from Roy Pearce, 1953, pp. 5 and 7 (III). On the assimilation of the Black to a domesticated animal, see the important work by Winthrop D. Jordan, 1968, pp. 1–91 (III).

20 See an extract from this text in Wright, 1965, pp. 115–33 (V). This work has a useful preface by the editor. Harriot's views on the Indians are summarised by Jacquot, 1952, pp. 170–4 (VI).

21 Purchas (1625), 1906, vol. 19, pp. 237–67 (V).

22 The treatise on herbal remedies is cited by Wright, 1965, p. 11 (V). The work in question is Monardes (1577), 1580 and 1596 (V). The journal of Simon Forman was edited by Rowse, 1974 (III).

23 Jankélévitch, 1971, p. 25 (VII).

24 Boaistuau (1560), 1961, p. 33 (V).

25 Jankélévitch, 1971, p. 19 (VII). On this point, Montaigne's position is that everything should be attributed to the creative power of God: the existence of monsters, marvels and things never seen is thus given some credence: 'Those which we call monsters are not so with God, who in the immensitie of his work seeth the infinitie of formes therein contained. And it may be thought that any figure [which] doth amaze us hath relation unto some other figure of the same kinde, although unknowne unto man': 1958, II, xxx, p. 691 (Florio trans., 1928, II, xxx, p. 445) (V). The whole of this text is pertinent to the present discussion. See also, in the 'Apologie de Raymond Sebond', the way nature is exalted. Shakespeare gives Polixenes a similar argument in his reply to Perdita (*The Winter's Tale*, IV, iv). Montaigne writes: 'And the industrie to enable, the skill to fortifie and the wit to shelter and cover our body by artificiall meanes, we have it by a kind of naturall instinct and teaching': 1958, II, iii, p. 435 (Florio trans., 1928, II, iii, p. 149 (V)).

26 [Jourdain], *Discovery of the Bermudas*, 1610 (V); The Council of Virginia, *True Declaration of the State of the Colonie in Virginia*, 1610; a letter from William Strachey, known under the title of *True Reportory of the Wreck*, dated 15 July 1610 and published by Purchas in 1625 (V). On these *Bermuda Pamphlets*, see Kermode in his preface to *The Tempest*, pp. xxvi–xxx (IV), and Bullough, vol. 8, 1975 (II) who cites a number of them. See also Hallett Smith, 1972, pp. 140–4 (VI).

27 Thomas Beard writes: 'nothing in the worlde commeth to passe by chance or adventure, but onely and alwaies by the prescription of his [God's] wil; according to the which he ordereth and disposeth by a straight and direct motion, as well the generall as the particular, and that after a strange and admirable order': 1597 (V), cited by Campbell (1930), 1961, p. 11 (VI).

28 See the essay entitled 'Figura' in 1959 (VII).

29 Todorov, 1969, p. 198 (VII).

30 'Of Plymouth Plantation', in Miller, 1956, p. 18 (III).

31 'Wonder-Working Providence of Sion's Saviour', *ibid.*, pp. 29–30.

32 Purchas (1625), 1905, vol. 1, pp. 1–45 (V).

33 On this point and other harmonics on the word 'delicate', see Brower, 1968 (VI).

34 Dubois, Edeline *et al.*, 1970, p. 120 (VII).

35 Styan, 1967, p. 136 (VI).

36 *Ibid.*

37 Kermode, preface to *The Tempest* (1954), 1958, pp. lxxiv–lxxvi (IV).

38 E. Welsford, cited by Kermode, *ibid.*, p. lxxiv.

39 See Leech, 1958 (VI); Marienstras, 1965, p. 912 (VI).
40 Bertrand Evans (1960), 1967, pp. ix and 324 (VI). See his analysis, pp. 323–37.
41 Brower, 1968, p. 155 (VI).
42 Here are some other proverbs related to the theme:

> Far folk fare best
> Far fowls have fair feathers
> Far from court, far from care
> Far from eye, far from heart
> Far from home, near thy harm
> Near neighbour is better than a far-dwelling kinsman
> Nearest way is commonly the foulest   Wilson, 1970 (II)

43 Vidal-Naquet, 1970, p. 1292 (VII).
44 On this distinction, see Marx (1964), 1970, pp. 61–5 (VI).
45 Kermode, preface to *The Tempest*, p. xlii (IV).
46 Vidal-Naquet, 1970, pp. 1283–4 (VII).
47 Preface to *Theatrum Poetarum* (1675), cited by Kermode, preface to *The Tempest*, p. xlvi (IV). Pierre Vidal-Naquet shows how one of the functions of the traveller's tale is to provide such a measure of what is human, by oscillating back and forth between excess and deficiency.
48 For an entirely negative view of the savage, see De Maistre, 1960, p. 66 (VIII).
49 Kermode, in preface to *The Tempest*, p. xxxiv (IV).
50 Cited by Cawley, 1937, p. 348 (VI).
51 The positions in this conceptual hierarchy are as follows: (1) men; (2) domesticated animals; (3) wild beasts. It is present in the *Odyssey* (Vidal-Naquet, 1970, p. 1288 (VII)) and, in the Elizabethan period, is in line with the ideology of the chain of being.
52 See Kermode, ed., *The Tempest*, p. 86, n. 17 (IV). See also Northrop Frye (1957), 1967, pp. 164, 286–7, 310–12 (VI).
53 'All his quality' might mean either 'his powers' or 'his gifts', or the other sprites who accompany Ariel. On the 'protean powers' of Ariel, see Donald A. Stauffer, 1949, p. 305 (VI).
54 This type of comparison, sequence by sequence, has, following Propp (1965), 1970 (VII), been used by Brémond, 1966 (VII), and by T. Todorov and C. Lévi-Strauss. On the relation between *The Tempest* and *Doctor Faustus*, see Appendices I and II.
55 F. D. Hoeniger, preface to *Pericles*, 1963, p. lxxii (IV).
56 See Lévi-Strauss, 1960, pp. 30–2 (VII).
57 Marienstras, 1965, pp. 899–917 (VI).
58 This chapter was read as a paper to the Congrès de la société des anglicistes de l'enseignement supérieur (1971) and has also appeared in *Le Voyage dans la littérature anglo-saxone*, Marcel Didier, Paris, 1972, since when it has undergone very few alterations. In *The Inconstant Savage: England and the North American Indian, 1500–1660*, Duckworth, London, 1979, Harry Culverwell Porter studies Anglo-Indian relations in depth.

8. Incest and social relations in *'Tis Pity She's a Whore*

1 In Bang, 1902ff, vol. 23, p. xii (IV), cited by Oliver, 1955 (VI). Although published for the first time in 1633, under the reign of Charles I, *'Tis Pity She's a Whore* may have been composed at any time between 1623 and 1633.

2 Oliver, 1955, p. 98 (VI).
3 A number of titles are given by Brian Morris in the introduction to his edition of *'Tis Pity She's a Whore*, 1968, p. x (IV). Others are to be found in Otto Rank, 1912 (VI), and above all in Brissenden, 1964 (VI).
4 Stavig, 1968 (VI).
5 See Sensabaugh, 1939 (VI).
6 See Thomas, 1971, p. 107, n. 2 (III).
7 Only one, mutilated, copy of this play exists; it is reproduced in Adams (1924), 1952 (IV), and in Anon., *Non-Cycle Plays* . . . , ed. N. Davis, 1970 (IV).
8 *'Tis Pity She's a Whore*, ed. Morris, 1968, I, i, 186 (IV). All the references to the text are to this edition. Maurice Maeterlink adapted it for the Théâtre de l'Oeuvre in 1894, under the title *Annabella*.
9 II, i, 16.
10 Burton (1621), 1964, vol. 1, pt 1, sec. 2, memb. 1, subs. 6, pp. 212–13 (V).
11 According to Maisch (1968), 1970 (VII), and Cuisenier, 1968 (VII), this explanation was assumed to have been first produced in the sixteenth century; but in truth it is more ancient: see Esmein, 1891, vol. 1, p. 338 (III).
12 Maine, 1886 (VII); Morgan, 1871 (VII).
13 *Love's Sacrifice*, in *Ford, Five Plays*, ed. H. Ellis, 1957, I, i, p. 267 (IV).
14 *Summa Theologica*, IIa, IIae, 9, CLIV, a9. Summarised, with useful commentaries, in the article 'Inceste' in *Dictionnaire de théologie catholique*, vol. 7, 2, 1937 (II). The prohibition itself evidently predated the writing of the *Summa Theologica*. See Esmein, 1891, in particular vol. 1, pp. 87–90 and 336–56 (III).
15 Fuzier reminded me of the importance of the theme of androgyny, the interest of which was pointed out by Kaufmann (1960), 1961, p. 371 (VI). N. W. Bawcutt notes, in the introduction to his edition of *'Tis Pity She's a Whore*, 1966, p. xix (IV), that the (neo-)platonic cult of beauty made popular in England at the end of the sixteenth century by Spenser (*Hymn in Honour of Beauty*) and by the translation of Castiglione's *The Courtier* (Book IV) provided a number of later texts with arguments in favour of incest – arguments which were, nevertheless, presented as fallacious or demoniacal. These constitute significant antecedents to Giovanni's speeches. One of the most common sources for these texts was the story of Myrrha in Ovid's *Metamorphoses*. A recent study of androgyny among the Greeks is that of Brisson, 1973 (VII). All the pertinent references are to be found in his article.
16 For the references for the Talmudic texts where these ideas are to be found, see *Encyclopaedia Judaica*, vol. 2, 1973, articles 'Adam' and 'Androgynos' (II).
17 De Rosset, 1619, pp. 256–81 (V). Davril, 1954 (VI) stresses the importance of this text (p. 165).
18 De Rosset, 1619, p. 256 (V).
19 *Ibid.*
20 Saint Augustine (1610), 1972, XV, xvi, 1, p. 623 (V).
21 *La Doctrine du mariage selon Saint Augustin*, G. Beauchesne, Paris, 1930, p. 158.
22 Margaret Mead, *Sex and Temperament in Three Primitive Societies*, G. Routledge and Sons, London, 1935, G. Morrow and Company, New York, 1935, cited by Cuisenier, 1968 (VII).
23 Maisch (1968), 1970 (VII), and Cuisenier, 1968 (VII).
24 Saint Augustine (1610), 1972 (V). One of L. Vives' notes refers to Cicero (*De finibus* . . . bk 5), in relation to love which is spread through the practice of

marriage. Another points out that, in contrast to the Romans, the gods (Saturn, Jupiter), the Egyptians and the Athenians all allowed incest (p. 554).

25 'For if it is wicked to go beyond the boundary of one's lands in the greed for increasing possession, how much more wicked is it to remove a moral boundary in the lust for sexual pleasure! It has also been our experience that even in our own days marriages between cousins were of rare occurrence because of moral scruples, although they were permitted by law; and that was because of the degree of kinship involved, only one step removed from that of brother and sister. Yet such unions were not prohibited by divine law and they had not yet been forbidden by the law of man. Nevertheless, an aversion was felt from an act which, though lawful, bordered on an illegality': Saint Augustine (1610), 1972, XV, xvi, i, pp. 624–5 (V).

26 Saint Augustine also attributes the prohibition of incest to custom. But his argument differs from that of Giovanni. The English translation of the period runs as follows: ' . . . custome is a great matter to make a man hate or affect any thing: and custome herein suppressing the immoderate immodesty of concupiscence, hath justly set a brand of ignominy upon it, as an irreligious and unhumaine acte . . . ': Saint Augustine (1610), 1972, p. 553 (V).

27   They are not ever jealous for the cause,
       But jealous for they are jealous: 'tis a monster
       Begot upon itself, born on itself.   *Othello*, III, iv, 158–60

28 Or, to use the term current at the time: lust. Among other recent commentaries on incest, we should mention two works by Thomas Mann, a novella: *Wälsungenblut* (Reserved Blood), and a novel: *Der Erwählte* (The Holy Sinner). In the novella two young Jews, brother and sister, enter into an incestuous relationship as much through 'affinity' as through rejection on the part of a non-Jewish society. In *Der Erwählte*, Willigis says to his sister Sybilla, 'For of us two no one is worthy, neither of you nor of me; worthy is the one of the other since we are wholly exceptional children, high of birth.' After the incest has been consummated, the spirit of story-telling comments: 'Of course, it is said: "When the bed has been gained, the right is obtained", but what was here obtained but unright and topsy-turviness to make one giddy? According to rule, the bed-lying goes before betrothal and wedding; but here it would have been madness and delusion to think, after the bed-gaining, of betrothal and marriage . . . She held the strange view, and spoke also in this sense to her left-hand spouse, that one who had belonged only to her brother had not become a wife in the common meaning, but rather was still a maid and wore with right the garland': trans. by H. T. Lowe-Porter, Penguin, Harmondsworth, 1972, pp. 19 and 27.

29 Jean Jacquot has drawn my attention to a marriage ritual that is somewhat similar, in Chapman's *The Gentleman Usher* (IV, ii).

30 De Rosset, 1619, p. 260 (V).

31 *Ibid.*, p. 261. The theme of enforced marriage is popular in the theatre of the first half of the seventeenth century. See Blayney, 1959 (VI).

32 Friar Bonaventura advises Giovanni to give up the idea of incest and indulge instead in lust with other women (I, i, 62–3).

33 '[I have] fashioned my heart to love him' (III, vi, 29).

34 See Lévi-Strauss' reflections on the Oedipus myth (1958, pp. 236–40 (VII)). Lévi-Strauss speaks of an 'overrating of blood relations' in incestuous relation-

ships, and of an 'underrating' in the murder of kin by kin. On a narrative level (Giovanni both sleeps with his sister and also kills her) these two aspects complement each other perfectly in Ford's play.

35 Stone, 1965 and 1972 (III).
36 Stavig, 1968, p. 121 (VI).
37 Northrop Frye (1957), 1967, p. 210 (VI).
38 Kaufmann (1960), 1961, p. 336 (VI).
39 Ovid, 1968 (VIII).
40

La Blanche Biche

Celles qui vont au bois
C'est la mère et la fille.

La mère va chantant
Et la fille soupire.

Qu'av'vous à soupirer,
Ma fille Marguerite?

J'ai bien grande ire en moi;
Et n'ose vous le dire.

Je suis fille le jour
Et la nuit blanche biche.

La chasse est après moi,
Les barons et les princes.

Et mon frère Renaud
Qui est encore bien pire.

Allez, ma mère, allez
Bien promptement lui dire

Qu'il arrête ses chiens
Jusqu'à demain ressie.

Où sont tes chiens Renaud
Et ta chasse gentille?

Ils sont dedans le bois
A courre blanche biche.

Arrête-les Renaud,
Arrête, je t'en prie.

Trois fois les a cornés,
O son cornet de cuivre.

A la troisième fois,
La blanche biche est prise.

Mandons le dépouilleur
Qu'il dépouille la biche.

Celui qui la dépouille
Dit: Je ne sais que dire.

Elle a les cheveux blonds
Et le sein d'une fille.

A tiré son couteau
En quartiers il l'a mise.

En ont fait un dîner
Au baron et aux princes.

Nous voici tous illec
Faut ma soeur Marguerite.

Vous n'avez qu'à manger
Suis la première assise.

Ma tête est dans le plat,
Et mon coeur aux chevilles

Mon sang est répandu
Par toute la cuisine,

Et sur vos noirs charbons,
Mes pauvres os y grillent.

In Henri Davenson (Alias Henri Marrou), 1946, pp. 197–9 (VIII). Henri Davenson writes: 'This song was found in the zone between the Vendée and eastern Normandy. Like many of our most beautiful tragic laments, it would appear to have originated in this western region and, more specifically, in Gallic Britanny where the Celtic genius for legend did so much to enrich French folklore. Nothing is known of its origins. The same theme apparently appears in a Swedish *vise*, "The Maiden transformed into a Troll" ' (p. 199). On relations between hunting, sacrifice and cannibal feasting, see 'Hunting and sacrifice in Aeschylus' Oresteia', in Vernant and Vidal-Naquet (1972), 1981 (VII).

Bibliography

Critics who write about Shakespeare are perhaps even more conscious than others of their debt to countless other scholars and writers. If a bibliography is to avoid becoming more weighty than the text it supports, it must be selective and, in many respects, no more than partial. It cannot take account of every single work consulted over the years in the course of research. In the present case the only works mentioned are works of reference, Elizabethan studies and methodological texts consulted, used or cited in putting together the various chapters of the present book.

I. Bibliographical works

Abstracts of English Studies, ed. Lewis Swain *et al.*, vol. 1, nos. 1–8, Boulder, Col., 1958, vol. 1, nos. 9– , Boulder, Col., National Council of Teachers of English, 1958–

Annual Bibliography of English Language and Literature, Bowes and Bowes, Cambridge, 1921–

Berman, Ronald, S., *A Reader's Guide to Shakespeare's Plays* (Scott, Foresman, Chicago, Ill., 1965) rev. edn Scott, Foresman and Company, Glenview, Ill., 1973

Bibliothèque Nationale, *Catalogue des ouvrages de William Shakespeare conservés au Département des imprimés et dans les bibliothèques de l'Arsenal, Mazarine, Sainte-Geneviève, de l'Institut et de l'université de Paris*, Paris, 1948

Ebisch, F. W. and Schucking, L. L., *A Shakespeare Bibliography*, Clarendon Press, Oxford, 1931

  Supplement for the Years 1930–1935 to a Shakespeare Bibliography (Oxford University Press, Oxford, 1936), reissued by Benjamin Bloom, New York, 1964

Elton, Geoffrey Rudolph, *The Sources of History: England 1200–1640*, Cornell Univ. Press, Ithaca, London, 1969

  Modern Historians on British History 1485–1945: A Critical Bibliography 1945–1969, Methuen, London, 1970

Harbage, Alfred, *Annals of English Drama, 975–1700* (Philadelphia Univ. of Pennsylvania Press, pub. in cooperation with the Modern Language Association of America; H. Milford, Oxford University Press, Oxford, 1940), rev. edn, ed. S. Schoenbaum, Methuen, London, 1964

Horn-Monval, Madeleine, *Traductions et adaptations françaises du théâtre étranger*, Centre National de la Recherche Scientifique, Paris, 1963, vol. 5: *Théâtre anglais, théâtre américain*.

Jaggard, William, *Shakespeare Bibliography* (Shakespeare Press, Stratford-upon-Avon, 1911), Dawsons of Pall Mall, Folkestone, 1971

Levine, Mortimer, *Bibliographical Handbooks: Tudor England*, Cambridge Univ. Press, Cambridge, 1968

McManaway, James G. and Roberts, Jeanne A., *A Selective Bibliography of Shakespeare: Editions, Textual Studies, Commentary*, published for the Folger Library by Univ. Press of Virginia, Charlottesville, 1975

Maxwell, Harold William, *A Bibliography of English Law to 1650*, Sweet and Maxwell's Complete Law Book Catalogue, vol. 1, London, 1925

Milward, Peter, *Religious Controversies of the Elizabethan Age: A Survey of Printed Sources*, foreword by G. R. Elton, Scolar Press, London, 1977

 Religious Controversies of the Jacobean Age: A Survey of Printed Sources, Scolar Press, London, 1978

P.M.L.A. Bibliography, published annually by the Modern Languages Association of America, 1884–

Quinn, Edward, Ruoff, James and Grennen, Joseph, *The Major Shakespeare Tragedies: A Critical Bibliography*, Free Press, New York, 1973

Read, Conyers (ed.), *Bibliography of British History: Tudor Period*, 2nd edn, Oxford Univ. Press, Oxford, 1959

Smith, Gordon Ross, *A Classified Shakespeare Bibliography, 1936–1958*, Pennsylvania Univ. Press, University Park, Pa., 1963

Thimm, Franz, *Shakespeariana from 1564 to 1864: An Account of the Shakespearian Literature of England, Germany, France and other European Countries during Three Centuries, with Bibliographical Introductions* (1865), Franz Thimm, foreign bookseller and publisher, 2nd enlarged edn, London, 1872

Velz, John W., *Shakespeare and the Classical Tradition: A Critical Guide to Commentary, 1660–1960*, Univ. of Minnesota Press, Minneapolis, 1968

Watson, George, *The New Cambridge Bibliography of English Literature*, vol. 1, *600–1660*, Cambridge Univ. Press, Cambridge, 1974

Wells, David M., *Guide to Shakespeare*, Barnes and Noble, New York, 1976

Also the periodic bibliographies for Shakespeare, published in:

The Shakespeare Association Bulletin (1924–9)

Shakespeare Jahrbuch (1865–1964), subsequently divided into *Shakespeare Jahrbuch* 1966– , in the West, and *Shakespeare Jahrbuch* 100/101 (1964–65) in the East

Shakespeare Newsletter, ed. Louis Marder, New York, 1951–

Shakespeare Quarterly, New York, 1950–72; Washington, 1972–

Shakespeare Survey, ed. A. Nicoll, then K. Muir, Cambridge, 1948–

Shakespearean Research and Opportunities (*S.R.O.*), New York, annual since 1965, ed. W. R. Elton

Year's Work in English Studies, Oxford, 1921, ed. Sidney Lee *et al.*

Also the specialised catalogues of some libraries: e.g. Folger, Birmingham, British Library.

II. Works of reference

Abbott, Edwin A., *A Shakespearian Grammar* (London, 1869), Dover Publications, New York, 1966

Bartlett, John, *A New and Complete Concordance or Verbal Index to Words, Phrases, and Passages in the Dramatic Works of Shakespeare with a Supplemen-*

tary Concordance to the Poems (London, 1894), reprinted St Martin's Press, New York, 1956

Bullough, Geoffrey, *Narrative and Dramatic Sources of Shakespeare*, 8 vols., Routledge and Kegan Paul, London, 1957–75

Campbell, O. J. and Quinn, E. G. (eds.), *A Shakespeare Encyclopaedia*, Methuen, London, 1966

Chambers, Edmund K., *The Elizabethan Stage*, 4 vols., Oxford Univ. Press, Oxford, 1923

The Compact Edition of the Oxford English Dictionary, complete text reproduced micrographically, 2 vols., Oxford University Press, Oxford, 1971

Cotgrave, Randle, *A Dictionary of the French and English Tongues*, London, 1611

Dictionary of National Biography (1885–1903), 22 vols., Oxford Univ. Press, Oxford, 1920

Dictionnaire de théologie catholique, general eds. A. Vacant, E Mangenot and E. Amann, Librairie Letouzey et Ané, Paris, 15 vols. (1899–1950) and Indexes (1951–72)

Enciclopedia dello spettacolo, 9 vols. and appendix, casa editrice Le Maschere, Rome, 1954–64

Encyclopaedia Britannica, 23 vols. and index, William Benton, Chicago, 1963

Encyclopaedia Judaica, 16 vols. and supplements, Keter Publishing House Jerusalem Ltd, Jerusalem, 1973

Encyclopaedia Universalis, 20 vols. and supplements, Encyclopaedia Universalis France, Paris, 1968

Florio, John, *Queen Anna's New World of Words* (2nd edn, London, 1611), facsimile edn, Scolar Press, Menston, 1968

Greg, Walter Wilson, *The Shakespeare First Folio: Its Bibliographical and Textual History*, Clarendon Press, Oxford, 1955

Halliday, Frank Ernest, *A Shakespeare Companion* (1964), Penguin, Harmondsworth, 1969

Hartnoll, Phyllis, *The Oxford Companion to the Theatre*, 3rd edn, Oxford Univ. Press, Oxford, 1967

Harvey, Paul, *The Oxford Companion to English Literature*, 4th edn, corr., Oxford Univ. Press, Oxford, 1969

Hinman, Charlton, *The Printing and Proof-Reading of the First Folio of Shakespeare*, 2 vols., Oxford Univ. Press, Oxford, 1963

Jowitt, William Allen (Earl Jowitt), *The Dictionary of English Law*, 2 vols., Sweet and Maxwell, London, 1959

Littré [Maximilian Paul], Émile, *Dictionnaire de la langue française* (1863–72), new edn, 7 vols., Jean-Jacques Pauvert, Paris, 1956–8

Muir, Kenneth and Schoenbaum, Samuel (eds.), *A New Companion to Shakespeare Studies*, Cambridge Univ. Press, Cambridge, 1971

Onions, Charles Talbot, *A Shakespeare Glossary* (1911), expanded edn, Clarendon Press, Oxford, 1958

Palsgrave, John, *Lesclarcissement de la langue francoyse* (1530), facsimile edn, Scolar Press, Menston, 1969

Partridge, Eric, *Shakespeare's Bawdy*, 2nd edn, Routledge and Kegan Paul, London, 1968

Schmidt, Alexander, *Shakespeare Lexicon* (1874), 3rd edn, 2 vols., Georg Reinier, Berlin, 1902, reprinted as *Shakespeare Lexicon and Quotation Dictionary*, Dover Publications, New York, 1971

Schoenbaum, Samuel, *William Shakespeare: A Documentary Life*, Clarendon Press, Oxford, 1975

William Shakespeare: A Compact Documentary Life, Oxford Univ. Press, Oxford, 1977

Skeat, Walter William, *A Glossary of Tudor and Stuart Words* (1914), Georg Olms Verlag, Hildesheim, 1968

Spevack, Marvin, *The Harvard Concordance to Shakespeare* (6 vols., 1968–70), Georg Olms Verlag, Hildesheim, 1973

Tilley, Morris P., *A Dictionary of the Proverbs in England in the Sixteenth and Seventeenth Centuries*, Univ. of Michigan Press, Ann Arbor, 1950

Wilson, F. P. (ed.), *The Oxford Dictionary of English Proverbs*, 3rd edn with an introd. by Joanna Wilson, Clarendon Press, Oxford, 1970

III. Political and social history, history of ideas

Allen, Don Cameron, *Doubt's Boundless Sea, Skepticism and Faith in the Renaissance*, Johns Hopkins Press, Baltimore, 1964

Allen, John William, *A History of Political Thought in the Sixteenth Century* (1928), Methuen, London, 1960

Ariès, Philippe, *L'Homme devant la mort*, Editions du Seuil, Paris, 1977

Ashley, Maurice, *England in the Seventeenth Century*, Penguin, Harmondsworth, 1952

Axton, Marie, *The Queen's Two Bodies. Drama and the Elizabethan Succession*, Royal Historical Society Studies in History, London, 1977

Beauté, Jean, *Un grand juriste anglais: Sir Edward Coke (1552–1634)*, Presses Universitaires de France, Paris, 1975

Bellamy, John G., *The Law of Treason in England in the Later Middle Ages*, Cambridge Univ. Press, Cambridge, 1970
The Tudor Law of Treason: An Introduction, Routledge and Kegan Paul, London; Univ. of Toronto Press, Toronto and Buffalo, 1979

Bibliothèque Nationale, *Les Sorcières*, Paris, 1973

Bindoff, Stanley Thomas, *Tudor England*, Penguin, Harmondsworth, 1950

Black, John Bennett, *The Reign of Elizabeth, 1558–1603*, vol. 8 of *The Oxford History of England*, 2nd edn, Clarendon Press, Oxford, 1959

Bland, A. E., Brown, P. A. and Tawney, R. H., *English Economic History, Select Documents* (1914), G. Bell and Sons Ltd, London, 1937

Bloch, Marc, *Les Rois thaumaturges* (1924), Armand Colin, Paris, 1961
La Société féodale (1939), Albin Michel, Paris, 1968

Bowen, Catherine (Drinker), *The Lion and the Throne, the Life and Times of Sir Edward Coke, 1552–1634*, Little, Brown and Company, Boston, 1957

Chadwick, Owen, *The Reformation*, vol. 3 of *The Pelican History of the Church*, Harmondsworth, 1964, rev. edn, 1972

Chew, Samuel Claggett, *The Crescent and the Rose: Islam and England during the Renaissance* (1937), Octagon Books, New York, 1965

Cobbett, William (ed.), *Parliamentary History of England*, 36 vols., London, 1806–20, vols. 1 and 2

Contamine, Philippe, *Azincourt*, Juillard, Paris, 1964

Cox, John Charles, *The Royal Forests of England*, Methuen, London, 1905
The Sanctuaries and Sanctuary Seekers of Medieval England, G. Allen and Sons, London, 1911

Daniel, Norman, *Islam and the West: The Making of an Image*, Edinburgh Univ. Press, Edinburgh, 1958
Islam, Europe and Empire, Edinburgh Univ. Press, Edinburgh, 1966

Davies, Godfrey, *The Early Stuarts, 1603–1660*, vol. 9 of *The Oxford History of England* (1937), 2nd edn, Clarendon Press, Oxford, 1963

Davis, David Brion, *The Problem of Slavery in Western Culture* (1966), Cornell Paperbacks, Ithaca, New York, 1970

Delumeau, Jean, *La Peur en Occident aux XIVe–XVIIIe siècles*, Fayard, Paris, 1978

De Mazzinghi, T. J., *Sanctuaries*, Stafford, 1887

Devèze, Michel, *La Vie de la forêt française au XIVe siècle*, 2 vols., S.E.V.P.E.N., Paris, 1961

Dickens, Arthur Geoffrey, *The English Reformation*, Batsford, London, 1964

Duby, Georges, *Les Trois Ordres ou l'imaginaire du féodalisme*, Gallimard, Paris, 1978

Dudley, Edward and Novak, Maximillian, E. (eds.), *The Wild Man Within: An Image in Western Thought from the Renaissance to Romanticism*, Univ. of Pittsburgh Press, Pittsburgh, 1972

Eccleshall, Robert, *Order and Reason in Politics; Theories of Absolute and Limited Monarchy in Early Modern England*, Oxford Univ. Press, Oxford, 1978

Elton, Geoffrey Rudolph, *England under the Tudors*, Methuen, London, 1955, new edn, 1962

    The Tudor Constitution, Cambridge Univ. Press, Cambridge, 1965

Ernle, Rowland E., Lord Prothero, *English Farming Past and Present* (1912), Heinemann Educational Books and Frank Cass, 6th edn, London, 1961

Esmein, Adhémar, *Le Mariage en droit canonique*, 2 vols., Paris, 1891

Fisher, William Richard, *The Forest of Essex*, London, 1887

Fitz Nigel, Richard, 'Dialogus de Scaccario', in *History and Antiquities of the Exchequer of the King of England*, ed. Thomas Madox, London, 1711

    De Necessariis Observantiis Scaccarii Dialogus, ed. Arthur Hughes, C. G. Crump and C. Johnson, Clarendon Press, Oxford, 1902

    The Course of the Exchequer, introd. and trans. by C. Johnson, Thomas Nelson and Sons, London, 1950

Gardiner, Samuel Rawson, *History of England from the Accession of James I to the Outbreak of the Civil War, 1603–1642*, 10 vols., London, 1883–4

George, Katherine, 'The Civilized West Looks at Primitive Africa: 1400–1880. A Study in Ethnocentrism', *Isis*, 49, 1958, pp. 62–72

Gierke, Otto Friedrich von, *Natural Law and the Theory of Society, 1500 to 1800*, trans. from the German by E. Barker, 2 vols., Cambridge Univ. Press, Cambridge, 1934

    The Development of Political Theory, trans. from the German by B. Freyd, Allen and Unwin, London, 1939

Haydn, Hiram, *The Counter-Renaissance* (1950), Evergreen Edition, New York, 1960

Henriques, Henry S. Q., *The Law of Aliens and Naturalization*, Butterworth and Co., London, 1908

    The Jews and the English Law, Oxford Univ. Press, Oxford, 1908

Hexter, Jack H., *Reappraisals in History*, Northwestern Univ. Press, Evanston, Ill., 1961

Hill, J. E. Christopher, *Puritanism and Revolution* (Martin Secker and Warburg Ltd, London, 1958), Panther edn, 1968

    Intellectual Origins of the English Revolution, Clarendon Press, Oxford, 1965

    The World Turned Upside Down, Temple Smith, London, 1972

Holdsworth, Sir William Searle, *A History of English Law*, 17 vols., Methuen, 1903–72 (vol. 1 of the 7th edn revised by S. B. Chrimes, 1956); vol. 4 and vol. 5 concern the reign of Elizabeth

Honour, Hugh, *L'Amérique vue par l'Europe*, Editions des Musées nationaux, Paris, 1976

Houston, S. J., *James I*, Longman, London, 1973

Howard, Clare, *English Travellers of the Renaissance*, John Lane, London, 1914

Howell, Thomas B., *A Complete Collection of State Trials*, 34 vols., London, 1809–28 (the first two volumes are relevant to the period)

Hughes, P. L. and Larkin, J. F., *Tudor Royal Proclamations*, 3 vols., Yale Univ. Press, New Haven and London, 1964–9

Janson, Horst Woldemar, *Apes and Ape Lore in the Middle Ages and the Renaissance*, Studies of the Warburg Institute, London, 1952

Johnson, Cuthbert William, *The Life of Sir Edward Coke*, London, 1837

Jones, Howard Mumford, *O Strange New World, American Culture: The Formative Years* (1964) Viking Press, Viking Compass Edn, New York, 1968

Jordan, Wilbur Kitchener, *The Development of Religious Toleration in England*, Harvard Univ. Press, Cambridge, Mass., 1932

Jordan, Winthrop D., *White over Black, American Attitudes Toward the Negro, 1550–1812*, Univ. of North Carolina Press, Chapel Hill, 1968

Joseph, Bertram Leon, *Shakespeare's Eden: The Commonwealth of England, 1558–1629*, Blandford Press, London, 1971

Kantorowicz, Ernst H., *The King's Two Bodies: A Study in Medieval Political Theology*, Princeton Univ. Press, Princeton, 1957

Kenyon, John Philipps, *The Stuart Constitution, 1603–1688: Documents and Commentary*, Cambridge Univ. Press, Cambridge, 1966

Kiralfy, Albert K. R., *A Source Book of English Law*, Sweet and Maxwell, London, 1957

Knafla, Louis B., *Law and Politics in Jacobean England – The Tracts of Lord Chancellor Ellesmere*, Cambridge Univ. Press, Cambridge, 1977

Lamont, William and Oldfield, Sybil (eds.), *Politics, Religion and Literature in the Seventeenth Century*, Dent, London, 1975

Larner, Christina, 'James VI and I and Witchcraft', in *The Reign of James VI and I*, ed. Alan Gordon R. Smith, Edward Arnold, London, 1973

Laslett, Peter, *The World We Have Lost* (1965), paperback, 2nd edn, Methuen, London, 1971

Lee, Sidney and Onions, Charles T., *Shakespeare's England: An Account of the Life and Manners of His Age*, 2 vols., Clarendon Press, Oxford, 1916

Le Goff, Jacques, *Pour un autre Moyen Age*, Gallimard, Paris, 1978

Levine, Mortimer, *Tudor Dynastic Problems 1460–1571*, Allen and Unwin, London, 1973

Lewis, Percival, *Historical Inquiries Concerning Forests and Forest Laws*, London, 1811

Liebermann, Félix, *Uber Pseudo-Cnuts Constitutiones de Foresta*, Halle a.S., 1894

Lipson, Ephraim, *The Economic History of England*: vol. 1, 12th edn, A. and C. Black, London, 1962, vols. 2 and 3, 6th edn, A. and C. Black, London, 1961

Lovejoy, Arthur O. and Boas, George, *Primitivism and Related Ideas in Antiquity* (1935), with supplementary essays by W. F. Albright and P. E. Dumont, Octagon Books, New York, 1965

Mackie, John Duncan, *The Earlier Tudors 1485–1558*, vol. 7 of *The Oxford History of England*, Clarendon Press, Oxford, 1952

Maitland, Frederic W., *The Collected Papers of Frederic William Maitland*, 3 vols., Cambridge Univ. Press, Cambridge, 1911

Mesnard, Pierre, *L'Essor de la philosophie politique au XVIe siècle* (1936), 2nd rev. edn, J. Vrin, Paris, 1951

Miller, Perry (ed.), *The American Puritans, Their Prose and Poetry*, Doubleday, Anchor Books, New York, 1956

Morris, Christopher, *Political Thought in England: Tyndale to Hooker* (1953), Oxford Univ. Press, London, New York, 1965

Neale, John E., *Queen Elizabeth I* (1934), Penguin, Harmondsworth, 1960
  The Elizabethan House of Commons (1949), rev. edn, Peregrine, Harmondsworth, 1963
  Elizabeth I and Her Parliaments (2 vols., 1953 and 1957), paperback, 2 vols., Jonathan Cape, London, 1965

Neaman, Judith S., *Suggestion of the Devil. Insanity in the Middle Ages and the Twentieth Century* (Anchor Books, New York, 1975), Octagon Books, London, 1978

O'Farrell, Patrick, *Ireland's English Question*, Schocken Books, New York, 1971

Patrides, C. A., ' "The Bloody and Cruell Turke": The Background of a Renaissance Commonplace', *Studies in the Renaissance*, 10, 1963, pp. 126–35
  'The Scale of Nature and Renaissance Treatises on Nobility', *Studia Neophilologica*, 36, 1964, pp. 63–9

Payne, Robert, *Hubris: A Study in Pride* (Heinemann, London, 1951), rev. edn, Harper, New York, 1960

Pearce, Roy Harvey, *The Savages of America: A Study of the Indian and the Idea of Civilisation*, Johns Hopkins Press, Baltimore, 1953 (reprinted as *Savagism and Civilization*, 1965)

Petit-Dutaillis, Charles, 'La Forêt et le droit de chasse en Angleterre au Moyen Age', study included in W. Stubbs, *L'Histoire constitutionnelle de l'Angleterre*, 3 vols., V. Giard and E. Brière, Paris, 1907–27
  'Les Origines franco-normandes de la forêt anglaise' in *Mélanges d'histoire offerts à M. Charles Bémont*, F. Alcan, Paris, 1913

Pocock, John Greville Agard, *The Ancient Constitution and the Feudal Law* (1957), Cedric Chivers Ltd, Bath, 1974
  Politics, Language and Time: Essays on Political Thought and History, Athenaeum, New York, 1971

Poliakov, Léon, *La Causalité diabolique. Essai sur l'origine des persécutions*, Calmann-Lévy, Paris, 1980

Pollock, F. and Maitland, F. W., *The History of English Law* (1895), ed., introd. and bibliog. by S. F. C. Milson, 2 vols., Cambridge Univ. Press, Cambridge, 1968

Prothero, G. W., *Select Statutes and Other Constitutional Documents Illustrative of the Reigns of Elizabeth and James I* (1894), 4th edn, Clarendon Press, Oxford, 1954

Quinn, David Beers, *The Elizabethans and the Irish*, Cornell Univ. Press, Ithaca, New York, 1966

Rich, E. E., 'The Population of Elizabethan England', *Economic History Review*, 2nd Series, 2, 3, 1950, pp. 247–65

Robbins, Rossell Hope, *The Encyclopedia of Witchcraft and Demonology*, Crown Publishers Inc., New York, 1959

Rowse, A. Leslie, *The England of Elizabeth* (1950), St Martins Library, London, 1964
  The Expansion of Elizabethan England, Macmillan, London, 1955
  The Case Books of Simon Forman, Sex and Society in Shakespeare's Age, Weidenfeld and Nicolson, London, 1974

Salzman, L. F., *England in Tudor Times*, Batsford, London, 1926

Schochet, Gordon J., *Patriarcalism in Political Thought*, Blackwell, Oxford, 1975

Schwoebel, Robert, *The Shadow of the Crescent: The Renaissance Image of the Turk*, B. de Graaf, Nieuwkoop, 1967

Shaw, R. Cunliffe, *The Royal Forest of Lancaster*, Guardian Press, Preston, 1956

Sheehan, Bernard, *Savagism and Civility; Indians and Englishmen in Colonial Virginia*, Cambridge Univ. Press, London and New York, 1980

Shyllon, Folarin, *Black Slaves in Britain*, Oxford Univ. Press, Oxford, 1974
  Black People in Britain 1555–1833, Oxford Univ, Press, Oxford, 1978

Simon, Marcel, *L'Anglicanisme*, Armand Colin, Paris, 1969

Skinner, Quentin, 'History and Ideology in the English Revolution', *Historical Journal*, 8, 2, 1965, pp. 151–78

Smith, Alan G. R., 'Constitutional Ideas and Parliamentary Developments in England 1603–1625', in *The Reign of James VI and I*, Macmillan, London, 1973

Southern, Richard William, *Western Views of Islam in the Middle Ages*, Harvard Univ. Press, Cambridge, Mass., 1962

Stone, Lawrence, *The Crisis of the Aristocracy, 1558–1641*, Clarendon Press, Oxford, 1965
  The Causes of the English Revolution, 1529–1642, Routledge and Kegan Paul, London, 1972
  The Family, Sex and Marriage in England, 1500–1800, Weidenfeld and Nicholson, London, 1977

Strutt, Joseph, *The Sports and Pastimes of the People of England*, ed. W. Hone, London, 1876

Stubbs, William, *L'Histoire constitutionnelle de l'Angleterre*, 3 vols., V. Giard and E. Brière, Paris, 1907–27

Summers, Montague, *The History of Witchcraft* (1956), University Books, Secaucus, N.J., 1971
  The Werewolf (1966), University Books, Secaucus, N.J., 1973

Tanner, J. R., *Constitutional Documents of the Reign of James I, 1603–1625* (1930), Cambridge Univ. Press, Cambridge, 1961

Tawney, R. H., *Religion and the Rise of Capitalism* (1926), Pelican, West Drayton, 1948

Tawney, R. H. and Power, Eileen, *Tudor Economic Documents*, 3 vols., Longman, London, 1924

Thirsk, Joan (ed.), *Agrarian History of England and Wales, IV, 1500–1640*, Cambridge Univ. Press, Cambridge, 1967

Thomas, Keith, *Religion and the Decline of Magic*, Weidenfeld and Nicolson, London, 1971

Thompson, Edward Palmer, *Whigs and Hunters: Origin of the Black Act*, Allen Lane, London, 1975

Thorne, Samuel E., *Sir Edward Coke*, Selden Society Lecture, 1952, published 1957

Trenholme, Norman Maclaren, *The Right of Sanctuary in England*, University of Missouri Studies, 1, 5, 1903

Turner, G. J., *Select Pleas of the Forest*, Selden Society, London, 1901

Turton, Robert Bell, *The Honor and Forest of Pickering*, 4 vols., North Riding Record Society, 1894–7

Walvin, James, *The Black Presence*, Orbach and Chambers, London, 1971
  Black and White – The Negro and English Society, 1555–1945, Allen Lane, London, 1973

Watson, R. W. H. Seton (ed.), *Tudor Studies Presented to A. F. Pollard*, Univ. of London, London, 1924

Wiener, Carol Z., 'The Beleaguered Isle. A Study of Elizabethan and Early Jacobean Anti-Catholicism', *Past and Present*, 51, May 1971, pp. 27–62

Willson, David Harris, 'King James I and Anglo-Scottish Unity', in *Conflict in Stuart England, Essays in Honour of Wallace Notestein*, ed. William A. Aiken and Basil D. Henning, Jonathan Cape, London, 1960, pp. 41–55

King James VI and I, Jonathan Cape, London, 1963

Wright, Louis B., *Middle Class Culture in Elizabethan England*, Univ. of Carolina Press, Chapel Hill, 1935

Zeeveld, W. Gordon, *Foundations of Tudor Policy*, Harvard Univ. Press, Cambridge, Mass., 1948

IV. Dramatic texts

Adams, J. Q., *Chief Pre-Shakespearian Dramas* (Houghton Mifflin Co., Boston and New York, 1924), Houghton Mifflin Co., Cambridge, Mass., 1952

Anon., *Everyman and Medieval Miracle Plays*, ed. A. C. Cawley, E. P. Dutton, New York, 1959

The Life and Death of Jack Straw, eds. Kenneth Muir and F. P. Wilson, Malone Society Reprints, Oxford, 1957

Ludus Coventriae or the Plaie called Corpus Christi (1922), ed. K. S. Block, E.E.T.S. extra-series 120, London, 1960

Non-Cycle Plays and Fragments, ed. Norman Davis, E.E.T.S., s.s. 1, Oxford Univ. Press, London, New York, Toronto, 1970

The York Plays, ed. Lucy Toulmin Smith, Clarendon Press, Oxford, 1885

Bang, W. (ed.), New Series, H. de Vocht (gen. ed.), *Materialien zur Kunde des älteren englischen Dramas*, Louvain, 1902ff

Beaumont, Francis and Fletcher, John, *Le Chevalier de l'ardent pilon*, introd. and trans. by M. T. Jones-Davies, Aubier éditions Montaigne, collection bilingue, Paris, 1958

Brooke, C. F. Tucker (ed.), *The Shakespeare Apocrypha* (1908), Clarendon Press, Oxford, 1967

Euripides, *The Bacchae*, trans. by G. S. Kirk, Cambridge Univ. Press, Cambridge, 1979

Ford, John, *John Ford's Dramatic Works*, in *Materialien zur Kunde des älteren englischen Dramas*, ed. W. Bang, vol. 23, Louvain, 1908; New Series, ed. H. de Vocht, vol. 1, Louvain, 1927

Ford, Five Plays, ed. H. Ellis, Hill and Wang, Inc., New York, 1957

Annabella, trans. and adapt. by Maurice Maeterlinck, 1894

'Tis Pity She's a Whore, ed. N. W. Bawcutt, Arnold, London, 1966

'Tis Pity She's a Whore, ed. Brian Morris, Ernest Benn, London, 1968

The Broken Heart, ed. D. K. Anderson, Edward Arnold, London, 1968

Kyd, Thomas, *Works*, ed. F. S. Boas, Clarendon Press, Oxford, 1901, expanded edn, 1955

The Spanish Tragedy, ed. Philip Edwards, The Revels Plays, Methuen, London, 1959

The First Part of Hieronimo and *The Spanish Tragedie*, ed. A. S. Cairncross, Edward Arnold, London, 1967

Lily, John, *Dramatic Works* (1858), ed. F. W. Fairholt, 2 vols., J. R. Smith, London, 1892

The Complete Works of John Lyly, ed. R. W. Bond, 3 vols., Clarendon Press, Oxford, 1902

Marlowe, Christopher, *The Works of Christopher Marlowe* (1910), ed. C. F. Tucker Brooke, Clarendon Press, Oxford, 1953

Shakespeare, William, *The First Folio of Shakespeare*, facsimile edn, Charlton Hinman, Norton, New York, 1968

William Shakespeare: The Complete Works, ed. Peter Alexander, Collins, London, Glasgow, 1951

William Shakespeare: The Complete Works, ed. C. J. Sisson, Odhams, London, 1954

All's Well That Ends Well, Arden Shakespeare, ed. G. K. Hunter, Methuen, London (1959), 1962

All's Well That Ends Well, ed. Barbara Everett, Penguin, Harmondsworth, 1970

As You Like It, New Variorum, ed. H. H. Furness, Lippincott, Philadelphia, 1890

As You Like It, ed. H. J. Oliver, Penguin, Harmondsworth, 1968

As You Like It, Arden Shakespeare, ed. Agnes Latham, Methuen, London, 1975

Coriolanus, Arden Shakespeare, ed. P. Brockbank, Methuen, London, 1976

Cymbeline, Arden Shakespeare, ed. J. M. Nosworthy, London, 1955

Cymbeline, New Shakespeare, ed. J. C. Maxwell, Cambridge Univ. Press, Cambridge, 1960

Hamlet, New Variorum, ed. H. H. Furness, 2 vols., Lippincott, Philadelphia, 1877

Hamlet, New Shakespeare, ed. J. Dover Wilson, Cambridge Univ. Press, Cambridge (1934), 1936

Julius Caesar, New Variorum, ed. H. H. Furness, Jr, Lippincott, Philadelphia, 1913

Julius Caesar, Arden Shakespeare, ed. T. S. Dorsch, Cambridge, Mass., 1955

King Henry V, Arden Shakespeare, ed. J. H. Walter, London, and Cambridge, Mass. (1954), 1960

King Lear, Arden Shakespeare, ed. K. Muir, Harvard Univ. Press, Cambridge, Mass., 1952, rev. edn, Methuen, London, 1959

Macbeth, New Variorum, ed. H. H. Furness, Lippincott, Philadelphia, 1873, rev. edn, 1903

Macbeth, Arden Shakespeare, ed. Kenneth Muir, Harvard Univ. Press, Cambridge, Mass., 1951; 9th edn, rev. and expanded, Methuen, London, 1977

Measure for Measure, Arden Shakespeare, ed. J. W. Lever, Methuen, London, 1965

Measure for Measure, ed. J. M. Nosworthy, Penguin, Harmondsworth, 1969

A Midsummer Night's Dream, New Variorum, ed. H. H. Furness, Lippincott, Philadelphia, 1895

A Misdummer Night's Dream, ed. Stanley Wells, Penguin, Harmondsworth, 1967

Othello, New Variorum, ed. H. H. Furness, Lippincott, Philadelphia, 1866

Othello, Arden Shakespeare, ed. M. R. Ridley, Harvard Univ. Press and Methuen, London and Cambridge, Mass. (1958), 1962

Othello, ed. Kenneth Muir, Penguin, Harmondsworth, 1968

Pericles, Arden Shakespeare, ed. F. D. Hoeniger, Methuen, London, 1963

Pericles, Prince of Tyre, New Shakespeare, ed. J. C. Maxwell, Cambridge Univ. Press, Cambridge, 1956

The Tempest, New Variorum, ed. H. H. Furness, Lippincott, Philadelphia, 1892

The Tempest, Arden Shakespeare, ed. Frank Kermode, Harvard Univ. Press, Cambridge, Mass., 1954; 6th edn, 1958

Titus Andronicus, New Shakespeare, ed. J. Dover Wilson, Cambridge Univ. Press, Cambridge, 1948

Titus Andronicus, Arden Shakespeare, ed. J. C. Maxwell, Methuen, London, 1953, amended edn, 1968

The Winter's Tale, Arden Shakespeare, ed. J. H. P. Pafford, Methuen, London, 1963

V. Sources and texts of reference

Anghiera, Pierre Martyr, *De orbe novo*, The First Decades, trans. by Richard Eden, London, 1555

Anon., *Certaine Sermons or Homilies, Appointed to be Read in Churches in the Time of the Late Queene Elizabeth of Famous Memory*, London, 1640
Certayne sermons or Homiles appoynted to be read in Churches, Clarendon Press, Oxford, 1822

Aristotle, *Nichomachean Ethics*, Loeb Classical Library, Heinemann, London; G. P. Putnam's Sons, New York, 1926

Atkyns, John Tracy, *Reports of Cases Argued and Determined in the High Court of Chancery in the Time of Lord Chancellor Hardwicke*, 3 vols., London, 1765–8

Aylmer, John (or Aelmer), *An Harborowe for Faithfull and Trewe Subiectes* (Strasbourg, 1559); annotated edn, by Philippe Cerf, mémoire de maîtrise, Institut d'anglais Charles-V, Université Paris VII, 1977

Bacon, Francis, *The Works of Francis Bacon*, eds. James Spedding, R. L. Ellis and D. D. Heath, 14 vols., London, 1857–74
The Advancement of Learning, Everyman's Library, London, 1950

Beard, Thomas, *The Theatre of Gods Judgements*, London, 1597

Boaistuau, Pierre, *Histoires prodigieuses*, preface by Yves Florenne, Club français du livre, Paris, 1961, reprint of 1560 original edn

Boccaccio, Giovanni, *The Decameron of Giovanni Boccaccio*, trans. by J. M. Rigg, introd. by E. Hutton, 2 vols., Everyman's Library, London, 1930–1

Bodin, Jean, *Method for the Easy Comprehension of History*, trans. by B. Reynolds with introd. and notes, W. W. Norton and Company for the Columbia Univ. Press, New York (1945), 1969

Bonet, Honoré, *L'Arbre des batailles*, ed. Ernst Nys, Brussels, 1883

Bouteiller [or Boutillier], Jehan, *Le Grand Coustumier et Practique du Droit civil et canon* (Bruges, 1479), new enlarged edn by L. Charondas Le Caron, chez Sebastien Carmoisy, Paris, 1621

Brook[e], Sir Robert, *Ascuns Nouell Cases de les Ans et Tempe Le Roy H. 8. Ed. 6 et la Royagne Mary . . . Anno Do, 1578*, London, 1578
Les Reports des Cases en les Ans des Roys Edward V, Richard III, Henrie VII & Henrie VIII, London, 1679

Browne, Sir Thomas, *Essai sur les erreurs populaires, ou examen de plusieurs opinions reçues comme vrayes, qui sont fausses ou douteuses* (an abbreviated French version of Browne's *Pseudoxia Epidemica*), trans. from English by J.-B. Souchay, 2 vols., Amsterdam, 1733
Works, ed. S. Wilkin, 4 vols., London, 1835
Religio Medici (1906), Everyman's Library, London, 1959
Works, ed. G. Keynes, 6 vols., Faber and Gwyer, London, 1928–31

Buchanan, George, *De Jure Regni Apud Scotos* (Edinburgh, 1579), trans. into English by Philalethes, 1680
The Powers of the Crown in Scotland, trans. and introd. by C. F. Arrowood, Univ. of Texas Press, Austin, Texas, 1949

Budé, Guillaume, *Traitte de la Venerie* (extract from *De Philologia*), ed. H. Chevreul, Paris, 1961

Bullinger, Heinrich, *Fiftie Godlie and Learned Sermons, Divided into Five Decades*

Containing the Chiefe and Principall Points of Christian Religion, 'translated out
  of Latine . . . by H. I. student in Divinitie', 4 vols. (London, 1587), ed. Thomas
  Harding, Cambridge, 1849–52
Burton, Robert, *The Anatomy of Melancholy* (London, 1621), 3 vols., Everyman's
  Library, London, 1932, reprinted 1964
Camden, William, *Britannia*, Latin text, London, 1586; English text, trans. Ph.
  Holland, London, 1610
Castiglione, Balthazar, *The Book of the Courtier*, trans. by C. S. Singleton, Anchor
  Books, Doubleday and Company, Garden City, New York, 1959; trans. by Sir
  Thomas Hoby (1561), introd. by J. H. Whitfield, Everyman's Library, London,
  1975
Coke, Sir Edward, *The Reports of Sir Edward Coke in Thirteen Parts* (1600–59), eds.
  J.-H. Thomas and J.-F. Fraser, 6 vols., London, 1826
  The Fourth Part of the Institutes of the Laws of England, London, 1644
  The Second Part of the Institutes of the Laws of England, 3rd edn, London, 1669
Cowell, John, *The Interpreter; or Booke Containing the Signification of Words*,
  Cambridge, 1607
Dalton, Michael, *The Countrey Justice*, London (1655), 1677
De Bueil, Jean, *Le Jouvencel*, biographical introd. by C. Favre, 2 vols., Paris, 1887–9
De Damhoudere, J. H., *La Praticque et enchiridion des causes criminelles . . .* ,
  Louvain, 1555
De Legnano, Giovanni, *Tractatus De Bello, De Represaliis et De Duello* (1630), ed.
  T. E. Holland, with an English trans. printed for Carnegie Institution,
  Washington by Oxford Univ. Press, Oxford, 1917
De Lery, Jean, *Histoire d'un voyage fait en la terre du Brésil, dite Amérique*, 4th edn,
  Geneva, 1599
De Rosset, François, *Les Histoires mémorables et tragiques de ce temps*, Paris, 1619
Doleman, R., *A Conference about the Next Succession to the Crowne of Ingland*
  (imprinted at N., 1594), facsimile edn, Scolar Press, Menston, 1972
Drayton, Michael, *Polyolbion, or a Chorographical Description of Tracts, Rivers,
  Mountains, Forests, and Other Parts of this Renowned Isle of Great Britain, with
  Intermixture of the most Remarkable Stories, Antiquities, Wonders, Rarities,
  Pleasures, and Commodities of the Same*, London, 1612/13, extended edn, 1622
Egerton, Thomas, Viscount Brackley (Lord Ellesmere), *The Speech of the Lord
  Chancellor of England, Touching the 'Post-Nati'*, London, 1609
Elyot, Sir Thomas, *The Book Named The Governor* (1531), Everyman's Library,
  London, 1962
Gifford, George, *A Discourse of the Subtill Practises of Devilles . . .* , London, 1587
  A Dialogue concerning Witches and Witchcraft, London, 1593, 2nd edn, 1603,
  reprinted 1842
Grevin, Jacques, *Deux livres des venins, ausquels il est amplement discouru des bestes
  venimeuses, theriaques, poisons et contrepoisons*, Antwerp, 1568
Grotius, Hugo, *On the Law of War and Peace, the Classics of International Law*
  (1625), trans. from Latin by F. W. Kelsey *et al.*, 2 vols., Oxford and London,
  1925
Hakluyt, Richard, 'Discourse on Western Planting' (1584), in *Documentary History
  of the State of Maine*, ed. Charles Deane, 2 vols., Cambridge, Mass., 1887
  Principall Navigations, Voiages, and Discoveries of the English Nation (1589),
  expanded edn, 3 vols., London, 1598–1600
  The Principal Navigations, 12 vols., Hakluyt Society, Extra Series, Glasgow,
  1903–5

Voyages, 8 vols., Everyman's Library, London (1907), 1967
Harrison, Williams, *Harrison's Description of England in Shakespeare's Youth*, ed.
F. J. Furnivall, London, 1877–81
Hearne, Thomas, *A Collection of Curious Discourses*, 2 vols., London, 1775
Holinshed, Raphael, *Holinshed's Chronicle as Used in Shakespeare Plays*, eds.
A. Nicoll and J. Nicoll, Everyman's Library, London (1927), 1963
Holinshed, Raphael, Harrison, William, *et al.*, *The First and Second Volumes of
Chronicles*, London, 1807–8
Holland, Henry, *A Treatise against Witchcraft*, Cambridge, 1590
Hooker, Richard, *Of the Laws of Ecclesiastical Polity*, 2 vols., introd. by Christopher
Morris, Everyman's Library, London (1907), vol. 1, 1958, vol. 2, 1960
Of the Laws of Ecclesiastical Polity, Folger Library Edition, vol. 1, Books I–IV,
1977; vol. 2, Book V, 1977; vol 3, Books VI–VIII, 1981. General editor:
W. Speed Hill, Belknap Press of Harvard Univ. Press, Cambridge, Mass., and
London, 1977–81
Hooper, John, *Later Writings of Bishop Hooper*, ed. Ch. Nevinson, Parker Soc.,
Cambridge, 1852
James I, *Demonology* (Edinburgh, 1597), London, 1603
Works, London, 1616
'The Trew Law of Free Monarchies' in *Political Works of James I*, ed. C. H.
McIlwain, Harvard Univ. Press, Cambridge, Mass., 1918
Jewel, John, *The Works of John Jewel, Bishop of Salisbury*, vol. 2, *The Reply to
Harding's Answer . . .* , ed. John Ayre, Parker Soc., Cambridge, 1847
Johnson, Edward, 'Wonder-Working Providence of Sion's Saviour', in Perry Miller,
ed., *The American Puritans*, Doubleday, Garden City, New York, 1956
[Jourdain, Sylvester], *A Discovery of the Bermudas otherwise called the Ile of Divels
by Sir Thomas Gates, Sir George Sommers and Capt. Newport* (1610), in L. B.
Wright, *A Voyage to Virginia in 1609*, Univ. of Virginia Press, Charlottesville,
1964
Knox, John, *The First Blast of the Trumpet against the Monstrous Regiment of
Women* (1558); *Declaration to Queen Elizabeth* (1559), ed. E. Arber, London,
1880
Le Roy, Louis, *De la vicissitude ou Variété des choses en l'Univers*, Paris, 1577
Lopez de Gomara, François, *The Conquest of the West India*, trans. by Thomas
Nicholas (1578), 1596
Machiavelli, Nicolas, *The Ruler*, trans. by P. Rodd, London, 1954
[Mandeville, Sir John], *Mandeville's Travels*, ed. and notes by M. C. Seymour,
Clarendon Press, Oxford, 1967
Manwood, John, *A Brefe Collection of the Lawes of the Forests . . .* , 1592, private edn
A Treatise and Discourse of the Lawes of the Forest . . . , London, 1598, 1st public
edn
A Treatise and Discourse of the Lawes of the Forest, London, 1599
A Treatise . . . , London, 1615, extended edn; 3rd edn, 1665, 4th edn, 1717, 5th
edn, 1741. The last two editions produced by W. Nelson are organised dif-
ferently from the earlier ones
'Project for Improving the Land Revenue of the Crown . . .', in *Observations on
the Land Revenue of the Crown*, London, 1787, App. 1 by [John St John]
Markham, Gervase, *Country Contentments* (1615), 6th edn, London, 1649
Martyr, Peter, 'The Decades of the newe worlde or West India, conteyning the navi-
gations and conquestes of the Spanyardes . . . wrytten in the Latin tongoue by
Peter Martyr of Anglera, and translated into Englysshe by Rycharde Eden'

(London, 1555), in Edward Arber (ed.), *The First Three English Books on America, [?1511]–1555 A.D.*, Birmingham, 1885

Mexia, Pedro [Messie, Pierre], *Diverses leçons*, Rouen, 1526

The Foreste, trans. Th. Fortescue, 1571 and 1576

Monardes, Nicholas, *Ioyfull Newes out of the newe founde worlde* (1577), London, 1580 and 1596

Montaigne, Michel de, *Essais*, Bibl. de la Pléïade, Paris, 1958 (Florio trans., London and Toronto, 1928)

Moryson, Fynes, *An Itinerary Written by Fynes Moryson, Gent . . .* (London, 1617), 4 vols., J. MacLehose and Sons, Glasgow, 1907–8

Navigatio Sancti Brendani abbatis, ed. C. Selmer, Publ. in Mediaeval Studies, 16, Univ. of Notre Dame Press, Notre Dame, Ind., 1959

Norden, John, *The Surveiors Dialogue*, London (1607), 3rd edn, 1618

Paré, Ambroise, *Animaux, monstres et prodiges*, Club français du livre, Paris, 1954
Des monstres et prodiges, critical edn and commentaries by Jean Céard, Droz, Geneva, 1971

Phillips, Edward, *Theatrum Poetarum Anglicanorum*, Canterbury, 1675

Plutarch, *The Lives of the Noble Grecians and Romans . . .* , trans. out of Greek into French by James Amyot and out of French into English, by Thomas North, London (1579), 1595

Porta, John Baptista, *Natural Magick in XX Bookes* (Naples, 1589), trans. from Italian, London, 1658

Purchas, Samuel, *Hakluytus Posthumus or, Purchas His Pilgrimes* (1625), 20 vols., J. MacLehose and Sons, Glasgow, 1905–7

Rabelais, François, *Oeuvres complètes*, Bibl. de la Pléïade, Paris, 1955, trans. by W. F. Smith, London, 1893

Ronsard, Pierre de, *Oeuvres complètes* (1950), Bibl. de la Pléïade, 2 vols., 3rd edn, Paris, 1958

Saint Augustine, *Of the Citie of God* (with notes from Vives) trans. by J[ohn] H[ealey], London, 1610; *City of God*, trans. by H. Bettenson, Pelican Classics, Harmondsworth, 1972

Saint Grégoire, *Les Morales de saint Grégoire Pape sur le livre de Job*, chez Pierre le Petit, Paris, 1669

Salkeld, William, *Report of Cases Adjuged in the Court of King's Bench*, 6th edn, London, 1795

Sandys, Edwin, *The Sermons of Edwin Sandys*, ed. John Ayre, Parker Soc., Cambridge, 1841

Scot, Reginald, *The Discoverie of Witchcraft* (London, 1584), ed. B. Nicholson, London, 1886; ed. M. Summers, Dover, New York, 1972

Shakespeare, William, *The Poems*, ed. F. T. Prince, Harvard Univ. Press, London and Cambridge, Mass., 1960

Siderfin, Thomas, *Le Second Part de les reports du Thomas Siderfin . . . Esteant plusieurs cases comme ils etoyent argue & adjudgees en le court de l'upper banc en les ans 1657, 1658 & 1659*, 2nd rev. edn, London, 1689

Smith, John, *Travels and Works of Captain John Smith* (ed. Edward Arber, 1899), reprinted in 2 vols. with introd. by A. G. Bradley, J. Grant, Edinburgh, 1910

Smith, Thomas, *De Republica Anglorum*, London, 1583

Spencer, T. J. B. (ed.), *Shakespeare's Plutarch*, Penguin, Harmondsworth, 1964

Spenser, Edmund, *The Faerie Queene*, ed. A. C. Hamilton, Longman, London, 1977

Stow, John, *A Survey of London* (1598), Everyman's Library, London, 1956

Strachey, William, *A True Reportory of the Wreck*, in Purchas, 1625, Bk IV, chap. 6; ed. L. B. Wright, *A Voyage to Virginia in 1609: Two Narratives*, Univ. of Virginia Press, Charlottesville, 1964

Turbervi[l]le, George, *The Noble Arte of Venerie or Hunting* (1575) (1611) (attributed to George Gascoigne: see C. T. and R. Prouty, 'George Gascoigne, *The Noble Arte of Venerie*' in *Joseph Quincy Adams Memorial Studies*, Washington, 1948, pp. 639–41), reprinted 1908, Tudor and Stuart Library, London

Twiss, Travers (ed.), *The Black Book of the Admiralty*, 4 vols., London, 1871–6

Vair, Léonard, *Trois livres des charmes, sorcelages ou enchantemens*, transl. from Latin by J. Baudon, Paris, 1583

Whetstone, George, *The English Myrror*, London, 1586

Wingate, Edmond, *Maximes of Reason. or, the Reason of the Common Law of England*, London, 1658

Wright, Louis B. (ed.), *The Elizabethans' America*, Stratford-upon-Avon Library, 2, Edward Arnold, London, 1965

VI. Literary studies and studies on the Elizabethan theatre

Adler, Doris, 'The Rhetoric of Black and White in Othello', *Shakespeare Quarterly*, 25, 2, 1974, pp. 248–57

Andersen, Peter S., 'Shakespeare's Caesar; The Language of Sacrifice', *Comparative Drama*, 3, 1969, pp. 3–26

Anderson, Ruth L., *Elizabethan Psychology and Shakespeare's Plays* (Univ. of Iowa, Iowa City, Iowa, 1927), Russell and Russell, New York, 1966

Armstrong, Edward A., *Shakespeare's Imagination* (Lindsay Drummond, London, 1946), revised edn, Peter Smith, Gloucester, Mass., 1963

Armstrong, William A., 'The Elizabethan Conception of the Tyrant', *Review of English Studies*, 22, 1946, pp. 161–81

Auden, W. H., 'The Dyer's Hand', *The Listener*, 53, 16 June 1955, pp. 1063–6
  The Dyer's Hand and Other Essays (Random House, New York, 1962), Faber and Faber, London, 1963

Bacquet, Paul, *Le 'Jules César' de Shakespeare*, Société d'édition d'enseignement supérieur, Paris, 1971

Bamborough, John Bernard, *The Little World of Man*, Longmans, Green and Co., London, 1952

Barber, Cesar Lombardi, *Shakespeare's Festive Comedy: A Study of Dramatic Form and its Relation to Social Custom*, Princeton Univ. Press, Princeton, 1959

Barroll, J. Leeds, 'Shakespeare and Roman History', *Modern Language Review*, 53, 1958, pp. 327–43

Bentley, Gerald E. (ed.), *The Seventeenth Century Stage, A Collection of Critical Essays*, Univ. of Chicago Press, Chicago, 1968

Bergeron, David M., *English Civic Pageantry: 1558–1642*, Edward Arnold, London, 1971

Bernheimer, Richard, *Wild Man in the Middle Ages: A Study in Art, Sentiment and Demonology*, Harvard Univ. Press, Cambridge, Mass., 1952

Bevington, David M., *From 'Mankind' to Marlowe*, Harvard Univ. Press, Cambridge, Mass., 1962

Blayney, Glenn H., 'Enforcement of Marriage in English Drama', *Philological Quarterly*, 38, 4, Oct. 1959, pp. 459–72

Bluestone, Max and Rabkin, Norman (eds.), *Shakespeare's Contemporaries*, Prentice Hall, Englewood Cliffs, N.J., 1961

Booth, Wayne, 'Shakespeare's Tragic Villain' (1951) in *Shakespeare's Tragedies*, ed. Laurence Lerner, Penguin, Harmondsworth, 1963

Bowers, Fredson T., 'The Audience and the Poisoners in Elizabethan Tragedy', *Journal of English and Germanic Philology*, 36, 1937, pp. 491–504
Elizabethan Revenge Tragedy 1587–1642 (1940), paperback edn, Princeton Univ. Press, Princeton, 1966

Bradbrook, Muriel C., 'Virtue is the True Nobility', *Review of English Studies*, New Series, 1, 1950, pp. 289–301
Shakespeare and Elizabethan Poetry, Chatto and Windus, London, 1951
Themes and Conventions of Elizabethan Tragedy (1935), Cambridge Univ. Press, Cambridge, 1960
Shakespeare the Craftsman (1969), Cambridge Univ. Press, Cambridge, 1979
The Living Monument (1976), Cambridge Univ. Press, Cambridge, 1979

Bradley, Andrew C., *Shakespearean Tragedy* (1904), Papermac, Macmillan, London, 1958
Oxford Lectures on Poetry (1909), preface by M. R. Ridley, Papermac, Macmillan, London, 1965

Brissenden, Alan, 'Impediments to Love: A Theme in John Ford', *Renaissance Drama*, 7, 1964, pp. 95–102

Brockbank, Philip, 'Upon such Sacrifices', *Proceedings of the British Academy*, 62, 1976, Lecture published by the British Academy, London, 1976

Brooke, C. F. Tucker, *The Tudor Drama*, Houghton Mifflin Co., Boston, 1911

Brooke, Nicholas, *Shakespeare's Early Tragedies* (1968), University Paperbacks, Methuen, London, 1973

Brooks, Cleanth, 'The Naked Babe and The Cloak of Manliness', in *The Well Wrought Urn* (Reynal and Hitchcock, New York, 1947), University Paperbacks, Methuen, London, 1968, pp. 17–39

Brooks, Harold F., 'Marlowe and Early Shakespeare' in *Christopher Marlowe*, ed. Brian Morris, Ernest Benn, London, 1968

Broude, Ronald, 'Roman and Goth in *Titus Andronicus*', *Shakespeare Studies*, 6, 1972, pp. 27–34

Brower, Reuben A., 'The Mirror of Analogy', in *The Tempest: A Selection of Critical Essays*, ed. D. J. Palmer, Macmillan, London and Glasgow, 1968

Brown, John Russel and Harris, Bernard, *Later Shakespeare*, Stratford-upon-Avon Studies, 8, Edward Arnold, London, 1966

Bush, Douglas, *The Renaissance and English Humanism*, Univ. of Toronto Press, Toronto, 1939
English Literature in the Earlier Seventeenth Century 1600–1660, vol. 5 of *Oxford History of English Literature*, Clarendon Press, Oxford, 1952

Campbell, L. B., *Shakespeare's Tragic Heroes, Slaves of Passion* (Cambridge Univ. Press, Cambridge, 1930), University Paperbacks, Barnes and Noble, New York, 1961

Carrive, Lucien, 'Le sentiment de la nature au début du dix-septième siècle', *Actes du congrès de Saint-Etienne de la S.A.E.S.*, Librairie Marcel Didier, Paris, 1975

Carroll, William Meredith, *Animal Conventions in English Renaissance Non-Religious Prose*, Bookman Associates, New York, 1954

Carson, David L., 'The Dramatic Importance of the Prodigies in *Julius Caesar*, Act II, Scene i', *English Language Notes*, 2, 1965, pp. 177–80

Cawley, Robert Ralston, 'Shakespeare's Use of the Voyagers in *The Tempest*', *P.M.L.A.*, 41, 1926, pp. 688–726

   The Voyagers and Elizabethan Drama, D. C. Heath, Boston and London, 1937

   Unpathed Waters, Princeton Univ. Press, Princeton, 1940

Chambers, Edmund K., *Shakespeare: A Survey* (London, Sidgwick and Jackson, 1925), Pelican, Harmondsworth, 1964

Charney, Maurice, *Shakespeare's Roman Plays*, Harvard Univ. Press, Cambridge, Mass., 1963

Cheney, Donald, *Spenser's Image of Nature: Wild Man and Shepherd in the 'Faerie Queene'*, Yale Univ. Press, New Haven and London, 1966

Clemen, Wolfgang, *The Development of Shakespeare's Imagery* (1951) (transl. from German: *Shakespeares Bilder*, Hanstein, Bonn, 1936), new edn and new preface, Methuen, London, 1977

Coleridge, Samuel T., *Shakespearean Criticism*, Everyman's Library, London, 1961–2

Colman, E. A. M., *The Dramatic Use of Bawdy in Shakespeare*, Longman, London, 1974

Craig, Hardin, *The Enchanted Glass: The Elizabethan Mind in Literature* (Oxford Univ. Press, New York, 1936), Blackwell, Oxford, 1952

Curry, Walter Clyde, *Shakespeare's Philosophical Patterns* (Louisiana State Univ. Press, Baton-Rouge, 1937), P. Smith, Gloucester, Mass., 1968

Cushman, L. W., *The Devil and the Vice in the English Dramatic Literature before Shakespeare*, M. Niemeyer, Halle, 1900

Danby, John F., *Shakespeare's Doctrine of Nature*, Faber and Faber, London, 1961

D'Avezac, M., *Les Îles fantastiques de l'océan occidental au Moyen Age*, Paris, 1845

Davis, Walter R., *A Map of Arcadia. Sidney's Romance in its Tradition*, Yale Univ. Press, New Haven and London, 1965

Davril, Robert, *Le Drame de John Ford*, Bibl. des Langues mod., 5, Didier, Paris, 1954

Desmonde, William H., 'The Ritual Origin of Shakespeare's *Titus Andronicus*', *International Journal of Psycho-Analysis*, 36, 1955, pp. 61–5

Dobree, Bonamy, 'The Tempest', *Essays and Studies by Members of the English Association*, 5, 1952, pp. 13–25

Doob, Penelope B. R., *Nebuchadnezzar's Children: Conventions of Madness in Middle English Literature*, Yale Univ. Press, New Haven and London, 1974

Doran, Madeleine, 'Good Name in *Othello*', *Studies in English Literature*, 7, 1967, pp. 195–217

Dyer, T. F. Thiselton, *Folk-Lore of Shakespeare* (1883), Dover Publications, New York, 1966

Eagleton, Terence, *Shakespeare and Society*, Chatto and Windus, London, 1967, reprinted 1970

Eliot, T. S., *Selected Essays*, Faber and Faber, London, 1934

Elliott, George R., *Flaming Ministers: A Study of 'Othello' as Tragedy of Love and Hate*, Duke Univ. Press, Durham, N.C., 1953

Ellrodt, Robert, 'Self Consciousness in Montaigne and Shakespeare', *Shakespeare Survey*, 28, 1975, pp. 37–50

Elton, William R., *'King Lear' and the Gods*, Huntington Library, San Marino, 1966, reprinted 1968

   'Shakespeare and the Thought of his Age', in *A New Companion to Shakespeare*

Studies, ed. K. Muir and S. Schoenbaum, Cambridge Univ. Press, Cambridge, 1971

Empson, William, *Some Versions of Pastoral* (1935), Peregrine Books, Harmondsworth, 1966

The Structure of Complex Words, Chatto and Windus, London, 1951

Evans, Bertrand, *Shakespeare's Comedies* (1960), paperback, Oxford Univ. Press, Oxford, 1967

Evans, Gareth Lloyd, 'Shakespeare's Fools: The Shadow and the Substance of Drama' in *Shakespearian Comedy*, Stratford-upon-Avon Studies, 14, Edward Arnold, London, 1972, pp. 142–59

Evans, K. W., 'The Racial Factor in *Othello*', *Shakespeare Survey*, 5, 1969, pp. 124–40

Farnham, Willard, *The Medieval Heritage of Elizabethan Tragedy* (1936), Barnes and Noble, New York, 1957

Shakespeare's Tragic Frontier (1950), Univ. of California Press, Berkeley and Los Angeles, 1963

Febvre, Lucien, *Le Problème de l'incroyance au XVIe siècle, la religion de Rabelais* (1942) revised edn, Albin Michel, Paris, 1962

Fiedler, Leslie A., *The Stranger in Shakespeare* (1973), Paladin Books, St Albans, 1974

Fluchère, Henri, *Shakespeare, dramaturge élisabéthain* (Cahiers du Sud, Toulouse, 1948), Gallimard, Paris, 1966

Foakes, R. A., 'Iago, Othello and the Critic', in *De Shakespeare à T. S. Eliot, mélanges offerts à H. Fluchère, Etudes anglaises*, 63, Didier, Paris, 1976, pp. 61–72

Foltinek, Herbert, 'Die wilden Männer in Edmund Spensers *Faerie Queene*', *Die Neueren Sprachen*, 10, 1961, pp. 493–512

Fry, Timothy, 'The Unity of the *Ludus Coventriae*', *Studies in Philology*, 48, 1951, pp. 527–70

Frye, Northrop, *Anatomy of Criticism* (1957), Atheneum, New York, 1967

A Natural Perspective: The Development of Shakespearean Comedy and Romance, Columbia Univ. Press, New York, 1965

Fools of Time, Univ. of Toronto Press, Toronto, 1967

Frye, Roland Mushat, *Shakespeare and Christian Doctrine* (1963), Princeton Univ. Press, Princeton, 1967

Fuzier, Jean, 'Kyd et l'éthique du spectacle populaire', *Les Langues modernes*, 59th year, 4, July–August 1965, pp. 451–8

'Carrière et popularité de *La Tragédie espagnole* en Angleterre', in *Dramaturgie et société*, ed. Jean Jacquot, Centre National de la Recherche Scientifique, Paris, 1968

Les Sonnets de Shakespeare, Armand Colin, Paris, 1970

Gardner, Helen, *The Noble Moor*, British Academy Lecture, 1955, Oxford Univ. Press, Oxford, 1956, reprinted in *Shakespeare Criticism 1935–1960*, ed. Anne Ridler, Oxford Univ. Press, Oxford, 1963, and in *Othello, A Collection of Critical Essays*, ed. John Wain, Macmillan, London, 1971

'*Othello*: A Retrospect, 1900–67', *Shakespeare Survey*, 21, 1968, pp. 1–11

Gauvin, Claude, *Un cycle du théâtre religieux anglais au Moyen Age*, Centre National de la Recherche Scientifique, Paris, 1973

Goddard, Harold C., *The Meaning of Shakespeare* (1951), 2 vols., Univ. of Chicago Press, Phoenix Books, Chicago, 1960

Goldsmith, R. H., 'The Wild Man on the English Stage', *Modern Language Review*, 53, 1958, pp. 481–91

Gorfain, Phyllis, 'Puzzle and Artifice: The Riddle as Metapoetry in *Pericles*', *Shakespeare Survey*, 29, 1976, pp. 11–20

Harbage, Alfred, *As They Liked It* (1947), Harper Torchbooks, New York, 1961

Harris, Anthony, *Night's Black Agents*, Manchester Univ. Press, Manchester, 1980

Harris, Bernard, 'A Portrait of a Moor', *Shakespeare Survey*, 11, 1958, pp. 89–97

Harrison, Thomas P., Jr, 'Aspects of Primitivism in Shakespeare and Spenser', *Studies in English*, Univ. of Texas Publ. no. 4026, 8 July 1940
    'The Literary Background of Renaissance Poisons', *Studies in English*, Univ. of Texas Press, 27, 1, June 1948, pp. 35–67

Hartsock, Mildred, 'The Complexity of *Julius Caesar*', *P.M.L.A.*, 81, 1966, pp. 56–62

Hawkes, Terence, *Shakespeare and the Reason: A Study of the Tragedies and the Problem Plays*, Routledge and Kegan Paul, London, 1964
    Shakespeare's Talking Animals, Edward Arnold, London, 1973

Hazlitt, William, *Characters of Shakespeare's Plays* (London, 1817), World's Classics, Oxford, 1955

Heilman, Robert Bechtold, *Magic in the Web*, Univ. of Kentucky Press, Lexington, 1956
    'To Know Himself: An Aspect of Tragic Structure', *Review of English Lit.*, 5, 1964, pp. 36–57
    'The Criminal as Tragic Hero: Dramatic Methods', *Shakespeare Survey*, 19, 1966, pp. 12–24

Heninger, S. K. Jr, 'The Renaissance Perversion of Pastoral', *Journal of the Hist. of Ideas*, 22, 1961, pp. 254–61

Henn, Thomas Rice, *The Living Image*, Methuen, London, 1972

Herndl, George C., *The High Design*, Univ. Press of Kentucky, Lexington, 1970

Hibbard, George R., '*Othello* and the Pattern of Shakespearian Tragedy', *Shakespeare Survey*, 21, 1968, pp. 39–46

Hill, R. F., 'The Composition of *Titus Andronicus*', *Shakespeare Survey*, 10, 1957, pp. 60–70

Holloway, John, *The Story of the Night* (1961), Univ. of Nebraska Press, Bison Books, Lincoln, 1966

Honigmann, Ernst A. J., *Shakespeare: Seven Tragedies: The Dramatist's Manipulation of Response*, Macmillan, London, 1976

Howarth, Herbert, *The Tiger's Heart. Eight Essays on Shakespeare*, Chatto and Windus, London, 1961

Hulme, Hilda M., *Explorations in Shakespeare's Language* (1962), Longman, London, 1977

Hunter, George K., 'Elizabethans and Foreigners', *Shakespeare Survey*, 17, 1964, pp. 37–52
    '*Macbeth* in the Twentieth Century', *Shakespeare Survey*, 19, 1966, pp. 1–11
    ' "Othello" and Colour Prejudice' (*Proceedings of the British Academy*, 53, 1967), Oxford Univ. Press, Oxford, 1968
    'Shakespeare's Earliest Tragedies: Titus Andronicus and Romeo and Juliet', *Shakespeare Survey*, 27, 1974, pp. 1–9

Hunter, Mark, 'Politics and Character in Shakespeare's *Julius Caesar*', *Transactions Royal Soc. Lit: Essays by Divers Hands*, 10, 1931, pp. 109–40; partially reproduced in *Julius Caesar, A Selection of Critical Essays*, ed. Peter Ure, Macmillan, London, 1969

Hyman, Stanley Edgar, *Iago, Some Approaches to the Illusion of his Motivation*, Atheneum, New York, 1970

Jacquot, Jean, 'Thomas Harriot's Reputation for Impiety', *Notes and Records of the Royal Society*, 9, May 1952, pp. 164–87

'La Pensée de Marlowe dans *Tamburlaine the Great*', *Etudes anglaises*, 6, 1953, pp. 331–45

'Problèmes et méthodes: l'exemple de Macbeth' in *La Mise en scène des oeuvres du passé*, ed. J. Jacquot and A. Veinstein, Centre National de la Recherche Scientifique, Paris, 1957

'De Richard II à Richard III au Royal Shakespeare Theatre', *Etudes anglaises*, 17, 4, Oct.–Dec. 1964, pp. 482–501

Jacquot, Jean (ed.), *Le théâtre tragique*, Centre National de la Recherche Scientifique, Paris, 1962

Jacquot, Jean in coll. with Elie Konigson and Marcel Oddon (eds.), *Dramaturgie et société, XVIe et XVIIe siècles*, 2 vols., Centre National de la Recherche Scientifique, Paris, 1968

Jacquot, Jean and Vigouroux, Nicole, '*Le Juif de Malte*', in *Les Voies de la création théâtrale*, 6, presented by Jean Jacquot, Centre National de la Recherche Scientifique, Paris, 1978

Johnson, Samuel, *Johnson on Shakespeare*, ed. A. Sherbo, vols. 7 and 8 of *Works of Samuel Johnson*, Yale Univ. Press, New Haven and London, 1968

Jones, Eldred, D., *Othello's Countrymen: The African in English Renaissance Drama*, Oxford Univ. Press, Oxford, 1965

Jones, Emrys, '*Othello*, Lepanto, and the Cyprus Wars', *Shakespeare Survey*, 21, 1968, pp. 47–52

Jorgensen, Paul A., 'Shakespeare's Coriolanus: Elizabethan Soldier', *P.M.L.A.*, 64, March, 1949, pp. 221–35

Shakespeare's Military World, Univ. of California Press, Berkeley, 1956

Lear's Self Discovery, Univ. of California Press, Berkeley, 1967

Kaufmann, Ralph J., 'Ford's Tragic Perspective', *Texas Studies in Literature and Language*, 1, printed 1960, reprinted in *Elizabethan Drama: Modern Essays in Criticism*, Oxford Univ. Press, New York and Oxford, 1961

Keen, Maurice, *The Outlaws of Medieval Legend* (1961), Routledge and Kegan Paul, London and Henley, 1977

Kirschbaum, Leo, 'The Modern Othello', *Journal of English Literary History*, 11, 1944, pp. 283–96

'Shakespeare's Stage Blood and Its Critical Significance', *P.M.L.A.*, 64, 1949, pp. 517–29

Klene, J., 'Othello: "A Fixed Figure for the Time of Scorn" ', *Shakespeare Quarterly*, 26, 3, 1975, pp. 139–50

Knight, G. Wilson, *The Wheel of Fire* (Oxford Univ. Press, Oxford, 1930), extended edn, Methuen, London, 1959

The Imperial Theme (Oxford Univ. Press, Oxford, 1931), Univ. Paperbacks, London, 1965

The Shakespearian Tempest (Oxford Univ. Press, Oxford, 1932), Methuen, London, 1960

The Crown of Life, Methuen, London, 1947

Knights, L. C., 'How Many Children Had Lady Macbeth' (1933), in *Explorations*, Chatto and Windus, London, 1946

Drama and Society in the Age of Jonson, Penguin, Harmondsworth, 1962

Some Shakespearian Themes and an Approach to 'Hamlet', Penguin, Harmondsworth, 1966

Kott, Jan, *Shakespeare notre contemporain*, trans. from Polish by A. Posner, Julliard, Paris, 1962, extended edn, Marabourt Univ. Press, Paris, 1965

'Les Deux paradoxes d'*Othello*', *Etudes anglaises*, 17, 4, Oct.–Dec. 1964, pp. 402–20

Leavis, F. R., 'Diabolic Intellect and Noble Hero: A Note on *Othello*', *Scrutiny*, 4, Dec. 1937, reprinted in *The Common Pursuit*, Chatto and Windus, London, 1952, and in John Wain, *Othello: A Selection of Critical Essays*, Casebook Series, Macmillan, London, 1971

The Common Pursuit (Chatto and Windus, London, 1952), Pelican, Harmondsworth, 1976

Leech, Clifford, *Shakespeare's Tragedies and Other Studies in Seventeenth Century Drama*, Chatto and Windus, London, 1950

'The Structure of the Last Plays', *Shakespeare Survey*, 11, 1958, pp. 19–30

Leech, Clifford and Craik, T. W. (eds.), *The 'Revels' History of Drama in English*, vol. 3, *1576–1613*, by J. Leeds Barroll, Alexander Leggat, Richard Hosley, Alvin Kernan, Methuen, London, 1975

Lerner, Laurence (ed.), *Shakespeare's Tragedies*, Penguin, Harmondsworth, 1963
Shakespeare's Comedies, Penguin, Harmondsworth, 1967

Lever, J. W., 'Shakespeare and the Ideas of his Time', *Shakespeare Survey*, 29, 1976, pp. 79–91

Levin, Harry, '*Othello* and the Motive-Hunters', *Centennial Review*, 8, 1, Winter 1964, pp. 1–16

The Myth of the Golden Age in the Renaissance, Faber and Faber, London, 1970
Shakespeare and the Revolution of the Times, Oxford Univ. Press, New York, 1976

Lewis, C. S., *English Literature in the Sixteenth Century Excluding Drama*, The Oxford History of English Literature, ed. F. P. Wilson and B. Dobree, Oxford Univ. Press, Oxford, 1953

Lewis, Wyndham, *The Lion and the Fox: The Role of the Hero in the Plays of Shakespeare* (Harper, New York and London, 1927), Barnes and Noble, New York; Methuen, London, 1966

Long, Michael, *The Unnatural Scene*, Methuen, London, 1976

McCallum, Mungo, *Shakespeare's Roman Plays* (1910), new edn, preface by T. J. B. Spencer, Macmillan, London, 1967

McGee, Arthur R., 'Macbeth and the Furies', *Shakespeare Survey*, 19, 1966, pp. 55–67

Mack, Maynard, Jr, *Killing the King*, Yale Univ. Press, New Haven and London, 1973

Madden, Dogson, H., *The Diary of Master William Silence: A Study of Shakespeare and Elizabethan Sport* (Longmans, Green and Co., London, 1897), 2nd edn, Longmans and Co., London, 1907

Maguin, Jean-Marie, 'Bell, Book, and Candle in *Macbeth*. A Note on I, 5, 61–62, II, 1, 31–32 & 62', *Cahiers élisabéthains*, 12, Oct. 1977, pp. 65–8

Marienstras, Richard, 'La Dégradation des vertus héroïques dans *Othello* et dans *Coriolan*', *Etudes anglaises*, 17, 4, Oct. 1964, pp. 372–89

'Prospero ou le machiavélisme du bien', *Bulletin de la faculté des lettres de Strasbourg*, May 1965, pp. 899–917

'L'Anglaise sous le règne d'Elisabeth', in *Histoire mondiale de la femme*, 3 vols., published under the editorship of P. Grimal, Nouvelle Librairie de France, Paris, 1966, vol. 2, pp. 399–454

'Les Personnages et les mécanismes narratifs dans *Les Joyeuses Commères de Windsor*', *Revue d'histoire du théâtre*, 3, 1972, pp. 251–68

'*Timon d'Athènes* et sa mise en scène par Peter Brook', in *Les Voies de la création théâtrale*, eds. Jean Jacquot and Denis Bablet, vol. 5, Centre National de la Recherche Scientifique, Paris, 1977, pp. 15–57

'*Jules César*, les élisabéthains et la crise du sacré', introduction to *Lectures de 'Jules Cesar' de Shakespeare*, coll. Dia, Belin, Paris, 1979a, pp. 6–16

'La forêt et le rite' (on the adaptation of *Macbeth* by Akira Kurosawa), *Positif*, Dec. 1979b, pp. 33–5

Marsh, Derick R. C., *Passion Lends Them Power: A Study of Shakespeare's Love Tragedies*, Manchester Univ. Press, Manchester, 1976; Barnes and Noble, New York, 1976

Marx, Leo, *The Machine in the Garden* (1964), Oxford Univ. Press, New York, 1970

Mason, Harold A., *Shakespeare's Tragedies of Love*, Chatto and Windus, London, 1970

Matthews, G. M., 'Othello and the Dignity of Man', in *Shakespeare in a Changing World*, ed. Arnold Kettle, International Publishers, New York, 1964, pp. 123–45

Merchant, W. Moelwyn, 'His Fiend-Like Queen', *Shakespeare Survey*, 19, 1966, pp. 75–81

Milward, Peter, *Shakespeare's Religious Background*, Sidgwick and Jackson, London, 1973

Muir, Kenneth, 'Image and Symbol in *Macbeth*', Shakespeare Survey, 19, 1966, pp. 45–54

Shakespeare's Tragic Sequence, Hutchinson University Library, London, 1972

Murray, W. A., 'Why was Duncan's Blood Golden?', *Shakespeare Survey*, 19, 1966, pp. 34–44

Murry, John Middleton, *Shakespeare* (1936), Jonathan Cape, London, 1955

Nuttall, Anthony D., *Two Concepts of Allegory: A Study of Shakespeare's 'The Tempest' and the Logic of Allegorical Expression*, Routledge and Kegan Paul, London, 1967

Oliver, H. J., *The Problem of John Ford*, Univ. Press, Careton, Melbourne, 1955

Owst, Gerald Robert, *Literature and Pulpit in Medieval England* (Cambridge Univ Press, Cambridge, 1933), 2nd edn, extended, Blackwell, Oxford, 1961, reprinted 1966

Palmer, John, *Political and Comic Characters of Shakespeare* (1945, 1946), Macmillan, London, 1965

Phillips, James Emerson, *The State in Shakespeare's Greek and Roman Plays* (1940), Octagon Books, New York, 1972

Plattard, J., 'L'Invective de Gargantua contre les mariages contractés "sans le sceu et adveu" des parents', *Revue du seizième siècle*, 14, 1927, pp. 381–8

Poisson, Rodney, 'Othello's "Base Indian": A Better Source of the Allusion', *Shakespeare Quarterly*, 26, 4, 1975, pp. 462–6

Poliakov, Léon, and Marienstras, Richard, *Autour du Colloque de Cérisy-la-Salle*, mimeographed lectures, Groupe d'études d'histoire du racisme. Maison des sciences de l'homme, 13, Paris, 1976, pp. 18–23

Proser, Matthew N., *The Heroic Image in Five Shakespearian Tragedies*, Princeton Univ. Press, Princeton, 1965

Rabkin, Norman, 'Structure, Convention and Meaning in *Julius Caesar*', *Journal of English and Germanic Philology*, 63, 1964, pp. 240–54

Shakespeare and the Common Understanding, Free Press, New York, 1967

Rank, Otto, *Das Inzest-Motiv in Dichtung und Sage*, F. Deuticke, Leipzig, 1912

Reese, Jack E., 'The Formalization of Horror in *Titus Andronicus*', *Shakespeare Quarterly*, 21, 1970, pp. 77–84

Reynolds, George F., '*Mucedorus*, Most Popular Elizabethan Play?', *Studies in English Renaissance Drama in Memory of Karl Julius Holzknecht*, New York Univ. Press, New York, 1959, pp. 248–68

Righter, Anne, *Shakespeare and the Idea of the Play* (1962), Penguin Shakespeare Library, Harmondsworth, 1967

Rogers, H. L., '*Double Profit*' in '*Macbeth*', Melbourne Univ. Press and Cambridge Univ. Press, Melbourne, 1964

Rosenberg, Marvin, *The Masks of Othello*, Univ. of California Press, Berkeley and Los Angeles, 1961

　The Masks of Macbeth, Univ. of California Press, Berkeley, Los Angeles and London, 1978

Rossiter, A. P., *Angel with Horns*, Longmans, Green and Co., London, 1961

Sahel, Pierre, 'Machiavélisme vulgaire et machiavélisme authentique dans *Macbeth*', *Cahiers élisabéthains*, 14, Oct. 1978, pp. 9–22

Sanders, Wilbur, *The Dramatist and the Received Idea: Studies in the Plays of Marlowe and Shakespeare*, Cambridge Univ. Press, Cambridge, 1968

Sanders, Wilbur and Jacobson, Howard, *Shakespeare's Magnanimity, Four Tragic Heroes, Their Friends and Families*, Chatto and Windus, London, 1978

Schanzer, Ernst, *The Problem Plays of Shakespeare* (1963), Schocken Books, New York, 1965

Schoenbaum, Samuel, *Internal Evidence and Elizabethan Dramatic Authorship*, Edward Arnold, London, 1966

Sensabaugh, G. F., 'John Ford and Platonic Love in the Court', *Studies in Philology*, 36, 1939, pp. 206–26

Shaheen, Nasceb, 'Like the Base Judean', *Shakespeare Quarterly*, 31, 1, 1980, pp. 93–4

Shakespeare's Hand in 'The Play of Sir Thomas More', Papers by A. W. Pollard, W. W. Greg, E. Maunde Thompson, J. Dover Wilson and R. W. Chambers, Cambridge Univ. Press, Cambridge, 1923

Shirley, Frances A., *Swearing and Perjury in Shakespeare's Plays*, Allen and Unwin, London, 1979

Siegel, Paul N., 'The Damnation of Othello', *P.M.L.A.*, 68, 1953, pp. 1068–78

Silhol, Robert, 'Magie et utopie dans *La Tempête*', *Etudes anglaises*, 17, 4, Oct.–Dec. 1964, pp. 447–56

　'Morale individuelle et morale sociale dans *La Tempête*', *Les Langues modernes*, 59th year, 1, Jan.–Feb. 1965, pp. 51–8

Simmons, John L., *Shakespeare's Pagan World*, Univ. Press of Virginia, Charlottesville, 1973

Siskin, Clifford, 'Freedom and Loss in *The Tempest*', *Shakespeare Survey*, 30, 1978, pp. 147–55

Smith, Gordon Ross, 'Brutus, Virtue and Will', *Shakespeare Quarterly*, 10, 1959, pp. 367–79

Smith, Hallett, *Shakespeare's Romances: A Study of Some Ways of Imagination*, Huntington Library, San Marino, California, 1972

Sommers, Alan, 'Wilderness of Tigers: Structure and Symbolism in *Titus Andronicus*', *Essays in Criticism*, 10, 1960, pp. 275–89

Spencer, Terence J.-B., 'Shakespeare and the Elizabethan Romans', *Shakespeare Survey*, 10, 1957, pp. 27–38

Spencer, Theodore, *Shakespeare and the Nature of Man*, Macmillan, New York, 1942

Spender, Stephen, 'Time, Violence and *Macbeth*', *The Penguin New Writing*, 3, Feb. 1941, pp. 115–26

Spivack, Bernard, *Shakespeare and the Allegory of Evil*, Columbia Univ. Press, New York, 1958

Spurgeon, Caroline, *Shakespeare's Imagery and What it Tells Us*, Cambridge Univ. Press, Cambridge, 1935

Starobinbski, Jean, 'Hamlet et Freud', preface to Ernest Jones, *Hamlet et Oedipe*, Gallimard, Paris, 1967

Stauffer, Donald A., *Shakespeare's World of Images: The Development of his Moral Ideas*, Norton, New York, 1949

Stauffer, Marianne, *Der Wald, Zur Darstellung und Deutung der Natur im Mittelalter*, Juris-Verlag, Zürich, 1958

Stavig, Mark, *John Ford and the Traditional Moral Order*, Univ. of Wisconsin Press, Madison and London, 1968

Stewart, John I. M., '*Julius Caesar* and *Macbeth*: Two Notes on Shakespearian Technique', *Modern Lang. Rev.*, 40, 1945, pp. 166–73

    Character and Motive in Shakespeare, Longmans, Green and Co., London and New York, 1949

Stirling, Brents, 'Or Else Were This a Savage Spectacle', *P.M.L.A.*, 66, 1951, pp. 765–74

    Unity in Shakespearian Tragedy, Columbia Univ. Press, New York, 1956

Stoll, Elmer E., 'Slander in Drama', *Shakespeare Quarterly*, 4, Oct. 1953, pp. 433–50

Styan, John L., *Shakespeare's Stagecraft*, Cambridge Univ. Press, Cambridge, 1967

Taylor, George C., 'Shakespeare's Use of the Idea of the Beast in Man', *Studies in Philology*, 42, 1945, pp. 530–43

Thiébaux, Marcelle, 'The Mouth of the Boar as a Symbol in Medieval Literature', *Romance Philology*, 22, 3, Feb. 1969, pp. 281–99

    The Stag of Love, Cornell Univ. Press, Ithaca and London, 1974

Tillyard, E. M. W., *Shakespeare's Last Plays* (1938), Chatto and Windus, London, 1964

    The Elizabethan World Picture, Chatto and Windus, London, 1943

    Shakespeare's History Plays (1944), Chatto and Windus, London, 1969

Traversi, Derek A., *An Approach to Shakespeare* (1938), 3rd edn, revised and expanded, 2 vols., Hollis and Carter, London, 1968

    'The Tempest', *Scrutiny*, 16, 2, June 1949, pp. 127–57

    Shakespeare: The Last Phase, Hollis and Carter, London, 1954

    Shakespeare: The Roman Plays (Stanford Univ. Press, Stanford, 1963), Hollis and Carter, London, 1963

Tricomi, Albert H., 'The Aesthetics of Mutilation in *Titus Andronicus*', *Shakespeare Survey*, 27, 1974, pp. 11–19

Ure, Peter (ed.), *Julius Caesar: A Selection of Critical Essays*, Casebook Series, Macmillan, London, 1969

Veit, Richard S., ' "Like the Base Judean": A Defense of an Oft-rejected Reading in *Othello*', *Shakespeare Quarterly*, 26, 4, 1975, pp. 466–9

Velz, John W., 'Clemency, Will, and Just Cause in *Julius Caesar*', *Shakespeare Survey*, 22, 1969, pp. 909–18

Vickers, Brian, *Toward Greek Tragedy*, Longman, London, 1973

Wain, John, *Othello: A Selection of Critical Essays*. Casebook Series, Macmillan, London, 1971

Waith, Eugene M., 'Manhood and Valor in Two Shakespearean Tragedies', *Journal of English Literary History*, 17, 1950, pp. 262–73
'The Metamorphosis of Violence in *Titus Andronicus*', *Shakespeare Survey*, 10, 1957, pp. 39–49
The Herculean Hero in Marlowe, Chapman, Shakespeare and Dryden, Columbia Univ. Press, New York; Chatto and Windus, London, 1962
Ward, Sir A. W. and Waller, A. R. (eds.), *The Cambridge History of English Literature* (1910), vols. 5 and 6, *The Drama to 1642* (parts 1 and 2), Cambridge Univ. Press, Cambridge, 1964
Watson, Curtis B., *Shakespeare and the Renaissance Concept of Honour*, Princeton Univ. Press, Princeton, 1960
'T. S. Eliot and the Interpretation of Shakespearean Tragedy in Our Time', *Etudes anglaises*, 17, 4, Oct.–Dec. 1964, pp. 302–21
Wells, D. A., *The Wild Man From the 'Epic of Gilgamesh' to Hartmann von Aue's 'Iwein'*, New Lecture Series no. 78, The Queen's University, Belfast, 1975
Whitaker, Virgil K., *The Mirror up to Nature*, Huntington Library, San Marino, 1965
White, R. S., ' "Now Mercy goes to Kill": Hunting in Shakespearean Comedy', *Durham Univ. Journal*, Dec. 1976, pp. 21–32
Wilson, Frank P., *The English Drama 1485–1585*, with bibliog. by G. K. Hunter, vol. 4, pt 1 of *The Oxford History of English Literature*, ed. B. Dobree and N. Davies, Oxford Univ. Press, Oxford, 1969
Wilson, Harold S., 'Action and Symbol in *Measure for Measure* and *The Tempest*', *Shakespeare Quarterly*, 4, Oct. 1953, pp. 375–85
On the Design of Shakespearian Tragedy, Univ. of Toronto Press, Toronto, 1957
Young, David, *The Heart's Forest: A Study of Shakespeare's Pastoral Plays*, Yale Univ. Press, New Haven and London, 1972
Zeeveld, W. Gordon, *The Temper of Shakespeare's Thought*, Yale Univ. Press, New Haven and London, 1974

VII. Methodological studies

Auerbach, Erich, *Mimesis, the Representation of Reality in Western Literature*, trans. by W. Trask, Doubleday, Anchor Books, New York, 1953
Scenes from the Drama of European Literature, Meridian Books, New York, 1959
Barthes, Roland, 'Introduction à l'analyse structurale des récits', *Communications*, 8, 1966, pp. 1–27
Bastide, R., article 'Sacrifice', in *Encyclopaedia Universalis*, Encyclopaedia Universalis France, Paris, 1968
Bellour, R. and Clément, C. (eds.), *Claude Lévi-Strauss*, Gallimard, Paris, 1979
Brémond, Claude, 'La Logique des possibles narratifs', *Communications*, 8, 1966, pp. 60–76
Brisson, Luc, 'Bisexualité et médiation en Grèce ancienne', *Nouvelle Rev. de Psychanalyse*, 7, Spring 1973, pp. 27–48
Cuisenier, J., article 'Inceste', in *Encyclopaedia Universalis*, Encyclopaedia Universalis France, Paris, 1968
Derrida, Jacques, *La Dissémination*, Editions du Seuil, Paris, 1972
Detienne, Marcel and Vernant, Jean-Pierre, *La Cuisine du sacrifice en pays Grec*, Gallimard, Paris, 1979
Douglas, Mary, *Purity and Danger*, Routledge and Kegan Paul, London, 1966
Dubois, J., Edeline, F. *et al.*, *Rhétorique générale*, Larousse, Paris, 1970

Girard, René, *La Violence et le sacré*, Grasset, Paris, 1972
 Des Choses cachées depuis la fondation du monde, Grasset, Paris, 1978
Hegel, G. W. F., *Hegel on Tragedy*, published with preface by Anne and Henry
 Paolucci, Anchor Books, New York, 1962
 Esthétique: L'Art classique (1, IV), trans. by S. Jankélévitch, Aubier-Montaigne,
 Paris, 1964
Hodgen, Margaret T., *Early Anthropology in the Sixteenth and Seventeenth Cen-
 turies*, Univ. of Pennsylvania Press, Philadelphia, 1964
Hubert, H. and Mauss, Marcel, 'Essai sur la nature et la fonction du sacrifice', *Année
 sociologique*, 2, 1899; text reprinted with two other works by Marcel Mauss in
 Oeuvres, vol. 1, Editions de Minuit, Paris, 1968, pp. 193–354
Jankélévitch, Vladimir, 'Ressembler ou dissembler', in *Tentations et actions de la
 conscience juive*, Presses Universitaires de France, Paris, 1971
Kaufmann, Walter, *Tragedy and Philosophy*, Doubleday, Garden City, New York,
 1968
Le Goff, Jacques, 'Le désert-forêt dans l'Occident médiéval', *Traverses*, 19, June
 1980, pp. 23–33
Le Goff, Jacques and Vidal-Naquet, Pierre, 'Lévi-Strauss en Brocéliande', *Critique*,
 325, June 1974, pp. 541–71; extended version in *Claude Lévi-Strauss*, collected
 by R. Bellour and C. Clément, Gallimard, Paris, 1979, pp. 265–319
Lévi-Strauss, Claude, *Anthropologie structurale*, Plon, Paris, 1958
 Leçon inaugurale, Collège de France, Paris, Jan. 1960
 La Pensée sauvage, Plon, Paris, 1962
 Anthropologie structurale deux (Plon, Paris, 1973), trans. by M. Layton, Penguin,
 1978
Maine, H. S., *Dissertations on Early Laws and Customs*, New York, 1886
Maisch, Herbert, *L'Inceste* (1968), trans. from German by E. Spivac, Laffont, Paris,
 1970
Marx, Karl, *Oeuvres*, ed. Maximilian Rubel, 2 vols., Bibl. de la Pléiade, Paris, 1965,
 1968
Merton, Robert K., *Social Theory and Social Structure*, Free Press of Glencoe,
 Glencoe, Ill., 1949
Morgan, L. H. *Systems of Consanguinity and Affinity of the Human Family*,
 Washington, 1871
Moscovici, Serge, *La Société contre nature*, Union Générale d'Edition, Paris, 1972
Nietzsche, Frederic, *La Naissance de la tragédie*, trans. from German by G.
 Bianquis, Gallimard, Paris, 1949
Poliakov, Léon (ed.), *Hommes et bêtes, entretiens sur le racisme*, Actes du colloque
 tenu de 12 au 15 mai 1973 au centre culturel international de Cérisy-la-Salle,
 Mouton, Paris, The Hague, 1975
 Le Couple Interdit, entretiens sur le racisme, Actes du colloque tenu en mai 1977
 au centre culturel international de Cerisy-la-Salle, Mouton, Paris, The Hague,
 New York, 1980
Propp, Vladimir, *Morphologie du conte*, followed by *Les Transformations des contes
 merveilleux* . . . trans. by M. Derrida, T. Todorov and C. Kahn, Editions du
 Seuil, Paris, 1965 and 1970
Sebag, Lucien, 'Le Mythe: code et message', *Les Temps modernes*, March 1975, pp.
 1607–23
Todorov, Tzvetan, 'La Quête du récit', *Critique*, 262, March 1969, pp. 195–214
Vacant, A., Mangenot, E. and Amann, E., article 'Sacrifice', in *Dictionnaire de
 théologie catholique*, Librairie Letouzey et Ané, Paris, 1935–72

Vernant, J.-P. and Vidal-Naquet, Pierre, *Mythe et tragédie en Grèce ancienne*, Maspero, Paris, 1972. Eng. trans. *Tragedy and Myth in Ancient Greece*, Harvester Press, Brighton, 1981

Vidal-Naquet, Pierre, 'Valeurs religieuses et mythiques de la terre et du sacrifice dans l'Odyssée', *Annales*, 5, Sept.–Oct. 1970, pp. 1278–98. *Le Chasseur noir*, Maspero, Paris, 1981, contains this article, revised

VIII. Various works and studies

Artaud, Antonin, *Le Théâtre et son double*, Gallimard, Paris, 1964

Bataille, Georges, *La Littérature et le mal*, Gallimard, Paris, 1957
   L'Erotisme, Editions de Minuit, Paris, 1957

Bédier, Joseph, *Le Roman de Tristan et Iseut* (1946), reprinted by H. Piazza, Paris, 1958

Bernanos, Georges, *Les Grands Cimetières sous la lune* (1938), Plon, Paris, 1955

Davenson, Henri (Marrou, Henri), *Le Livre des chansons*, La Baconnière, Neuchâtel, 1946

De Maistre, Joseph, *Les Soirées de Saint-petersbourg*, introd. by L. A. de Gremilly, Ed. du Vieux-Colombier, Paris, 1960
   'Lettres à un gentilhomme rusee sur l'Inquisition espagnole', Extracts in *Du pape et autres oeuvres*, J. J. Pauvert, Paris, 1964

Klingender, Francis, *Animals in art and Thought to the End of the Middle Ages*, eds. E. Antal and J. Hartan, Routledge and Kegan Paul, London, 1971

Mann, Thomas, *The Blood of the Walsunds* (*Wälsungenblut*, 1905), Stones of Three Decades, London, 1946
   The Holy Sinner (*Der Erwählte*, 1951), trans. from German by H. T. Lowe-Porter, Penguin, Harmondsworth, 1972

Melville, Herman, *Billy Budd*, 'Postface' by Willard Thorp, New York, 1961

Ovid, *Metamorphoses*, Loeb Classical Library, Heinemann, London, 1968

Péguy, Charles, *Oeuvres en prose, 1904–1914*, Bib. de la Pléiade, Gallimard, Paris, 1961

Rowland, Beryl, *Animals with Human Faces, A Guide to Animal Symbolism*, Allen and Unwin, London, 1974

Voragine, Jacques de, *La légende dorée*, trans. by J.-B. M. Roze, 2 vols., Garnier-Flammarion, Paris, 1967

Index

Bold figures indicate the more important references. The plays discussed in detail in this book are indexed under their titles (as are anonymous works); other works are indexed under their authors. Entries for characters are not subdivided; for greater detail the reader should consult the entries for the plays in which they appear.

Aaron (first high priest of the Israelites), 51
Aaron the Moor (*Titus Andronicus*), 40–6 *passim*
absolutism, 24–5
Acteon, 45, 46
adultery, see under *'Tis Pity*...
Alarbus (*Titus Andronicus*), 40, 42
allegiance, 4, **105–10**, 112, 118, 123
Allen, J. W., 25
Alonso (*Tempest*), 171–3, 178–82 *passim*
Alves Pereira, B., 191
Amadine (*Mucedorus*), 11–13
America, 160, 162, 177
Annabella (*'Tis Pity*...), 6, 186–99 *passim*
ante nati, 101
Antonio (*Tempest*), 6, 161, 170–83 *passim*
Antony (*Julius Caesar*), *see* Mark Antony
Ariel (*Tempest*), 174, 178–85 *passim*
Ariès, Philippe, 213n43
Aristotle, 163, 175
Armada, 102
Artaud, Antonin, 44
asylum, *see* sanctuary
Auerbach, Erich, 50, 167
Augustine, Saint (bishop of Hippo): *De Genesi ad Litteram*, 190; *The City of God*, 191–2, 198
authority, 10, 199; see also under *Macbeth*

Babington, Anthony, 102
Bacon, Sir Francis, 100; and classification of foreigners, 10, 116, 118, 122; on royal sovereignty, 4, 24, 111–12
banquet, 179; see also under *Tempest*, *'Tis Pity*...

Banquo (*Macbeth*), 78, 81–4, 89, 91
barbarians, *see* primitive peoples
Barthes, Roland, 82
Bassianus (*Titus Andronicus*), 40–6 *passim*
bear, 11, 203n1
beasts of the forest, *see under* forest; *see also* seasons
Bergetto (*'Tis Pity*...), 193–7 *passim*
bestial, the, opposed to the human, see under *Othello*, *Tempest*
blackness, see under *Othello*; *see also* Blacks
Blacks, 136, 163, 176, 177–8, 227n39, 227n41
Blackstone, Sir William: *Commentaries*, 118
Blackwood, Rev. Dr: *Apologia pro Regibus*, 24
Blanche Biche, La, see *White Doe, The*
Bloch, Marc, 117
blood, 117, 118, 221n85, 222n89; see also under *Julius Caesar*, *Macbeth*
Boaistuau, Pierre: *Histoires prodigieuses*, 136, 165
boar, 32
Boccaccio, Giovanni, 14
Bolingbroke (Henry IV), 10
Bosch, Hieronymus, 164
Brabantio (*Othello*), 128, 130–46 *passim*
Bracton, Henry de, 21, 27, 111
Bradford, William, 167
Bradley, Andrew C., 73, 81, 87
Brandan (Brendan, Brenainn), Saint, 161
Brandt, Sebastian: *Ship of Fools*, 161
Bremo (*Mucedorus*), 11–15, 176
Brockbank, Philip, 41
Brook[e], Sir Robert, 123–4
Brooks, Cleanth, 87